AdWords Terms

Ad position: The placement of an ad on the Google search results pages. Position #1 is at the top of the first page.

Bid price: The maximum amount of money an advertiser is willing to pay for a click from a given keyword.

Call to action: Directions within an ad or a Web page for the reader to take an action.

Conversion: A desirable action by a Web-site visitor, including joining a mailing list, buying a product, calling a phone number, or downloading a file.

CPC (cost per click): The amount an advertiser is charged for a single click. Different keywords cost different amounts, depending on competition.

CTR (click-through rate): The number of clicks an ad receives divided by the number of impressions. The higher the CTR, the more effective Google considers the ad.

Impression: The display of an ad on a Web page.

Landing page: The first Web page shown after an ad is clicked. The page is constructed to appeal to the same desire as the ad.

PPC (pay per click): The advertising model that charges advertisers only when their specific ads are clicked.

Split test: Test that divides online traffic randomly between two or more creative approaches (ad, Web site, e-mail, and so on) and measures which one generates more conversions.

Traffic: The number of visitors to your Web site.

Visitor value: How much money, on average, a single visitor to your Web site is worth.

Campaign-Optimization Tips

- **Separate Google, Search Partners, and Content Network traffic into different campaigns.** Keep your traffic streams separate so you can track the visitor value from each stream individually; optimize your sales funnel for each group.

- **Create tightly focused ad groups with closely related keywords.** Avoid sloppy ad groups with thousands of words all pointing to some loosely related ad. Group common desires and mindsets; send each to a targeted landing page.

- **Place underperforming keywords in new ad groups and optimize the ads for those keywords.** If one of your top traffic keywords in an ad group is getting a significantly lower CTR than the rest, move it to its own ad group and write an ad with that keyword in the headline (and perhaps in the URL).

- **Build ad groups with enough traffic to split-test in a timely fashion.** Don't take too long to declare split-test winners.

- **Add long-tail keywords to decrease CPC and increase traffic.** Three- and four-word phrases tend to have less competition and represent buyers rather than lookers.

- **Focus your energy on the changes that will make the biggest difference.** Before managing and optimizing your account, sort campaigns, ad groups, and keyword lists by impressions. Start where the most traffic is so your improvements lead to increased or more qualified visitor flow.

For Dummies: Bestselling Book Series for Beginners

AdWords® For Dummies®

Cheat Sheet

Landing Page Elements to Test

- **Headline:** Use the results from your ad split tests to inform different headlines. Proclaim a big benefit, ask a question, start telling a story, make a scary prediction, and so on.

- **Offer:** Do your visitors prefer an e-book, a newsletter, a mini-course, a sales quote, a CD, a return phone call, a cheat sheet, or a suitcase filled with unmarked $100 bills? (Just kidding about the suitcase.)

- **Location of opt-in form:** Try the opt-in form on the right or the left, above the scroll, every four paragraphs, and so on.

- **Graphics:** Test different photos of the product. Add shadow. Make the pictures bigger or smaller. Experiment with removing the header graphic. Try different colors and fonts for text and hyperlinks.

- **Background color:** Try lighter or darker colors, warmer or cooler, with or without repeating background graphics.

- **Multimedia:** Test adding audio or video to your page to orient, instruct, and win over your visitor.

Free AdWords Resources

AdWords Home Page: https://adwords.google.com to sign up for AdWords and to log in to your account.

AdWords Help Center: https://adwords.google.com/support for answers to frequently (and not-so-frequently) asked questions.

AdWords Learning Center: www.google.com/adwords/learningcenter for text and multimedia AdWords lessons. You can watch short videos, take quizzes, and even become a Qualified Google Advertising Professional.

AdWords Editorial Guidelines: https://adwords.google.com/select/guidelines.html reminds you what not to put in your ads.

Google Group for AdWords Help: http://groups.google.com/group/adwords-help to connect with over 11,000 AdWords users to ask questions and receive answers from Google-approved experts (free registration required).

Free Keyword Tool: www.askhowie.com/freewords gives you the top 100 searches related to a given keyword.

Free Split-Tester: www.askhowie.com/freesplit allows you to enter statistics for two ads and determine whether you have a winner.

Companion Web Site for This Book: www.askhowie.com includes updates, an AdWords tips newsletter, free teleseminars, video tutorials, and information about AdWords consulting, coaching, and campaign management.

For Dummies: Bestselling Book Series for Beginners

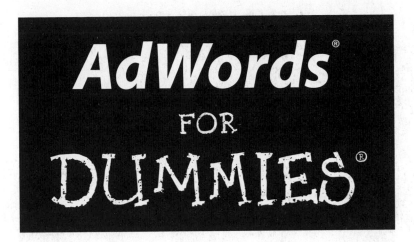

AdWords® FOR DUMMIES®

by Howie Jacobson, PhD

BICENTENNIAL
1807
WILEY
2007
BICENTENNIAL

Wiley Publishing, Inc.

AdWords® For Dummies®

Published by
Wiley Publishing, Inc.
111 River Street
Hoboken, NJ 07030-5774
www.wiley.com

WILEY

About the Author

Howie Jacobson, PhD, has been an Internet marketing strategist since 1999. He specializes in helping clients use Google AdWords to grow their businesses. Due to the fact that he was forced to study statistical methods in graduate school, Jacobson took to direct marketing as soon as he tripped over it in 2001.

He is the creator of "Leads into Gold," a home-study course that teaches small-business owners how to become their own direct-marketing agencies. He is also co-creator of The System Seminar's home-study course, "Internet Marketing for Smart Beginners," along with System founder Ken McCarthy and Cindy Kappler.

Jacobson has presented at several System Seminar events, at Perry Marshall's AdWords Seminar, and at workshops and seminars around the world. He is a regular contributor to HorsesMouth.com, a performance-improvement site for financial advisors, as well as a former writer for Vault.com. He is the second-tallest member of Perry Marshall's AdWords Coaching faculty, and has worked with Marshall since 2003. He leads telephone seminars on beginner and advanced AdWords topics and provides online coaching and support at his Web site, www.askhowie.com.

Jacobson also runs www.loweryourbidprice.com, a company that produces software tools that help AdWords advertisers and AdWords consultants save time, reduce costs, and increase profits.

Luckily for you, Jacobson began his career as a schoolteacher. He learned through trial-by-fire how to be engaging, clear, and entertaining while providing value and motivating results. He is also a business coach and trainer, skilled in turning learning into action, helping his own clients and a horde of others in association with Bregman Partners, Inc., and The Avoca Group.

Jacobson combines his marketing expertise with his background in and passion for health and fitness at FitFam.com, a resource for parents struggling to raise fit and healthy kids in a crazy-busy world.

He lives in Durham, North Carolina, with his wife, two kids, big goofy dog, and little mountaineering hamster. His lifelong ambition is to bring about world peace through marketing — and after that's accomplished, to play Ultimate Frisbee in the 2044 Olympics in Maui.

Dedication

This book is dedicated to the people I annoyed and ignored the most during the writing of it: my children Yael and Elan, and my wife. Mia, I love you more than any of my favorite song lyrics can say. Yael, continue to strive for justice and keep making the world a more beautiful and unpredictable place. Elan, keep growing strong and true, and share your belly laugh with everyone you meet.

I also dedicate this book to my mother, Lucie Jacobson, whose example reminds me to give generously and live big, and the memory of my father, Joel R. Jacobson, a courageous man with a kind heart and a great squash serve.

Author's Acknowledgments

If I were to properly acknowledge on one page all the help I received while writing this book , I'd be using Times New Roman 0.01-point font and you'd be reading this with an electron microscope.

My wonderful editors at Wiley Publishing: Melody Layne, Steve Hayes, Jean Rogers, and Barry Childs-Helton. They have been patient with my whining, accepting of nothing but my best, and always ready with advice and reassurance.

My technical advisors at Google, Jason Rose, Fred Vallaeys, and Emily Harris, answered my frequent volleys of questions with celerity and grace. We haven't met, but I like to think of them riding their Segways from the office to the gourmet lunch rooms at the Googleplex.

Big hugs to the many AdWords experts who shared their wisdom, stories, and sometimes even keywords. Perry Marshall is such a fine AdWords teacher, business associate, and friend that I wonder what good deeds I performed in my previous life to deserve him. David Bullock and Glenn Livingston shared their best stuff with me freely and often — I apologize to their clients and spouses for all the time I monopolized while asking them questions. David even agreed, in a moment of weakness, to become the technical editor for the book. Luckily, I asked and he agreed just before he was featured in Black Enterprise Magazine and became the most sought-after Taguchi expert in the country.

Timothy Seward, my neighbor in North Carolina, has taught me more about Analytics than I thought there was to know. If I'd been paying for his time, he'd be retired by now. The fabulous Joy Milkowski shared her methodologies with me and helped me rewrite the chapter about creating compelling ads. The friendship we developed during this project has been an added bonus. Don Crowther, one of the cleverest and under-the-radar marketers on this or any other planet, shared more cool ideas with me than I could ever have hoped.

Bryan Todd and I have argued and philosophized about metrics more than either of us cares to admit. Kelly Muldoon shared her experience with geographic targeting, and always has the right amount of sympathy and chocolate for any situation. Michael Katz, the world's expert on e-newsletters, was so helpful during this project that I almost forgive him for being funnier than me. Thanks also to my many clients who shared case studies with me — sorry about all the ones I couldn't use.

Rob Goyette, Steve Goyette, and Erik Wickstrom were never more than a cell-phone call away whenever I had a question about PHP, HTML, or the MLB MVP. Working with these talented programmers and marketers is like having three genie-filled lamps.

Ken McCarthy is, quite simply, the source. He understood the potential of the Internet long before the dotcom craze, and he has been quietly creating business leaders and success stories for over 14 years. The combination of masterful teacher and brilliant business strategist is a rare one; throw in loyal friend and passionate righter of wrongs and you have Ken.

Brad Hill believed in me enough to get this whole adventure in motion, and he has encouraged me to become the writer my elementary school teachers always said I'd become. Danny Warshay has been a business and life mentor since we met as roommates in Jerusalem in 1986. And Peter Bregman gave me my introduction to the business world when I was a naïve, befuddled PhD freshly minted from grad school. He always encouraged me to ask questions, no matter how stupid, and except for that time when I asked the HR Director from American Express what exactly she meant by "P&L," it all worked out. Without Peter's guidance and wicked humor, my life would be unimaginably less rich.

Publisher's Acknowledgments

We're proud of this book; please send us your comments through our online registration form located at www.dummies.com/register/.

Some of the people who helped bring this book to market include the following:

Acquisitions, Editorial, and Media Development

Project Editor: Jean Rogers

Senior Acquisitions Editors: Melody Layne, Steven Hayes

Senior Copy Editor: Barry Childs-Helton

Technical Editor: David Bullock

Editorial Manager: Kevin Kirschner

Media Project Supervisor: Laura Moss-Hollister OR Laura Atkinson

Media Development Specialist: Angela Denny, Josh Frank, Kate Jenkins, OR Kit Malone

Media Development Associate Producer: Richard Graves

Editorial Assistant: Amanda Foxworth

Sr. Editorial Assistant: Cherie Case

Cartoons: Rich Tennant (www.the5thwave.com)

Composition Services

Project Coordinators: Adrienne Martinez, Jennifer Theriot

Layout and Graphics: Carl Byers, Stephanie D. Jumper, Christine Williams

Proofreader: ConText Editorial Services, Inc.

Indexer: Potomac Indexing, LLC

Anniversary Logo Design: Richard Pacifico

Publishing and Editorial for Technology Dummies

Richard Swadley, Vice President and Executive Group Publisher

Andy Cummings, Vice President and Publisher

Mary Bednarek, Executive Acquisitions Director

Mary C. Corder, Editorial Director

Publishing for Consumer Dummies

Diane Graves Steele, Vice President and Publisher

Joyce Pepple, Acquisitions Director

Composition Services

Gerry Fahey, Vice President of Production Services

Debbie Stailey, Director of Composition Services

Table of Contents

Introduction

· ·

*M*ost business owners I meet have never heard of Google AdWords. My prediction: If you aren't advertising your business in Google within two years, you're not going to stay in business. The age of the Yellow Pages is coming to an end, and online advertising — led by AdWords — is taking over.

For those who take the time to master this new advertising medium, it's an exciting time. AdWords represents a revolution in the advertising world. For the first time ever, businesses large and small can show their ads to qualified prospects anywhere in the world, when those prospects are hungriest for their products and services. AdWords allows fine geographic targeting, like a Yellow Pages ad, but (unlike the Yellow Pages) *also* allows advertisers to edit, pause, or delete their Google ads any time they like, in real time.

Unlike a traditional advertisement, Google ads cost money only when they are clicked — that is, when a live prospect clicks the ad to visit your site. And perhaps most important, AdWords enables advertisers to test multiple ads simultaneously and to track the return on investment of every ad and every keyword they employ.

Since a click can cost as little as a penny and each click can be tracked to a business outcome, even small, cash-strapped businesses can find AdWords an effective way to grow without betting the farm on untested marketing messages. Google's ads reach across the entire Internet; in addition to the 200 million Google searches per day (almost 60% of all Internet searches), Google provides search results for AOL, Earthlink, Netscape, and other big Internet service providers. And through its AdSense program, Google's ads appear on sites all across the Internet — in thousands of newspaper Web sites and hundreds of thousands of blogs, as well as on Gmail pages.

Yet few small businesses have ever advertised through AdWords. The pay-per-click technology, combined with the unfamiliar form of direct-response marketing, has so far kept most small businesses away from the potential benefits of AdWords. If few businesses are using it, even fewer are using it wisely. Marketing executives at large companies have been slow to embrace the direct-response model, having been trained in brand advertising that has little place in a results-accountable medium like AdWords.

About This Book

I've consulted with hundreds of AdWords clients over the past several years, working with everyone from complete beginners who didn't know how to set up their account to power users spending over a million dollars a month in clicks. Nothing in this book is theoretical — every concept and strategy has been tested under fire in some of the most competitive markets on Earth. When you play the AdWords game, you don't have much room to spin failure into success. You either make money or lose money, and the numbers tell the story.

This book strives to explain clearly, in layperson's terms, the AdWords mechanics and best practices for businesses large and small. You will discover how to build smart and elegant campaigns based on an understanding of the direct-marketing principles.

This book isn't meant to be read from front to back. (I didn't even write it from front to back.) It's more like a reference. Each chapter is divided into sections, so you can jump in anywhere and find out how to accomplish a specific AdWords task.

You don't have to remember anything in this book. Nothing is worth memorizing, except the mantra, "Thank you, Howie." The information here is what you need to know to create and manage successful AdWords campaigns — and nothing more. And wherever I mention a new term, I explain it in plain English. When the movie comes out (I'm thinking Kevin Spacey plays me, although Daniel Day Lewis would also be a good choice), these explanations will be in bold subtitles. I rarely get geeky on you, because AdWords is by and large a user-friendly interface. Occasionally I do show off by explaining a technical phrase — feel free to skip those sections unless you're preparing for a big game of Trivial Pursuit — Cyber Edition.

Conventions Used in This Book

I know that doing something the same way over and over again can be boring (the opening credits of *The Brady Bunch* comes to mind), but sometimes consistency can be a good thing. For one thing, it makes stuff easier to understand. In this book, those consistent elements are *conventions*. In fact, I use italics to identify and define the new terms.

Whenever you have to type something, I put the stuff you need to type in **bold** type so it's easy to see.

When I type URLs (Web addresses) within a paragraph, for the rare snippets of code I show you, and for keywords, I use a monospace font that looks like this: `www.dummies.com`.

What You Don't Have to Read

This is the hardest part of the book for me, because each word I wrote is my baby, and they're all wonderful. Nevertheless, I am contractually obligated to let you off the hook at least a little, so here goes.

You can skip all the paragraphs marked with the Technical Stuff icon. I just put that in because I like the icon, and to give you confidence that I know what I'm talking about. The sidebars aren't crucial to the plot either, although many of them feature tips and examples from very sharp AdWords users.

If you already have an AdWords account, you can actually skip Chapters 2 and 3, which show you how to set up Starter and Standard Edition accounts, respectively. I discuss the principles behind the settings in these chapters, so if your account is running on the Google default settings, you may want to skim these chapters just to avoid some classic beginners' mistakes.

Foolish Assumptions

As I gaze into my polycarbonate ball (crystal balls are breakable, and I can be clumsy), I see you as clearly as if you were sitting here with me in this hotel lobby in Wisconsin at 5:30 in the morning. You have a barely noticeable scar just above your right elbow where you cut yourself against a pool wall when you were eleven, and you are wearing a plaid watch band.

The foolish assumptions that informed my writing include the guess that the main market for your ads reads and speaks English. If not, no big deal: Just substitute Spanish or Russian or Azerbaijani for English as you read (although the reference to Azerbaijani muffins may confuse you).

I'm also assuming that your AdWords goal is business-related, especially in the way I talk about the desired outcomes of your campaigns — that is, leads, sales, profits, and so on. If you're advertising on behalf of a nonprofit, you can easily substitute your own desired outcomes, including signatures on an online petition, additions to your mailing list, or attendance at an event. Your outcomes can be nonmeasurable as well, such as convincing Web-site visitors to reduce their energy consumption, support a political candidate or position, eat healthier food, and so on.

I make several foolish assumptions about your level of computer savvy. I assume you can make your way around a Web site, including clicking, typing in Web addresses, completing forms, and so on. I assume you have access to a working credit card (no, you can't borrow mine) so you can sign up and pay for AdWords.

I don't assume that you're using a PC or a Mac. You can benefit from this book whatever computer platform you use: Mac, PC, Linux, Hairball (all right, I made that last one up). Some third-party software works on Windows PCs only, but you can accomplish 99% of the tasks in this book using just a Web browser and text editor.

I also assume you can get Web pages created. You don't have to create them yourself, but either through your efforts or someone else's, you can design, upload, name, and edit simple HTML Web pages.

How This Book Is Organized

I sent my editor an unabridged dictionary and told her all the words from the book are in it, and she could decide which ones go where (that's her job, after all). It turns out I was wrong: Google wasn't even in the dictionary (the one I got for my college graduation in 1987), so it was back to the drawing board.

On my next try, I divided this book into parts, which I organized by topic. Google AdWords is the big topic, but much of the book focuses on what you have to do before and after AdWords in order to be successful. You don't have to read it in order. In fact, every time I wrote "as you saw in Chapter 4," my editor sent a slight electric shock through the Internet into my keyboard. So start anywhere you like, and go anywhere you like. If you're looking for information on a specific AdWords topic, check the headings in the table of contents, or skim the Table of Contents.

By design, this book enables you to get as much (or as little) information as you need at any particular moment. Having gotten through college English by reading the jacket blurbs of great novels (this was before Google appeared in the dictionary), I understand the value of strategic skimming. By design, *AdWords For Dummies* is a reference that you reach for again and again whenever you encounter a new situation or need a fresh poke of inspiration.

Part I: Becoming a Google Advertiser

Before you drive your AdWords vehicle to success, let's get you pointed in the right direction. Forget everything you learned about marketing in business school, and understand that AdWords is fundamentally a direct-marketing medium. You'll discover what that means, and how it differs from the brand advertising that we see all around us, and how to play the direct-marketing game to win.

Once you're oriented and pointed toward success, I show you how to start your engine — first with training wheels if you wish (with the simple Starter Edition), then with the full-featured and powerful Standard Edition.

Part II: Launching Your AdWords Campaign

The two bricks of your AdWords campaign (to switch metaphors abruptly) are keywords and ads. Before you activate your first campaign, I introduce you to the single most important element of AdWords (actually, of just about all online marketing): choosing the right keywords. I show you how to do this through various online research tools and methods, most of which are quick, free, and easy.

Next you master the ads themselves. Since AdWords is the most competitive advertising space in existence (slapping your ad in the middle of 20 others offering more or less the same thing), you must deploy advanced strategies for creating compelling, action-triggering ads. Otherwise no Web traffic, no leads, no money. I focus on text ads, since they are the most common and (in their simplicity) provide the best opportunity to illustrate direct-marketing principles. I also cover image ads, video ads, and local business ads connected to Google Maps.

Part III: Managing Your AdWords Campaigns

Keywords and ads are the bricks. If you hired me to build you a house and I just dropped a dump truck full of bricks on your empty lot, you wouldn't be happy. The chapters in this part give you the blueprints to turn your bricks into a sound and effective structure, and the tools to build and maintain it.

You'll learn how to structure campaigns and ad groups, manage keyword bids, and target the right traffic.

Part IV: Converting Clicks to Clink

This is my favorite part of the whole book, the part where my family dragged me away from my keyboard as I kicked and screamed, "Wait, I haven't told them about live chat yet." Once you've set up your campaigns and paid for visitors to your Web site, you learn how to use lead-generating magnets to collect contact information from visitors — and to use e-mail to stay in touch and build a relationship. I also cover Web site strategies to extract maximum value from each visitor.

Part V: Testing Your Strategies and Tracking Your Results

Actually, this is my favorite part of the whole book (okay, my other favorite) because I show you how to fail your way to success inexpensively, quickly, and predictably. When you test multiple approaches, one is almost always better than the other. As long as you keep testing properly and paying attention to the results, you can't help but achieve constant incremental (and sometimes enormous) improvement in your profitability.

Part VI: The Part of Tens

Part of my hazing in the *For Dummies* fraternity included creating top-ten lists that will, alas, never make their way onto Letterman. They include beginners' mistakes you want your competitors to make instead of you, and case studies that bring the principles of the book to life. The Part of Tens is a resource you can use whenever you're stuck, except for wedding toasts and term papers about the causes of World War I.

Be sure to check out www.dummies.com/go/adwords to see this book's two bonus chapters as PDF files. These two bonus chapters provide you with top ten lists of the best AdWords tools available and tips for writing great ads.

Icons Used in This Book

Unfortunately, I could not convince my editor to let me use an icon of a sumo wrestler wearing a tutu hurtling toward you on ice skates to indicate "this paragraph makes absolutely no sense, but you should pay close attention to it anyway." So I stuck with the standard *For Dummies* icons:

Hopefully my tips don't hurt as much as the one in the icon, but are just as sharp. I use this bull's-eye to flag concepts that can cut months from your AdWords learning curve.

I use this icon to remind you to remove the string that's cutting off the circulation to your index finger. (What were you thinking?) Also, this icon highlights points and items that should be on your AdWords to-do list; little tasks that can prevent big problems later on.

I've heard too many stories of AdWords beginners turning on their campaigns, going to bed, and waking up to $16,000 craters in their credit cards. I use the bomb icon when a little mistake can have big and nasty consequences.

I'm probably less geeky than you are. I've learned enough code writing to be dangerous (ask my Webmaster, who probably has installed a one-click backup for my sites by now), but not enough to be useful. So I use this icon only to impress you with my knowledge of certain geeky terms, and when I share a snippet of code that your Webmaster can deal with if you don't want to.

I've created a companion Web site to this book at www.askhowie.com. Many of the processes you'll implement can be hard to describe on paper, but simple to show in a video tutorial. (If you're not sure what I mean, try describing to someone how to tie their shoes.) I include video footage of my own computer screen, so you can see and hear exactly how to do what I tell you to. Also, the Web addresses of articles, resources, and tools change from time to time. When I suspect that the current URL won't be valid by the time you read this, I send you to my site, which will either automatically redirect you to the right location, or provide an even better resource that wasn't available when I was writing the chapter.

Where to Go from Here

I'm thinking that a nice bowl of gazpacho would be nice right about now. Fresh Roma tomatoes, cilantro, onions, some cumin, and maybe a few chunks of cucumber, sweet corn and avocado floating on top. Wanna join me?

You can start reading wherever you want, but I'd like to point out a couple of fundamental chapters that you will want to understand fully before spending money on AdWords. Chapter 1 gives you the direct-marketing mindset you need to use AdWords effectively, while Chapter 4 guides you to a deep understanding of your market. Skim Chapters 10 and 11 before turning on the traffic to your Web site.

Once you have the lay of the land, you may want to implement the tracking described in Chapter 14 as soon as you've set up a Standard Edition account (explained in Chapter 3). Knowing the profitability of each element of your AdWords campaign makes everything easier and more fun.

The companion Web site www.askhowie.com is a good place to go for more information, detailed video tutorials, updates, and an e-mail newsletter on AdWords tips and strategies. If you encounter something online that is different from the book, check the Web site section devoted to that chapter for an update.

If you're aching to tell me how much you love this book and how you'd like to fly me, first-class, to Cape Town, Fiji, or Maui to teach a workshop, give a keynote, or just enjoy a well-deserved vacation, feel free to e-mail me at howie@askhowie.com.

Part I
Becoming a Google Advertiser

The 5th Wave — By Rich Tennant

"Look—you can't just list an extraterrestrial embryo on AdWords without using some catchy phrases or power words to make it seem interesting and unique."

In this part . . .

This part introduces Google AdWords and shows you how to get started. While almost everyone is familiar with the Google search engine, few people understand how easy it is to pay to display your ad listing on the coveted first page of search results — and how challenging it can be to do so profitably.

Chapter 1 discusses online search as a revolution in advertising and reveals the marketing-mindset shifts required for success. You'll discover how to get into your customers' minds and see through their eyes, so your advertising will be customer-centric and effective.

Chapters 2 and 3 take you through the mechanics of creating — and immediately pausing — a single campaign. (Patience, grasshopper.) Chapter 2 begins with the Starter Edition. (The Starter Edition was recently released, and it gives you a much simpler, though less powerful, way to use AdWords. It's a good way for the hyper-nervous to begin.) Chapter 3 goes step-by-step through creating an account with the Standard Edition. These chapters provide the foundation upon which your AdWords success is built — customized campaigns whose settings support the achievement of your goals.

Chapter 1

Profiting from the Pay-Per-Click Revolution

*H*ave you ever bought an ad in the Yellow Pages? I remember my first time — I was terrified. I didn't know what to write. I didn't know how big an ad to buy. I wasn't sure which phonebooks to advertise in. I had no idea what headings to list under. I had to pay thousands of dollars for an ad I wouldn't be able to change for the next 12 months. And I had recurring nightmares that I mistyped the phone number and some baffled florist in Poughkeepsie got thousands of calls from my customers.

Why am I telling you this? (Aside from the fact that my therapist encourages me to release negative emotions?) Because I want you to appreciate the significance of Google AdWords as a revolution in advertising.

You can set up an AdWords account in about five minutes for five dollars. Your ads can be seen by thousands of people searching specifically for what you've got, and you don't pay a cent until a searcher clicks your ad to visit your Web site. You can change your ad copy any time you want. You can cancel unprofitable ads with the click of a mouse. You can run multiple ads simultaneously and figure out to the penny which ad makes you the most money.

You can even send customers to specific aisles and shelves of your store, depending on what they're searching for. And you can get smarter and smarter over time, writing better ads, showing under more appropriate headings, choosing certain geographic markets and avoiding others. When your ads do well, you can even get Google to serve them as online newspaper and magazine ads, put them next to Google Maps locations, and broadcast them to cell phones — automatically.

AdWords gives you the ability to conduct hundreds of thousands of dollars of market research for less than the cost of a one-way ticket from Chapel Hill to Madison. And in less time than it takes me to do five one-arm pushups (okay, so that's not saying much).

AdWords can help you test and improve your Web site and e-mail strategy to squeeze additional profits out of every step in your sales process. It can provide a steady stream of qualified leads for predictable costs. One recent bestseller by Timothy Ferriss, *The Four Hour Work Week: Escape 9-5, Live Anywhere, and Join the New Rich* (Crown Publishers), teaches a very achievable AdWords-based system for becoming financially independent in just a few months.

But AdWords can also be a huge sinkhole of cash for the advertiser who doesn't understand it. I've written this book to arm you with the mindsets, strategies, and tactics to keep you from ever becoming an AdWords victim.

Introducing AdWords

The Google search engine, found at `www.google.com`, processes hundreds of millions of searches per day. Every one of those searches represents a human being trying to solve a problem or satisfy an itch through finding the right information on the World Wide Web. The AdWords program allows advertisers to purchase text and links on the Google results page (the page the searcher sees after entering a word or phrase and clicking the Google Search button.

You pay for the ad only when someone clicks it and visits your Web site. The amount you pay for each visitor can be as low as one penny, or as high as $80, depending on the quality of your ad, your Web site, and the competitiveness of the market defined by the word or phase (known as a *keyword* even though it may be several words long) typed by the visitor.

Each text ad on the results page consists of four lines and up to 130 characters (see Figure 1-1 for an example ad):

 ✔ **Line 1:** Blue underlined hyperlinked headline of up to 25 characters

 ✔ **Line 2:** Description line 1 of up to 35 characters

 ✔ **Line 3:** Description line 2 of up to 35 characters

 ✔ **Line 4:** Green display URL (URL stands for Uniform Resource Locator, the way the Internet assigns addresses to Web sites) of up to 35 characters

Figure 1-1:
This
AdWords ad
targets
parents
whose
children
suffer from
asthma.

Goodbye Asthma and Colds
How to Raise Healthy and Fit Kids
Free Downloadable Action Guide
www.FitFam.com

The fourth line, the display URL, can differ from the Web page your visitor actually lands on. I cover this in detail in Chapter 6.

Where and When the Ads Show

You can choose to show your ads to the entire world, or limit their exposure by country, region, state, and even city. You can (for example) let them run 24/7 or turn them off nights and weekends. You also get to choose from AdWords' three tiers of exposure, described in the following sections.

Google results

When someone searches for a particular keyword, your ad displays on the Google results page if you have selected that keyword (or a close variation) as a trigger for your ad. For the ad shown in Figure 1-1, if someone enters `kids asthma prevention` in Google, they can view the ad somewhere on the top or right of the results page (see Figure 1-2).

Search partners results

Your ads can also show on Google's search partners' network. Companies such as AOL and Earthlink incorporate Google's results into their own search pages, as in Figure 1-3.

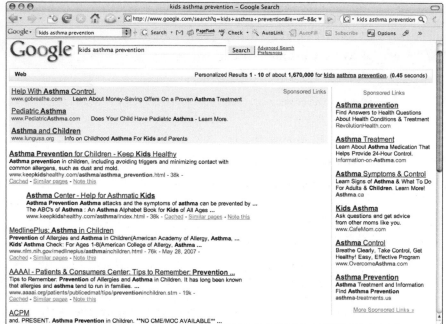

Figure 1-2:
AdWords
results are
labeled
Sponsored
Links at the
top and
right.

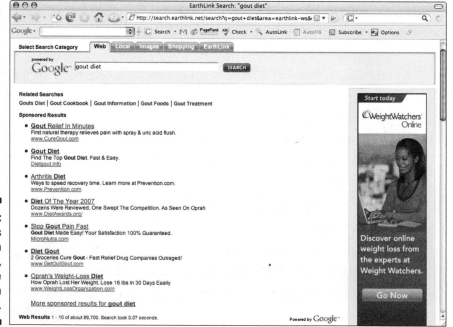

Figure 1-3:
AdWords
ads shown
by Earthlink,
a Google
search
partner.

A partial list of Google search partners includes

- **America Online (AOL):** www.aol.com
- **AT&T Worldnet:** www.att.net
- **Ask.com:** www.ask.com
- **CompuServe:** http://webcenters.netscape.compuserve.com/menu
- **Earthlink:** www.earthlink.net
- **Netscape Netcenter:** www.netscape.com
- **Shopping.com:** www.shopping.com

AdSense sites and Gmail

Additionally, hundreds of thousands of Web sites show AdWords ads on their pages as part of the AdSense program, which allows Web site owners to get paid by showing AdWords ads on their sites. (See Figure 1-4 for an example.) Think of an online version of a newspaper or magazine, with ads next to the editorial content. The content of the page determines which ads get shown. On sites devoted to weightlifting, for example, Google shows ads for workout programs and muscle-building supplements, rather than knitting and quilting supplies. Google lets you choose whether to "syndicate" your ads on these "syndication" networks.

While anyone with a Web site can use the AdSense program, Google has a special relationship with some of the most popular content sites on the Web, including

- **About:** www.about.com
- **business.com:** www.business.com
- **Food Network:** www.foodnetwork.com
- **HGTV:** www.hgtv.com
- **HowStuffWorks:** www.howstuffworks.com
- **InfoSpace:** www.infospace.com
- **Lycos:** www.lycos.com
- **The New York Times:** www.nytimes.com
- **Reed Business:** www.reedbusiness.com

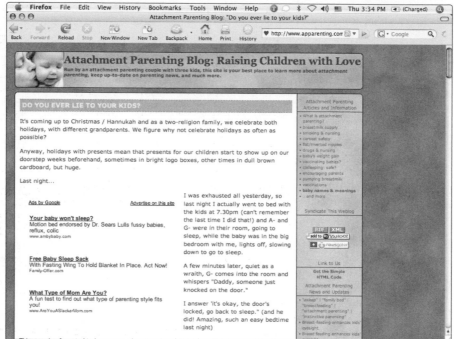

Figure 1-4:
AdWords
ads on a
Web page.

Gmail is Google's Web-mail service. It displays AdWords results to the right of the e-mails you receive. If you choose to syndicate your ads, your prospects who use Gmail may see them if the text of the e-mail is deemed relevant to your offer. For example, Figure 1-5 shows an e-mail that I (almost) sent to the MacArthur Foundation, humbly explaining why I should receive one of their "genius grants." To the right, you can see ads for small business grants, a Cow Ringtone, triggered by my mention of a self-esteem program for cows, and two resources for college grant-seekers.

AdWords in the Total Google Context

Google rose from nothing to become the world's most popular search engine in just a few months because it did one thing faster and better than all the rest: help Internet searchers find what they were looking for. I don't want to overload you with the details of Google's search algorithm (especially since it's a such a secret that if I told you, I'd have to kill you, as well as the fact that I would have to understand words like *eigenvector* and *stochastic* in order to explain it), but you will become a better Google advertiser when you get the basic principles. The most important word in Google's universe is *relevance*.

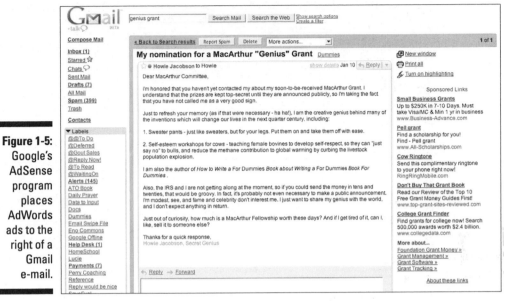

Figure 1-5: Google's AdSense program places AdWords ads to the right of a Gmail e-mail.

When you type a word or phrase into Google, the search engine asks the World Wide Web for the best page to show you. The big innovations Google uses are a couple of calculations: One, called PageRank, is basically a measure of the popularity of a particular page, based on how many other Web pages link to that page and how popular *those* pages are. (Sort of like high school — the definition of a popular kid is one who is friends with other popular kids.) The other calculation is known as Page Reputation, which answers the question, "Okay, this page may be popular, but for which topic?" The Page Reputation of a Web page determines whether it will appear in a given search; the PageRank determines whether it will be the first listing, the third, or the four million and eleventh.

The entire Google empire is based on this ability to match the right Web pages, in the right priority order, with a given search phrase. The day Google starts showing irrelevant results is the day *after* you should have sold all your Google stock.

When Google started, it only showed the results of its own calculations. These results are known as *organic listings*. Organic listings appear on the left side of the Google results page (see Figure 1-6, which includes organic listings only, and no AdWords entries).

Figure 1-6:
Google's
organic
listings
appear on
the left of
the results
page.

In the early days of AdWords, your ad was shown based on a combination of two numbers: your *bid price,* or how much you were willing to pay for a click (that is, someone clicking your ad and visiting your Web page), and a very important metric called Click-Through Rate (CTR): the percentage of searchers who clicked your ad after seeing it. Now, Google also takes into account the quality of the fit between the ad and your Web site. If searchers exit your site so fast they leave skid marks, Google figures that they didn't find what they were looking for, and you get penalized for irrelevance.

Pay Per Click: Your Online Gumball Machine

AdWords is a PPC (Pay Per Click) advertising medium. Unlike other forms of advertising, with PPC you pay only for results: live visitors to your Web site.

AdWords allows you as the advertiser to decide how much you're willing to pay for a visitor searching on a given keyword. For example, if you sell vintage sports trading cards, you can bid more for `Babe Ruth rookie card` than `John Gochnaur card` if you can make more money selling the Babe Ruth card.

A really short history lesson

The first Pay Per Click (PPC) search engine, `goto.com` (whose name changed to Overture and now is known as Yahoo Search Marketing), ran on a straight auction basis. Whoever wanted to show an ad in the top position simply bid more per click than everyone else for a given keyword. Google rose to preeminence in the PPC world because it figured out that letting badly written, unappealing ads rise to the top just because an advertiser was willing to spend a lot of cash was bad for everyone. Bad for the search engine, because the search engine doesn't get paid unless a Web visitor likes the ad enough to click it. Bad for the advertiser, because unappealing ads usually come from the same lazy or confused thinking that produces unappealing and unprofitable Web sites. And most important, bad for the search-engine user, who was now getting unappealing and irrelevant listings muddying the results page, and would therefore start searching for a better search engine.

AdWords elegantly solved this problem by rewarding advertisers whose ads were popular with searchers. If your ad was twice as popular as a competitor's (meaning it got clicked twice as often), your cost per click (the amount of money you paid Google when a searcher clicked your ad and visited your Web site) was half what your competitor was paying for the same position on the page.

For example, suppose you and your competitor both bid $1.00 on the keyword `elephant ride`, and 1000 people see each ad. Forty people click your ad, and 20 people click your competitor's. Your ad would appear *above* your competitor's for a cost per click of around $0.51 — if it's twice as popular, it costs half as much.

Highly relevant and compelling ads rose to the top of the page, while unappealing ads faded away as they proved unprofitable. Google also began AdWords with a cutoff on CTR: If your ad couldn't compel at least 5 out of the first 1000 viewers to click it, Google would disable it and make you rewrite it before it could be shown again. They also instituted a three strikes and you're out rule — after the third disablement, you had to pay $5.00 to resuscitate your ad.

Over the years, Google has been tweaking the AdWords program to provide more and more relevant search results to its users. This book contains the very latest updates as I write, but please realize that Google never stops moving. While it's impossible to predict the exact changes Google will implement, you can be sure that it's always moving in the direction of greater relevance for its users. If your ads and Web pages always provide real value to real people, and don't exist just to "game" the AdWords machine, you're probably going to be just fine no matter what Google dreams up next.

For many businesses, advertising is like a slot machine: You put in your money, pull the handle, and see what happens. Sometimes you do well; sometimes you don't. Either way, you don't learn much that will help you predict the results of your next pull. PPC has changed all that for businesses with the patience and discipline to track online metrics. Just as a gumball machine reliably gives you a gumball every time you drop a quarter, PPC can reliably deliver a customer to your Web site for a predictable amount of money. Once you run your numbers (explained in Part V), you know exactly how much, on average, a visitor is worth from a particular keyword. You may find that you make $70 in profit for every 100 visitors from AdWords who searched for `biodegradable wedding dress`. Therefore you can spend up to $0.70 for each click from this keyword and still break even or better on the first sale.

The Direct-Marketing Difference: Getting Your Prospects to Do Something

Direct marketing differs from "brand" marketing, the kind we're used to on TV and radio and newspapers, in several important ways. AdWords represents direct marketing at its purest, so it's important to forget everything you thought you knew about advertising before throwing money at Google.

Direct marketers set one goal for their ads: to compel a measurable response in their prospects. Unlike brand marketers, you won't spend money to give people warm and fuzzy feelings when they think about your furniture coasters or ringtones or South Carolina resort rentals. Instead, you run your ad to get hot prospects to your Web site. On the *landing page* (the first page your prospect sees after leaving Google), you direct your prospect to take some other measurable action — fill out a form, call a phone number, initiate a live chat, drop everything, race to the airport and hop on the first plane to Hilton Head, and so on.

On the Web, you can track each visitor from the AdWords click through each intermediate step straight through to the first sale and all subsequent sales. So at each step of the sales cycle, on each Web page, in each e-mail, with each ad, you ask your prospect to take a specific action right now.

Brand advertisers rarely have the luxury of asking for immediate action. The company that advertises home gyms during reruns of *Gilligan's Island* has no illusion that 8,000 viewers are going to TiVO the rest of the episode and drive, tires squealing, to the nearest fitness store to purchase the GalactiMuscle 5000. They count on repetition to eventually lead to sales.

Contrast that approach with infomercials, which have one goal: to get you to pick up the phone NOW because they realize that once you get distracted, they've lost their chance of selling to you.

The Internet outdoes the immediacy and convenience of the infomercial by maintaining the same channel of communication. Instead of jumping from TV to phone, AdWords and your Web site function together as a seamless information-gathering experience.

You can measure your results

Because your prospects are either doing what you want them to do or not, you can measure the effectiveness of each call to action. For example, let's say you sell juggling equipment to left-handed people. You show your ad to 30,000 people in one week. Your ad attracts 450 prospects to your Web site, at an average CPC of $0.40. Your landing page offers a 5% off coupon in exchange for a valid e-mail address, and by the end of the week your mailing list has 90 leads — 20% of all visitors. You follow up with an e-mail offer that compels 10 sales totaling $600.00.

The following table shows an example of an AdWords ad campaign's overall metrics.

Metric	Total cost or percentage
Total advertising cost	$180 (450 × $0.40)
Sales total	$600
Return on investment (ROI)	333% ($600 ÷ $180)
AdWords ad CTR	1.5% (450 ÷ 30,000)
Landing-page lead conversion	20% (90 ÷ 450)
E-mail sales conversion	11% (10 ÷ 90)
Cost per visitor	$0.40
Average visitor value	$1.33 ($600 ÷ 450)
Cost per lead	$2.40 ($180 ÷ 75)
Average value of a lead	$8.00 ($600 ÷ 75)
Cost per sale	$18.00 ($180 ÷ 10)
Average value of a sale	$60 ($600 ÷ 10)

What does this horrific flashback to SAT prep mean to your business? These numbers give you control over your advertising spending, allow you to predict cash flow (just play a game of Monopoly with my daughter if you don't appreciate the value of positive cash flow!), and enable you to assess additional market opportunities by comparing them to this pipeline. (If you're not rubbing your hands together and going, "Muahahaha" like a cartoon villain, I still have some explaining to do.)

In this hypothetical case, you have found a gumball machine that gives you $1.33 every time you drop 40 cents into the machine. You've set it up once, and it happens automatically as long as Google likes your credit card. ROI is a metric that simply converts your input amount to a single dollar, so you can easily compare ROI for different campaigns and markets. ROI answers the question, if you put a dollar into this machine, how much comes out? ROI of 333% means that you get $3.33 out for every dollar you put it. If you found a gumball machine that managed that trick, you'd never go back to slot machines again.

Now suppose the market becomes more competitive, and your CPC rises. If you were advertising in your local newspaper and the ad rep told you that prices were going up by 25%, what would you do? Would you keep advertising at the same level, or cut back, or stop showing your ads in that paper completely? Unless you're measuring the ROI of your ads, you have no way to make a rational decision.

Say your AdWords CPC from the example shown in the preceding table increases by 25%. Now your cost per visitor is 50 cents. Do you keep advertising? Of course — you're still paying less for a lead than the value of that lead — 83 cents less. Your ROI is down from 333%, to a still respectable 267% (total advertising cost is now 450 × $0.50 = $225, and $600 ÷ $225 = 267%).

But wait — there's more! (Did I mention how much I enjoy a good infomercial?) AdWords makes it simple not only to see your metrics, but also to improve your profitability by conducting tests. The ability to test different elements of your sales process is the next important element of direct marketing.

Keep improving your marketing

So far in this chapter, I've only discussed inputs (how much you pay to advertise and how many Web site visitors) and outputs (how much you receive in sales). But it's really the intermediate metrics (called *throughputs* by people like me who sometimes find it useful to pretend we went to business school) that give us an opportunity to make huge improvements in our profitability.

For example, imagine you improve the CTR of your ad from 1.5% to 2.2% without lowering the quality of your leads. Big whoop, right? An improvement of 0.7% — who cares? Actually, it's an improvement of 68% — for the same $180 advertising spend, you now get 660 visitors instead of 450. If everything else stays the same, your visitor value of $1.33 means your sales increase to $880, for an ROI of 489%.

But wait — there's more! What's to stop you from improving your landing page by 20% by testing different versions? Instead of getting 20 leads out of 100, you're now collecting 24. Six hundred sixty visitors now translate into

158 leads. If 11% of them make a purchase from your e-mail offer, that's 17 sales. At an average of $60 per sale, you've now made $1020.

But wait — there's more! How about testing your e-mail offer too? Let's say you get a 36% improvement, and now 15% of e-mail recipients make a $60 purchase. That's 23 sales at $60, for a new total of $1380.

Thanks to the miracle of compounding, the three improvements (68% × 20% × 36%) give you a total improvement of 230%. This isn't pie-in-the-sky math either — when you test the elements of your sales process scientifically, it's hard not to make significant improvements. See Chapter 13 for the stunningly simple explanation of how to do it.

It's dating, not a shotgun wedding

In case you got a little lost in the numbers in the previous section, I want to make sure you got the moral of that direct marketing story: It's a process of multiple steps. Seth Godin (marketing guru and author) compares direct marketing to dating. You wouldn't walk up to a stranger in a museum and propose marriage. (If you did, and you're happily married 17 years later, please don't take offense; I'm not talking about you.) In fact, there are a lot of things you wouldn't suggest to a stranger in a museum that you might very well suggest to someone who knew you a little better. (If you're not sure what these are, check out Dr. Ruth's contribution to the *For Dummies* series.)

Direct marketing operates on the premise that you have to earn your prospects' trust before they become your customers. As with dating, you demonstrate your trustworthiness and likeability by asking for small commitments with low-downside risk. Your ad, the first step in the AdWords dating game, makes a promise of some sort while posing no risk. Your visitor can click away from your Web site with no hassle or hard feelings. AdWords' Editorial Guidelines commit you to playing nice on your landing page: an accurate display URL, no pop-ups, and a working Back button so your visitors can hightail it back to their search results if they don't like your site.

Your *landing page* makes a second offer that involves getting permission from your prospects to communicate with them in the future. Here's the deal you're offering: "I'll give you something of value if you let me contact you in the future. And any time you want me to stop contacting you, just let me know and I'll stop. And I'll never share your contact information with anybody else who might try to contact you."

Sometimes you can go right for the sale on the landing page, and sometimes it's better to focus on turning your visitor into a *lead* — someone with whom you can follow up later. Chapter 10 offers guidelines for creating an effective landing page.

As your prospect gets to know you and trust you, you increase the value you provide while asking for larger and larger commitments. Depending on your business, your sales/dating process could consist of surveys, reports, free samples, try-before-you-buy promotions, teleseminars, e-mails, live chat, software downloads, and more. When you ask for the sale you are, in effect, proposing marriage — or a long-term relationship, anyway.

Following up with your best prospects

Direct marketing focuses on prospects — people who raise their hands and tell you they're interested in what you've got. When someone clicks your AdWords ad, they've just identified themselves to you as someone worth developing a relationship with. Returning to the dating analogy, this is like a stranger smiling at you at the museum. You respond by striking up a conversation about the artwork you're both looking at ("Do you think the green splotch in the upper-left-hand corner represents a rebirth of hope or an exploding drummer?") If the two of you hit it off, you don't want to leave the building without getting a phone number.

In dating, the phone number is the litmus test of interest. If you can't get the phone number, or if you call it and discover you've really been given the number for the West Orange Morgue (now why are you assuming that actually happened to me?), you know that relationship has no future.

Your prospect has the online attention span of a guppy. When we go online, we typically multitask, we have multiple windows open, we're checking e-mail, IMing, watching videos, listening to MP3s, and searching and browsing and surfing. Not to mention answering the phone, opening the mail, eating and drinking, and dealing with other people. How many times have you visited a Web page, gotten distracted, and never found it again? How many times have you bookmarked a Web page, intending to visit again, and haven't gotten around to it?

Get the prospect's e-mail address as soon as you can. Before they get distracted. Before they browse back to Google and click one of your competitors' ads. Before they spill a cappuccino latte all over the keyboard.

With their e-mail address and permission to follow up, you've done all you can to inoculate yourself from the short Internet attention span. You now have a chance of continuing the conversation until it leads to a sale.

How to Think Like Your Prospect

I began this chapter with a pathetic rant about my experiences as a Yellow Pages advertiser. Now let's look at the Yellow Pages from the point of view of the user — the person searching for a solution to a problem. But I'm done whining, so I'm not going to complain about figuring out which heading to look under, deciding which listing to call, dealing with voice mail (no, really, I'm done whining). Instead, imagine a totally new experience: the Magic Yellow Pages.

In the Magic Yellow Pages, you don't have to flip through hundreds of pages. In fact, the book doesn't *have* any pages — just a blank cover. You write down what you're looking for on the cover, and then — Poof! — the listings appear. The most relevant listings, according to the Magic Yellow Pages, appear on the cover. Subsequent pages contain more listings, in order of decreasing relevance.

But wait — there's more! The listings in the Magic Yellow Pages don't have phone numbers. Instead, touch the listing and you're magically transported to the business itself. Don't like what you see? Snap your fingers and you're back in front of the Magic Yellow Pages, ready to touch another listing or type another query.

This is how AdWords functions from the point of view of your prospects: They have all the power. They conjure entire shopping centers full of competing shops by typing words — and they window-shop until they find what they want or give up.

Their search term represents an itch that they want to scratch at that very moment — some unsolved problem. They are looking for the shortest distance between their itch and a good scratch. Maybe they want information. Maybe they want a product. Maybe they want to be entertained. Maybe they want to be told that their problem isn't so bad.

It's your job to figure out what they really want, based on the keyword they type, and give it to them quicker and more obviously than your competitors. In the Magic Yellow Pages, the rules are, "Give the prospect what she wants and nobody gets hurt." Winning the game of AdWords comes down to figuring out what your prospect — the person you can help — is thinking and feeling as they type their search. When you understand this, you bid on the right keywords, you show compelling ads, and you present clear and irresistible offers on your Web site. See Chapter 4 to discover how to conduct quick and easy keyword research, so you can become the champion itch-scratcher in your market.

Chapter 2

Setting Up Your Starter Edition Account

*I*n late 2006 Google figured out that the standard AdWords interface was freaking some people out: lots of steps, too many choices, and not enough guidance before the machine started cranking and costing them money. In its wisdom, Google created a Starter Edition that eliminates all but the most basic steps and decisions.

In this chapter, I describe the limited functionality of the Starter Edition to help you figure out if you should start slow or jump into the Standard Edition right off the bat. If you decide to skip to Standard, you can skip the rest of this chapter (no refunds, though).

I take you through the signup process and show you how to proceed if you have your own Web site, and even if you don't. (I told you this was the Starter Edition!) I'll take you on a guided tour of the Starter Edition Control Panel (if you want, you can hang a tape recorder around your neck and wear sunglasses and a Hawaiian shirt to enhance authenticity), and then show you how to manage and — when you're good and ready — activate your account. Finally, I help you decide when to take the plunge into the Standard Edition, so you can continue to read and benefit from this riveting book.

Who Should Start with the Starter Edition

When I was a boy, there was no Starter Edition and we walked 10 miles to school uphill through broken glass every day. We toughed it out, and it made us stronger — or not. But those days are over. Now you have a choice.

The Starter Edition is just that — a place to start out. It has quite a few limitations when compared to the Standard Edition (see Chapter 3 if you want to jump right in with the Standard Edition).

The Starter Edition is a good place to start advertising with AdWords if

- ✔ **You only sell one product and have one Web page:** The Starter Edition is for advertisers who want to send all their traffic to a single Web page and can target an entire country. If you have more than one product (for example, clown noses in both red and blue), or more than one sales funnel (for example, you sell red noses to clowns and politicians), the Starter Edition will be too limited.

- ✔ **You want to sell your product in just one region:** If you want to advertise to multiple geographic regions, you must start with the Standard Edition. If you can begin by showing your ads to one region only, the Starter Edition is fine. With the Starter Edition you can target as follows:

  - • Entire Country (for example, United States)

  - • Entire State (for example, North Carolina)

  - • Metropolitan Area (for example, Raleigh-Durham-Fayetteville)

  - • City (for example, Durham)

  If you need to show different ads to Durham and Chapel Hill, you'll need the Standard Edition. (Having lived in this college-basketball-worshipping part of the country for two years, I don't recommend trying to sell Duke Blue Devil sweatshirts to UNC Tarheel fans, even if the two campuses are only 7 miles apart.)

- ✔ **You don't want to sift through complex reporting:** Choose the Starter Edition if you aren't ready to look at the really interesting numbers, like cost per lead and return on investment. The only metrics you'll have to deal with in the Starter Edition are how many people saw your ad, how many clicked it, and how much you paid Google for the privilege. If you want to find out how much money each of your ads and keywords makes for you, you need the Standard Edition.

In order to use the advanced *conversion tracking* (meaning, how many of your visitors did what you want them to do), you'll need a way to put HTML code on your Web site. If you don't know how to do that yourself or have access to a Webmaster, these advanced features will be unavailable to you in any case.

- ✔ **You want to use text ads only:** With the Starter Edition, you show only plain vanilla text ads (no pretty pictures, video, cell phone ads, or dancing monkeys). Most advertisers find that text ads are the bread and butter of their online advertising, so this may not be a big deal for you. Even if you plan to make graphical and video ads eventually, I strongly recommend you start with the text ads to get your message right — before you jump into expensive and slow-to-change media such as art and video.

- ✔ **You want simple keyword bidding:** The Starter Edition does not allow you to bid higher for some keywords than others. If you want precise control of your spending on each keyword, you need the Standard Edition.

- ✔ **You don't need to choose specific Web sites to show your ads:** With the Starter Edition, you can't show your ads on Web sites that belong to Google's Content Syndication (AdSense) network. If you sell something that people aren't actively searching for and will only stumble upon accidentally, you need the Standard Edition.

Of course, you can always begin with one simple campaign and upgrade to the Standard Edition when you've gotten the hang of it.

Signing Up Couldn't Be Easier

Got 10 minutes, a credit card at least $5 shy of your credit limit, and a connected Web browser? Then you're ready to play. If you already have a Web site that you use to sell your product, keep reading. If not, skip to the later section, "If you don't have a Web site."

If you have a Web site

You already have a Web site where you sell your product, and now you're interested in advertising with Google's AdWords. To start out with the Starter Edition, follow these steps:

1. **Point your browser to http://adwords.google.com and click the Click to Start button, as shown in Figure 2-1.**

    (The button could also be labeled Begin or Start Now. I've gotten all three — Google appears to be testing which button text works best.)

2. **Select the Starter Edition radio button.**

3. **Select the I Have a Webpage radio button.**

Figure 2-1:
The
gateway
page to a
world of
AdWords
fun.

4. Skip down to the bottom of the page and click the Continue button.

You are taken to the simplified one-page signup form, consisting of six sections.

5. In the Location and Language section, enter your region and select a language preference.

If you are advertising within the United States, you can target the entire country or type a city name or Zip code in the Search for a City Name or Postal Code text box and click the Search United States button. Here are some acceptable formats:

```
South Orange, NJ
Madison, Wisconsin
27705
```

Google then provides you with options based on your selection (see Figure 2-2). Choose the geographic area that most closely matches your chosen market.

If you select the radio button for Another Language, you'll get a menu with about 20 different languages you can choose. For the purposes of this book, I'm going to assume you'll stick with English for now, as my Portuguese is rather rusty. Aprovação?

Figure 2-2:
Geographic
options
for search
term 27705.

6. **In the Write Your Ad section, enter your landing page.**

Enter the URL of the page that your visitor will land on after clicking
your ad. This is the page that will convince them, within seven seconds,
to stay and look around or click away forever. (I talk about landing
pages, with much sagacity and long-windedness, in Chapter 10.)

Unless you really know what you're doing, don't change the prefix from
`http://` to `https://`. The `s` in `https://` means the Web site is secure
from an e-commerce standpoint. The data you enter is encrypted, so
online criminals have a hard time charging your card for their new 48-
inch plasma TV screen. You can tell if a site is secure by looking for a
small lock icon at the bottom right of the screen, in the status bar.

There's almost never a reason to send a visitor to a page that asks for
their credit card right away. Slow down and get to know each other
before going for the wallet.

I once spent hundreds of dollars of Google traffic that I sent to the wrong
page and didn't realize it for weeks. Make sure the URL is exactly right by
opening another browser window and typing the URL into the address bar.
When your Web page appears, copy the URL in the address bar, switch
back to the Google AdWords page, and paste the URL into the text box.

Don't worry about duplicating the `http://` prefix; Google automatically formats your URL properly.

7. **Write your ad copy.**

   Whoa, Bessie! All of a sudden, out of the blue, Google is asking you to think! (Don't you hate when that happens?) Don't worry — you can just enter some placeholder text right now. As long as you don't break Google's rules (no profanity, no superlatives, no abbreviations, no drugs from Canada without Square Trade certification, no unproven claims, that sort of thing), you can pretty much write whatever you want. So don't sweat this. Think of Paul McCartney's placeholder lyrics when he began to compose the Beatles' hit song "Yesterday": "Scrambled eggs, oh my baby, how I love your legs."

   You can enter the headline and two lines of text yourself, or click the radio button in the Give Me Ideas tab and follow the Google Wizard of AdWords. If you decide to do it yourself, just place your cursor anywhere in the box and start typing. The existing text will conveniently disappear.

   The Google Wizard takes 10 steps — you can skip any of the questions that don't make sense to your business. Feel free to accept any of Google's suggestions for now — you'll improve them before any of your prospects see them.

   Google allows you 25 characters in your headline and 35 characters in your next two lines. (Think Haiku, not Tolstoy.)

8. **Choose your keywords.**

   Enter a single keyword in the text box. Don't worry about brainstorming. Just pick the first one that comes to mind to describe what you're selling. Google offers a short tutorial here, tantalizingly titled *Top secret keyword tips* (which, by the way, is an excellent model for your ad headline). I know you want to read it — go ahead, it's quite smart, but there's no need to get ahead of yourself. Signing up for an AdWords account is like getting a Ph.D.: Quality is irrelevant; the only thing that matters is whether you're done or not. (Hey, it worked for me. Stop looking at me like that.)

9. **Choose your currency.**

   Choose the currency you use to buy groceries. This is about your account, not your customers.

10. **Set your monthly budget.**

    Play it safe here and click the radio button next to $30 per month, or choose an even lower number next to the bottom radio button. You'll set your actual budget when you've done more research and are ready to go live.

    If you set a budget lower than Google likes, you'll receive a pop-up warning when you complete the form by clicking the Continue button. Ignore it by choosing OK.

Your initial advertising budget is entirely for testing. Don't expect to make money from your first ads and campaigns. I'm not saying you won't, but counting on it is like counting on winning at roulette in Las Vegas to pay your plane fare home. You are paying for cheap market research.

Once you've used AdWords to figure out your market and adjust your sales process to profitability, you no longer care about limited your budget. Once you can buy a dollar for 60 cents, you want to make that deal as many times as Google will let you.

11. **Decide how much contact you want with Google.**

   At the bottom of the page, you'll see two prechecked boxes offering you personalized ideas for improving your ad performance and AdWords newsletters with generic tips. Your inbox, your call. At least Google doesn't send you 200 V!@gra offers every hour.

12. **Click the Continue button to go to your account.**

   You'll land on a page like that shown in Figure 2-3.

Figure 2-3:
Linking to an existing Google account or setting up a new one.

13. **Set up your AdWords account.**

   Google wants to know if it knows you already. If you already have an account for any of the three billion other Google services (like Gmail, AdSense, Orkut, Google Docs and Spreadsheets, Picasa, and so on), you can link your AdWords account to the same login. Google will give you the choice of using your existing account for AdWords, or creating a brand new one. If this is your first brush with Google's personalized services, or if you want to create a completely new account, Google gives you that option.

To use an existing Google account:

a. Select the radio button next to I Have an E-mail Address and Password I Already Use with Google Services Like AdSense, Gmail, Orkut, or the Personalized Home Page.

b. Enter your e-mail and password and click the Continue button.

To create a new Google account:

a. Select the radio button next to I Do Not Use These Other Services. Enter your e-mail, enter your password twice, and type the funny-looking characters you see in the box to prove you're not a malicious or annoying software program. If you are visually impaired and can't make out the letters, click the Handicapped icon to the right for an auditory equivalent. You'll hear male muttering in the background, and a female voice reading out some numbers for you to type.

b. Once you're done, and you've carefully examined the Terms of Use and the Privacy Policy, click the Create Account button.

You'll be taken to a page like the one shown in Figure 2-4, with instructions to check your e-mail to verify your account.

Figure 2-4:
You've
created
your
account;
now go
check your
e-mail.

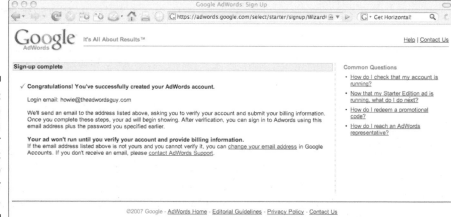

14. **Verify your account by clicking the link in the e-mail message from Google AdWords.**

Check your inbox for an e-mail from `adwords-noreply@google.com` (see Figure 2-5), and click the link that looks like this:

```
https://www.google.com/accounts/VE?service=
    adwords&hl=en-US&c=-46587411630718875627
```

The bottom of the e-mail contains your AdWords account number, a 10-digit number that looks something like 123-456-7890. Write this down somewhere — you'll need it if you ever need to contact AdWords about your account.

Figure 2-5:
Click the link
in the e-mail
message.

15. **Click the Click Here to Continue button to keep riding this wild AdWords roller coaster.**

    You'll arrive at the very first screen we started at. You may ponder the philosophical implications of this fact, with a little help from T.S. Eliot:

    > *We shall not cease from exploration*
    > *And the end of all our exploring*
    > *Will be to arrive where we started*
    > *And know the place for the first time.*

    Or, you can just log in, using the e-mail address and password you created. You did write them down and hide them in a safe place, right?

    You'll find a friendly page welcoming you to AdWords. It displays your ad below an invitation to either enter your billing information and activate your ad, or review it.

16. **Click the Review Ad First button to enter — drum roll please — your AdWords Control Panel.**

If you don't have a Web site

Google will help you create a basic "Yellow Pages" Web page for your business. You won't be able to make online sales on this Web page, but you can provide enough information on the page for your visitors to call you, send you an e-mail, or visit your actual business location.

If you run a local business and conduct all transactions in person, this simple Web site may be all you need for a little while. When you get to the Web page where you enter your business information, you can click the See a Sample Page link to check out the Mario Loves Pasta, Inc. page, which gives you an idea of what your one-page Web site can look like. Note the live e-mail link, hours of operation, phone numbers, address, and payment accepted. The ziti look great, don't they? Sadly, the phone numbers aren't real. I wonder if Mario will respond to e-mail?

To set up your Starter Edition account if you don't already have a Web site, follow these steps:

1. **Point your browser to `http://adwords.google.com` and click the Click to Start button (refer to Figure 2-1).**

   (The button could also be labeled Begin or Start Now. I've gotten all three — Google appears to be testing which button text works best.)

2. **Select the Starter Edition radio button.**

3. **Select the I Don't Have a Webpage. Help Me Create One radio button, and then scroll down and click the Continue button.**

   Google takes you to a page where you enter the information you want on your business's AdWords Web page.

4. **In the Provide Basic Business Information area, enter your business's name, address, phone, and e-mail address in the appropriate text boxes.**

   Enter your business name and address in the text boxes. Click the Test Address link to see if it maps properly. The page refreshes to include a close-up map of your location. You can choose further down the page to include this map or not.

   Enter the e-mail address and phone number you want Web visitors to use. If you check the box next to Help Me Count the Calls I Receive FREE, Google does a very neat thing for you. They assign a phone number to your Web page that forwards to your actual business line, and they give you statistics on how many calls your Web site generates. You can choose a local or toll-free number.

   Imagine if the Yellow Pages did that for you! You could stop paying for ads in the directories that don't lead to calls, and buy bigger ads in the books that generate business.

5. **Select the check boxes of all the payment methods your business accepts in the What Forms of Payment Does Your Business Accept? area.**

   You get a baker's dozen of choices, including a check box for you to add other methods Google didn't include, like Discover, local credit cards, and "will work for back massages."

6. **Select whether you want the page to show your business's operating hours in the What Are Your Operating Hours at This Location? area.**

   When you select the I'd Like to Specify Operating Hours radio button, the page immediately updates to enable you to enter the business hours for each day of the week. You can input different hours for each day of the week, close or open your shop with a check in the Closed check box, and even use military time if you think there's a danger of some confused soul showing up at 3:00 am wondering why she can't buy a leopard-skin lion tamer's costume.

   If you want to take a lunch break, put a check in the check box that says Enter Two Sets of Hours for a Single Day, just below the days. Your page will refresh with double start and end times.

7. **Write a few paragraphs about your business in the Describe Your Business section.**

   As you write the description, think about three things:

   a. What do your prospects need to know to help them make a decision?

   b. What differentiates your business from their other choices?

   c. What action do you want your Web visitor to take after viewing this page?

   Include details that support your claims, and communicate in a style that represents how your establishment actually feels to customers. If you want prospects to physically visit you, give a clear description of your location, and where to park. Think about how you decide whom to call or where to shop. You're probably looking for the first ad that answers your burning questions and ends your confusion. Provide that information to your Web visitors.

8. **Include a clear Call to Action in your business description, such as**

   • E-mail me for today's specials

   • Mention coupon code "405" for a 10% discount on your first order

   • Call to find out which water filter is right for you

9. **Select a radio button to determine the layout of your Web page in the Choose a Layout area.**

   You can choose to include a map, a picture, both, or text only. If you include a picture, you can upload one from your computer. Click the Browse button to bring up your computer's files, and find the picture you want. It must be in .jpg or .gif format, and can't be larger than 500k. If you're not sure what any of this means, find a graphics person to help you get the best picture into an appropriate file format.

10. **Select a radio button in the Choose a Background Color area.**

    Your choices include gray, rose, blue, or yellow. You can go back and change this at any time. Click the Preview My Webpage link to preview the page you created (note that you'll need to disable any pop-up blockers).

11. **Click the Continue button.**

    Now you'll continue creating your ad and the rest of your account, as described in the earlier section, "If you have a Web site." The only difference is, the URL of your ad will begin with `http://biz.googlepages.com` and will end with a suffix of your choosing, up to 15 characters.

Touring Your Starter Edition Control Panel

When you log in for the first time, Google will show you the ad you created and the keyword you selected, along with your monthly budget, language and geographic range of the ad. (See Figure 2-6.)

The alerts at the top

Your new account arrives with an alert at the top of the page, which will remain until you dismiss it. This first alert is simply an invitation to read Google's Frequently Asked Questions (FAQs) about the Starter Edition. Once your campaign starts running, the alerts are likely to be more relevant: Your credit card is about to expire, some ads have been disapproved, Google has changed a policy, things like that. It's a good idea to dismiss the old alerts, both to give yourself more room on the screen for campaign management, and to train yourself to pay attention to them.

The ad

Your ad appears near the top left of the Control Panel, enclosed in a thin rectangle. It looks just as it will look in the Google search results on the right side of the page.

Testing your ad

Before you do anything else, click your ad and see where Google takes you. Is it where you want to send your visitors? Does it reach your home page instead of a specific landing page? Does it go to Page Not Found? Does it go to a different Web site entirely? I've seen all these calamities cost advertisers dearly — this quick check should nip the problem in the bud.

If your ad takes you somewhere you don't want to go, click the Back button to return to AdWords; then click the Edit link below the ad to fix the URL.

Editing your ad

To change an existing ad, click the Edit link below the ad. You'll see the same screen you used to create the ad in the first place. Make any changes you like and click Save.

By default, Google displays your root URL only — that is, only up to the `.com` or `.org` or `.whatever` — in the fourth line of the ad. Use your URL to attract visitors to your Web site. For example, if you sell red staplers and are advertising on the keyword `red stapler`, the second URL below would be more attractive to prospects:

```
www.StaplerHeaven.com
www.StaplerHeaven.com/Red-Staplers
```

Change the URL by clicking the Edit link next to the fourth text box (the one with your Web site name in green) near the bottom of the page. Your display URL (the one that shows in your ad) doesn't have to be identical to your landing URL (the page your visitors go after clicking). See Figure 2-7 for an example.

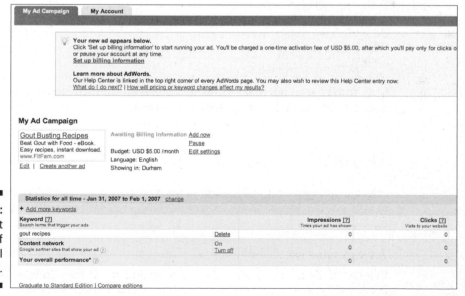

Figure 2-6: Your first glimpse of the Control Panel.

Figure 2-7:
The landing
URL and
the display
URL are
different, but
both point to
the same
Web site
(www.fit
fam.com).

Writing a second ad

As I will repeat until you're sick of hearing it, the key to success in Internet marketing is ongoing split testing. (*Split testing* is creating two variations [in this case, of your ad], sending half your traffic to each, and seeing which one generates a better response.) Not only that, the key to success in Internet marketing is ongoing split testing. The Starter Edition gives you the ability to create a second ad to run alongside the first by following these steps:

1. **In the Control Panel page, click the Create Another Ad Variation link below your existing ad.**

   You'll get a choice on the next page — whether to create a variation on your current ad or a brand new ad for a different set of keywords.

2. **Click the radio button next to A Variation on My Current Ad.**

3. **Scroll down to make any changes you want to the existing text, and click Save.**

Google will return you to the campaign Control Panel. You'll immediately notice a new tab: Ad Variations. Now you can monitor the difference between your two ads by counting clicks. One of the ads will probably receive more clicks than the other. When your ads have accrued enough clicks to make a statistician happy, you can replace the "losing" ad with another challenger. For the full sermon on split testing, please turn in your hymnal to Chapter 13.

The Keywords

The keyword tab allows you to add and delete keywords, and see which ones are getting impressions and clicks.

Adding keywords

Click the Add More Keywords link, and then add two variations of your existing keyword. Put one in square brackets and the other in quotes (as in Figure 2-8).

Figure 2-8:
Add the
exact and
phrase
match
variations
of your
keyword.

The brackets limit the search to an exact match — only someone who typed that exact phrase in that exact order, with nothing before or after it, will see the ad. The quotes limit the search to a phrase match — that exact phrase must appear in the search, but it can be part of a longer search string. For example:

Keyword	*Search that will trigger the ad*
gout recipes	Gout Recipes
	recipes for gout
	what recipes fight gout?
	gout recipies
"gout recipes"	vegetarian gout recipes
	gout recipes for a Superbowl party
[gout recipes]	gout recipes

See Chapter 5 for everything you wanted to know about keywords, but weren't sure how to search for it.

Once you've saved your additions, Google returns you to the campaign Control Panel. You'll notice a difference right away: the column headers, Keyword, Impressions, Clicks, and Total Cost are now blue, clickable links. If you click one of them, you sort the entire table based on that column. A downward-facing triangle appears next to the word you clicked. Your table is sorted in descending order of that column's values. Click the same word again and the triangle flips. Now the table shows the ascending order. This comes in very handy when you're managing large campaigns with hundreds of keywords.

Deleting keywords

Delete keywords by — this tip is worth the whole price of the book right here — clicking Delete next to the keyword you want to delete. Don't thank me — I'm just doing my job.

Monitoring keyword performance

As your campaign runs, you'll notice some interesting things. Some keywords will register lots of impressions and others very few. Some will get lots of clicks while others get ignored. For now, just notice these data points. The Starter Edition doesn't really give you enough information to make good business decisions. When you're ready to start acting on the market trends, it's time to remove the training wheels and graduate to the Standard Edition.

Content network

Below your keyword list, you'll see a row heading called Content Network. This doesn't refer to a bunch of satisfied people who all know each other — I'll pause while you smile grimly and consider chucking this book across the room — but rather the Web sites that have signed up to show Google ads in the middle of their content.

You can let it run for a bit just for curiosity's sake, but a best practice is to turn it off for now. Here's why: You may get a lot more content searches than keyword searches, which can overwhelm your monitoring. Keyword searches, because they're tied to specific words, give you much better market data than impressions and clicks from a bunch of Web sites that are unknown to you.

Once your campaigns are humming based on keywords, see Chapter 7 to find out how to set up content network campaigns that won't muddy your reporting.

Deploying the Goldilocks maximum CPC strategy

In addition to ad copy and keywords, you have control over one more aspect of your campaign: how much money you agree to give Google for each visitor it sends to your Web site.

You can let Google's Budget Optimizer do it for you, which is the default option. Google will try to give you as many clicks as possible for the monthly budget you've chosen. I recommend overriding Google's control over your bidding. You can learn a lot from bidding too high and too low, if you perform experiments and pay attention to the results. The just-right bid will hover around the average value of a visitor to a Web site in your market. Visitor value, which I cover in Chapter 14 until you beg me to stop, is perhaps your most important business number.

Testing your bids can benchmark you against your competitors to determine how profitable your Web site is, once someone lands on it, compared to others in your space. If your Web site is considerably better at making money from a visitor than your competitors, you can offer to buy their traffic from them and pay them more as your reseller than they'd make selling their own stuff!

If you want to set the maximum CPC yourself, click Edit Settings in the main campaign Control Panel, and next to Bidding, uncheck the Budget Optimizer option. Enter a bid in the box next to the currency, and save your settings at the bottom of the page. Pay attention to format here — 25 translates into $25.00, not $0.25. Don't get careless and saddle yourself accidentally with a $4,000 bill to pay.

Impressions, clicks, and cost

These three crucial numbers, shown in Figure 2-9, are at the heart of your campaign. Smart advertisers pay close attention to those numbers to save time, money, and heartache.

Impressions

Technically, an impression is a single instance of a search results page that contains your ad. It doesn't mean the searcher has seen the ad, just a search results page with your ad on it. If the searcher has a small screen with high resolution and your ad appears below the scroll (meaning they'd have to scroll down in order to view it), it's still counted as an impression. If they click the first listing they see, before they've looked at yours, it still counts.

Figure 2-9:
Impressions,
clicks, and
total cost
for three
keywords
on the third
day of a
campaign.

Impressions can indicate the potential size of your AdWords market. If you are bidding on popular keywords, you can expect lots of impressions. But if your bidding strategy places your ad very low in the ad rankings, and it shows up on page 4 of the listings, you'll see very few impressions — even though the market itself may be huge.

Clicks

A click is a single instance of a unique visitor clicking your ad and arriving at your landing URL. Clicks are good, right? The more clicks, the more visitors to your Web site. Well, not so fast. Clicks cost you money, remember? You make that investment back only when the visitor buys something from you. The goal of your ad is twofold:

✔ To get all the people who will eventually buy from you to click your ad

✔ To discourage all the people who will never buy from you from clicking your ad

Obviously, you can't know in advance who will buy and who won't. But you can make some pretty good guesses until you graduate to the Standard Edition and implement conversion tracking (see Chapter 14).

For example, if you're advertising a pony tail holder worn by Paris Hilton, and you mention Paris Hilton in your ad and select `Paris Hilton` as a keyword, chances are you'll find a lot of visitors who have no interest in your hair accessory but a lot of interest in, shall we say, a multimedia Paris Hilton experience.

As you gain AdWords experience, you'll learn how to turn the prospect tap higher or lower to maximize profits.

Cost

Your cost equals the total number of clicks multiplied by the average cost per click. If you are paying $2.05 per click and your campaign has racked up 17 clicks, your cost so far will be $2.05 \times 17 = $34.85.

You should track how long it takes you to use up your monthly budget. If it's all gone in 3 days, you're looking at 27 days with no activity. You should also track, as best you can, whether an increase in AdWords spending produces more sales and profits for you.

After you graduate to the Standard Edition, you'll benefit from much more powerful reporting tools that show you the profitability of each ad and each keyword.

You can change the date range to see how your campaign has performed at different times. On the campaign management Control Panel, click the Change link next to the date range at the top left of the green header. You'll be given a choice of presets: all time, today, yesterday, last 7 days, last week (Mon-Sun), last business week (Mon-Fri), this month, or last month. You can alternatively click the second radio button to select any range you want. This second option is useful if you've changed something on January 17 and you want to compare the 5 days before and after the change.

The statistics don't represent what your prospects are doing in real time. Google cops to a three-hour delay in click reporting. You can see impressions faster than that, usually. But don't panic because your expected traffic surge hasn't materialized two minutes after writing that irresistible ad. Patience, Grasshopper.

Graphs and reports

If you're a visual sort of person, check out the Graphs tab on the right of the green header bar. You will be shown clicks, cost, and impressions per day.

If you want to view your campaign data in beautiful printed form for some late night reading in bed, or want to share some statistics with colleagues without having them log in to the account, you can download reports of impressions, clicks, and costs by keyword and ad. You get a choice of formats; chances are, if you have Microsoft Excel installed on your computer, you'll choose .csv (for Excel).

Activating Your Account

Are you ready to spend some coin and take your campaign live? Click Activate Account and complete the form that comes up, as shown in Figure 2-10.

Figure 2-10:
Activating
your
account.

To activate your account, follow these steps:

1. **Use the drop-down list to select your billing country.**

   The most common choices are at the top, followed by long list of just about every country there is.

2. **Select your country from the Time Zone Country or Territory drop-down list, and then select your time zone from the Time Zone drop-down list.**

   Google won't let you change your time zone once you've set it, so be careful here. No second chances!

3. **Enter the promotional code at the back of this book to recoup the cost of this book in free clicks.**

4. **Click the Continue button.**

5. **Choose a payment method.**

   Google charges your credit card on a pay-as-they-click system. Chances are, your only real choice here *is* a credit card: JCB, American Express, MasterCard, or Visa. I spent about 10 minutes searching for a country that allowed other options, and gave up after pretending to be from the USA, Canada, UK, Norway, Netherlands, China, Azerbaijan, and Brunei Darussalam. (If you happen to live in a country from which Google accepts PayPal or silver or yak cheese, please let me know for the second edition.)

6. **Accept Google's Terms and Conditions.**

   Google's long and complex Terms and Conditions constitute a legal contract, so read it carefully before agreeing. I'm not a lawyer, so you'll get no guidance from me on this one. I just signed up and hoped for the best.

7. **Click OK.**

   You'll be taken to a screen where you can fill out billing information. If you've ever bought anything online, that process will be straightforward and simple.

   Google's preferred phone-number format includes dashes, but no parentheses or periods:

   ```
   919-555-3167
   ```

   not

   ```
   (919) 555-3167
   ```

   Once you complete the form, your account is live — and your ad should start showing on the right side of the Google search results page for the keywords you've selected.

After you complete your account setup, wait 15 minutes, and then browse to www.google.com and do a search on your keyword.

Look at the top and the right of the search results page. If you don't see your ad, scroll down and click the More Sponsored Links link. Keep going through the pages until you see your ad or you get to the end of the listings. This exercise gives you an idea of the competitiveness of your market. If you see a lot of competitors, don't get discouraged. It means a lot of people think they can make money here. The information in this book will put you way ahead of most of them. When you see no or few competitors for a keyword, that may indicate a market that's too small or too unresponsive.

When nobody can see your ad

If your ad doesn't appear in the right column within 30 minutes of account activation, you may have a problem. Usually, correcting it is simple — once you've figured out what it is.

If your ad isn't receiving any impressions (indicated by a 0 in the last row of the Impressions column), you may be a victim of one of the following:

- **Editorial disapproval:** Have you violated Google's editorial guidelines? If you throw exclamation points around like crazy, promise "the best" or "the cheapest" stuff, capitalize like you're screaming in a chat room, use copyrighted terms, offer cheap drugs from Canada or $25 Rolexes or nuclear-weapon-making instructions, or commit any of a dozen other infractions, your ad won't show.

Google lays out their rules here:

- *Editorial Guidelines:* `https://adwords.google.com/select/guidelines.html`

- *Content Guidelines:* `https://adwords.google.com/select/contentpolicy.html`

✔ **Low ad rank:** Based on your monthly budget, which you set when you created the account, and your optional choice of a maximum bid price, which you can edit at any time, your ad may be relegated to page 19 of search results, the equivalent of scribbling it onto the back of a gas station receipt in yellow crayon and tossing it into a dumpster.

In the Standard Edition, you can see exactly in what positions your ads show. At this point, you can try raising your minimum bid — and monthly budget — and see if that gets you onto the first page of search results.

✔ **Poor keyword performance:** If your keyword is `pink slippers big enough to fit an African elephant` or some other phrase that few or no people would ever search for, you could wait a long time before seeing a single click. In Chapter 5, I'll introduce you to the spy tools that help you find out exactly what people are typing into their online searches.

When just you can't see your ad

Sometimes your ad is receiving impressions, but try as you might, you can't find it yourself. Before you start humming the *Twilight Zone* theme, consider the possibilities described in the following subsections.

Google thinks you're searching outside your geo-targeting

Remember when you first set up your account and you had to choose a geographic location within which to advertise? Google may be interpreting the information it's reading on your computer (specifically, its Internet Protocol [IP] address, to mean you yourself are outside of your targeted area). IP addresses are loosely connected to different parts of the world.

To find out where the Internet thinks you are, go to `www.ipligence.com` and scroll down until you can see the map at the bottom right, shown in Figure 2-11.

There are many reasons why Google could get confused about where in the world you are. First, IP addresses aren't exact — they're not like Zip or postal codes. Second, if you are connecting to the Internet through a service that's somewhere other than where you are, Google can be misled. Third, little green aliens from outer space sometimes take over my fingers when I'm typing stuff I really don't know anything about so that the paragraphs look long enough to be authoritative.

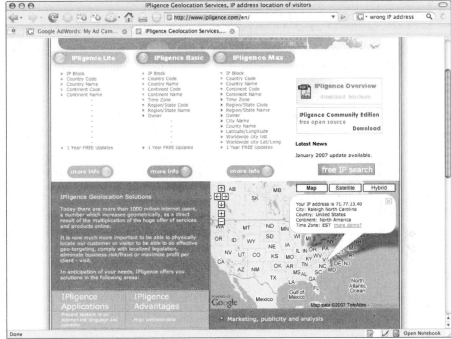

Figure 2-11:
Here
ipligence.com
shows me
where the
Internet
thinks my
computer
resides.

Every machine connected to the Internet has a unique IP address, a string of four numbers separated by dots. Google's IP address, for example, is 216.239.51.100. The IP address is the "real" Internet address. We humans give Web sites names, like Google and WalletEmptyingJunk.com, so we can find them more easily. The Internet machines map these names onto the numbers to send our browsers and e-mails to the right places.

Confused? Try this experiment: Open a Web browser, type **216.239.51.100** into the address bar, and press Enter. If you've entered the numbers and dots correctly, you should arrive at Google's home page.

Your IP address may be unique to your computer, shared by other computers on your network, or even shared by many of the computers served by your Internet service provider (ISP).

You chose a different language

If you have chosen to advertise in Spanish (for example), you may not be able to find your ad if your Google searching preference is set for English. To change it (you can always change it back), go to www.google.com and click Preferences next to the search box. Click the radio button Search Only for Pages Written in These Language(s) and put a check next to the relevant language. Click Save Preferences to return to your search.

Managing Your Account

The final frontier of the Starter Edition is the My Account tab at the top left. Click it and you'll see three subtabs: Billing Summary, Billing Preferences, and Account Preferences, as shown in Figure 2-12. Explore them at your leisure — they're pretty self-explanatory.

Figure 2-12:
The My Account tab for keeping track of your spending, adding and changing credit cards, and setting your e-mail notification preferences.

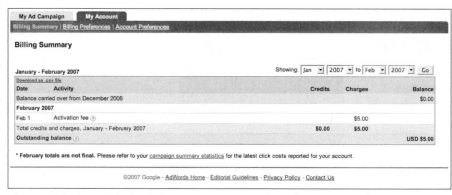

If you run an online pharmacy, you'll need a PharmacyCheckerID before Google will let you advertise. Go to the Account Preferences subtab, find the PharmacyCheckerID section, and click the Edit link to go to a new page. Click the Read Our FAQ link to find out how to apply.

Upgrading to the Standard Edition

If you've created and activated a Starter Edition Account, written two ads, selected three keywords, and set a monthly budget and minimum CPC, I hereby declare you ready to upgrade to the Standard Edition.

At the bottom of any page in the Campaign Management tab, click the Graduate to Standard Edition link. Chapter 3 gives all the details about moving up to the Standard Edition.

Chapter 3

Setting Up Your Standard Edition Account

· ·

In This Chapter

▶ Graduating from the Starter Edition

▶ Starting with the Standard Edition

▶ Navigating the setup process

▶ Introducing AdWords Mission Control

· ·

You're about to set up a fully functioning AdWords account! Whether you took my humble advice and created a starter account first, or decided to skip the training wheels and climb directly on the two-wheeler, I congratulate you on this momentous step in your online advertising career. I'm so glad I'm here to share it with you.

In this chapter, I walk you through setting up a Standard Edition account, both as an upgrade from the starter edition and from scratch. If you already have an existing account, you can skip ahead to the "Running Mission Control with the Campaign Management Tab" section, where you explore the three basic features of the Standard Edition: campaign management, keyword selection, and ad writing.

Setting Up Your Standard Edition Account

If you already have a Starter Edition account, you see Google's pitch to try the full-featured Standard Edition front and center every time you log in. If that's you, keep reading. If you've decided to jump right into the Standard Edition, good for you — skip to the "Opening a new Standard Edition account" section, later in this chapter.

Graduating from the Starter Edition

You can graduate from the Starter Edition to the Standard Edition at any time, simply by clicking the link at the bottom of any page of your account. On the next page, review the benefits of the upgrade, and note the warning at the bottom: You can't go home to the Starter Edition again. When you're ready to take the leap (this really isn't a big deal, I promise), click Continue.

The next page reminds you yet again that the change to Standard Edition is permanent. Boldly click the Yes, Graduate link and hum "Pomp and Circumstance" as the next page loads. Congratulations, you've done it! Skip to the "Running Mission Control with the Campaign Management Tab" section, later in this chapter, to find out how to use your awesome new powers responsibly. (Can you tell I just watched *Spider-Man 3?*)

Opening a new Standard Edition account

If you've decided to jump straight into the Standard Edition, follow these steps:

1. **Open your Web browser and go to** `http://adwords.google.com`.

2. **(Optional) Choose a language other than English (US) from the drop-down list at the top right, and Google will translate the page into that language.**

3. **Click the Start button at the top right.**

   (Sometimes the button is labeled Click To Begin or Let's Get Started. I've never seen it read Drink Me, but I'm hopeful . . . .)

4. **Select Standard Edition and click the Continue button.**

5. **(Optional) Select one or more languages from the list box.**

   If you'll be advertising exclusively in English, do nothing. To choose multiple languages, hold down the Ctrl key while you click (for PC users) or the ⌘ key (for Mac users).

6. **Leave the Countries and Territories radio button selected, and click the Continue button.**

   With the Standard Edition, you can target your ads with flashlight-like (not really laser-like) precision. I'll show you how to do this in Chapter 7.

7. **Select the country or countries where you'd like your ads to be seen:**

   a. Select the country in the Available Countries and Territories list box, and then click the Add button to copy your selection to the Selected Countries and/or Territories list box.

   Select multiple countries just as you would choose more than one language, by Ctrl+clicking or ⌘+clicking.

b. To remove a country or territory from the Selected Countries and/or Territories list box, select it and click the Remove button.

c. When you're done, click the Continue button.

8. **Fill in the text boxes to create an ad; click the Continue button when you're finished.**

Now Google wants you to create your first ad. What, you're not ready to whip out a masterpiece of persuasive prose at the drop of a cursor? No worries. Type pretty much anything here — you won't show it to the world for a while yet. The following list provides guidance on what to enter in those text boxes:

- In the Headline text box, type the problem or opportunity.

- In the Description Line 1 text box, enter a short description of big benefit.

- In the Description Line 2 text box, write a short description of your product/service.

- In the Display URL text box, type your Web site's name.

- In the Destination URL text box, enter the URL of the exact Web page you want customers to visit first.

The display URL is what your prospect sees in the ad itself. It must be "real" enough to go somewhere relevant if they were to type it in, but it doesn't have to be the same as the actual destination URL. Think of the display URL as the name of your online store; would you rather buy a CN Netcom amplifying phone headset from `www.StuffThatSitsOnYour Desk.com` or `www.PhoneSupplies.com/Netcom-Headsets`? You can use the destination URL to track your Web-site traffic and to show different pages to different markets.

See Figure 3-1 for an example. But please don't sweat it at this point. Just write something that doesn't violate Google's editorial or content guidelines (see Chapter 2) and move on.

9. **Type your chosen keywords into the list box and click the Continue button when you're finished.**

For now, just type a single keyword that someone searching for your business might type; for example:

```
used cars
glow in the dark poker chips
functional fitness training
```

Next to the box where you input keywords, Google asks if you want more. If your URLs point to a working Web site, Google quickly scans the site and suggests other keywords, based on your Web site copy and Google's database of related searches. If it can't find your Web site, you can enter your main keyword and Google will give you variation and related searches from its database.

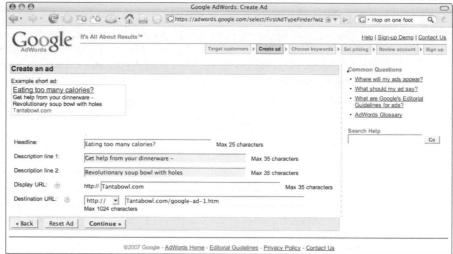

Figure 3-1:
Write your
first ad.

Google is, at its core, a very large data processor. By tracking the behavior of searchers, it gets smarter all the time — and can offer better suggestions to advertisers and better search results to shoppers. Google notices, for example, how long a person will stay away after clicking an ad or free listing. If you click my ad, look at my Web page for 3 seconds and then click back to Google for another search, that tells Google you didn't think much of my site. Enough data like that, and my bid prices will increase to penalize me for not giving Google's users what they want.

The keyword-suggestion tool can be helpful, but don't use it right now. Until you understand how to create tightly focused ad groups, the tool will create a messy and unfocused campaign. Use the tool later to refine your campaigns. Right now, just pick one or two closely related terms, if you like, and continue.

10. **Select your currency from the Pay for This Account Using drop-down list, and then type how much you're willing to spend in the Enter Your Daily Budget and the Enter Your Maximum CPC text boxes.**

Ready to have some fun? It's trial-and-error time, thanks to Google's Traffic Estimator. Enter any numbers you like for daily budget and maximum CPC and click View Traffic Estimator. It will show you estimated CPC, the position of your ad (1 puts you at the top of the first page, 9–10 put you at or near the bottom of the first search-results page or top of the second page, and 11+ puts your ad squarely on page 2 or worse), the likely number of clicks per day, and your daily cost.

Typically, an ad on page 2 gets one-tenth the impressions of the same ad on page 1, so (unless the clicks are ridiculously expensive on the first page), page 1 is where you want to be.

To view the maximum traffic you could possibly expect from that keyword, enter a maximum CPC of $100 and a daily budget of $10,000.

Make sure you change these back before continuing!

Google will show you the most you'll pay for a click if your ad is in the top position, and the maximum number of clicks each keyword will generate in a day. Keep in mind, your ad may out- or under-perform this estimate, depending on how well it connects with your prospects.

Settle on a CPC you can live with financially that puts your ad somewhere on the first page. You can make adjustments when you have actual results to base them on.

11. **Click the Continue button.**

12. **Review your selections on the next page, decide whether you want e-mail from Google about AdWords strategies and tips, choose an appropriate answer from the How Did You First Hear about Google Adwords drop-down list, and finally, click the Continue to Signup button.**

If you don't have a Google Account, you're prompted to create one. If you already have a Google Account for Gmail or other Google services, you can use it for your AdWords account. If you are a Gmail junkie, for example, you'll want to connect the accounts so you don't sign yourself out of AdWords every time you check your mail.

For more information about navigating the Google Account business, see Chapter 2.

The rest of the setup process is exactly the same as the Starter Account process described in Chapter 2. After you click the link in your activation e-mail, you'll get to the login page. Enter the e-mail address and password you selected, and you're ready to explore the Standard Edition AdWords control panel.

Your ads won't show up on-screen until you activate your account by giving Google five bucks and a working credit-card number. You can do that now by clicking the link in the warning box with the reddish-pink background and following the account activation wizard (Google is very user-friendly when it comes to taking your money), or take the tour first and pay later. Even if you activate now, you can pause your campaigns so you don't get charged for a lot of traffic before you know what you're doing.

Running Mission Control with the Campaign Management Tab

The first screen you'll see when you go to `http://google.com/adwords` and enter your user name and password is the Account Snapshot screen (shown in Figure 3-2), unless Google decides it's a bad idea and drops it after this book is published. The snapshot screen shows the summary statistics of all the campaigns in the account: total cost, total number of clicks, total impressions, and overall CTR. My first impression: This information is essentially useless. The only number that makes sense to summarize over all campaigns is total cost. The rest of the numbers only make you smarter when you break them down to individual campaigns, ad groups, ads, and keywords.

Figure 3-2:
The
Account
Snapshot
page that
may or may
not be
around by
the time you
read this.

You'll spend the majority of your AdWords time in the Campaign Management tab. After this chapter, most of the book shows you how to improve your online advertising using its various features. For right now, I'll show you the cockpit without asking you to go for a test flight.

You can view your account from three levels, from overview to granular. The All Campaigns view lists your campaigns and gives you basic metrics on each one. The individual campaign view provides the same level of detail about the different ad groups in a particular campaign. The ad group view shows you the finest details about every ad and every keyword in that ad group. This last view is where you'll spend most of your time. Use the other two views to help you prioritize which ad group will give you the biggest return for time spent.

All Campaigns view

The main campaign summary page lists your campaigns and gives summary data about each of them. When you create your second campaign, all the column headings (Campaign Name, Current Status, and so on) become clickable so you can sort your campaigns in various ways. For example, you probably want the campaigns that cost the most to be in your face more; click the Cost heading to sort from most to least costly. Click Cost again to reverse the order.

Campaign Name

By default, AdWords assigns your campaign exciting and informative names like `Campaign #1` and `Campaign #2`. For your own sanity, please replace these generic names with descriptions that will still make sense when you're running dozens of campaigns at once. You can change the name of a campaign by selecting the check box next to the name and then clicking the Edit Settings button above the list of campaigns.

Current Status

Campaigns can be active, paused, or deleted by checking the box next to the campaign or campaigns you want to change, and clicking the Pause, Resume or Delete buttons above the list of campaign names.

- **Active:** Active campaigns currently display your ads to searchers. They cost you money and bring visitors to your Web site.

- **Paused:** Paused campaigns are on hold, but can be reactivated by a single click. Pausing a campaign automatically pauses all the ad groups in that campaign. No impressions, no clicks, no visitors.

- **Deleted:** Deleted campaigns can also be reactivated by a single click. So what's the difference between pausing and deleting a campaign? Beats me. If you delete a campaign, you can't actually make it go away. You can hide it by choosing Show All But Deleted Campaigns from the drop-down list that currently reads Show All Campaigns (see Figure 3-3). This can be helpful if you don't want to clutter your screen with old campaigns, but still want to see active and paused campaigns. Also, it's helpful to delete campaigns if you're writing *AdWords For Dummies* and you don't want the world to see every detail of your AdWords account in your screen shots.

Current Budget

Google shows you the daily budget you set for each campaign. It's grayed out and bracketed in paused and deleted campaigns. You can change your daily budget for any campaign by checking the box next to the campaign name and clicking the Edit Settings button above the list of campaigns.

Clicks

A click represents one person clicking your ad and arriving on your landing page. Google doesn't count multiple clicks from the same computer on the same day (or tries very hard not to) — that's so your competitors can't sit behind their desks and develop carpal tunnel syndrome trying to bankrupt you by clicking your ad repeatedly. Two clicks equals two unique visitors to your site.

Figure 3-3:
You can
hide paused
and/or
deleted
campaigns
to simplify
your screen.

1mpr.

Impr. is short for *impressions,* or the number of times your ad was included on a page that Google showed to a searcher.

CTR

CTR (Click-Through Rate) is the ratio of clicks to impressions, expressed as a percentage. It's one of your most important AdWords numbers, so if you're confused, take a little time to get clear. You can calculate CTR by dividing clicks by impressions. For example, if 200 people see your ad, and 12 of them click it, here's the math:

```
12 ÷ 200 = .06 = 6.00%
```

You'd then brag at the AdWords Saloon, "My CTR is six percent." And everyone would understand that your ad was so compelling, 6 out of every 100 people who saw it ended up on your Web site.

Avg. CPC

The Avg. CPC (Cost Per Click) column tells you how much, on average, you paid Google to get a visitor to your Web site. You may have different average CPCs by campaign, ad-group, keyword, and ad. A big part of AdWords management is deleting or improving elements of your advertising that cost you more than you make back, so your average click cost is an important metric.

Cost

Your cost is simply all the money you've spent on clicks. In this screen, it's broken down by campaign. When you drill deeper, you can see how much each ad and each individual keyword costs you. (After you've set up conversion tracking, described in Chapter 14, you can also track how much each ad makes you.)

You can change the date range in the All Campaigns or any other view by selecting one of the presets in the drop-down list just below the date, or by selecting the lower radio button and inputting any two dates. For some reason, Google insists that your start date be before your end date (that's a little un-quantum-physics, don't you think?). Get into the habit of checking your date range first, whenever you work on campaign management. Otherwise you panic if you see only six clicks, when the cause isn't a broken campaign, but a view set to Today instead of This Month.

Individual Campaign view

Click your campaign name to see your account at the ad-group level. You can see all your ad groups' statistics, including two new columns: Default Bid and Avg. Pos.

- **Default Bid:** Your default bid is the maximum CPC you selected when you created the account. You can change this bid for specific campaigns, the ad groups, or even individual keywords. You can also bid more or less based on the source of the traffic: Google, search partners, or content partners. In Chapter 7, you'll discover smart strategies for bidding different amounts on different keywords.

- **Avg. Pos:** The average position of your ad refers to where it appears in relation to all other ads showing for the same keyword. At the ad-group level, an average position of 5.7 means that on average, your ad shows most often in position 6, less often in position 5, and occasionally higher or lower. If your average position is greater than 8, your ads are not showing nearly as much as they might — only very determined searchers ever go on to the second page of Google results.

You can see some trends, even with extremely small numbers. For example, my new Cold Calls ad group (in Figure 3-4) has received 2 clicks out of 41 impressions, for a rather nice 4.87% CTR. This CTR translates into 49 visitors to my Web site for every thousand people who view the ad after searching for keywords in the Cold Calls ad group. Each click cost me just under $0.20 on average, so I can expect to pay $9.80 for those 49 visitors.

Don't make any assumptions or decisions based on numbers as low as I'm describing here. As a general rule, you want to see at least 30 total clicks before ascribing validity to the data. I know of one business owner who drove his business into the ground making knee-jerk changes based on tiny numbers. See Chapter 13 for more than you ever wanted to know about statistical significance.

As in the All Campaigns view, once you have more than one ad group in a campaign, the column headers will turn clickable and sortable.

Individual ad-group view

In the Individual Campaign view, click the name of an ad group to drill down to the most detailed and powerful view, the individual ad group (see Figure 3-4).

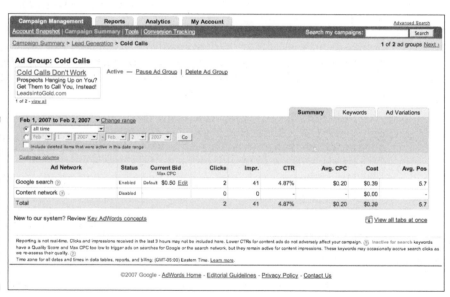

Figure 3-4: Clicking an ad group's name takes you into the powerful Individual Campaign ad-group view.

Summary tab

The summary tab shows you several things at a glance:

- Look below the ad for an indication that you are running more than one ad. In Figure 3-4, you can see 1 of 2 — View All. That's good — you almost always want to be running two ads simultaneously, to find out which one is better (I'll show you how to do this in Chapter 13). For now, you'll see 1 of 1.

✔ Check the date range at the top left of the green header bar. You can change it by clicking the Change Range link, amazingly enough.

✔ Check how your ads are doing by network. In this example, my Google search results are 2 clicks and 41 impressions, and my content network is disabled.

Keywords

The real power of this view resides in the Keywords tab, located just to the right of the active Summary tab. Click Keywords right in the tab to move into keyword view. In Chapter 5 you discover the power of this screen — and learn to drive it like a pro.

Ad variations

One tab to the right from Keywords is the Ad Variations tab. Click it to view your ad. (Figure 3-5 shows an ad group with two ads running simultaneously, to give you a taste of what's in store.) You'll see how that ad is doing, and on what networks it's been showing.

Click the ad itself to go to your landing page. Click the Edit link under the actions column to change the ad. Delete it by marking the check box to its left and clicking Delete. Create a new text ad by clicking the Text Ad link next to Create New Ad just below the date range.

Figure 3-5:
You can compare two ads' performance and replace ineffective ads with new challengers.

The numbers are far too low to take seriously at this point — but notice the difference in CTR: 8.69% to 0%. If the first ad gets 10–15 clicks while the second ad hasn't gotten a single one, I'd declare the second ad DOA and try to beat my control with a new one. By the way, what's the difference between the two ads? Can you see it? The first ad has a comma in the Description Line 2 while the second has doesn't. When you only have 130 characters to play with, little things matter!

Part II
Launching Your AdWords Campaign

The 5th Wave   By Rich Tennant

"Maybe your keyword search, 'legal secretary, love, fame, fortune,' needs to be refined."

In this part . . .

This part is dedicated to finding and counting your prospects, so you can determine whether you have a business that can benefit from AdWords (or any other online-traffic-generation program), and then connecting with your prospects on an emotional level, so they see your ads and Web site and immediately get the urge to reach for their wallets. The biggest business mistake is ignoring your market and trying to sell what you've got, regardless of whether anybody needs or wants it.

Chapter 4 introduces you to the underground world of online market research. You'll see how to assess the profitability of a market in an afternoon, so your online adventures can be close to risk-free.

You explore the heart and soul of online marketing in Chapter 5: keywords. Keywords are the words and phrases that people type into search engines, YouTube, and eBay when they're looking for something to read, watch, or buy. When you understand the keywords your prospects use to find you, and the hidden desires represented by those keywords, you will be successful.

Chapter 6 builds on the keyword foundation and shows you how to write ads that inflame the desires represented by keywords. It covers fundamentals, clever variations, and even some sneaky tricks to make your ads more compelling and profitable.

Chapter 4

Discovering Your Online Market

*T*he Internet is the ultimate spy tool — (ahem) I mean, *market-research opportunity*. If you know where to look (and you will by the end of this chapter), you can determine pretty precisely how many people are looking for your product, how much they're willing to pay for it, and how much money your competitors are making from those people. You can also see how your competitors are marketing — their ads, Web sites, e-mails, promotions, pricing, customer service — and learn a lot about what works and what doesn't. On the Internet, we're all marketing naked. In this chapter, you'll learn how to become a peeping tom of prospects and competitors. Enjoy the view!

Assessing Market Profitability (Don't Dive into an Empty Pool)

In the movie *Field of Dreams,* the Ray Kinsella character builds a baseball diamond in his Iowa cornfield based on a voice that mysteriously repeats, "If you build it, he will come." That philosophy made for a great movie, but I don't recommend it as a customer-acquisition strategy. If you build it, you're probably end up with a garage full of it — unless you take the time to figure out whether anybody's going to want it enough to pay for it.

Ken McCarthy, creator of The System Seminar for Online Marketing (www.thesystemseminar.org), once asked during a lecture, "If you were an Olympic diver, what would be the most important skill you could possess?" The answers varied — the ability to hold a triple gainer, strong core alignment, powerful legs, and so on — but Ken kept shaking his head no to each try. Finally, when we were getting really frustrated, he shared his answer: "The ability to tell if there's enough water in the pool before diving."

In other words, find out if there's a market before you commit large amounts of time and money to creating a business or a product (or to learning fancy marketing tricks to attract buyers). As Perry Marshall points out, amateur marketers create a product and then look for people to sell it to — while professional marketers *find customers* and then look for something to sell them.

Whether you are starting a new venture online, or you have an existing business that you're looking to expand online through AdWords, don't spend any time writing ads or creating Web sites or sourcing products or setting up factories or hiring employees or printing letterhead *until* you've looked into the pool and determined that you can dive without hitting the concrete floor at 60 miles per hour.

In the old days of business, that sort of market research was a drag. Labor-intensive, expensive, imprecise, and slow. But if you want to sell online through paid search, you can save yourself months of agony and thousands of dollars in less time than it takes to fly from Bath, New York to Bath, England.

Glenn Livingston, a former consultant to Fortune 100 companies, has been doing online market research on a do-it-yourself budget with impressive results: he has entered 12 online markets and achieved profitability quickly in all 12. That's quite a batting average, considering that 78.6% of all new businesses fail within six months. (See *Conveniently Making Up Statistics For Dummies* for a full explanation of this calculation. Actually, I have no idea what the failure rate is, and neither does anyone else.) Considering that Glenn offers seven hours of free audio training on his state-of-the-art market-research techniques at www.ultimateadwordsresearch.com, I'm glad he was able to boil down those techniques to four critical factors for inclusion in this book:

"Traditional marketing wisdom says you make your money when you choose your market. Any fisherman will tell you that the best rod and bait in the world won't do you any good in a mud puddle, so let's talk about how to find the best fishing holes.

"While there are literally dozens of factors to consider when choosing a market, here are four of the absolute most important things to know before you go fishing . . .

"How big is your market? (Market Size)

"How much is the average visitor worth? (Average Spend)

"What's the total dollar volume? (Market Size x Average Spend)

"How stable is the market? (Market Stability & Trends)"

Glenn boils down initial market research into one key question: "Are other people making money there?" Because the Internet is so decentralized, nobody knows exactly how big and juicy a given market is. And, as the diet ads say, individual results may vary. Glenn created some guidelines that allowed him to evaluate a market on a lazy Sunday afternoon, and have a very good idea of the potential profitability of the market by dinnertime.

Remember when your high school Social Studies teacher got mad at you for skipping all the comments on your essay and just flipping to the letter grade on the last page? You're about to discover why — in the case of PPC (Pay Per Click) marketing, the "letter grade" — the potential profitability of the market — can get you into a lot of trouble if you don't understand the data behind it. For example, certain markets can be profitable for advanced marketers and not beginners. Some markets can produce good results with a dozen keywords, while others require tens of thousands. No tool can ever replace your own judgment.

Determining market size by spying on searches

Would you like to know how many times people searched for keywords related to your business last month? How about which keywords were the most popular? And suppose you could do it in about 20 seconds — are you willing to spend the time before setting up your AdWords campaigns?

The number of searches is a critical number if you plan to make AdWords a significant part of your business acquisition strategy. Think Yellow Pages again — if no one is looking for the listing *Unicycles*, then a unicycle shop that relies on the Yellow Pages is going to have trouble paying the rent. Of course, many items and services are sold that aren't searched for — just not with AdWords. For example, lots of people buy CDs with guided meditations. But very few people searched for them (about four a day), so you could reasonably expect one sale every one to two months from AdWords traffic if your ad and Web site were very good. And with that tiny trickle of traffic, your testing of alternate ads (see Chapter 13) and landing pages (Chapter 15) will provide conclusive results some time around the next ice age.

Go to www.askhowie.com/freewords, type a keyword into the search box, and click Research. After a few seconds, you'll see a list of the top 100 keywords that include the one you typed, as shown in Figure 4-1. Select and copy the entire list, including search volume numbers. Then open an Excel spreadsheet, highlight cell A1, and paste. You should see one column of numbers and another of keywords.

Quickly scan the keywords and delete any rows unrelated to your market. For example, if you sell books and supplies to rabbit owners, you will remove terms like Velveteen Rabbit and Who Framed Roger Rabbit from the list. Examine the remaining keywords, paying attention to several things:

- ✔ Which keywords are more popular (higher on the list) than others?

- ✔ Are there just a few keywords that result in the vast majority of searches?

- ✔ Do some of the keywords represent sub-markets within the main market (for example, rabbits for hobbyists versus rabbits for commercial purposes — Pets or Meat)?

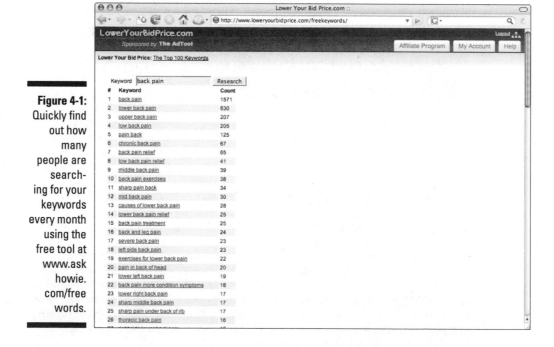

Figure 4-1: Quickly find out how many people are searching for your keywords every month using the free tool at www.askhowie.com/freewords.

Google doesn't make the number of searches public information, so you will have to use a different source to estimate the size of the AdWords search market. Yahoo! currently makes its numbers available at http://inventory. overture.com, but the tool has been unreliable and disappears from time to time. Check www.askhowie.com/chapter-4 for updates and locations of the best free and paid keyword research tools. I've configured www.askhowie. com/freewords to redirect to whatever keyword tool is working best at any given time. The one in Figure 4-1 gets its data from the $70 per month Keyword Discovery database. I find that these numbers must be multiplied by 100–300 to predict actual Google search impressions.

Figure 4-1 shows that people searched for back pain 1,571 times the previous month. The top related terms include lower back pain (630), upper back pain (207), and low back pain (205). This information is helpful — not just now, while you're assessing the potential risks and rewards of entering the market, but later on, when you choose keywords and write sales copy. For example, over three times as many people searched for lower back pain than low back pain. If you were writing the headline of a Google ad promising relief from back pain, that information would lead you to choose lower back pain as the term that mirrors the language of your market. You would also use that information to create the copy on your Web site, and in offline marketing materials such as brochures, print ads, business cards, and so on.

The total number of searches for the top 100 keywords, which appears at the bottom of the page, is a good indication of whether it's a good market to enter. Beginning AdWords marketers should stay between 500 and 5,000 searches per month (which translates into 50,000–1,500,000 Google searches). After you've had success in these less competitive but still vibrant markets, you can begin to tackle markets with more than 5,000 monthly searches in the free keyword tool.

Estimating profitability by snooping on your competitors' keyword bids

Most smart businesses will spend money on customer acquisition until they reach the break-even point. If you know that every time a Google user visits your Web page, you make 35 cents (on average, not for every single visitor), and you have the ability to sell additional products and services to that customer in the future, you probably would be willing to pay 35 cents to get the Google user to visit. That is, you're willing to break even on the first sale to gain a valuable business asset: a customer with whom you can build a relationship. (Chapter 14 celebrates the break-even concept to your heart's content.)

If you are selling a product that promises customers will save or make money by using it, you can usually charge more for it than if the product does not promise financial reward. It's hard to translate money into happiness. It's easy to compare the price of the product (say, a $750 AdWords telephone consultation with me) with the thousands of dollars you'll save on your AdWords campaigns. That's why marketing consultants make more than life coaches. Keep this distinction in mind as you explore your markets.

If the average bid is under a dime, you can assume that very few people have figured out how to sell high-ticket or high-margin products or services. For example, about 75,000 people search for home remedies each month, yet the average bid hovers around 10 cents. Home remedy seekers are do-it-yourselfers, looking for cheap and ingenious tips rather than expensive do-it-for-me solutions. Compare that to starting a business, which goes for over two dollars a click. This comparison points out an important distinction between markets: the "buying dollars for dimes" market versus everything else.

In some markets, bid prices bear little relation to the value of a visitor. Big companies (which I define as any organization where the person in charge of AdWords campaigns isn't using a personal credit card to pay) tend to over-bid. Some businesses are so good at earning money from visitors that they can afford to lose money to acquire a customer. But in general, the average bid price for a keyword gives you a good idea how much a click is worth, on average, to your competitors.

Google doesn't share its bid prices publicly, but you can estimate them using the Traffic Estimator tool in your AdWords control panel. The tool is erratic in its ability to predict your actual bid prices, but as long as you're using it to compare markets in a very preliminary "Is this worth my time?" sort of way, you needn't worry about pinpoint accuracy.

Sizing up the entire market by tallying total advertising spend

By doing a little keyword research and entering your results into the MPG calculator that you can download from www.askhowie.com/mpg, you can assess the Total Market Health (TMH) — man, am I a fabulous acronym builder (FAB) or what? — of your market by combining the total number of bids with a weighted average of bid prices. This gives you a rough estimate of how much money is being spent in the market by PPC advertisers.

The process will take you fewer than ten minutes per market (I've done it so often I can do it in under five minutes), and it looks more complicated than it is. If you've never used a spreadsheet program before, you may want to have an Excel jockey friend on hand to help you the first time.

1. **Go to www.askhowie.com/mpg and download the MPG Calculator.**

   You'll need Microsoft Excel or the free spreadsheet Calc available at www.openoffice.org to open the MPG.

2. **Once you've downloaded and opened the MPG, enter the keyword you searched using the free keyword tool described in the "Determining market size by spying on searches" section, earlier in this chapter.**

3. **Enter the total monthly search volume from the spreadsheet with the top 100 keywords into the MSV column of the MPG.**

4. **Log in to your account at http://google.com/adwords.**

5. **Click the Tools link and choose Traffic Estimator from the Optimize Your Ads section.**

6. **From the spreadsheet with the top 100 keywords, select and copy the entire column containing the keywords.**

   Do not include the search volume numbers, just the keywords themselves.

7. **Paste those 100 keywords into the box at the top of the Traffic Estimator.**

8. **Leave Max CPC and Daily Budget blank, select the language and location targeting based on the market you've going after, and click Continue.**

9. **Above the table on the next page, look for the Average CPC for those keywords.**

10. **Divide the Average CPC in half and enter that number in the Maximum CPC field. Click Get New Estimates.**

11. **Keep reducing your Maximum CPC until the Estimated Ad Positions are 4–6 for the majority of your highest volume keywords.**

12. **Now take the Average CPC estimated by Google and paste it into the CPC column of the MPG.**

The MPG calculates the TMH for the market defined by that broad keyword. It will be a number between 0 and 5000 (some markets may top out above

5000, but that will be rare). Try this exercise with different markets, and especially with different variations of your main keywords. Which appears more profitable: `car insurance` or `auto insurance`? `Back pain` or `back ache`? `Beekeeper` or `apiarist`?

What sort of TMH are you looking for? The longer you do this, the better your feel will become, but for right now you can follow Glenn's rule of thumb: AdWords beginners should enter niche markets with TMHs between 100 and 200. At 200, the markets become more competitive, and below 100, there's not enough money to go around. One exception to this rule is the "dollars for dimes" market. If you're helping people make or save money, you can probably make a go of it with a TMH between 50 and 200.

Don't get freaked out if Google's Traffic Estimator tool initially predicts very high CPCs — those numbers are the bid prices for the top positions, which you probably don't want, and reflect the "ignorance tax" Google imposes on advertisers who don't follow the strategies you're learning here. (See the "Bid persistence: Will you still love me tomorrow?" section, later in this chapter.) Chris Carpenter, creator of the popular Google Cash e-book (available at `www.google cash.com`), cautions against making market profitability predictions in markets where lots of newbie advertisers are failing on a daily basis. His reasoning:

> There are tons of newbie advertisers that enter the market everyday. They throw up an ad for a day and then when they lose money, they take the ad down.

> So if you went to the Google Traffic Estimator and saw that people are spending $1 or even several dollars per click for a keyword (`health insurance`, for example), you might think that they're making money in that market. But there is a good chance that they are not.

> For many keywords, especially broad, high-traffic keywords that have bid prices of $1 per click and up, nobody is making money.

> I have been monitoring over 100,000 keywords for the last six months using software that I created. It shows me for each keyword, which Adwords ads have shown up consistently day in and day out, and which have been put up and taken down right away, or a couple of days later.

> There are many keywords where I see a new ad coming and going every day, but no ads staying up there day in and day out. So that means that even though some of these keywords cost over $1 per click, no one has a profitable Adwords campaign using these keywords.

At press time, Chris's tool, Google Cash Detective, wasn't available to the general public. If you're interested in advanced predictive PPC market research, check `www.askhowie.com/detective` for the latest on the public availability of the tool.

Giving your market a stress test to determine future health

If Oprah ever reads my hilarious yet touching and wise essay, *Manifesto of an Average Ultimate Frisbee Player,* surely she will invite me to be a guest on her show. For several weeks after this, many people will search online for `Oprah Frisbee guy` and a few variations. But would it be wise to build a business based on that keyword family? Probably not, since my fame (and it is coming, I tell you) is likely to be fleeting. If your business success depends on short-lived trends or fads, you'll never turn your AdWords campaigns into business assets. They won't be reliable. Similarly, if your market is trending downward (Ken McCarthy discovered that very few people in the 21st century are searching for `buggy whips` anymore, even though they had been all the rage 100 years earlier), you can't rely on past data.

Luckily, Google publicly shares a tool that allows you to view trends in your market to help you decide whether it's stable, growing, or declining.

Visit Google Trends (`www.google.com/trends`) and search for the major keywords in your market. Is the traffic stable over the past few years? Trending upward? Good. If it's trending downward, beware. You'll see seasonal cycles in the Google Trends graphs, as shown in Figure 4-2. Don't worry about dips that occur regularly each year. Be worried if the overall graph trends downward.

Aside from being fascinating and addictive (at least for people who subscribe to *American Demographics* magazine), Google Trends gives you a longer-term picture of your market. Why, for example, did searches on `back pain` spike in July of 2005? I don't know, but I'll but some chiropractic market analyst has an answer. The cities, regions, and language tabs provide more useful information. For instance, the regions tab reveals that 9 of the 10 countries ranked for most `back pain` searches were part of the British Empire at one point in their history. Coincidence? Maybe.

Sometimes, Google superimposes news headlines on the graph, as in Figure 4-3. William Shatner's hospitalization for back pain in October 2005 (point B on the graph) appears to have triggered little additional interest, but the December 2006 ABC news report on lower back pain and yoga (point C) either anticipated or sparked another explosion of interest going into the new year. I don't know what any of this means, but if I were selling products to help your aching back, I would spend a lot of time looking at graphs like these. And whatever your market, I recommend you do the same.

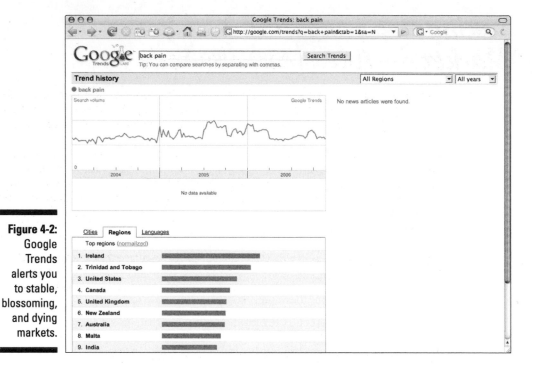

Figure 4-2:
Google
Trends
alerts you
to stable,
blossoming,
and dying
markets.

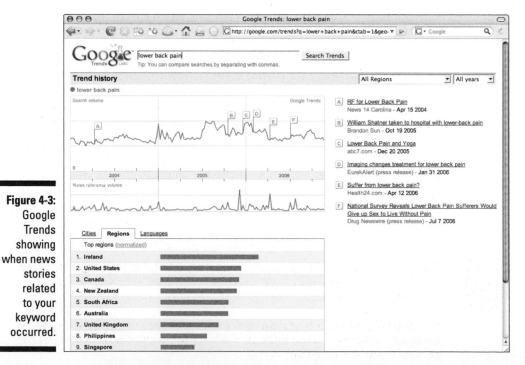

Figure 4-3:
Google
Trends
showing
when news
stories
related
to your
keyword
occurred.

Taking the Temperature of Your Market — Advanced Methods

The search data described in the preceding section represents the demand side of your market. The following sections look at the supply side — information about the businesses selling in that market, and how much they're making.

To continue paying homage to Ken McCarthy's swimming-pool metaphor, it's not enough for the Olympic diver to be able to tell that the pool contains 660,253.09 gallons of water. If the water is frozen solid, diving in is not a good idea. If the market consists of hundreds of thousands of monthly searches *but no buyers,* you're diving in a frozen market — and it won't feel good when you land on your head (or your empty wallet).

The average bid price, described earlier in this chapter, is one indicator of the responsiveness of a market. But this issue is so important that you should take some time and corroborate your first impression with several other data sources.

Number of advertisers on Google

In the popular imagination, entrepreneurs get rich by creating products and services that nobody else has ever thought of. In real life, that rarely happens. Truly original products and services often languish for years until they catch on. Rather than celebrating when you discover that no one else is selling what you want to sell, you should become somber and a little nervous. Then take a deep breath, relax your shoulders, and continue with your day. (I didn't want to leave you all nervous and tense — you might get back pain, and I'm not selling anything in that market. Much better for me if you get gout.)

Go to www.google.com, search for your keyword, and count the number of sponsored listings. You can do this by clicking More Sponsored Links just below the column of AdWords ads on the right (see Figure 4-4). The first 10 listings appear on that page. Click the Next button at the bottom to bring up listings 11-20. Keep clicking Next on each subsequent page until you run out of Next links to click. Figure 4-5 shows the end of the long line of ads for the keyword lower back pain. Seven ads on Result Page 9 translates to 87 ads.

For some reason, Google doesn't always display the More Sponsored Links link the first time you search. Refresh the page until that link appears by choosing View⇨Refresh or View⇨Reload in your browser.

You'll see slightly different results depending on your geographic location — a number of listings in my example were for local chiropractors — but the general trend will be clear.

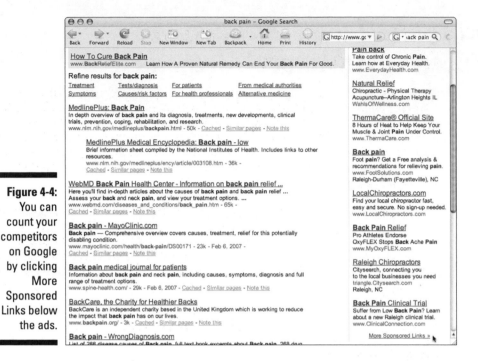

Figure 4-4:
You can count your competitors on Google by clicking More Sponsored Links below the ads.

Glenn Livingston (of www.ultimateadwordsresearch.com) cautions AdWords beginners to avoid competing on keywords with more than 25 competitors. Once you've cut your teeth in less competitive markets, you can begin to assault the lofty domains of high profit. After all, if someone's doing well there, why not you?

Figure 4-5:
Looks like 87 advertisers are competing for the term "lower back pain."

Bid persistence: Will you still love me tomorrow?

Beware of markets full of here-today-gone-tomorrow advertisers. After all, advertisers are trying new things all the time, thanks to Google's no-commitment, low-cost model. Just because you can gather more market data on a Sunday afternoon than Procter & Gamble was able to amass during the entire Carter administration doesn't mean the data is stable. Bids especially are vulnerable to sudden change, since each bid represents not an entire market segment but one merchant's decision that day.

A simple way to establish bid persistence is to print out the first two pages of the sponsored listings, and then print out the listings again at least three weeks later. To reduce your risk as much as possible, repeat this exercise again three weeks after that. If you see that the listings are stable over those six weeks, it means that these folks are either very careless or they're making money.

Going deeper with the AdWords Keyword Tool

Earlier in this chapter, I describe how to use the Traffic Estimator to assess Total Market Health. Now I show you how to use another AdWords tool to figure out if you can afford to use AdWords to test your initial sales process. Google is famous for being wildly inaccurate in predicting your actual bid prices, because your actual bid depends on the quality of your Web site (as well as on the invisible hand of capitalism). The Keyword Tool, like the Traffic Estimator, gives you a dollar amount based on the history your competitors have amassed, which makes it more, not less, valuable at this point in your research.

To use the AdWords Keyword Tool, follow these steps:

1. **Log in to your Standard Edition AdWords account and navigate to an individual Ad Group by entering the Campaign Management area, clicking a campaign name, and then clicking an ad group within the campaign.**

2. **Select the Keywords tab and click the Keyword Tool link (see Figure 4-6).**

3. **Enter your main keyword, select Cost and Ad Position Estimates from the Choose Data to Display drop-down list, and click the Get More Keywords button.**

Figure 4-7 shows the estimated CPC for `back pain` and — hundreds of related keywords — as well as the position you can expect for that CPC. If your default CPC for that ad group is too low, enter a higher Max CPC in the box and click the Recalculate button. You can also enter smaller CPCs and recalculate to find out how little you can expect to pay for various positions. The lower the CPC, the less profitable it has been in the past for other AdWords advertisers. You're looking for a sweet spot, where the Max CPC is low enough that you can afford to pay for enough clicks to test and improve — and high enough that you can be sure others are making money in this market.

Discovering buying trends at online stores

Another source of Internet market data are the popular online stores. To different degrees, they reveal what their merchants are selling and/or what their patrons are buying.

PayPal

Many online merchants conduct business using PayPal as their Web host and merchant account. PayPal graciously provides us with revealing glimpses of their bloomers by listing the number of sales each shop has made (which is one reason not to use PayPal shops if you're in a competitive market).

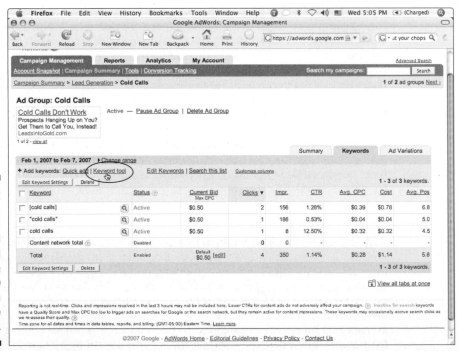

Figure 4-6:
The Keyword Tool (indicated by the little hand icon) includes a bid price estimator.

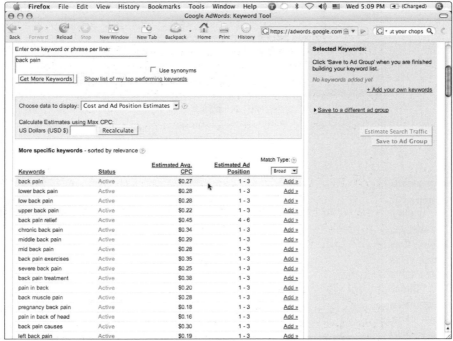

Figure 4-7:
Google estimates that bids of around 20 to 50 cents will get you on the first page for back pain keywords.

To score this data, go to www.paypal.com and click the tiny Shops link near the bottom of the page. On the next page (see Figure 4-8), you can enter a keyword and search for shops, or you can browse the category listings to the left. In most cases, the category listings are too broad to help you assess the strength of a niche market. You can see 16 pages of PayPal shops — at 25 listings per page, that's a minimum of 376 merchants selling products related to back pain.

Spend some time looking at which merchants are making the most — and fewest — sales. Mattresses and magnetic wraps (passive devices) seem to be more popular than hypnosis products and advice (products that require active participation). Save yourself the grief of creating another failing online store by making sure that at least a few people are making sales of products similar to yours.

Amazon

Remember way back when Amazon.com was just a bookstore? Now it sells electronics, kitchen gadgets, outdoor furniture, clothes, shoes, musical instruments, groceries, jewelry, sporting goods, toys, and pretty much everything else that can be put in a box and sent by UPS. Amazon has succeeded partly because it analyzes every bit of customer data it collects. If you've shopped at Amazon before, and you have its cookie on your computer, it'll show you a home page calculated to vacuum the maximum amount of money from your wallet, based on what it thinks you'll want to buy next.

Figure 4-8:
PayPal
shows you
exactly how
many sales
its PayPal
Shops
merchants
have made.

You want to search Amazon anonymously — so if you, too, get a personal greeting from Amazon (and you thought you were special, huh?), click the link at the top that says `If you're not Jack Bauer, click here`. On the sign-up page that follows, don't fill anything in. Instead, click the amazon.com tab at the top left to re-enter the site as a stranger. Now, when you search, Amazon won't filter the results based on your shopping history. Instead, it'll serve you the most profitable products in each category.

A *cookie* is a tiny piece of code that a Web site will store in your computer so the Web site will recognize you in future visits. Amazon always greets me by name when I log on, and shows me the items I looked at last, along with new recommendations. If I delete all my cookies in my Web browser Options or Preferences menu, the next time I show up, Amazon will treat me like a new customer, about whom it knows nothing.

As in PayPal Shops, you can type in a search term or just browse by category. A category search of Exercise & Fitness (see Figure 4-9) shows the three most profitable products front and center: a stationary bicycle, a treadmill, and an elliptical trainer. On the right, it offers a low-cost item (a yoga mat) and a slightly higher-priced step system.

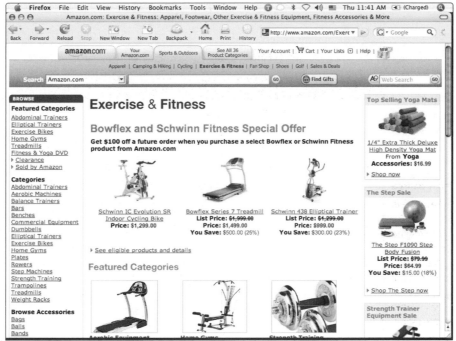

Figure 4-9:
Shopping anonymously at Amazon.com puts millions of dollars of market research at your fingertips.

Drill down into categories and subcategories to see what Amazon knows it can sell in each market niche. You can also search by keyword; a search for `back pain` on the entire Amazon.com site (shown in Figure 4-10) displays, on the left, 28,000 books, 1436 products in Health and Personal Care, 211 items in Sports and Outdoors, 88 in Home and Garden, and so on. Click each category to find the bestselling items within it.

I want to see what's hot in Health & Personal Care related to back pain. When I click that category, Amazon shows me the most popular items it or its partner stores carry (see Figure 4-11). In this case, it's a Spine-Worx Back Realignment Device, a Body Back Buddy — which presumably can double as a coat rack, and lumbar support for the cheap desk chair your company buys because ergonomically sound chairs cost too much.

You might be tempted to throw in the towel if you see the product you want to sell, or a very similar one, listed on Amazon for 30% less than you can buy it for. Don't worry — you have a huge competitive advantage over Amazon if you've chosen a specific market niche. Amazon will bid on AdWords, but your ads will be better. Your campaigns will be more efficient and more tightly targeted, and you will understand your customers' fears and desires better than Amazon does.

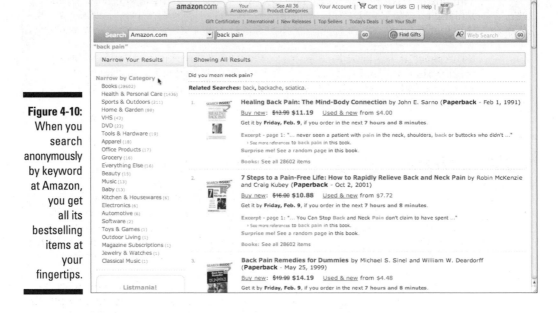

Figure 4-10: When you search anonymously by keyword at Amazon, you get all its bestselling items at your fingertips.

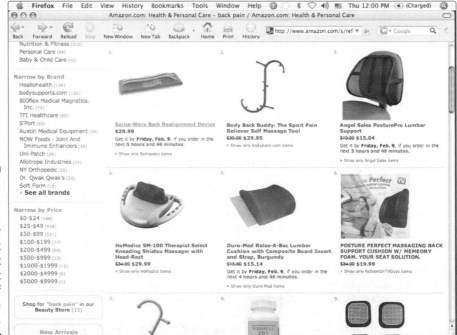

Figure 4-11: Amazon tells you exactly what's hot by putting it on the first page of the search results.

The bottom line of all your research is to answer the question, "Are people making money online in this market using PPC?" If the answer is no, let go of this market for now, and repeat the research process with a different market.

If the search volume is high enough, and the customers are ready to spend money, then you're ready to go to a higher and more intensive level of research, to find out what your prospects want — and what drives them crazy about their current situation.

Eavesdropping at the Watering Hole

The size and temperature of your market tell you whether to enter that market. Knowing how many people are searching and buying doesn't help you market to them yet. You just know they're out there, poking around and buying stuff from your competitors. The next three research questions guide you to develop the right product and sell it using the right concepts.

Your future customers will tell you what they want to buy, how they want to buy it, what color and size and shape it should be, what kind of delivery options they prefer, and how much you should charge for it. They will talk for hours about what bugs them about other options, and what the perfect solution to their problems would be. All you have to do is find out where the conversations are happening, sit down, and start listening.

Remember those nature specials on public television that show all the animals gathered around the watering hole in the savannah? They're all hanging out, drinking, socializing, eating some grass, sharing the day's gossip. Your market has a watering hole where your buyers gather, too. If you want to find out what to sell to your market and how to sell it, you've got to hang out at the watering hole.

Your market's watering hole is where your prospects come to gather information and develop relationships that will help them in their business. The offline component of a watering hole includes lunches, golf meetings, conferences, phone calls, trade journals, water cooler gossip (a literal watering hole!), and the daily routines of business. The online component has two big parts: online groups and the *Blogosphere* (a cool word meaning "the world of blogs").

Online groups

The two big providers of free groups are Yahoo! and Google. Spend some time on each site, searching for groups related to your keywords and your market.

Join the most active groups, read the message archives, and follow the daily threads. Verify that the people in the groups are your prospects.

Resist the urge to do any selling in these groups. You're at their watering hole, remember? If you start pitching your product or services, or contribute comments that are off-base or self-serving or unhelpful, you've just identified yourself not as a zebra, giraffe, springbok, or wildebeest, but as a crocodile! If you want to come back and sell to these groups later, after you've mastered their jargon and understood their concerns, they'll freeze you out if you pushed too hard at the beginning.

Yahoo! Groups

Begin at `http://groups.yahoo.com`. To join Yahoo! Groups, you need a free Yahoo! account. If you don't yet have one, you'll be prompted to create one. You can start searching for groups without an account, but you'll need to create an account before you can join a group. If you have a Yahoo! account, log in and start searching. You can apply to join groups right away.

After you've done some searching, you'll discover why Google, not Yahoo!, is the preferred search engine. Yahoo! focuses exclusively on keywords, and ignores meaning and context. When I typed **Juggling** into the Groups search box, the first two groups listed (shown in Figure 4-12) were a support group for work-at-home moms and another for Christian homeschoolers with more than two children. They were in the top positions not for relevance, but because they were the two largest groups that had the word *juggling* in their description. Both groups, of course, used the term *juggling* metaphorically. So neither is a particularly useful watering hole to learn about your prospects' views on replaceable wicks for juggling torches or the proper weight of a silicon stage ball. The next three groups, however, are closer to the mark: a group dedicated to Contact Juggling, a group of Christian clowns, and the main Yahoo! juggling group. The Contact Juggling group's archives are public, while the other four groups require membership.

In addition to the keyword search, Yahoo! also gives you a directory of categories that may be more useful. At the top of Figure 4-12, you can see the categories Hobbies & Crafts > Hobbies > Juggling. Click Juggling to view 192 different juggling-related groups. The first two groups look familiar. When you click juggling2, you're taken to the group's home page, where you can read a description of the group, see how active the members are (by viewing the message-history chart), and decide if it's worth your time to join this group. To join, click the Join This Group! on the right. On the next page, select the e-mail address you want linked to this group, choose how you want to receive messages (individual e-mail, daily digest, or Web only), select the e-mail format, copy some text to prove you're a human and not a software program, and click Join. I recommend choosing the daily digest over individual e-mails — if it's an active group, you could easily spend your entire day dealing with off-topic threads about whether other threads are off-topic, and nonsense like that. You can always change your preferences after you've joined, and you can also quit any group easily.

Once you join, you can read through the archives and view profiles of group members. Figure 4-13 shows posts in the Juggling2 group.

If you wanted to launch a competing product to the Dube Airflight Clubs, you could gain valuable insight into what people like and don't like about them. The posts shown in Figure 4-13 indicate that clubs striking in midair is a problem for some jugglers.

If you wanted to (say) sell against Airflight, you could create thinner clubs less likely to bang into each other, or softer clubs that wouldn't hurt so much if they hit people in the head. And you would save this post in an idea file for when you started writing AdWords ads. You might come up with an ad that targets the problem you found:

```
Clubs hitting in midair?
Tired of getting bonked on the head?
Try Thin and Soft Juggling Clubs
www.SoftThinClubs.com
```

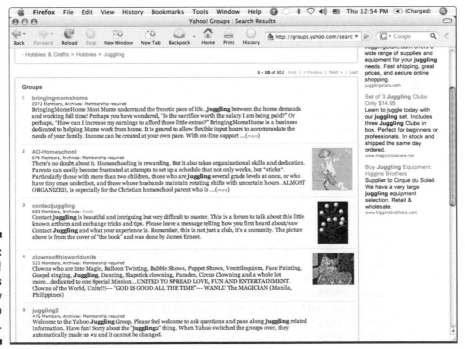

Figure 4-12:
Yahoo!
Groups
supposedly
related to
juggling.

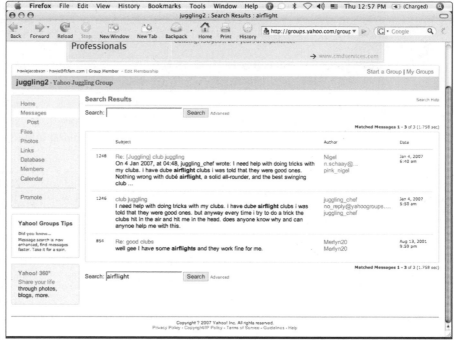

Figure 4-13:
Members of
the Juggling
Yahoo!
Group
discussing a
particular
brand of
clubs.

Google Groups

To search Google Groups, go to `http://groups.google.com`. Google Groups hasn't been around as long as Yahoo! Groups, so you won't find Google communities as established as the Yahoo! ones. But Google Groups get direct feeds from many of the independent "usenet" groups that have existed since the late 1980s, and so provide much more comprehensive coverage of the market. When you search Google Groups for `juggling`, you don't get the irrelevant listings that Yahoo! served up. The first groups Google shows you are a unicycling group, a non-Google group called `rec.juggling` (which I talk about in a minute), and a discussion list for the Vancouver Juggling Club (shown in Figure 4-14).

To join a Google Group, click Apply for Group Membership on the right. If you're logged in to your Google account, you get taken to a signup page where you choose your e-mail delivery schedule, provide a nickname, and apply.

Once you've been approved for membership, you can read and reply to messages, search the message archive by keyword, and post new questions. Google formats its group messages on the Gmail template — meaning that replies are kept next to the original message in chronological order. (See Figure 4-15.)

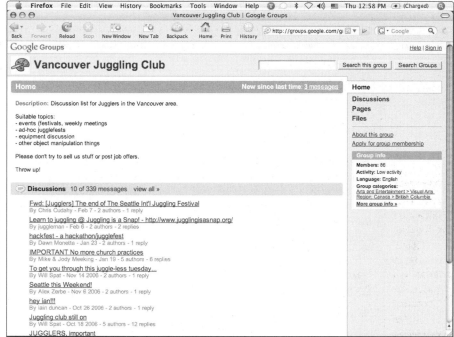

Figure 4-14:
The home
page of a
Google
Group, with
a list of
recent
messages.

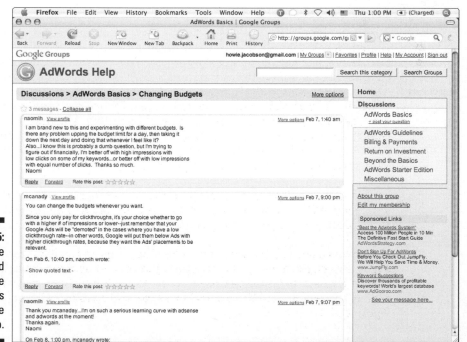

Figure 4-15:
A message
thread
on the
AdWords
Help Google
Group.

Other free and paid subscription groups

The Yahoo! Juggling Group moderator sent a welcome e-mail informing me that the group doesn't get much activity these days, and if I wanted to be in the thick of the juggling watering hole, I should try `www.jugglingdb.com/news`, a portal to `rec.juggling`, a forum independent of Yahoo! or Google. In fact, I already saw a link to this group for the Google Groups search results.

The first page of messages on that forum is shown in Figure 4-16.

Even before joining this group, you can read all the posts, search for members by country (useful for figuring out geographic ad targeting in AdWords), and look at the Juggling FAQs and lists of current vendors. If you're starting or expanding an online business, this sort of homework is required if you prefer making money to gambling. And it's so cheap and easy and quick, I hereby grant you no excuses for not doing it.

Figure 4-16:
This hopping Juggling forum received 14 posts already today.

The Blogosphere

When a technology merits a *For Dummies* book, you know it's important. Blogging has now achieved *For Dummies* status, with good reason. By July of 2006, Technorati was tracking over 50 million blogs, and estimated that 175,000 new blogs are created each day. Granted, many (most?) of these blogs are completely irrelevant to everyone but their creator and two or three friends, but that still leaves hundreds of blogs written by professionals in any given industry for other professionals in that industry. Other blogs touch on issues related to your product and service every now and then.

Blogs are great places to learn about your customers because, for some reason, people write blogs like online diaries — little held back, little left to the imagination. When they rant about a vendor or a product they don't like, they go all out. Also, bloggers love to link to and comment on one another's blogs in a particular market space, so true conversations develop. Arguments, discussions, reviews, comparisons — read influential bloggers' posts and you'll quickly feel the pulse of a market segment's desires.

How do you find the blogs and blog posts relevant to your business? Two sites are particularly helpful: Technorati and Google's Blog Search.

Technorati

Technorati is a search engine for blogs. Go to www.technorati.com and enter your keyword at the top. Technorati gives you three ways to search for blog posts:

- ✔ **Search for posts with your keyword in the text:** Choose In Blog Posts from the drop-down list to the left of the Search button.
- ✔ **Search for posts tagged with your keyword:** Choose In Tags.
- ✔ **Search for your keyword in the description of the entire blog:** Choose In Blog Directory.

I find the Blog Directory search to be most helpful — it returns a list of often-influential blogs that deal with your market. The list in Figure 4-17 shows several blogs that write about home gym equipment. If you're selling home gym equipment, go visit them (by clicking their URL) and find out what they're ranting about and what's tickling their fancy. Pay attention to visitor comments, if any (few comments probably means few readers and not much influence), and follow the *blogroll* — the list of blogs that this blog thinks is important.

Figure 4-17:
Technorati blog search results can help you find the pulse and the opinion makers in your market.

The top listing for Home Gym Equipment is a post called Track Your Walks. Technorati shows us that 257 other blogs link to this one, making it highly authoritative. When you click the post title, you're taken straight to that post. In this case, it's the Walking expert for About.com at `http://walking.about.com`. Since a lot of people read and rely on About.com for advice, you'd want to read this blogger's reviews of home exercise equipment before entering that market.

You can sort the blogs by relevance (based on how closely the blog's description matches your keyword) or by authority (a measure of how many other blogs link to that blog). Because the Blogosphere represents a network, you can usually find your way to the center of that network just by observing who's quoting whom. Blogging expert Dave Taylor (of `www.askdavetaylor.com`) likens the Blogosphere to a giant party. The person in the middle of the room surrounded by gaping hangers-on is probably the most influential person. Sidle over to that group and you'll learn a lot about your market. On the other hand, you can also find blogs that don't link to other blogs, that just try to sell you stuff, that rant and rave but have no influence whatsoever. That's like a person loudly talking at a party, but no one is listening.

Technorati isn't very smart about returning relevant search results in blog posts — it will look at individual words rather than the meaning of the whole phrase. If your keyword is more than one word, put quotes around your search term to ensure that all the words appear together in the post.

Google blog search

`http://blogsearch.google.com` returns results not only from blogs, but also online forums. It works just like a regular Google search, without the Web pages, and sorted by relevance or date.

Say you invented a device that improves automobile and truck gas mileage by adding supplemental hydrogen to the engine's air intake valve. Enter your big keyword, `hydrogen boost`, into Google's Blog Search to return the results shown in Figure 4-18.

Clicking the first post leads us not to a blog, but to a forum dedicated to really big Toyota trucks and SUVs: `www.ih8mud.com`. The posts on the forum indicated that many doubted whether the hydrogen-boost kit would actually work as advertised, that the kit required too much power from the alternator, and that price tag of $900 seemed too steep.

By reading over the posts, you can get a sense of the objections you'll have to overcome in your sales process. Second, you see the specifications that you need to improve: Instead of 20–30 amps, can you design a unit that draws only 8–10? Third, you see that $900 is more than this segment of the market is willing to pay for a product like yours.

Figure 4-18:
Google Blog Search lists blog posts mentioning hydrogen boost.

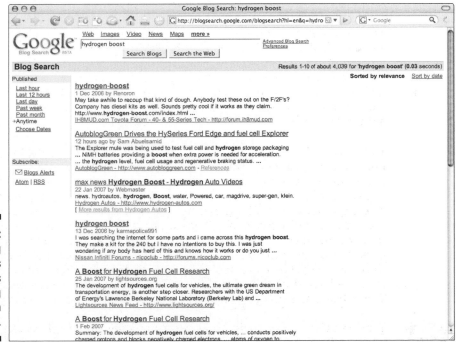

Loitering on Web sites

Your competitors' Web sites are great places to learn what to do and what not to do. When I talked about bid persistence earlier in this chapter, I advised you to print out a list of the top AdWords advertisers in your market three times over six weeks. Grab those printouts now, and circle the Web sites that appear on all three pages — both the sponsored and organic listings. It's time to hang out with successful businesses and see what they're up to.

First, look at your competitor's Web site as if you're a potential customer. Can you find what you're looking for? Does the site confuse or bore you? Is it easy to contact the site owner and ask questions? Do you trust the site? Can you order easily?

Remember that the home page may not be the landing page you get to by clicking its ad. Check out its landing page, and see how it draws you in — or not. Pay attention to how that landing page connects to the rest of the site. Does it try to make a sale, or capture your contact information? What are the featured products? What are their shipping and return policies?

Also, do other sites link to your competitor's Web site? Google loves sites with a lot of "inbound links." You can find out who's linking to a Web site by typing **link:** and then the URL in Google. For example: `link:www.monkeybargym.com` returns 71 linking pages (see Figure 4-19). The top few are from the site itself, but the rest are from other Web sites. A high number of inbound links will help to increase their organic Google traffic — as well as decrease their PPC bid prices.

Sleeping with the enemy

But wait, there's more! Don't just float around on your competitors' sites — if you can afford it, become their customer. Get into their sales funnel. Discover how they treat their customers, and whether (and how) they try to grow the relationship. You may discover that their initial sale is a *loss leader* — that is, they lose money on the front end because they have an effective system for selling additional products on the back end.

Do they send e-mail offers for additional products? Do they give coupon codes for dollars off? Do they request feedback? Do they ship promptly? Does the merchandise do what they say it does?

So what do you do if your competitors do everything right? Here's a little online marketing secret: Your competitors are also your best potential business partners. If you can figure out how to share customers, everyone can increase profits by promoting different offers to different market segments. You can play nice with competitors only when you can figure out ways to differentiate yourself from them.

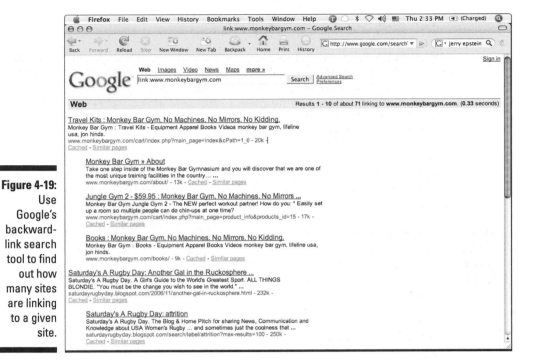

Figure 4-19:
Use
Google's
backward-
link search
tool to find
out how
many sites
are linking
to a given
site.

Cutting Through the Clutter with Positioning

You know how big your potential market is. You know how hungry they are. You've discovered what they care about — and what frustrates them about the existing situation and options. You've figured out what kind of pricing structure and market response you need to be profitable. And you've scoped out the competition to see what needs are not yet being filled.

Armed with this information, you're now ready to construct the most important sentence in the life of your business: your positioning statement.

Marketing master Ken McCarthy (TheSystemSeminar.org) explains positioning this way:

"Successful marketing is a multi-dimensional process. What do I mean by that? Remember the three dimensional chess board featured on Star Trek? Instead of one board and two dimensions, there were multiple boards on different levels and pieces could move up and down in space as well as backwards and forwards.

Many advertisers obsess about THEIR product and THEIR advertising. That's all well and good, but what these business owners fail to include in their calculations is the total space of the market they hope to enter. Rarely do prospects see only your product and your advertising. They're usually aware of other offers that — on the surface — appear similar to yours. Further, because we're all so busy and have so many things on our minds, we don't have a lot of extra processing power to think deeply about any company's offer.

Here's the key: You can't expect your prospects to do any heavy mental lifting. If it's not crystal clear why your offer is unique, it will be added to the rummage sale pile in their minds where all the other products go that they don't quite understand and will probably never buy.

Your goal as a business is very simple: You want your offer to occupy a completely unique place in the cubbyhole system of your prospect's mind and you want to figure out how to telegraph that unique value in seconds.

Better marketing and advertising is not just about building a better mousetrap (or creating a better ad), it's about figuring out where your offer fits in the market space and why you're uniquely qualified to hold a place in it, then communicating that message simply and powerfully, over and over again.

Let me give you two examples of how this works. The ultimate romantic city destination for lovers — what place pops into your mind? Probably Paris.

An innovative computer hardware company that's especially friendly to creative types — which company is already there staking out that space? Probably Apple.

A good rule of thumb is that there's probably only one space per category in everyone's mind. Second place is the same as last place.

Your mission as a smart marketer is to go boldly where few marketers tread and figure out what place your offer can own and then make sure every ad you run reinforces that message. Positioning is the thing that separates the marketers who are standing on the winner's platform from the ones who are perennially treading water."

Your ad copy, your Web site, your e-mails, the way you answer your telephone — all these marketing elements must flow out of your positioning. The easiest way to establish top positioning is to carve up a market segment that no one else has claimed. For example, there are many competing merchants in the fitness space. That niche is far too big to attack with limited resources. What about home gym equipment? Also big — and full of established competitors. What about home gym equipment for parents with young children? Indoor playgrounds the size of a home gym that both parents and toddlers can enjoy safely — and that parents can use for a real workout while watching their kids? No company I've ever heard of has told *that* story before.

If your research tells you that parents with young children are frustrated about their exercise options, you may stake your fitness-industry positioning on catering to that market. You may find that your initial idea doesn't fly — they don't have enough room in their house for a gym that big, or they doubt that it's safe for kids. But as you watch the market, you'll discover things they *will* search for and buy. And your positioning, based on those discoveries, will make you the obvious choice when they see your Google ad.

Ken McCarthy likens online market research to sitting next to a busy road and watching the cars go by. First you find the potholes, by seeing what people want and aren't getting. Then you create products and marketing messages to fill those potholes.

This concept of positioning as the foundation of your entire business is hugely important for your success, but if I gave it all the pages it deserves, this book would be called *Weightlifting For Dummies*. Instead, I've asked Ken to make his copywriting, positioning, and marketing strategies available online. Go to `http://positioning.thesystemseminar.org` to get it for free.

Chapter 5

Choosing the Right Keywords

*Y*ou're in control of most parts of your online marketing. You write your ads. You design and create your Web site. You write checks for advertising. You set your prices, hours of operation, and policies. But one of the most important elements of your online strategy isn't created by you at all, but by your prospects: the keywords they use to search for your solution to their problem. Your job isn't to invent keywords, but to identify the keywords they are already typing. If you can't find those keywords, the AdWords game is over before it starts. No keywords means no impressions, no clicks, no leads, no sales.

After you've discovered those keywords, however, your job isn't over. Now you've got to figure out "the want behind the word." Each keyword represents a different mindset — a different set of assumptions about how to fulfill a need, and a different state of buying readiness. For example, the singular and plural keywords can imply huge differences. Someone searching for used car is probably closer to buying than someone who types used cars. The plural searchers typically are at the early stages of their quest, while the singular searchers have, in their minds, a picture of one item that they'll buy when they find it.

I use the singular/plural example because it's surprising, perhaps, that one letter can make such a big difference. Other keyword variations, such as synonyms, are equally significant:

- ✔ car **versus** auto
- ✔ used **versus** pre-owned

If you've ever received high-quality sales training, you know to pay attention to prospect cues and clues before making your pitch. You might steer one prospect to a 1991 Mustang convertible, a second to a 1985 Mercedes sedan, and a third to a 2002 Odyssey minivan. With AdWords, your prospects' keywords are your only initial clues to their innermost desires. Different keywords should trigger different ads, take prospects to different landing pages, and make them different offers.

This chapter shows you how to interpret keywords to help you read your prospects' minds. Armed with this fundamental understanding, you'll discover how to conduct keyword research to find the words and phrases that will bring you qualified search traffic. You'll learn how to manage your keyword lists in AdWords, separating them into ad groups and using the positive and negative keyword formats to get as many good prospects as possible while discouraging nonbuyers from seeing and clicking your ads.

Decoding Keywords to Read Your Prospects' Minds

The golden rule of marketing, in my book (hey, this *is* my book — cool!), was first articulated by Robert Collier in his 1934 book, *The Robert Collier Letter Book:* "Join the conversation already going on in your prospects' mind." His example: If you want to sell a winter coat to a man walking down the street talking with a friend, don't jump out and interrupt him with a statement about what a great winter coat you've got here. Instead, start walking along with the pair, listening and nodding at their conversation. Here and there ask a question, offer a relevant comment, and watch for an opening. When talk comes around to vacations, steer it gently to trips to cold climates. Once your prospect is primed, you can show him your coat. (Please remember that's a metaphor, not a suggestion to lurk in doorways and stalk strangers!)

Since Google has not (yet) hooked up electrodes to our brains while we browse the Web, the keyword is your best guide to the conversation already going on in your prospects' heads.

Perry Marshall of www.perrysmarshall.com is fond of saying that every keyword represents an unscratched itch. We search to solve a problem. Maybe we literally itch and are looking for an ointment. Maybe we're bored and are looking for excitement. Maybe we're worried and looking for peace of mind. Maybe we accidentally dropped our cell phone in a cup of coffee. Maybe we want to find a summer camp for our kid. Whatever it is, the fact that we're searching means we don't have enough information to take action immediately. There's a gap between what we know and what we need to know in order to make a decision.

`www.squidoo.com`, a nifty Web site created by Seth Godin, says it well:

> *We believe that when you go online, you don't search. You don't even find. Instead, you are usually on a quest to make sense.*
>
> *That's the goal of most visits to Google or Yahoo! or blogs or Wikipedia. How do you make sense of the noise that's coming at you from all directions?*
>
> *You won't take action, you won't buy something, book something, hire someone, or take a position on a political issue until you've made sense of your options.*
>
> *Searching online should really be called poking online. Because that's what you do. You poke around. You poke in Google and you poke at some ads. After looking at a bunch of links and pages, then, finally, you get it. You understand enough to take action — to buy something or make a decision.*

Your mission as an AdWords advertiser is to help your prospects make sense of their options. And to do it faster and more completely than anyone else. The word *client* comes from the Middle Ages, where it originally meant, "person seeking the protection or influence of someone powerful." Think of yourself as the expert in your market, the protector of the hordes of confused seekers, the one who will take your prospects by the hand and guide them through the hype and confusion and lies, and take them to the promised land of clarity and truth.

Squidoo's description suggests that "poking" is often inefficient because the searchers encounter lots of false starts and dead ends, confusion, frustration, and mistrust. What if you were able to figure out, just by the keywords they used, where your prospects are and what paths they need to follow to achieve understanding? Then you become their protector, and they become your clients — trusting you to show them the next piece of information they need to make a decision and act on it. That's the ultimate goal of your AdWords strategy — to show each prospect that you understand him or her, and can give them what they want each step of the way — including the part where they pull out a credit card and pay you for it. You achieve this goal by learning how to interpret keywords. Your best teachers will be Google, your own practice of empathy, and the data you collect.

Learn from Google

Google won the search-engine wars, in part, because it got very good at figuring out what people were looking for based on what they were typing. And the more data Google collects, the smarter it gets. Every time you perform a Google search and click a link, Google follows you and adds your actions to its database. It knows which sites you visit as part of your search. It knows how long you stay and how many pages you browse. If the advertiser has installed Google analytics or conversion tracking or Web site optimizer,

Google knows if you've signed up for a mailing list, or bought something, and even how much you spent. The next time someone searches on that or a similar keyword, Google tweaks the search results to reflect what you told Google through your actions.

To fully appreciate the differences that Google has discovered, try this experiment: Perform a search on any keyword and print the first page of search results. Then search for a synonym and print *that* page. Compare the two pages — what percentage of the listings has changed? For example, try searching for vermiculture and then its synonym worm farming.

If you take the time to visit the landing pages on each results page, you will learn something of what Google knows about the mindset difference between vermiculture and worm farming. Perhaps one group is professional, while the other is made up of amateurs. Maybe vermiculturists are just worm farmers with more education and higher credit limits. Could be that vermiculturists are into composting, while worm farmers are into selling fish bait. (If I didn't have 12 more chapters to write — and had some worm-farming supplies to sell — I might spend the time to find out.)

If you are preparing to advertise your business on Google, researching the keyword differences in your market will significantly increase your chances for success.

Decision mindset

Perform Google searches for the top keywords in your market and scan the results for clues. In particular, look for clues about what values will dominate their decision-making process. What data will they consider before making a decision, and how will they evaluate and prioritize that data? What's the first question they need answered to alleviate feelings of impatience, confusion, or frustration?

The following subsections help you determine your potential customers' mindsets.

Buyer or tirekicker

Are they serious about buying or just fantasizing? Big mansion sounds like a dream, while 9 BR Colonial Princeton NJ looks like a serious quest.

Market-savvy or innocent beginner

Are they familiar with standard industry terms, or new to the industry? For example, whenever I go to the home-improvement store, I have to describe the tool or part I'm looking for with lots of hand gestures, analogies, and facial contortions, because I don't know the name of anything in the store except for *hammer*, *Snickers bar*, and *toilet-bowl flange* (please excuse me as I process this flashback). Whether I walk out with a frown or a ratcheting 11mm box wrench depends on the patience, empathy, and experience of the clerk I manage to find hiding in Aisle 53. (Do they hide from you, too, or it is just me?)

For example, someone who wants to make their own beer might search for `beer making` or `homebrew`. The very fact that some folks are familiar with the "insider" term *homebrew* suggests they are at least somewhat market-savvy. The savvier the prospect, the more knowledgeable *you* must appear about the market and the product choices. Even experts are looking for leadership.

Discretionary or nondiscretionary purchase

How badly does your prospect want or need what you've got? How hard do you have to work to convince that person to buy? Imagine a long sales letter, an e-mail follow-up course, a video demonstration, and an hour of audio testimonials for . . . a box of large paper clips. Overkill. Paper clips are an office necessity, needed when they're needed. Compare that to motivational posters for the office, a product that didn't even exist until some entrepreneur figured out that managers are lousy at motivating employees and would pay money to get a picture to do it for them.

Problem-conscious or solution-conscious

For example, `get more clients` represents the problem (not enough clients), while `CRM software` (CRM stands for Customer Relationship Management) is one solution to that problem. Your ads can focus on problems (empathizing, agitating) or solutions (describing, proving, advocating). Remember: Join the conversation already going on in your prospect's mind.

Suppose that every prospect is searching for a solution, and you have a competing solution to the same problem. In that case, you start by talking about the solution they're already thinking of. My Leads into Gold campaign does this with prospects searching for `cold calling scripts`. One ad headline reads, "Stop cold calling." Another: "Cold Calling Doesn't Work." You can also raise questions about the solution: "Does Cold Calling Work?" Or position yourself as an expert above the fray: "Cold calling scripts compared."

Solution-conscious shoppers think they know what they need, but are often wrong. To the extent that your ads and Web site can educate them through a consultative approach, you can shift them away from preconceptions that are limiting their thinking. Problem-conscious shoppers typically open their minds to a broader array of solutions.

Price shopping or feature shopping

If someone searches for `Canon Digital Rebel XT 8MP Digital SLR Camera with EF-S 18-55mm f3.5-5.6 Lens (Black)` you can bet they're looking for a price, shipping info, and a store they can trust. Compare that to a search for `8 MP SLR digital camera` — which indicates more of an interest in general camera types (and possibly price *ranges*) than in specific brands and features.

Need it now or planning for future need

Your prospects' time frame is important, because you always have a choice to send them to a "buy now" page, or a "sign up for my 56-day e-mail course" page. Don't pitch a course on avoiding plumbing emergencies to someone with a busted pipe flooding their basement. And don't try, on the landing page, to sell a luxury beachfront property in Tasmania to someone searching for `retirement property`.

Sale or service

As I mention earlier in this chapter (unless you're reading it backward, in which case "retpahc siht ni retal noitnem I sa"), singular and plural keywords often point to big differences in desired outcome. Someone who wanted to teach a pet cockatiel to stop eating the curtains, for example, would probably begin with `cockatiel` rather than with `cockatiels`. Someone looking to buy several cockatiels would be more likely to begin with the plural.

Practice thinking like your prospect

Following the Google trail is a start. The next step is to put yourself into your prospect's head, walk a mile in their moccasins, see through their eyes, and feel through their kidneys (or whatever), for all of them and each of them.

Why did they type those particular search terms at that moment? What went through their minds during the seven seconds prior to the search? What were the triggers? How long have they been thinking about this problem? What tasks did they just interrupt to conduct this search? What environmental distractions are competing for their attention right now?

Who are they? What do they care about? What are their hopes, fears, dreams? What are their deepest, most secret desires? Can I stop writing romance-novel back-cover teaser questions?

 The practice of market empathy is one of the hardest marketing tasks you'll ever have to accomplish. Before you can pretend to be someone else, you first have to pretend you aren't you. You, after all, are a very small but very loud market sample, and the more you listen to yourself, the less room you have in your brain for thinking about others. When you think your prospect is the same as you, the "Market to Yourself Syndrome" follows: You speak in industry jargon, you assume everyone knows the purpose and history and significance of your product, and you believe everyone can see the dramatic differences between your product and the competition. Since it's obvious you're talking to yourself, your prospects politely ignore you.

The more words in the keyword phrase, the more information you have about your prospect. Look at the following four-word keywords, each including the words `treatment for gout`. What differences might exist in the minds of the three different searchers?

✔ natural treatment for gout

✔ alternative treatment for gout

✔ symptom treatment for gout

I'm intrigued by the difference between "natural" and "alternative" — the two terms overlap a lot. I feel the alternative seeker is more desperate than the natural seeker. Natural implies high standards, while alternative tells me that conventional treatments haven't worked. "Symptom" may be a quick-fix tell, a searcher who wants immediate relief rather than to address the root causes.

What can you do with this information? If my livelihood depended on selling as much stuff as I could to these three people, I might craft my ad pitches accordingly:

Keywords	*Ad Pitch*
natural treatment for gout	Natural Gout Treatment — no side effects
alternative treatment for gout	Gout Treatment Your Doctor Doesn't Know
symptom treatment for gout	Quick Relief from Gout Pain

My landing page would immediately indicate that I understand them. For example:

Keywords	*Landing-Page Text*
natural treatment for gout	"Are you worried about the side effects from the pills your doctor prescribed for your gout flare-ups? Would you like to be drug-free? Would you like to prevent future attacks naturally?"
alternative treatment for gout	"You've tried the drugs, and they didn't work. You wonder whether Western Medicine really knows how to treat gout. Your doctor just keeps prescribing higher doses of the same stuff. Would you like to get off the drug treadmill completely, and discover a treatment that attacks the causes of gout, and not just the symptoms?"
symptom treatment for gout	"You live in fear of a sudden onset of painful symptoms, and you're always wondering when your next attack will occur. Instead of treating the symptoms when you're already in agony, would you like to learn how to prevent flare-ups in the future?"

Mastering the Three Positive Keyword Formats

You can't possibly guess all the variations of keywords your prospects will type when they're trying to find you. Fortunately, Google doesn't force you to be specific, although it allows you to be. AdWords lets you input positive keywords (that is, keywords that will trigger your ad, as opposed to negative keywords that will prevent your ad from showing) three different ways: broad match, phrase match, and exact match. They look like this:

- **Broad match:** Buddha statue
- **Phrase match:** "Buddha statue"
- **Exact match:** [Buddha statue]

Broad match

Broad match keywords show your ad when the actual keyword is similar to yours. Buddha statue shows for the following actual searches (note the differences in spelling and capitalization):

- Buddha statue
- statue of the Buddha
- Buddah statue
- Korean statue of buddha
- Buddhist statues

Broad-match keywords are useful when you don't know what people are searching for, and you want to make sure you capture all relevant searches. The downsides of broad matching are the inability to match ad copy to the keyword, as well as lower CTR and higher bid prices.

Phrase match

Putting the broad match in double quotes converts it to *phrase match,* meaning the characters between the quotes must appear exactly as they are somewhere in the actual search. "Buddha statue" matches the following searches:

- Buddha statue
- "Buddha Statue"

✔ `Chinese Buddha statue`

✔ `grinning Buddha statue`

Phrase matches generally have higher CTR and lower CPC than broad matches, because they eliminate synonyms and changes in tense, number, and order. The most accurate matching occurs with the third syntax: exact matching.

Exact match

You indicate an exact match with square brackets, generally found to the right of the P key on your keyboard. `[Buddha statue]` will only show for the following searches:

✔ `Buddha statue`

✔ `buddha Statue`

✔ `"Buddha statue"`

Exact-match keywords are the most precise. You know exactly what the searcher typed when you register an exact match impression.

If you include the broad, phrase, and exact matches of the same keyword in your ad group, phrase trumps broad — and exact trumps both. In other words, if your keyword list includes

✔ `Buddha statue`

✔ `"Buddha statue"`

✔ `[Buddha statue]`

and someone searches for `life-sized Buddha statue`, that searcher triggers the phrase match (in quotes), but not the broad or exact match. And `Buddha statue` triggers the exact match.

The goal: From vague to specific

Exact match is a powerful way to exclude searches you don't want to attract. But it's a double-edged sword — exact match can also eliminate searches you do want, but haven't thought of yet. In a perfect AdWorld, the vast majority of your traffic comes from exact matches (since this means you know what your prospects are thinking and typing) and you still capture other relevant searches. When you start advertising on AdWords, you may not have enough traffic for your exact matches, so you'll have to use broad- and phrase-match keywords for a while. If you keep track of the actual search terms people use to get to your Web site (see the later section, "Using your server log to get smarter"), you'll be able to replace broad-match keywords with the exact keywords that triggered your ads.

Over time, you replace keyword guesswork with precise knowledge. For example, if you sell used Toyota trucks and your only keyword is `used Toyota trucks`, you may be getting traffic from a lot of other keywords, including these:

- ✔ `used Toyota pickup trucks`
- ✔ `used Toyota Tacoma trucks`
- ✔ `used Toyota trucks for sale`
- ✔ `used Toyota trucks for sale in Hawaii or Guam`
- ✔ `pictures of used Toyota trucks 4wd`

After you start seeing these searches in your server log, you add them as phrase- and exact-match keywords. The number of impressions for `used Toyota trucks` goes down as these keywords pick up the slack. Eventually, you may be able to retire your broad-match keywords entirely.

"Why would I want to retire my broad-match keywords?" I hear you ask. Well, do you want to sell used Toyota trucks to customers in Guam or Hawaii? (Remember, this is a hypothetical — I'm not assuming you sell used Toyota trucks. Just play along, okay?) If not (say, because you'd have to ship the goods overseas), then you're attracting the wrong prospects — and needlessly lowering your CTR and increasing your bid price for clicks. So how can you turn off your ad for the Hawaii and Guam searchers? One solution, which I cover later in this chapter, is the use of negative keywords. You can add `-Hawaii` to your keyword list to tell Google, "Hide my ad if the word *Hawaii* is in the keyword."

Oh, and you'll have to do that for Guam as well. And maybe Papua, New Guinea? Patagonia? Tikrit, Iraq? Instead of spending all your time defending your CTR against every possible place name where you don't want to do business, you may eventually be able to eliminate these searches by choosing only the keywords that *qualified* prospects are typing.

I show you how to move from vague to specific keywords later in this chapter, in the "Sorting Keywords into Ad Groups" section.

Researching Keywords: Strategies and Tools

In the perfect AdWords campaign, every click leads to a sale, and you don't miss any clicks that *could* have led to a sale. In real life, of course, such a perfect campaign is impossible. But it's the goal of everything you're doing. Your keyword selection represents a balancing act between hyper-aggressive and hyper-conservative:

- ✔ **Hyper-aggressive:** If you choose every keyword in the universe, you won't miss anybody, but your CTR will be microscopic and your bid prices will be astronomical.

- ✔ **Hyper-conservative:** If you bid only on the very obvious keywords, you'll miss a lot of sales from prospects who approach the search process differently from you.

The ideal balance point is the one that maximizes your business goals, whatever they are. If you are advertising a for-profit business, your goal may simply be the highest possible profits. You may sacrifice some profits for quality of life, and go for the highest ROI. If you're building a company to sell, you may prefer to build a huge subscriber base to earning profits up front.

Whatever the goal, the same three-part strategy applies:

1. Start with the obvious keywords.

   Make a list of the keywords you would search if you were your customer.

2. From there, go laterally into synonyms and related searches.

   Conduct the research described in Chapter 4, use the Google Keyword Suggestion Tool, and one or more of the tools described a little later in this chapter.

3. Tweak or fire underperforming keywords — and keep looking for new ones.

Part III shows you how to manage your AdWords campaigns to continually improve your results.

Eventually, you'll have a stable of reliably profitable keywords pointing to the appropriate ads, taking visitors to effective Web sites.

The Free Keyword Tool

You can use the Free Keyword Tool (mentioned in Chapter 4 in the section on the size and health of your online market) at www.askhowie.com/freewords to generate related search terms. Simply type the main keyword in the box and click Submit to receive a list of 100 related terms. You can research each of the top 100 terms by clicking it — the tool will return the keywords (and their search volumes) for all keywords that include the one you typed. You can explore the keyword landscape, and download keywords to your computer in a file that you can open in a spreadsheet program such as Microsoft Excel or Google Spreadsheets.

Google's keyword tools

In Chapter 4 you used the Google Keyword Tool that's part of your AdWords Standard Edition to get the "lay of the land" of your market. You can use that tool to find thousands of keywords related to your main ones. Google searches Web sites similar to yours and references its huge search database to help you discover the words other people have used to get what you can give them.

KeywordDiscovery and WordTracker sites

These two Web-based services, available at www.keyworddiscovery.com and www.wordtracker.com, respectively, are comprehensive and competing keyword research tools. Every serious AdWords user I know relies on one of these not-so-cheap tools. They both give you hundreds — or thousands — of keywords related to broad search terms. They tell you how many times the keywords have been searched in the recent past. They allow you to download keywords and counts into spreadsheets or text files. They let you create projects to store your words.

Neither is cheap, although WordTracker thoughtfully offers a week-long subscription for around $30.

Thesaurus tools

Remember the frantic high-school-essay writer's best friend, *Roget's Thesaurus*? It got us through some pretty rough papers by giving us 12 ways to say *accomplish* and 19 ways to say *want*. (Although my history teacher thought *hanker* too colloquial and *prefer* too wishy-washy.) Well, the old thesaurus is now online, in two free incarnations, and can lead you to keywords you would otherwise miss.

Online Thesaurus

Go to http://thesaurus.reference.com to access the online version of Roget's New Millennium Thesaurus. Type your keyword (one word, generally) into the text box near the top of the page and click the Search Button.

For example, when you type the keyword insurance, one of the synonyms, coverage, can open up a huge new set of keywords. Just about anywhere you can use insurance, you can now use coverage:

✔ health insurance and its synonym health coverage

✔ automobile insurance Omaha Nebraska and its synonym automobile coverage Omaha Nebraska

Every synonym in the online thesaurus is hyperlinked to a list of its synonyms. Clicking `coverage` takes you to another set of results for the word `compensation`.

For your purposes, the majority of thesaurus results are irrelevant. Look for words that jog your brain into thinking, "Oh, *that's* a good keyword, too."

LexFN.com

The Lexical FreeNet connected thesaurus, located at `www.lexfn.com`, can perform several cool tricks. Type a keyword into the Word 1 box, select the Show related radio button, and click the Submit Query button. You will find synonyms, words that are triggered by your word, more specific and more general categories related to your word, and words that are part of your keyword and words that your keyword is a part of, as shown in Figure 5-1.

If you sell stage makeup for theatrical performers, several of the results of this LexFN search will point you in promising directions (`greasepaint`, for example), while others will help you brainstorm negative keywords (see the later section, "Deploying Negative Keywords").

KeyCompete.com

If you're serious about using AdWords, KeyCompete.com is one of several paid tools I recommend highly. Go to `www.keycompete.com` and type a keyword in the search box; then click the Search button. You're taken to a list of Web sites bidding on that keyword, as shown in Figure 5-2. Click any of the Web site links to see a long list of *their* other keywords.

In other words, if your competitor has done a good job of researching keywords, you can use this sneaky tool to take advantage of all their hours of hard work. You can buy individual keyword results for $5, or purchase a single day's access for $19. An annual subscription is $299. If you need to compete against established competitors in an AdWords market, this tool is a no-brainer.

Using your server log to get smarter

Quietly, uncomplainingly, your Web site has been storing a gold mine of visitor data, patiently waiting for you to realize its value. If your Web site has been welcoming visitors for any length of time and you haven't perused your server log yet, you're in for a treat. Among lots of other useful data, your server log will tell you exactly what search terms visitors typed to land on your site. All the tools I've talked about in this section are useful as idea generators — but only your server log tells you exactly what keywords are *already* getting people to your site.

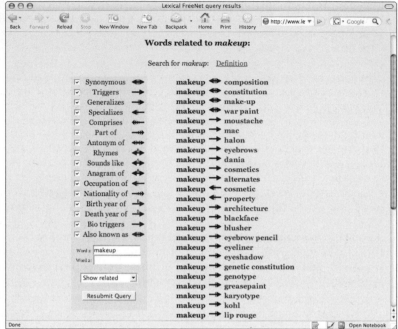

Figure 5-1:
The term
makeup is
related to
several
different
categories.

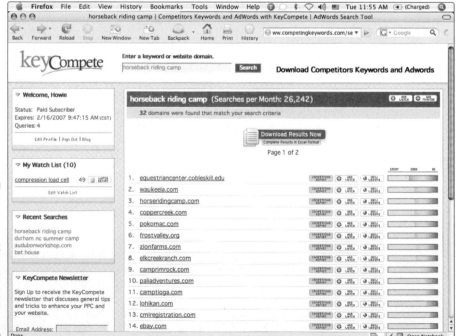

Figure 5-2:
KeyCompete.
com
returns a list
of Web sites
currently
bidding on
the same
keyword.

Because Web servers differ significantly, unfortunately I can't tell you exactly how to find and read your own server logs. If you are technically savvy about your Web site, you already know where to find the server log. If you're not sure how to view your server logs, contact your hosting provider.

What you want to look for in your server logs are the key phrases and keywords that people typed into a search engine just *before* visiting your site. You want to select a reporting period that makes sense (last month, last year, and so on). Figure 5-3 shows the server logs for key phrases and keywords that lead visitors to my site, `www.leadsintogold.com`, for one year. Some of the keywords with very few clicks are potential long-tail keywords I can add to my AdWords campaigns.

Long-tail keywords refer to phrases that are rarely typed, and will therefore bring you very few visitors, but collectively can generate many sales. The concept of the long tail (the phrase itself refers to the shape of the graph of the statistical distribution of events) was popularized in the book *The Long Tail*, by Chris Anderson, who argued that in a digital world with no production or shipping costs, the combined profits generated by long-tail products can be greater than the profits from the blockbuster bestsellers. Amazon.com, for example, can be more profitable than brick and mortar bookstores because such a large proportion of Amazon's sales come from obscure books that physical stores wouldn't be able to stock due to shelf space limits.

Figure 5-3: My server log shows me rarely searched keywords that have brought visitors to my Web site.

TIP

Similarly, long-tail keywords, as long as you don't spend too much time generating or managing them, can give you the slight edge that leads to market domination over time. Here's how: The long-tail keywords are very cheap, with almost no competition. This traffic stream lowers your average bid price, giving you more visitors for the same amount of money. Assuming you convert these visitors to sales at a rate equal to or higher than that of your other visitors (a pretty good assumption, since they're coming in on very targeted and specific keywords), you make more money per visitor. You can afford to advertise more — and to pay more for advertising — compounding your slight edge into a real lead. Finally, the increased traffic means you can split-test and improve all the elements of your sales process (see Chapter 13 for more on split-testing) more rapidly than your competition, leapfrogging you ever farther ahead over time.

Finding Sneaky Variations for Fun and Profit

So far you've been looking at semantic variations — keywords with similar but slightly different meanings. Now you can explore the wide world of sneaky variations — slight keyword tweaks that can mean the difference between lackluster and sizzling campaigns.

Some quick ways to vary keywords

For openers, here are a couple of simple sources of keyword variation — geographic location and human typographical error:

- ✔ **Geography:** As we saw in the used Toyota trucks example, keywords sometimes include geographical terms. If you ship home gym equipment anywhere in the U.S., you want to capture searches for home gym Alaska to home gym Vermont. You may even want to get more granular than the state level: home gym Chicago and Chicago home gym.

- ✔ **Misspellings:** Let's face it — we all couldn't win the spelling bee in elementary school. And we're often typing so quickly, we mess up wodrs and phraess (oops) as we search. Don't take my word for it — check out this hilarious page, courtesy of Google, that lists the misspelled searches for Britney Spears over a three-month period:

      http://www.google.com/jobs/britney.html

If you bid on misspellings that your competitors ignore, you have a twofold advantage:

- ✔ **Significantly decreased competition:** When I search for `low cholesterol recipes` in Google, I find 12 sponsored listings. When I enter `low cholesterol recipies` I see only two. Ten advertisers, including heavyweight Lipitor.com (a Pfizer Web site about its cholesterol medication), did not think to show their ad for a common misspelling. You have a much higher chance of compelling a click if you're in a beauty pageant against only one or two other competitors.

- ✔ **Lower CPC:** Because there's less competition, you don't have to bid as much to appear on the coveted first page. In the `low cholesterol recipies` example, the misspelled keyword costs about half as much as the correctly spelled term.

Misspellings won't generate huge search traffic. The Britney Spears example shows the correct spelling receiving almost half a million searches, and the most popular misspelling (*britanny*) getting 10% of that. Most of the misspelled keywords (have you ever noticed how the word "misspelled" just doesn't look right?) occurred four times or fewer. The goal in using misspellings isn't to double your traffic. Instead, it's to *lower your average cost of customer acquisition*. The goal of the AdWords game — as with a lot of business — is to turn cheap raw materials (in this case, clicks) into valuable products (in this case, hungry customers with working credit cards). You can use misspellings to lower your average CPC slightly and increase your traffic slightly, which gives you slightly more money to spend on advertising and slightly more traffic to run through your split-testing machine (see Chapter 13) — and become slightly better at turning visitors into customers. The cumulative effect of all these slight advantages is enough to snowball into market dominance.

Let's say you bid on one keyword only: `mortgage`. To show in Ad Position 6, you must bid an average of $1.45. Assuming 1852 clicks, you pay a total of $2,685.40.

Your competitor can also afford to bid an average of $1.45, but let's say they also bid on the term `morgage`. They must bid $0.23 to show in position 6, and they receive only 14 clicks on the misspelling. They pay an extra $3.22 for those clicks, giving them a grand total of 1866 clicks for $2,688.62 (your total plus their extra 14 clicks). Their average CPC is $1.44 — one cent lower than yours. That single penny, over many thousands of clicks, can put them firmly in Position 6, while you can only afford Position 7. Now they get more clicks than you because they're closer to the top of the page. Their CTR may be in a higher postition, so their quality score shifts to reflect the improved performance. Their bid price, relative to yours, goes lower again. One misspelled keyword won't make much difference, but if you take the time to discover a few dozen more discount variations, you can convert that slight edge into a significant advantage.

Different versions

If you sell different versions of the same basic product, you will improve your CTR by including specific search terms. A business selling light bulbs might bid on the following general terms:

- ✔ fluorescent light bulb
- ✔ compact fluorescent light bulb
- ✔ flood light
- ✔ floodlight
- ✔ lightbulb
- ✔ floursescent bulb

Their customers may be searching for much more specific items:

- ✔ 36" fluorescent light bulb
- ✔ dimmable compact fluorescent light bulb
- ✔ 14 watt compact fluorescent light bulb
- ✔ red 150 watt flood light
- ✔ green 150 watt flood light

If you sell 20 different colors or shapes or sizes or types of a product, be sure to include *all* those variables in your keyword list.

Different points of view

A realtor may advertise for the keyword real estate Carrboro NC and miss the following keywords that include the perspective of different searchers:

- ✔ buy real estate Carrboro NC
- ✔ buying real estate Carrboro NC
- ✔ sell real estate Carrboro NC
- ✔ selling real estate Carrboro NC
- ✔ looking for real estate Carrboro NC
- ✔ shopping for real estate Carrboro NC
- ✔ house hunting real estate Carrboro NC

A regular verb and a gerund (the verb with *-ing* at the end) can signify completely different mindsets. Until you're sure you don't want the customer with a particular mindset, include them all.

Singular and plural

The difference between a singular and plural word can mean a lot of things. Sometimes, people looking for information type the plural (`digital cameras`), while more serious shoppers use the singular (`digital camera`). If the plural keyword is significantly cheaper to bid on than the singular, you know that other advertisers have found it harder to make money from the less-expensive keyword. If you optimize your sales process to bring the information-seeker to the point of purchase, you can take advantage of the cheap, plentiful "pre-transaction" keywords such as general plural terms.

.com

Every year, the number of Internet users grows. Since a steady stream of Web newbies are searching for your products, you can profit by knowing the search "mistakes" they often make. Web neophytes can confuse the Google Search box with the Address Bar (where you type the URL of the Web site). So if you sell red flood lights, you can snag some inexpensive traffic by bidding on (say) `redfloodlights.com`.

LowerYourBidPrice.com — sneaky keywords made easy

I've developed a keyword-manipulation tool, the AdTool, which makes it easy to generate thousands of "sneaky" keyword variations from a single keyword. You can add U.S. cities and states before and after all your keywords, you can substitute synonyms with the click of a button, you can add hundreds of misspellings, convert singular to plural and vice versa, add `.com` to the end of your keyword, and add quotes and brackets automatically (if you're as bad a typist as I am, this one feature will save you hours).

Let's say you've brainstormed 1000 keywords that all contain the word `mortgage`. Now you discover that 5% of searchers spell *mortgage* without a "t" as *morgage*. The AdTool will let you replace `mortgage` with `morgage` in all 1000 keywords — and add *those* new 1000 keywords to your campaigns.

You can also use it to generate hundreds of keyword phrases using the phrase combiner. For example, someone who sells collegiate team clothing might sell 20 different items (hats, jerseys, sweatshirts, and so on) related to 12 different sports (baseball, basketball, lacrosse, and so on) for 150 colleges and universities (Duke, UNC, Princeton, and so on) $20 \times 12 \times 150 = 36{,}000$ keywords.

In Figure 5-4, I've included four colleges, five sports, and five items. The AdTool instantly generated 209 variations, including two-word phrases like `Duke hat` and `Princeton sweatshirt`.

Figure 5-4:
The AdTool's combiner feature generates hundreds or thousands of keywords based on the elements you input.

The AdTool is available for a full-featured 21-day trial for $3.95 at www. loweryourbidprice.com. It includes many other features that I don't want to hurt your brain with right now. But since I developed it for my own personal use, it's grown to do just about everything I recommend in this book.

Sorting Keywords into Ad Groups

After you've generated your keywords, your next step is to organize them into ad groups. Your mission, should you choose not to waste money and time, is to match your ad closely with the keywords in that group. In the first part of this chapter, I emphasize that each keyword has a mindset that goes with it. The *mindset* represents what the searcher wants and how she or he wants it; if you put all your keywords into a single ad group, you can't write an ad that will appeal to all those different mindsets. I'll give you six reasons to organize your keywords into coherent groups:

✔ **You can scratch the right itch:** Perry Marshall puts it this way: "Think of a group of keywords as a bundle of desires. Some desires go together better than others. Some are alike and some are very different. Each ad group must clump together the most similar desires, so the ad can mimic and inflame those desires. You want every one of the people who views your ad to say, 'Yeah, that's for me.'"

Say you run an online golf store, selling clubs, balls, bags, shoes, instructional books and videos, training aids, and so on. You can bid on thousands of keywords and send them all to your home page, www.jimsgolfemporium.com. The keywords could include

• golf

• golf clubs

- putters

- golf shoes

- improve your golf swing

- improve your golf game

- correcting a slice in golf

and many others. Each of these keywords represents an "itch." The search results page is nothing other than a race among all the listings to scratch that itch first. If your ad is a generic golf ad, you can't compete with an ad that names the itch and promises to scratch it good.

If you had typed `left-handed titanium drivers`, which headline would catch your eye — Golf Clubs and Clothing or Lefty Titanium Drivers?

The big reason to separate similar keywords into ad groups — to show an ad that scratches the itch — is supported by other reasons:

✔ **Google bolds keywords in the search results:** Type any word or phrase into Google and look at the results page. Every keyword you typed (except for *a, an, the, for,* and suchlike) appears in bold in every listing, whether sponsored or organic. Bold text catches the searcher's eye.

✔ **Talk to your prospects in their language:** If your prospect is searching for `foods that prevent gout` and you put that exact phrase in the headline, you've scored an empathy point. The way they search is the way they talk to themselves. Tap into their lingo and you demonstrate understanding.

✔ **Improve your ads by split testing:** If you don't segment your market, you're missing key split test data. Maybe you have two ads running neck and neck (see Chapter 13 for the details on split testing), with a CTR of 1.4. In actuality, Ad #1 has a CTR of 3.6 with people who typed `tiger woods putter` and only 0.03 with people who typed `golf shoes`.

✔ **Show visitors the right landing page:** The golfer searching for left-handed titanium drivers doesn't want to land on your home page and have to play hide-and-seek with your site navigation. Google has made us impatient and lazy — your visitors will go back to Google before trying to make their way through a confusing site. With a tight ad group, you can send all the traffic to a perfectly matched landing page — either for a selection of left-handed titanium drivers, or the best-selling men's and women's drivers, or an article on how to choose a left-handed titanium driver. The easier you make it for your visitors, the more likely they are to follow your lead.

✔ **Easy campaign management:** Managing different ad groups is easier than handling one larger group. If your AdWords campaign consists of 1000 keywords, all in one ad group, you'll have a miserable time trying to manage that campaign. You'll have trouble comparing keyword performance because you'll have too much data to look at. You may end up spending time inputting keywords you already have but can't find.

Divide keywords into concepts

Separating the list of golf keywords into concepts, or "bundles of desires," you get big groups and smaller groups within the big groups. The big buckets are

- Clubs
- Accessories
- Clothing
- Instruction

You can divide, say, Clubs into the following categories:

- Left-handed and right-handed
- Men's and women's and juniors'
- Putters, drivers, fairway woods, irons, and wedges
- Power and accuracy
- Different brands

The combination of these splits could be the ad groups:

- Left-handed men's putters
- Right-handed women's drivers
- Junior fairway woods

For accessories, a big subcategory is "golf balls." Your ad groups are probably named for the brands. Pay special attention to the most-searched brands.

Don't get paralyzed here, looking for the one right way to organize your keywords. You can't know for sure at this point. Your data will help you optimize your campaign over time — right now, take your best guesses (the market research described in Chapter 4 will help here), and create ad groups that are tight enough to be coherent and not so numerous as to defy effective management.

Spend more time on the high-traffic keywords than the long tails. Think of the high-traffic keywords as your prize pumpkins, the ones that can win you a gold medal at the state fair. The low-traffic keywords are the apples on the trees in the orchard — collectively, they are valuable, but you couldn't spend 10 minutes a day on each apple.

Organizing your keywords

I manage my keywords for all my AdWords campaigns with three tools: a text editor, the AdTool (from `www.loweryourbidprice.com`), and Microsoft Excel.

Step 1: Collect keywords with a text editor

As I'm doing my initial market research, I just copy and paste all my keywords into a text file. Your PC or Mac almost certainly comes with a text editor. Notepad is bundled with PCs and can be accessed by choosing Start⇨All Programs⇨Accessories⇨Notepad. On the Mac, the default editor is called TextEdit, and can most easily be found by typing **textedit** into the Spotlight search box at the top right and choosing the application called TextEdit. I prefer a simple text editor to a complicated word processing program like Microsoft Word because the word processors sometimes add funny stuff (formatting commands, invisible characters, whatever) to the text. With plain text, what you see is what you get.

If you're so familiar with Word that you can't bear the thought of learning another program, just save the Word file as `.txt` instead of `.doc` in the drop-down menu in the Save screen. Don't forget to save the text file somewhere you can find it easily — and remember: Word won't show you files that end in extensions other than `.doc` unless you specifically ask it to.

Step 2: Input the words into the AdTool and generate new ones

Copy the keywords list in your text editor and paste them into the AdTool. You can then Peel and Stick the Keywords into individual Excel sheets by ad group.

One of the AdTool's tabs is called *Peel & Stick*. This phrase entered the AdWords landscape courtesy of Perry Marshall, who used it initially to describe the process of removing a single keyword from an ad group and building a new ad group around that one key keyword. More broadly, *peeling and sticking* refers to tightening ad groups by moving keywords into new ad groups — and writing ads that more specifically target those keywords.

The AdTool's Peel and Stick function allows you to peel keywords out of your giant keyword bucket according to common words or letters.

After you've generated all your keywords, go to the Peel & Stick tab. Choose a word that is contained by all the keywords you want to peel out of the big group. For example, suppose I peel keywords containing `course` for the golf ad campaign and then e-mail them to myself. I can then stick them straight into AdWords, edit them further, or save them for future work. For that matter, instead of e-mailing the list, I could copy it to my Clipboard and paste it into a text or spreadsheet file.

Step 3: Sort the keywords with Excel

I use Excel to help me view my keywords as sorted by ad group. The first sheet is my summary sheet. It includes the names of all my ad groups, and the search volume for each group. Figure 5-5 shows a very neat division of ad groups in the Golf Lesson market, courtesy of Glenn Livingston of www.ultimateadwordsresearch.com.

	A	B	C	D
282	Golf Lesson	60113		
283	Golf Lesson Local Search	10420		
284	Online Golf Lesson	7533		
285	Free Golf Lesson	2889		
286	Golf Lesson Video	2405		
287	Golf Lesson Tips	1895		
288	Golf Swing Lesson	1771		
289	Golf Lesson Plans	1252		
290	Child Golf Lesson	1251		
291	Golf Lesson International	1139		
292	Golf Lesson Las Vegas	879		
293	Golf Lesson Florida	853		
294	Golf Lesson Atlanta	757		
295	Golf Lesson San Diego	739		
296	Golf Lesson Beginner	734		
297	Golf Lesson New York	706		
298	Golf Lesson Chicago	705		
299	Golf Lesson Instruction	702		
300	Golf Lesson LA	627		
301	Golf Lesson Putting	620		
302	Golf Lesson Grip	569		
303	Golf Lesson California	528		
304	Golf Lesson Arizona	493		
305	Austin Golf Lesson	480		
306	How To Play Golf Lesson	438		
307	Golf Lesson Boston	432		

Summary   Golf   Golf Instruction Beginners   Golf Instruction   DVD Golf   Golf Instructio

Figure 5-5: The summary sheet of the spreadsheet includes every ad group with a search count.

Each subsequent sheet shows the keyword list for that ad group, as in Figure 5-6.

A spreadsheet laid out this neatly makes it a breeze to input the keywords into AdWords. Just select column A by clicking the A at the top of the column, copy the entire column, and paste it into the AdWords Add Keywords tool.

Go to www.askhowie.com/keywords5 for a video demonstration of using Excel for keyword management.

Use each keyword only once in your AdWords account. If you include the same keyword in two different ad groups, or campaigns, Google will show only one ad, based on the keyword's quality score. Google won't let you compete against yourself by showing both ads. Also, when you have duplicate keywords, your campaign management becomes a mess. You can't be sure how much traffic your keywords are getting, because the traffic is divided among your ad groups. If you want to delete a nonperforming keyword, you have to hunt for it in more than one place. So begin your account with a clean structure; you'll find it easy to follow through with best practices later on.

◇	A	B
1	arizona and golf and fitness lesson	10
2	arizona golf in lesson	14
3	arizona golf lesson	436
4	arizona golf lesson 20	5
5	arizona+golf+lesson	1
6	golf lesson arizona	3
7	golf lesson in arizona	3
8	golf lesson mesa arizona	1
9	golf warehouse golf car golf lesson arizona golf	4
10	phoenix scottsdale arizona golf lesson	16
11		
12		
13		493
14		
15		
16		
17		
18		

Figure 5-6: This ad group, called Golf Lesson Arizona, contains just 10 keywords.

Deploying Negative Keywords

In the movie *The Verdict*, Paul Newman plays Frank Galvin, an outgunned lawyer representing an injured client in a medical malpractice lawsuit. When Galvin realizes that the defendant is hiding incriminating evidence, he requests delivery of the damning documents. The defendant delivers the evidence in a way that ensures (he hopes) it won't be found before trial — buried somewhere in truckloads of meaningless paper. Your AdWords traffic is the same — there are a few gems (your future customers and referrers) buried in a giant stream of nonbuyers. Negative keywords are your first line of defense, a filtration system that keeps the wrong folks away while letting the right folks see your ad.

Let's say you sell wooden kits for building bat houses. You bid on the keywords `bat` and `bats` and discover that, for some reason, you're getting large numbers of impressions but very low CTRs. What's going on? Are your ads ineffective? Maybe. But the first problem you've got to solve is related to keywords, not ads.

Who else might be searching for `bat` or `bats`? Go to `www.lexfn.com` and type **bat** in the search box labeled Word 1. Click Submit Query, as shown in Figure 5-7.

Baseball, cricket, and squash fans are also typing `bat` into Google, without the remotest interest in attracting mosquito-eating flying mammals by building houses for them. The actual search numbers for the top 10 bat-related keywords, according to LowerYourBidPrice.com, are shown in Table 5-1.

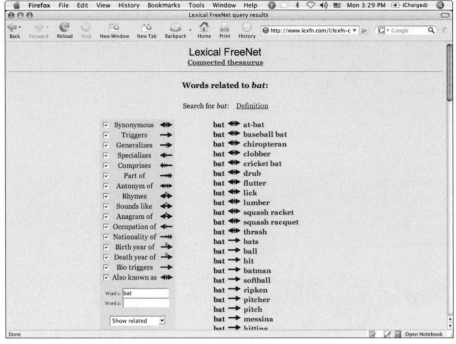

Figure 5-7:
The term bat occurs in many contexts other than flying mammals that can echolocate their prey and (allegedly) turn into vampires.

Table 5-1	Searches for Top 10 Bat-Related Keywords over a 12-Month Period
Search Term	*Number of Hits*
baseball bat	420,784
softball bat	380,614
bat	147,129
the bat	73,019
easton baseball bat	35,204
bat softball	24,984
milken softball bat	22,484
bat house	22,297
easton bat	19,159

If you are bidding on bat as a broad match, you're going to show your ad to a lot of the wrong people. If they don't click, they don't cost you money directly, but by lowering your CTR, they have a negative impact on your quality score. The lower your quality score, the more you need to bid to remain in a desirable position. Fortunately, Google provides a solution to help you filter out traffic you don't want: negative keywords.

Negative keywords are words and phrases that automatically disqualify your ad from showing should they appear in a search. In the `bat house` example, you would designate the following negative keywords:

- ✔ `baseball`
- ✔ `softball`
- ✔ `ball`
- ✔ `easton`
- ✔ `milken`

You don't need to include `base ball` or `soft ball` because `ball` already takes care of all variations in which `ball` is a separate word.

Brainstorming negative keywords

You should spend some serious time finding negative keywords. One of the most common and costly AdWords mistakes is focusing all your attention on positive keywords. Positive keywords *bring* you traffic, while negative keywords *filter* it for you so only the quality searchers ever get to your ad. A comprehensive list of negative keywords will increase the quality of your traffic and improve your CTR significantly. Several sources of negative keywords are discussed in the following subsections.

Thinking about who isn't your customer

No database or tool can replace your own insight and common sense. For example, `bath house` may be a reasonable typo of `bat house` — you may want to include the negative keyword `bath`. Consider other searches that may be triggered by your broad-match keywords. Do you want to show your ad to people concerned about bat bites, for example? They may be searching for an exterminator or a medical Web site, but perhaps you can entice them with an ad like this:

```
Bat Problems?
Don't kill them - Help them move!
Bat House Kits - vs. Yard Pests.
www.BatHouseKits.com
```

If your best efforts at selling to `bite` keywords fail, then turn `bite` into a negative keyword and move on.

Scraping LowerYourBidPrice.com for negative keywords

You can generate a more complete list by looking at the top 100 search terms from the free LowerYourBidPrice.com tool. What searches are unrelated to your market or your offering? Include those as negative keywords to keep those searchers away.

Searching Google for negative keywords

For example, a Google search on bat brings up the following concepts, all unrelated to flying mammals:

- ✔ British American Tobacco (BAT) company
- ✔ The BAT! Email Client
- ✔ Balanced Audio Technology
- ✔ Infogrip BAT Keyboard
- ✔ Brockton Area Transit (BAT) Authority
- ✔ BATch files

Finding negative keywords with the AdWords keyword tool

First, go to the ad group you're working on, by logging in to your account, and choosing the campaign and ad group from the Campaign Summary screen. From within that ad group, click the Keywords Tab and select the Keyword Tool. Enter your keyword, making sure the Use Synonyms check box is checked, and click the Get More Keywords button. (See Figure 5-8.)

Figure 5-8: Some of Google's keyword suggestions make excellent negative keywords.

In this example, the suggestion tool yields several more negatives:

- ✔ `file`
- ✔ `glove`
- ✔ `gloves`
- ✔ `command`

What about `guano` and `vampire`? Both terms relate to your kind of bat, but may bring you high school students looking for articles to rip off for term papers (or, for that matter, *Buffy the Vampire Slayer* fans). Can you turn them into customers? Perhaps — but you'll want to keep these traffic streams separate from the others so you can send them to the appropriate landing pages (and then track your success).

Adding negative keywords

Add negative keywords quickly to your keyword list by clicking the Keywords tab from within an ad group, then selecting Quick Add, just below the date range. You add negatives to your keyword list by typing a hyphen before the word or phrase, as shown in Figure 5-9.

Figure 5-9: Put a hyphen before your negative keywords when adding them to your keyword list.

Adding, Deleting, and Editing Keywords

All these keywords won't do you any good until you place them in your ad groups. If you've opened up an AdWords account, you have at least one keyword in each ad group. Here's a look at how to add, subtract, edit, and manage keywords in the individual ad-group interface.

Log in to your AdWords account and navigate to an individual ad group. Click the Keywords tab at the right to view the list of all your keywords, as shown in Figure 5-10.

Growing your keyword list

In your AdWords account, you can add keywords to your ad group in two ways:

- ✔ **Quick Add:** Add keywords by clicking the Quick Add link, just above the keyword list. Google gives you a text box into which you can type or paste keywords, one word or phrase per line, as shown in Figure 5-11. You can add them straight away by clicking the Save button, or you can see how much traffic Google expects to give you for each of them by clicking the Estimate Search Traffic button.

  Don't worry about adding a keyword that you already have in your ad group — Google kindly filters out duplicates for you.

- ✔ **Keyword Tool:** The Keyword Tool link, next to the Quick Add link, allows you to type or paste keywords or let Google do it for you.

  I strongly recommend using Google's vast keyword capabilities *before* you get to this point. Don't let Google add words directly into your account. Instead, use this tool to generate lots of keywords, and then manipulate and filter them in a text file or spreadsheet.

Editing your keywords

Click the Edit Keywords link (next to the Keyword Tool link) to bring up your entire list in a text box. Here you can remove, add, and change keywords, as well as change your default bid (the amount you'll pay for a click unless you set specific maximum CPCs for individual keywords). Note that negative keywords do not trigger bids, so you don't need to worry about bid prices for them.

Below the Save Changes button, Google instructs you on changing cost-per-click bids and destination URLs manually. That's right — each non-negative keyword can have its own bid *and* its own landing page.

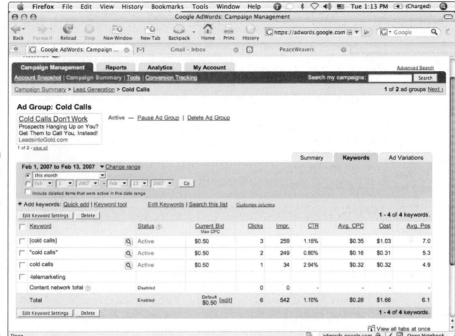

Figure 5-10:
The
Keywords
tab within
an ad group
shows you
each
keyword
along with
its status
and history.

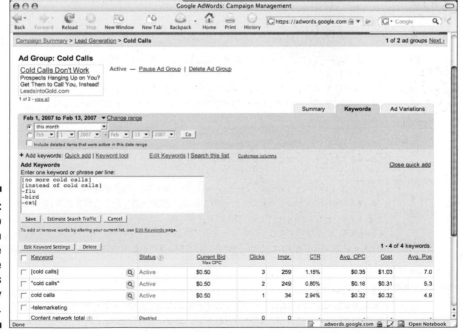

Figure 5-11:
I add two
exact match
and three
negative
keywords
to my
existing list.

Individual CPC bids

Use Google's syntax `keyword**0.25` to override your default bid for a specific keyword (see Figure 5-12 for an example). You can accomplish the same task much faster, with less possibility of typing or syntax error, through the Edit Keywords interface on the main ad group page.

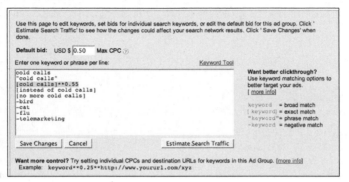

Figure 5-12:
The exact match [cold calls] now has a bid of $0.55 instead of the ad group default of $0.50.

To change bids easily and safely, select the keyword or keywords you want to re-bid by clicking the check box to the left of each keyword. To select all the keywords, check the Keyword check box at the top of the column. Now click the Edit Keyword Settings button just above the keyword column to find a page like the one shown in Figure 5-13.

Figure 5-13:
You can change maximum CPCs and destination URLs with Google's Edit Keyword Settings page.

Keyword	Status	Search Bid Max CPC	Destination URL		Clicks	Impr.	CTR	Avg. CPC	Cost
[cold calls]	Active	$ 0.55	http://		3	259	1.15%	$0.34	$1.03
"cold calls"	Active	$ 0.55	http://		2	249	0.80%	$0.16	$0.31
cold calls	Active	$ 0.55	http://		1	34	2.94%	$0.32	$0.32
[instead of cold calls]	Active	$ 0.55	http://		0	0	-	-	-
[no more cold calls]	Active	$ 0.55	http://		0	0	-	-	-
-flu									
-cat									
-telemarketing									
-bird									

Change bids by replacing the number next to the currency sign. Google tells you which bids are too low to show on page 1, marking each one with a V icon.

Individual landing pages

You can change destination URLs (landing pages) for each keyword as well. Since each keyword represents a slightly different mindset — and buying readiness — the perfect AdWords campaign would send each visitor to a landing page tailored specifically to his or her keyword. In a perfect world, however, you would have so much money you wouldn't be reading this book (and I would be playing Ultimate Frisbee instead of writing this book), so let's not get carried away by fantasies of unlimited resources. Fact is, you have a certain amount of time to spend on AdWords, and no more. Creating individual landing pages for low-traffic keywords is not the best way to spend your precious AdWords minutes.

At this point, you may be wondering why Google bothers you about different landing pages at the same time you set your bids. It's because the fit among your keyword, ad, and landing page helps determine your ad's Quality Score — which determines your minimum CPC for Google and the search network. In other words, if your ad isn't showing on the first page of search results, your only option isn't to raise your bid. You can also improve your ad, improve your landing page, and find a better keyword. Raising your bid is simply the quickest and least time- and energy-consuming way to get back onto the first page.

In the old days (pre-2004), Google would disable keywords that didn't achieve a minimum 0.5% CTR. Now they impose a lazy-tax on advertisers who show uncompelling ads that invite searchers to unhelpful and irrelevant landing pages. So instead of being disabled, your ads are now dubbed Inactive. Like a *maitre d'* angling for a tip to get you a table at a "full" restaurant, Google holds out its palm and says, "You wanna show your ad to my people? That'll be 10 bucks a click."

In the Edit Keywords tool, you can change the URL after a keyword, like so:

```
keyword**http://www.yoururl.com/xyz
```

In Figure 5-14, I've added two keywords whose traffic I'm sending to www.leadsintogold.com/fa, a Web page I set up specifically for financial advisors who work for big houses such as Smith Barney and Morgan Stanley.

In the Edit Keyword Settings screen, change destination URLs by typing the new URL in the long text box next to http://.

Figure 5-14:
Those
searching
for
"financial
advisor cold
calling"
(and
alternate
spellings)
are taken to
a different
Web page.

Use this page to edit keywords, set bids for individual search keywords, or edit the default bid for this ad group. Click 'Estimate Search Traffic' to see how the changes could affect your search network results. Click ' Save Changes' when done.

Default bid: USD $ 0.50 Max CPC ⑦

Enter one keyword or phrase per line: Keyword Tool

```
financial advisor cold calls**http://leadsintogold.com/fa
financial adviser cold calls**http://leadsintogold.com/fa
cold calls
"cold calls"
[cold calls] ** 0.55
[instead of cold calls]
[no more cold calls]
-bird
-cat
-flu
-telemarketing
```

Want better clickthrough?
Use keyword matching options to better target your ads.
[more info]

keyword = broad match
[keyword] = exact match
"keyword" = phrase match
-keyword = negative match

[Save Changes] [Cancel]   [Estimate Search Traffic]

Want more control? Try setting individual CPCs and destination URLs for keywords in this Ad Group. [more info]
   Example: keyword**0.25**http://www.yoururl.com/xyz

Chapter 6

Writing Magnetic Ads

This sentence contains the same number of characters — 130, including spaces — that Google allows you in an ad.

You get four lines of 25, 35, 35, and 35 characters to tell enough of your story to compel the right people to choose your ad over all the other ads and organic listings on the Google search page. If you're advertising on the content network, your ad is competing with articles, videos, games, and more. I've heard professional copywriters say that the Google ad is the most challenging form of salesmanship-in-print they've ever attempted.

Depressed? Don't be. Writing effective ads is hard for everyone, not just you. Spend some time preparing, practicing, and (especially) testing your ads, and you'll quickly rise to the top of your industry. As business philosopher Jim Rohn says, "Don't wish it were easier — wish you were better."

This chapter helps you stop wishing and start improving. First, I explain the three-pronged goal of your ad. Most advertisers focus on one prong only, to their detriment. You discover how to balance the first two goals for maximum profits by bringing in the right kind of traffic (not just the maximum possible traffic), and how to reach the third goal of setting visitor expectations so your prospects are primed for your Web site. Next, you discover how to tune your ad to your prospect's radio station, WII-FM (What's In It For Me?), based on their keyword. I share with you the missing link between your ad and your Web site — the call to action. I cover some basic strategies for effective ad writing, as well as a few top-secret (until now!) "black belt" techniques that you'll need if you're playing in a hyper-competitive market. Finally, I introduce you to some alternatives to the standard text ad: image, mobile text, local business, and video ads.

Understanding the Three Goals of Your Ad

A good ad attracts the right people — your best prospects — to your Web site. Your ad has three goals:

✔ Generating clicks from qualified visitors

✔ Discouraging the people who are unlikely to become your customers from clicking your ad

✔ Setting your prospects' expectations so that your Web site satisfies (and possibly even delights) them

The following sections discuss these three goals in detail.

Attracting the right prospects while discouraging the wrong people

The AdWords medium encourages a stepladder approach. The job of the ad is to deliver a drooling prospect to your Web site. They don't even have to be drooling over what you want to sell them, just over what you're offering them in the ad. Sometimes the ad offer and the first sale are identical — selling a product they're searching for by name and model. Other times, you're dangling a magnet that will attract the quarters and ignore the wooden nickel. (I talk more about lead-generating magnets in Chapter 10.)

Your four-line ad can't make a sale, any more than a door-to-door salesperson can ring the doorbell, utter one sentence, and sell a $1000 vacuum cleaner. The first sentence is meant to make the prospect listen to the second sentence. Likewise, the Google ad isn't long enough to capture the prospect's attention, pique their interest, stroke their desire, and make them pull out their credit card. Let your Web site and e-mails and phone calls accomplish the heavy lifting. Craft your ad to make or imply a promise that your landing page can keep.

The rest of this chapter shows you how to write an attractive ad. Right now, though, I'm going to tell you how to make your ad unattractive. After all, a click means you just paid Google. Clicks from the wrong people can cost you a lot of money without putting any of it back in your pocket.

You may remember magazine ads that featured a huge red headline of the word sex, with the subhead, "Now that I've got your attention . . ." The ad would go on to sell some product totally unrelated to the headline. Similarly, many people use names of celebrities (Britney Spears and Paris Hilton, for example) in their ads to grab attention. Don't try that with AdWords. In cyberspace, folks are serious about their searches. If they feel misled by your ad, they'll cost you a click and never visit you again. For example:

```
Free Britney Spears Pics
Hundreds of exclusive photos
and videos - all completely free!
www.BootzRus.com/BritneyGoesWild
```

If your site actually sells custom inserts for cowboy boots, this ad will almost certainly achieve a higher CTR than the more traditional ad that follows:

```
Custom Cowboy Boot Inserts
Instant relief of bunions and corns
Cures athlete's foot - free shipping.
www.BootzRus.com/CowboyBootInserts
```

But how qualified is the traffic from the first ad? Aside from their anger at being duped when they arrive at a site featuring cowboys with corns and not the celebrity gossip or racy pictures they expected, how likely would they have been to *want* boot inserts in the first place?

The Britney mistake doesn't usually look that stark and ridiculous, but I see it all the time in my clients' campaigns. Big promises are great, but when they're too vague, they attract the wrong people. For example, Nova-Mind.com sells mind mapping software to help writers and others brainstorm creatively and efficiently. Here's an ad I made up that would probably beat all their other ads' CTRs, but wouldn't lead to many sales:

```
Be More Creative
Amazing Technique Helps You
Brainstorm Brilliant Ideas
www.Nova-Mind.com
```

This ad promises a big benefit — one that the software theoretically can deliver on — but doesn't qualify the benefit with any information that would allow someone to say, "Oh, that's not for me."

Here's one of their real ads:

```
Mind Map Software
Organize your Creative Thoughts and
Mind. Download a Free Trial now!
www.Nova-Mind.com
```

The headline states what the product is and by implication disqualifies people who don't own or like or use computers. The free trial offer is appealing, but suggests that the product itself isn't free. *Free* is a powerful word, and must be used cautiously in AdWords. People who have no desire to pay for something will still take one if it's free. If the ad had promised a free download without qualifying it as a *trial*, they would have increased CTR at the expense of the quality of the traffic.

Writing a personals ad

Think of your ad like a personals ad. If you're putting personals ads in local papers or Match.com, your goal isn't to attract every bozo in the county. Instead, you want to weed out the incompatibles and make every date a potential winner. Personals ads achieve this qualification by stating who should not apply:

> *Divorced White Male, 53, in good health, seeks Single White Female, non-smoker, under 45; no cats or whistling cockroaches; must not be allergic to peanuts or mangos; must like Berlioz, Bartok, and organic kohlrabi.*

Negative qualifiers not only weed out the wrong folks; they also attract the right folks: ("He's right — I could never live with a whistling cockroach. We're a lot alike. I wonder what he looks like. . . .")

Your ad can qualify based on location (Roslindale IT Consultant), price (Downloadable Book — $17.77), limited options (Red and Gold Only), platform (Not Mac-Compatible), profession (For Teachers), personality (No Whiners!), and many other characteristics. Brainstorm a list of qualifiers by answering the question, "Who shouldn't buy from me?" If you sell a stand-alone version and a prospect is searching for an enterprise edition, don't even waste a nickel of your cash or a minute of their time. If your negative keywords didn't turn them away (see Chapter 5), let your ad do it before they cost you money.

Which side do you want to err on?

Every ad has to choose between Mistake #1 and Mistake #2. Mistake #1 is the false positive: Someone clicks who isn't your customer. You've just wasted the click price. Mistake #2 is the false negative: You send away someone who would have bought from you.

Which mistake is worse depends on how much each mistake costs you and how often it occurs. If your clicks cost five cents and your average sale is $800, you can afford a lot of false positives ($800 \times 20 = 16,000$ to be exact) for each sale. On the other hand, if clicks cost $32 each, your campaign can hemorrhage cash if you aren't very particular about who, exactly, you invite to your site.

Ultimately, the decision to widen or narrow the ad comes down to the value of a visitor from that ad to your Web site. One ad will simply make you more money (after subtracting your advertising spend) than all the others. Your mission is to keep writing ads until you find that one.

Telling your visitors what to expect

The third goal of your ad is to *manage expectations*. If your ad conveys play-fulness, don't send your visitor to a dry and hyper-professional-looking land-ing page. If you advertise a free download, make it easy to find that download. If you highlight a benefit, focus the landing page on that benefit. Show your prospect that you keep your promises, even the little ones you make in your ads.

Tuning Your Ad to the Keyword

Imagine that your goal is to sell a photocopier to a local business owner named Al Schmendrick. Which ad headline has the best chance of success?

A. Big Sale on Business Machines This Week

B. Are You Tired of Clearing Paper Jams from Your Old Copier?

C. Hey, Al Schmendrick: Are You Tired of Clearing Paper Jams from Your Old Copier?

If my kids' college tuition depended on the sale, I'd choose headline C in a heartbeat. Why? It's all about the prospect, and it's very likely to get his atten-tion. In fact, if Al Schmendrick doesn't read the paper that day, or skips the page that contains my ad, I'd bet that one of Al's friends will tell him about it.

The meta-message of your ad to your best prospect is, *"This ad is all about you."* Marketing consultant Dan Kennedy talks about the "message-to-market match." The keyword defines the market — who they are and what they want. Your ad is the message that must address their self-identity and desires. As I talk about in Chapter 5, the tighter your ad groups, the more precisely your tone, message, and offer can match what each market will respond to.

Marching to a Different Drummer

AdWords is arguably the most competitive advertising real estate on earth. Where else can you find dozens of competitors crammed sardine-like into the same space, vying for eyeballs and actions? If you said "the Yellow Pages," you're almost right. AdWords functions like the Yellow Pages, except in four important respects that make AdWords far more competitive:

- ✔ In the Yellow Pages, customers might find your ad on the third page of listings, but it could be the very first ad they see. Position is less important than size and look. An AdWords ad on page 8 is essentially invisible.

- ✔ The Yellow Pages separates the free and paid listings into white and yellow pages. Google shows both on the same page. I've heard from AdWords clients who also have first-page organic rankings who tell me that their organic listing generates three times as many clicks as their ad.

- ✔ Because AdWords is a results-accountable medium (meaning, you can tell when your ad works and when it doesn't), many AdWords competitors have become proficient through trial and error. Most Yellow Pages ads are just plain awful, because businesses haven't discovered the direct-marketing principles that allow for continuous improvement. (For more on this, visit my Web site www.leadsintogold.com.)

- ✔ In the Yellow Pages, you don't pay less or move to a better position if your ad is more effective than a competitor's. The Yellow Pages is like golf: Your score doesn't directly affect your competitor's score. AdWords rewards relevance with lower prices and higher position, making it more like tennis.

The most important rule when trying to stand out in a crowd is, "When they zig, you zag." As you compose your ad, keep your prospect's big question in mind: "Why should I click your ad instead of all the other ads and organic listings on this page, instead of typing a different search term — and instead of blowing off this search entirely and just logging on to *Second Life* for three hours?"

Studying your competition

Search for your top 5–10 keywords and print the results pages. Study these sheets — they may represent hundreds of hours and tens of thousands of dollars of market research and testing. Get a notebook and jot down your observations about each of the ads:

- ✔ What's the big promise?
- ✔ What's the tone?
- ✔ What's the emotional appeal?
- ✔ What's the logical appeal?
- ✔ How does each ad position itself as different from the rest?
- ✔ What features are highlighted?

✔ What proof is offered?

✔ What is the call to action?

Positioning your offer

Different isn't enough — your ad must be better. Your goal is to write an ad that sets you apart from the other ads in a way that connects you with your market. For example, say you sell industrial fans. You check out the AdWords competition and discover that the keyword `industrial fan` brings up ads that focus on models, features, and price. You can differentiate your company by writing an ad citing benefits and ROI.

You can position your offer as unique in many ways. Your market research (detailed in Chapter 4) can give you ideas about what your market wants and what the competition is currently providing and talking about. Now you can apply Ken McCarthy's "Holes in the Road" theory from Chapter 4 and write ads that address unmet needs.

When most businesspeople think of competition, they think first of price. If you can produce your goods and services more efficiently than others, you can compete on price. After all, Wal-Mart does it. But being the cheapest isn't usually the most compelling sales argument. Do you want the cheapest flooring in your living room? Do you want to drive the cheapest car? Do you want the cheapest heart surgeon operating on you? Besides, price wars often end up as a damaging race to the bottom for all involved, including the customer who finds that the business can't deliver quality at the price quoted.

If a segment of your market is searching for a particular model, like the Lifeline USA Power Wheel or the Canon PowerShot S400 Digital ELPH, they may have decided on that particular model already, and are now comparison-shopping for the best deal. In that case, an ad that mentions price can be effective.

Two fundamental ways to position your ad

One way to position your ad is to *slice the niche differently*.

For example, if you sell martial arts training videos, books, and equipment, you might assume that the entire world of martial arts students and enthusiasts is your market. If you claim a slice of that market and speak to them specifically — for example, college-age women, senior citizens, bouncers — you can position yourself as their supplier of choice. Each of those niches might be small, but you can own all of them if they self-identify with their keywords.

The second way to position your ad is to *make a better first offer*.

Even though the goal of the ad is to make a first sale, you can offer other things that your prospects may want or need before they buy. Reviews, free samples (physical, informational, or software), advice, video demonstration, discussion, and so on can be dangled in front of prospects who haven't yet made up their minds. As long as the "magnet" attracts your prospects and leaves non-prospects cold, you can generate the right clicks by offering an intermediate step of value.

No matter what you sell, you can always position yourself as an expert in the field. Search, by definition, implies some gap between your customers' desires and the information they have about how to fulfill those desires. If your ad offers to guide and educate, rather than simply to sell, your offer can stand out.

Motivating Action in Four Lines

Everyone makes decisions rationally, right? People weigh the pros and cons, consider their values and priorities, and maximize benefits while minimizing costs. People balance risks and rewards, and get better over time as they learn from their experiences.

That doesn't sound like anybody I know.

The truth is, all people make decisions emotionally, in their guts. They justify those decisions using logic, but the part of the brain that can handle matrices and cost-benefit analyses is just slower than the part that acts out of fear and greed. Before they consciously ponder, that old reptile brain decides instantly whether someone is friend or foe, prey or predator.

The AdWords ad heightens the emotional aspect of decision making because the rational brain has very little to go on: three lines of text and a Web address. Marketing consultant David Bullock, of www.davidbullock.com, puts it this way:

> *How do you connect to the "right" click?*

> *One second is all that you have to get the attention of your online visitor. That's it.*

> *The fastest way to meet your revenue goal is to figure out what to say, write, or display in this little 1-inch space to get, hold, and motivate the viewer to click your AdWords ad.*

> *Simply, the idea is to develop a stunning emotional appeal that gets the "right" click.*

> *By definition, emotional appeal is the mental state that arises spontaneously rather than through conscious effort and is often accompanied by physiological changes; a feeling: the emotions of joy, sorrow, reverence, hate, and love.*

As you boil it down, most of the decisions people make are based on fear and desire. All emotional states arise from one of these two states. We are either moving toward something or away from some situation.

Your ad has to hit the visitor/searcher right between the eyes, make an instantaneous connection and move the visitor to spontaneously gravitate towards your offer. It is not a matter of logic. Your visitor has no time to think about not *clicking your AdWords ad. Your goal is to get them to your landing page and move forward in your customer-acquisition process.*

Either you hit the mark or you are off. You either get the click or you don't. Period. End of story.

Your four lines must focus on emotions first and logic second. Your prospect will use logic to construct a search strategy (choosing keywords, searching for information, refining the search to longer and most specific keywords, and so on), but moves toward and away from search results and Web sites based on a subconscious emotional response.

To write effective ads, you have to understand the conversation that just took place inside the head of your prospect as they typed the keyword that brought your ad to them. What is their story? What are they telling themselves about their situation and how to improve it?

And I mean *story* quite literally. Go check out a book of fairy tales, or rent a couple of Disney movies to remind yourself what a story contains: a hero (that's them), a problem, a trigger to action, obstacles and villains, and a happy ending. If your ad can connect to the right place in their story, you can grab their attention and lead them the rest of the way.

Figure 6-1 shows the top ten ads for the keyword home based business. Which ads plug into compelling stories?

Figure 6-1: Each ad addresses a different story the searcher may be narrating to her- or himself.

Home-based business offers tap into the business opportunity market, which is actually several different markets, each with its own set of motivations and internal stories. Examine the first four ads to identify what they're up to:

- **Home Business:** A no-nonsense ad that uses words like *legitimate* and *serious* to emphasize the soberness of this opportunity. The syntax implies that the entrepreneur in question is already doing this, making it by definition "do-able." The ad connects with the prospect whose story is, "I don't believe in something for nothing. If I want to be successful, I have to be willing to work for it. (But not too hard, I hope.)"

- **I Was Scammed 37 Times:** This ad allows the reader to bond with Danny over his misfortunes, and to feel superior to him even as they take his advice. The word *scammed* appears three times, tying into the cynicism of the serial opportunity seeker who too has felt scammed yet keeps hoping that the perfect business opportunity is just around the corner. The word *absolute* is a powerful emotional trigger, making the tone one of righteous indignation. Prospects who subconsciously want a protector will be drawn to this ad.

- **Home Based Business — Free:** The emotionally laden phrase in this ad is, "You won't get rich." The word *realistic* and the modest income claims support the notion that this opportunity, unlike others, is achievably modest. It is designed to give hope to those who have been burned or turned off by big promises. This ad connects with the story, "If something's too good to be true, it probably is." The URL reflects the theme of realistic expectations by calling it a project and promising a payday rather than a windfall.

- **Don't Lose $49 Bucks:** This ad is similar to the second one, but speaks directly to the prospect's fear of loss by concretizing and quantifying the risk. Even without knowing how they might lose this $49, the prospect for this ad is suspicious enough to want to find out. The ad appeals to the "cautious risk-taker" who believes that having inside information can make them safe. Their story goes like this: "The world is a dangerous place for suckers, but I will be rewarded for my educated boldness."

The two ads at the bottom of the right column (Home Income Opportunity and Your Passport to Wealth?) are interesting because of their choices of emotionally laden words. *CEO* implies power and status, and speaks to a frustrated employee of a large company who envies and probably resents the CEO. The word *passport* attracts prospects who view exotic travel as market of success. They crave movement and excitement over security.

An old marketing acronym, AIDA, names the four states that have to occur, in order, in your prospect before you can make a sale:

- **Attention:** Attention is compelled by a headline that names the prospects or their pain, or connects with one of the big three motivators: greed, fear, or curiosity.

✔ **Interest:** Interest is raised by naming features and benefits (price, free shipping, options, works in zero gravity, you know the drill).

✔ **Desire:** The desire is the happy ending, or a promised step in that direction. (They can't slay the dragon until they find the enchanted sword.)

✔ **Action:** The action is the click, to go from the Google results page to your landing page.

All this highfalutin' theory is great, but let's get down to business. You have four lines to accomplish these marketing tasks. The following sections break down the task of each line so you can begin to create magnetic ads.

Grabbing them with the headline

The goal of the headline is to get your prospects' attention while leaving everyone else unimpressed. Classic headline gambits include the following:

✔ **Name Them:**

- Considering a Unicycle
- Mind Maps for Teachers
- Actor's Disability Insur.

✔ **Mirror Their Itch:**

- Suffering from Gout?
- Rotten-Egg Water Odors?
- Disorganized?

✔ **Pick Their Scab with a Provocative Question:**

- Suffering IBS for Years?
- Do You Hate Filing?
- Got a Jerk for a Boss?

✔ **Arouse Curiosity:**

- Are You Right-Brained?
- Are You a Slacker Mom?
- Copywriting Secret #19

✔ **Warn Them:**

- I was scammed 37 times
- Howie Jacobson Exposed
- Biodiesel Scandal

✔ **Make a Big Promise:**

- Write and Publish a Book

- The "Beat Gout" Diet

- Jump Higher in 14 Days

✔ **Offer Unbiased Information:**

- 8 Shower Filters Tested

- Flat-Panel TV Reviews

- Compare Autoresponders

Use the keyword if appropriate

If you include the keyword in your headline, you can almost always increase your ad CTR. For example, an ad with the headline "Homebrew for Beginners" achieved a 3.88% CTR for the keyword [homebrew] but pulled only 1.01% for [home brew].

Matching the ad to the exact keyword tells your prospects that you understand them (even if you don't). NLP (Neuro-Linguistic Programming) experts tell us that we build rapport by using the same words as others rather than para-phrasing. Also, Google bolds keywords on its results page. If you search for healthy recipe you'll see several advertisers who take advantage of this fact, while others offer healthy recipes and don't get the benefit of bolding.

If your competitors are all using the keywords in their headlines (or, in the case of keywords of 20–25 characters, as their headlines), then you'll want to choose a different strategy to stand out. But it's a rare ad that won't benefit from inclusion of keywords somewhere in the headline, description, or URL.

Develop a swipe file

A *swipe file* is a collection of successful advertising pieces from which you can draw inspiration. Professional copywriters rarely invent headlines and bullets from thin air; instead, they modify old standards. For example, John Caples famously (among direct marketing geeks, anyway) sold a piano home study course with the headline, "They laughed when I sat down at the piano but when I started to play . . . !" Today, copywriters model this formula in selling everything from baking magazines ("They laughed when I got up to bake") to dog training ("They laughed when I issued my $10,000 dog-trainer challenge . . .").

Perry Marshall recommends building your own AdWords swipe file quickly and inexpensively by visiting your local library or supermarket and copying the text on the covers of popular magazines. If you prefer to stay at home, go to www.magazines.com to view covers of current issues. Here are some headline formulas from this week's issues of *Cosmo*, *O*, *Woman's Day*, and *Vogue*, followed in parentheses by possible AdWords adaptations:

- 19 dresses that show who's boss (7 skateboards that show who's boss)

- The season's hottest styles (The season's hottest cameras)

- Weird male behavior decoded (Weird dog behavior decoded)

- Break your bad food habits (Break your bad skiing habits)

- Shhh! We've got a big secret to less stress (Shh! A big packaging secret)

Using the description lines to make them an offer they can't refuse

AdWords consultant Joy Milkowski (www.adwordstoolbox.com) has put together a menu of ad elements you can deploy in your two description lines. She recommends choosing two, plus a call to action. (See the "Sending Out a Call to Action" section for more information.)

Take some time and brainstorm a few elements for your ad for each of the following menu items. Don't worry yet about fitting your copy into the AdWords space restrictions. Just get the concepts first, and whittle away the extra words later.

Your menu of ad elements

I'm going to find examples of Joy's ad elements in phrases from real ads for a single keyword: data recovery.

- **Address a Pain Point:** If your customers are searching because they want to prevent or alleviate a problem, you can stoke their interest and build rapport by showing them you understand their situation.

  - Lost data?

  - No Need to Panic

- **Offer a Solution:** It's a marketing cliché that people buy holes, not drills, yet businesses routinely neglect to advertise the solutions they provide. One way to get at the solution your customers want is to fill in the blanks, "We provide _____ to _____ and what this means to you is _____." What you wrote in the last blank is the solution. The solutions listed as follows are tame. I would enliven them by adding a "what this means to you" phrase (in parentheses following each solution).

  - Restore Lost or Deleted Data (so you can keep billing your customers)

  - Fast data recovery for SQL Server (so you can keep your business running)

✔ **List Features:** If your product or service is significantly different from your competitors' offerings, list the differentiating features. Banks that are open on Sunday and late on weekdays, environmentally friendly dry cleaners, and single-volume print-on-demand presses are all examples of companies seeking an advantage by doing things a little differently.

- HD, RAID, Tape, CD/DVD, Memory Card
- 24/7 Support
- On-Site Clean Room

✔ **Short Value Proposition:** A value proposition is the answer to the question, "What do you do that makes you the best choice for me?" The first example is a no-quibble guarantee, while the second sets out a specific performance goal.

- No Data, No Cost
- We Recover Most Data in 24 Hours

✔ **Differentiator:** You can compare your business favorably to others, either overtly or by implication. Google generally frowns upon superlatives (*best*, *cheapest*, *biggest*), but usually is OK with qualifiers such as *better*, *cheaper*, *bigger*. Two of the following examples trash the competition by implication: "We actually do it" implies that others don't, while "no junk fees" suggests that competitors tack on extra charges to pad their margins.

- Others say $379, we actually do it!
- Fastest Turnaround Time
- No Junk Fees

✔ **Price:** In a price-sensitive market, you can signal that you're the best deal by naming a specific price, by telling your prospect that you have low prices, or by offering free shipping. For some reason, free shipping is a very popular online feature. People will pay $20 for the product if they can avoid a $7.95 shipping fee (not consciously, but it happens all the time).

- $379
- Low Flat Rates
- Free Shipping

✔ **Sale/Promotion:** Do you have anything free or on sale? Can you offer two for the price of one? What about throwing in a copy of *AdWords For Dummies* with every purchase? (Just a thought.) Retail stores have attracted customers with sales since Grog drew a crowd by offering a free club with every spear.

- Free Evaluation!
- Free Consulting
- Free Trial

✔ **Credentializer:** You can mention any awards you've received, well-known clients, certifications, media mentions. For example, when I searched for diet tips, the phrase "As Seen on Oprah" appeared twice in the first eight sponsored listings.

- Since 1980

- Industry-Leading 90% Success Rate

- 12 yrs. Crashed Hard Drive Recovery

- Experts on RAID

Benefits before features

No one formula for effective ad writing exists, and you have to make sure the elements you combine make sense together and all pull in the same direction. In general, though, you won't go wrong by putting the big benefit on the first line and the differentiating feature on the second line. The second line will also contain the other crucial element of your ad: the call to action.

Sending Out a Call to Action

You usually want your prospect to click your ad. (In some cases, you may prefer that they phone; if so, include your phone number in the ad. Several of the data-recovery ads had phone numbers, probably on the assumption that someone typing data recovery is in a state of near-hysteria and wants to contact a real person ASAP.) Joy Milkowski suggests two tactics to compel the click: Offer something in exchange for action and create a sense of urgency.

Making an offer with action words

When you offer something, use action words. Your prospect is searching with a "gatherer" mentality. Offer something bright and shiny to shift them into "hunter" mode. Active action words include

✔ *Get, buy,* or *purchase*

✔ *Order, call,* or *sign up*

✔ *Try* or *download*

More passive action words help the prospect make a decision:

✔ *See, learn, compare,* or *discover*

✔ *View, listen,* or *watch*

The following examples are from ads that appeared when I searched for the keyword `data recovery`. Note how they all begin with action words.

- Get a Quote Today
- Call 1-800-555-1212 for Free Analysis
- Discover reliable data recovery.
- View demo — whitepaper

Fanning desire with urgency qualifiers

Ken McCarthy points out that nothing stokes desire as much as unattainability. If we can't have it, we want it all the more. Joy uses urgency words to compel immediate action:

- Now
- Today
- By (date)
- While it lasts (in conjunction with a sale price)

Mastering the Medium and Voice at Haiku U.

Once you've chosen your approach and selected elements that will compel action from the right prospects, you've got to fit that content elegantly into 135 characters. Joy Milkowski calls this step, "Sell to me in 10 words or less." Stop thinking sales pitch and start thinking haiku — the Japanese poetic art that paints a compelling mental picture in 17 syllables.

First, forget everything your high-school English teachers taught you about grammar. Your ad must read like a conversation, not an essay. Notice that Joy didn't use the more grammatically correct construction, "Sell to me in 10 words or fewer." Write like you talk — or better yet, write like your *market* talks.

Apple Computer is running very effective ads featuring two actors portraying a Mac and a PC. The Mac actor is a hip young dude, while the PC actor is a pocket-protector-wearing nerd who awkwardly stumbles and bumbles through life. If huge multinational companies develop personalities in the minds of consumers, your business too needs a voice. Your ads are the first words in this voice that your prospects will hear.

The best business personalities are slightly exaggerated but basically accurate extensions of the business owner or leader. Start adopting that voice in your ads. An Internet marketer calling himself "The Rich Jerk" used the following ad when the name of another Internet marketer (whose name I've omitted) was typed as a keyword:

```
I'm Rich. You're Not.
How much money did [name] make?
Who cares? I make millions.
therichjerk.com
```

This ad works both to attract a certain type of person and to strongly repel everyone else. In some markets (like Internet marketing, for example), your tone can be brash. In others, you must come across as professional and no-nonsense. You can be caring, efficient, funny, angry, matter-of-fact, exasperated, excited, clinical, or poetic. Test different voices to find out which one connects best with your market. But your best voice will most often be your genuine voice — just smoothed and amped a bit to cut through the clutter of Timid Timmies and Me-Too Mollies. Your prospects are looking for authenticity in a world full of fakeness. Connect to them as your unique self and you're already cutting through the clutter.

Almost everything about your business can be copied, except for you. No one else has your thoughts, your experiences, your unique point of view. Most businesspeople hide this aspect of themselves to appear professional. It's possible to do both — be real *and* be professional. Take advantage of your only true differentiator and be yourself whenever possible.

AdWords consultant Garrett Todd of www.impresscallers.com cautions against rampant creativity. Extensive testing has shown him that classic direct-marketing approaches outperform offbeat, creative ads. He shared his top two formulas with me:

✔ **Who Else Wants to . . .**

```
Music On Hold
Who Else Wants to Reduce Hang-Ups
and Impress On-Hold Callers?
www.Impress-Callers.com
```

✔ **If . . . Then . . .**

```
Music On Hold
If You Want to Reduce Hang-Ups
Then Try Custom Music On Hold.
www.Impress-Callers.com
```

Garrett reports that the first ad generates an impressive 11.02% CTR. Note that his display URL includes a hyphen; he found that separating the two words increased CTR. The www prefix also improved CTR.

Rob Goyette of `www.vaelos.com`, another crackerjack AdWords user, found that his most successful problem headline was

```
Got [problem]?
```

For example:

```
Got Gout?
```

Naming Your Online Store Effectively

Many advertisers spend dozens of hours brainstorming and agonizing over their headline and two description lines, and never play with their URLs. That's a big mistake; your URL makes up 25% of your entire ad, and is often the most important line. Your URL is the name of your store. It conveys lots of meta-information about who you are and whom you serve.

For example, I used to funnel some `cold calling` traffic to `Free-Lead-Generation-Course.com`, which offered a 7-day e-mail course instead of a sales-letter Web site. My CTR was comparable to ads that sent traffic to `LeadsintoGold.com`, but the free course generated about half as many sales.

Buying more domain names

Even if you have one main Web site, you can buy other URLs and test them in your ads. Domain names cost about $8.00 a year these days (I use `www.getgoingonline.com`). You can redirect the extra URLs to your main site. As long as the display URL takes your prospect somewhere relevant, Google doesn't mind.

Glenn Livingston offers the examples shown in Figure 6-2 of huge differences in CTR due solely to changes in the display URL:

Figure 6-2:
Different
Display
URLs can
double CTR.

Microwave Oven Mania
If You're Looking For A Microwave
Oven This Is For You!
www-Microwave.com
29 Clicks | 10.9% CTR | $0.49 CPC
Served - 31.2% [more info]
Edit - Delete

Microwave Oven Mania
If You're Looking For A Microwave
Oven This Is For You!
www.SharpUSA.com
64 Clicks | 6.2% CTR | $0.73 CPC
Served - 27.3% [more info]
Edit - Delete

Buying A Piano?
Please Don't Buy Your Piano Before
You Take A Serious Look At This.
www-Piano.com
46 Clicks | 6.7% CTR | $0.52 CPC
Served - 52.9% [more info]
Edit - Delete

Buying A Piano?
Please Don't Buy Your Piano Before
You Take A Serious Look At This.
www.PianosByRosch.com
20 Clicks | 3.3% CTR | $0.68 CPC
Served - 47.1% [more info]
Edit - Delete

The domain suffixes also tell a story. The business-focused `.com` sometimes can be beaten by the non-profit `.org`, and even `.org` domains can in fact front for-profit businesses. If you offer reviews or comparisons, `TheAntiWrinkleInstitute.org` may pull better than `JanesWrinkle BustingCream.com`.

Adding subdomains and subdirectories

Joy Milkowski improved her die-cutting client's CTR by changing the display URL from `www.MyClient.com` to `www.MyClient.com/die-cut`. (Her client's URL wasn't actually `myclient.com` — most successful AdWords advertisers view their ads and keywords as maps to secret fishing holes, kept close to the chest and never shared with potential competitors. And with AdWords' low barrier to entry, pretty much everyone is your potential competitor.)

In the preceding example, `/die-cut` is a subdirectory, or folder, within the Web site. You can also test subdomains, which look like this:

```
die-cut.myclient.com
```

If you're not sure how to create subdomains or subdirectories, ask your Webmaster.

Testing capitalization and the www prefix

Check out the two ads shown in Figure 6-3. The top ad received 4.64% CTR, compared to only 2.22% CTR for the second ad. The only difference was the URL.

Figure 6-3: Two ads with different CTRs.

> Get started Beekeeping.
> Set up hives, harvest honey - be
> safe and have fun! Family activity.
> www.Beekeeping-Secrets.com
>
> Get started Beekeeping.
> Set up hives, harvest honey - be
> safe and have fun! Family activity.
> beekeeping-secrets.com

The top ad included the www and capitalized the first letter of each keyword — and attracted more than twice as many clicks per impression as the lower ad.

Wielding "Black Belt" Techniques for Hyper-Competitive Markets

I know you bought this book to learn the basics of AdWords, to get into the game. But if your market is highly competitive, you have to start at Big Leagues level just to get any impressions on your keywords. If your keywords are expensive, you may need one of more of the following three techniques just to stay solvent as you crack the AdWords code:

 ✔ **The "fake" www domain** is easy enough to try, as long as someone else in your market hasn't thought of it already. (Hey, here's an idea: Buy up every copy of this book you can find, just to make sure your competition doesn't learn about this technique.)

 ✔ **Dynamic keyword insertion** is almost a Google secret. For good reason — do it wrong and you're looking at an AdWords bill that could fund a flight to Mars. So read carefully — and don't even consider using it until you've installed and mastered conversion tracking and analytics on your Web site.

 ✔ **Subdomain redirects** were pioneered by Perry Marshall, who has many happy clients using it for all their domains. It's a way to test hundreds of URLs without having to buy them. This technique is a little complicated, but worth it in many cases.

The fake www-domain technique

You may have noticed the trick that Glenn Livingston of `www.ultimateadwords research.com` used in creating his winning display URLs earlier in this chapter. He added `www-` to a popular keyword and showed that to searchers.

It works because it tricks the eye into seeing your domain as the "main" Web site in the category. Someone searching for `digital cameras` will view `www.DigitalCameras.com` as the most relevant and authoritative domain to visit. Glenn bought the domain `http://www.www-digitalcameras.com` and simply omitted the "real" `www` from the display URL. The searcher sees `www-DigitalCameras.com` and can easily confuse it for `www.DigitalCameras.com`.

This technique is a cheap trick, but it's possibly worth the price of several cases of this book.

Dynamic keyword insertion

Do you ever wonder how eBay and Amazon manage to bid on practically every keyword in existence and show those keywords in their ads? They don't have thousands of employees creating millions of different ads. Instead, they use a special format to stick the keyword right into a generic ad, as shown in Figure 6-4. And now you can do it too!

Figure 6-4:
These ads
dynamically
insert the
keyword.

> **David Broza** at Amazon.com
> Low prices on new & used music.
> Qualified orders over $25 ship free
> Amazon.com/music
>
> CD's, DVD by **David Broza**
> Large selection of Israeli CD's
> Listen Online before You Buy!
> www.orlysbookstore.com
>
> **David Broza**
> Looking for **David Broza**?
> Find exactly what you want today.
> www.eBay.com

To use dynamic keyword insertion, first make friends with the squiggly brackets. On most keyboards, you can find them by using the Shift key with the square bracket keys, just below the - and = keys near the top right. They look like this:

{ left squiggly bracket

} right squiggly bracket

Dynamic keyword insertion requires two decisions:

✔ How you want to handle capitalization of keywords?

✔ What do you want to appear on-screen in case the keyword is too long to fit into the ad?

Let's say you sell mobile phone ringtones, and you know lots of people are searching by typing their favorite performer or composer or type of music followed by the word ringtone. The list of potential keywords could be enormous. Without dynamic keywords insertion, you would either spend hundreds of hours creating tightly focused ad groups (see Chapter 5), like Mozart ringtone, Beethoven ringtone, Bach ringtone, Beyonce ringtone, and so on, or you would have a few big ad groups with thousands of those keywords and very vague ads with headlines like these:

✔ Classical Music Ringtones

✔ R&B Ringtones

✔ Hip-Hop Ringtones

To use dynamic keyword insertion, create medium-sized ad group buckets:

- Classical Music
- Pop Music
- Country Music
- Rap Music

and so on. Put all your classical music terms — `Beethoven`, `Hilary Hahn`, `violin concerto`, `Leonard Bernstein`, `Philharmonic` — in the Classical Music ad group. Then create the following headline:

```
{KeyWord:Classical Music Ringtones}
```

Note that the colon is not followed by a space!

Now if someone searches for one of your keywords, they will see that keyword in the headline if it contains 25 characters or fewer:

- Hilary Hahn Ringtones
- Bach Requiem Ringtone
- Missa Solemnis ring tone

If the keyword is too long (`Alicia de Larrocha Mozart piano sonata in C ringtone`), they will see the default keyword `Classical Music Ringtones` instead.

To capitalize every word of the keyword, capitalize the K and W in `KeyWord`:

```
{KeyWord:Alternate Text}
```

Capitalize just the first word by capitalizing the K only:

```
{Keyword:Alternate Text}
```

If you want the keyword to appear in all lowercase, don't capitalize any letters:

```
{keyword:Alternate Text}
```

If their keyword doesn't fit, the alternate text will appear exactly as you've typed it — capitalized or not.

If you are careless about your keyword list, you could end up spending a lot of money that you won't make back. An extreme example to make the point: Let's say my friend Battery Bob accidentally includes `Paris Hilton` in the keyword list for his cell phone battery ad group.

Without dynamic keyword insertion, the worst that happens is a million teenagers looking for gossip or racy photos see and ignore the following ad:

```
Cell Phone Batteries
All Makes and Models
Low Prices - Same Day Shipping
www.BatteryBob.com
```

But with dynamic keyword insertion, here's what they might see:

```
Paris Hilton Videos
All Makes and Models
Low Prices - Same Day Shipping
www.BatteryBob.com
```

Uh-oh, Battery Bob. You just spent $12,000 on clicks in about six hours, with no sales to show for it. (The real Battery Bob would never make such a mistake, of course.)

You can deploy dynamic keyword insertion not only in the headline and description lines, but also in the display URL for marketing purposes and the destination URL for advanced conversion tracking. Rob Goyette has written an excellent technical introduction to this tactic, available at www. vaelos.com/dk.

Subdomain redirects

The third "black belt" ad technique gives you a chance to test hundreds of display URLs for the price of one. A *subdomain* is the part of your URL that can appear before the main domain name. For example, books is the subdomain of this Web site:

```
http://books.fitfam.com
```

Using a Web service called www.zoneedit.com, you can quickly and easily create new subdomains without needing to know Web design or HTML or server architecture or how to make vegan oatmeal cookies. (I actually do know how to make delicious vegan oatmeal cookies — send a blank e-mail to cookies@fitfam.com for the recipe — but I assure you I could still work ZoneEdit.com without this knowledge.)

My wife sells handmade soap featuring different essential oils and other natural ingredients. Her main Web site address is www.comfortsoap.com. Let's say she wants to test a different domain that works well with various subdomains, www.soapforyourfamily.com:

```
lavender.SoapForYourFamily.com
oatmeal.SoapForYourFamily.com
cruelty-free.SoapForYourFamily.com
```

Using ZoneEdit.com, which is free for the first five domains (not subdomains, so their free service may be all you'll ever need), she can create subdomains and then redirect them to specific pages on her `www.comfortsoap.com` Web site. She can even mask the pages so the subdomain is what appears in the visitor's browser's address and title bars. Using this method, she can test different URLs (which is better, `Natural.SoapForYourFamily.com` or `ChemicalFree.SoapForYourFamily.com`?). She can also use different display URLs in different ad groups: the lavender group, the Shea-butter group, the neroli group, and so on.

Visit `www.askhowie.com/zoneedit` for a video tutorial on using `www.zoneedit.com` for subdomain redirection.

Following Google's Text-Ad Guidelines

I'll warn you about some commonly broken rules in the following sections, but you should still take ten minutes to read Google's editorial guidelines at

```
https://adwords.google.com/select/guidelines.html
```

Punctuation

Google's rules for punctuation in your AdWords ads are pretty simple:

✔ No more than one exclamation point in your text, and not in the headline.

✔ No repeated punctuation (Tired??!!).

✔ No unnecessary punctuation ($$ instead of *money* or $#!! standing in for an expletive).

Capitalization

The capitalization rules for AdWords ads are that you can't use excess capitalization such as *FREE* or *SIDE EFFECTS*.

However, you can capitalize acronyms (MPH) as well as the first letter of each word in your ad and in your display URL (`LeadsIntoGold.com` is acceptable; `LeadsintoGOLD.com` is not).

Spelling and grammar

Google doesn't like ads that look like they were written by toddlers. Make sure all words are spelled correctly. If you don't have an ear for grammar, get someone who does to take a look at your ad. Spell checkers can't pick up mistakes like using *than* for *then* or *weather* for *whether*.

Copyright and trademark usage

You can't use copyrighted and trademarked terms in your ads without the permission of the rights holder.

This is a thorny and complicated issue for Google. If you sell one brand of mobile phone, can you compare it to a competing brand in your ad? Can you use copyrighted terms in your URL? In my experience, Google has not consistently enforced these rules. When I was advertising a natural approach to certain health problems, I ran ads that mentioned the names of prescription drugs. Google disallowed those ads, probably because the pharmaceutical company that makes the drugs had already complained to Google (or perhaps threatened a lawsuit). In other cases, I used copyrighted and trademarked terms without a problem.

Competitive claims

If you say your business is the best, fastest, cheapest, most successful, and such, you need to prove it to Google (and the world) on your landing page.

Offers

If you offer it in your ad, your visitor must be able to get it easily from your landing page. Giving away a free trial download? Put the link in an obvious place on the landing page. If Google's editors visit your site and decide your offer is fraudulent, your ad will be disallowed.

No offensive language

Unlike George Carlin, I *can't* tell you the seven words you're not allowed to use on Google. But if they get bleeped out of movies on TV, that's a pretty good clue to omit them from your ads.

If you want to be offensive, find acceptable synonyms. Perry Marshall found that replacing *sucks* with *stinks* revived a disallowed ad in 2005. Yet The Rich Jerk has been getting away with "Gurus Suck" as his headline for several months, so maybe Google is loosening up.

Links

Your display URL must "accurately reflect" (to use Google's exact language) the URL of your Web site. You can't display a URL that you don't own and aren't sending traffic to. That is, if someone typed your display URL into their browser instead of clicking your ad (thoughtfully saving you money!), they should still get to the same Web site, if not the exact same landing page.

Your destination URL must work properly and must resolve to a working Web page, as opposed to an e-mail address or document or multimedia file.

Exploring the Other Ad Formats

Google is constantly exploring new places and media for their ads. You can now create graphical ads for Web sites, text ads for mobile phones, local business listings that appear on search results pages and next to Google Maps, and video ads.

Getting the picture with image ads

Image ads are graphical files that display on content sites, but not on Google's or their search partners' results pages. Publishers can choose to display image ads instead of text ads. Perry Marshall has found that image ads typically generate higher CTRs than text ads, but convert to leads and sales at a much lower level. If you're a Web site publisher who gets paid for clicks on the Google ads on your site, image ads can be very profitable because of their high CTRs. For you, the AdWords advertiser, the high CTR can be a double-edged sword. Unless you monitor ROI from each ad, you may be funding Google's expansion at the expense of your own.

Joy Milkowski of www.adwordstoolbox.com offers the following four suggestions if you decide to try image ads:

1. Focus on a Pain or Problem

The same principles apply to this format as to all your marketing material — does it clearly suggest/address a pain or problem? Often I see adds trying to "feature dump" instead of offering to solve an issue in simple, easy to read language.

2. Keep the Design Clean and Simple

Are you trying to be too busy or use colors that are too bold in order to try to get noticed? If yes, chances are you may be turning prospects OFF. Our eyes are drawn to clean, easily decipherable images and language. Image ads, normally, are not the place to go "Las Vegas."

3. Show People, Not Products

Careful with using pictures of your product on the ad — often the space is so small that you end up either confusing the viewer or making your product seem less than adequate. Instead, I recommend using people. Get the viewer looking at a person — it's hard to NOT notice a person looking right at you!

4. Include an Offer and a Call to Action

Your image ad needs an irresistible offer as well as a compelling call to action. Remember, you're still in a direct response world. Don't let your ego look at the pretty pictures and elevate branding above measurable response.

Compared to text ads, image ads are more expensive and time-consuming to create, more expensive to display, and take longer to generate results. For these reasons, test your message, tone, offer and call to action with text ads before creating image ads.

Making the phone and the doorbell ring with mobile text ads

Google is going mobile, creating content that can be accessed and acted upon seamlessly from your smart mobile phone (and even from your mobile phone of average intelligence but with a nice smile). If your ad includes a link to a Web site, you have to make sure the site is created in a phone-compatible way. If you just want prospects to pick up the phone and call, or drive over and pay you a visit, create your ad and include an offer and call to action.

To create a mobile text ad, click the Mobile Text Ad link from within the Ad Variations tab of an ad group.

You can view your mobile text ad from your SMS-enabled phone by first registering your phone with Google at `http://google.com/mobile`. You can do this from your computer, or just point your phone's browser to `http://mobile.google.com`. You'll be able to conduct searches and view maps, as well as access several other Google services such as Gmail and Google News.

Waving to the neighbors with local business ads

If your business caters to a local market, you can still use AdWords to attract clients and customers. For instructions on using regular text ads for geographically limited markets, see Chapter 7. Right now you'll see how to create a local business ad that will appear as Google Maps business listings as well as other search results.

From within the Ad Variations tab of an ad group, click the Local business ads link just above the ad variations. On the next page, enter the business name and address. If you have multiple locations, you have the option to add additional addresses to your ad. If your business is not yet listed in Google's Local Business Center, you'll receive the following error message:

```
No businesses matched the address you entered.
```

In that case, visit `https://www.google.com/local/add/login` to add your business.

If your business is listed (mine isn't, so I'm going to use the Dogstar Tattoo Co. in Durham, NC as an example in Figure 6-5), you can continue to create your ad.

You can add a business image and even change the icon that appears next to your ad. Figure 6-6 shows what the ad will look like on the Google search page.

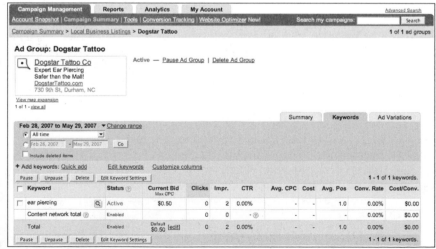

Figure 6-5: Creating a local business ad for a business already in Google's Local Business Listing.

Figure 6-6:
The local business ad on the Google search page looks like a regular listing. The business name is the headline, and the city is the fifth line.

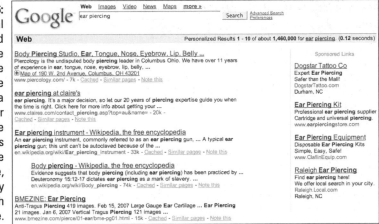

When someone searches for your keyword in a local area on Google Maps (http://maps.google.com), your ad may appear on the left, below, or above the business listings. Clicking it brings up the ad (including phone number and image) as a callout from the map location, as shown in Figure 6-7.

Figure 6-7:
Clicking the sponsored link on the left brings up the local business ad within the map on Google Maps.

Going Hollywood with video ads

To create a video ad that shows on content pages, click In-Line video ad from within the Ad Variations tab of an ad group. On the next page, you'll choose an image (Google is very picky about the size of this image, so make sure your graphic designer knows the dimensions Google will accept), enter display and destination URLs, name your ad, and upload your video.

My nine-minute, 30MB QuickTime video took about seven minutes to load with a fast cable-modem connection, so have a book handy if you plan on uploading lots of large videos.

Adriel Brunson of www.rfyvideo.com, a video advertising expert of many years, studied and experimented with Google video ads in 2006, and sent me this evaluation:

> When Google offered video ads in AdWords, everyone who understood the power of video on the Web cheered. Unfortunately, we may have cheered too soon.

> We wanted video ads in AdWords campaigns on Google search pages. What we got were video ads that only played on AdSense sites that allow graphical ads. Nothing for regular Google search pages.

> Google's AdWords video program does offer powerful options. You can create both keyword and site-targeted campaigns. You can search for AdSense sites matching your keywords. If you find any that allow graphical AdSense ads, you can target those sites.

> However, few AdSense publishers allow graphical ads. Most choose the default text-only option. Even the AdSense experts recommend text-only ads to blend in with the site navigation and content. No graphical ads, no video.

> My recommendation is to create regular AdWords campaigns and drive traffic to a page with a good headline, a good video, and well-written sales copy.

> With a regular Google AdWords keyword-targeted campaign, you'll get more control over the traffic, plus you can test everything in the chain — the keywords, the ad, the headline, the video placement, the text and links around the video. You can even test different video edits if you want.

> With Google AdWords video ads, you have little or no control over these elements.

> Go with a tested AdWords campaign and a landing page with good video. It's a much better option all the way around.

Because Google runs a *blind* advertising network based on keyword search (meaning you as an advertiser can't tell in advance where your ads will show, and the publishers can't predict accurately which ads will display on their pages), I recommend using Google video — if you must — only in site-targeted campaigns (more on this approach in Chapter 7).

You can expect big changes from Google video now that Google has bought YouTube. Stay abreast of those changes by subscribing to Adriel's newsletter at www.rfyvideo.com.

Part III

Managing Your AdWords Campaigns

The 5th Wave   By Rich Tennant

"And tell David to come in out of the hall. I found a way to adjust our ad budget estimate."

In this part . . .

The AdWords fantasy is that you find the perfect keyword, write the perfect ad, and retire to Fiji while the money rolls in relentlessly. The reality is that as important as keywords and ads are, the structure of your AdWords campaigns will determine success or failure.

In Chapter 7, you find out how to navigate a dizzying array of settings, including which network(s) will display your ads, how to budget and set bid prices, where in the world and what time of day to show the ads, and others.

Chapter 8 covers the strategy most neglected by AdWords users: creating tight Ad Groups of similar keywords and relevant ads. You discover how to perform ongoing tune-ups of your keyword lists, bids, and ads, so your AdWords vehicle runs ever more powerfully and efficiently.

Chapter 9 introduces you to the tools that Google has thoughtfully provided to make your AdWords life easier and more fulfilling. Okay, just easier.

Chapter 7

Deciding Where and When to Show Your Ads

*W*hen I install a piece of software on my computer, I often get a screen that asks me whether I want to go ahead with the Typical Installation (always recommended) or the Custom Installation (for advanced users only). To my recollection, I've never chosen Custom. I always worried that I would install a version of Microsoft Word that wouldn't let me type the letter M, or didn't have a built in English-to-Esperanto translator, or would omit some other crucial feature.

Google gives you an overwhelming number of choices for configuring AdWords campaigns — but it doesn't really bring them to your attention. Google isn't trying to bamboozle you; instead, the default settings are designed to protect clueless advertisers from themselves. But you, my friend, are no longer a clueless advertiser. By virtue of buying this book (or at least spilling coffee on it at Barnes & Noble), you are hereby officially dubbed "clueful advertiser."

In this chapter, you see how to tweak the AdWords default settings that aren't appropriate for power users. You discover how to bid intelligently on your own, instead of relying on Google to set your bids for you. (I know Google's motto is "Don't Be Evil," but I still wouldn't give them complete control over my advertising spending.) And you learn how to show your ads to different geographic areas with laser precision, and how to separate your search and content traffic for maximum clarity and ROI.

Getting the Most Out of Your Campaigns

If you want to set up one AdWords campaign, put it on autopilot, and never look at it again, feel free to skip this section. The changes I suggest will usually mean more, not less, work for you — more decisions, more overseeing, more risk, even, if you drop the ball. Google gives you a vehicle with an automatic transmission that does your thinking for you. On highways it works fine, although it will never be as efficient as a well-handled manual transmission. When you take it out for a race, though, you're going to need precision control based on experience - something no computer can do for you. Ready to strap on your AdWords seatbelt and hit the track?

Changing the default campaign settings

From within your AdWords account, choose a campaign and click Edit Campaign Settings. You'll see a page where you can change various settings for that particular campaign, as shown in Figure 7-1. Some of these options are shown to you when the campaign is born, while others hide on this page, waiting for you to find them. Let's explore the options that you haven't yet seen.

Figure 7-1:
You can edit the default campaign settings to gain more control over where and when your ads show.

Delivery method

If you exceed your daily budget on a regular basis, you have two choices: tell Google to pace your ads evenly through the day (standard), or show the ads as often as possible until you run out of money (accelerated).

Both methods can make sense, depending on the viewing patterns of your market. If your market is global, you probably want to show your ads evenly so you can get your message to your prospect in Singapore as well as the one in Saskatoon. If you run a local campaign for office workers, you may want to accelerate the ad showing if more people buy in the morning than the afternoon.

However, the choice begs an important question: why are you limiting your advertising spend? The concept of a budget for advertising doesn't make sense if each ad is making money. If I offered you a dollar bill in exchange for your half-dollar, how many times would you want to complete that transaction? Does *infinity* sound about right to you? It wouldn't make sense for you to say, "Let's only trade my 50 cents for your dollar 24 times, because my daily budget is 12 dollars."

Limit your daily budget for testing purposes, when you're not yet profitable and you're adjusting your keywords, ads, and Web-site sales process to become profitable. Another case where limiting your budget makes sense is if demand exceeds supply and you can only service so many paying customers. Or if you work for a big company used to advertising that's not directly tied to results, and you're given an ad budget. Or if you haven't read this book and don't yet know what you're doing.

(In fact, as you're assessing the competition, if you find that their ads disappear and reappear on the Google search results page as you refresh the page, you can be fairly confident that a) they aren't profitable yet; or b) they don't understand results-accountable marketing and won't be much of a threat to you.)

Keyword bidding

Keep the default here (Default bidding – maximum CPC) if you're going to pay attention to your keywords and monitor your account on a regular basis. Don't let Google optimize your budget.

Ad scheduling

Click the Turn On Ad Scheduling link and gasp to discover that Google gives you the option to schedule your ads by 15-minute increments, any day of the week, as shown in Figure 7-2. You can run your ads from midnight to 2:45 a.m. Monday, 3:00–3:15 a.m. Tuesday, and so on. By clicking the Switch to Advanced Mode link near the top of the page, you can even adjust your maximum bids by time period. You may want to be in a higher position on weekends, or just after *The Daily Show,* or during *Monday Night Football,* and so on.

Figure 7-2:
You can
schedule
when your
ads appear
by time and
day of the
week.

Position preference

If you select the Enable Position Preferences check box and save your changes, you are taken to a position preference introduction page. When position preference is activated, you can designate a position range for each keyword, accomplishing two goals: your ad will not show for a given keyword unless it falls within that position range, and Google will try to keep your ad within that range, given your budget limitations.

Essentially, position preference is like setting your maximum CPC, except you focus on the outcome (position) instead of the input (how much you're willing to pay for that position). I prefer to control the money — rather than the position — since the only metrics that matter at the end of the day are money in and money out.

To play with position preference, drill down into the Keyword tab of an ad group, and make sure the settings are showing for each keyword. (If the cell at the top of the column reads Show Settings, click it.) Then click the Edit link in that column for the keyword whose position you want to set (see the cursor position in Figure 7-3).

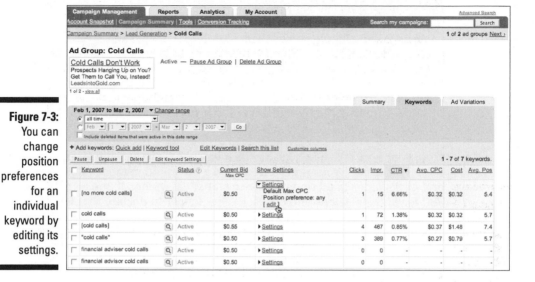

Figure 7-3:
You can
change
position
preferences
for an
individual
keyword by
editing its
settings.

In Figure 7-4, I've configured the keyword [no more cold calls] to trigger ads that appear between positions 4 and 8 (including both endpoints).

Figure 7-4:
This
keyword will
now show
only when
its ad is
between
positions
4 and 8.

Ad serving

Hold on for a short fire and brimstone sermon about the Ad Serving setting: Please do not Optimize your ads. I don't care where you are. Run, don't walk to a Web browser, log in to your account, choose a campaign, click the Edit Campaign Settings link, and move the radio button from Optimize to Rotate (refer to Figure 7-1). Then click the Save Changes button.

Done? Okay, now I can get rational and calm again. Let me explain why you made this change, and why it's so important. When you run two ads in the same ad group, Google shows them to different people and gives you statistics on how each ad performed (see Chapter 13 for the gory — er, *glorious* — details of split-testing). If Google optimizes your ad serving, the ads with lower CTR get shown less and the ads with higher CTR get shown more. Eventually, the poor performer stops showing, and Google declares a winner by default. You set the test up once, and it runs without you from then on. What could be bad?

First, your tests take much longer when you don't give each ad an equal chance to be "voted on" by searchers. You need a threshold number of impressions and clicks for each ad to determine a statistical winner. If one ad gets fewer and fewer impressions and clicks, it takes longer to declare that winner.

When you can't declare winners as they happen, you learn slower. Think of how fast bacteria adapt to antibiotics — because they go through so many generations in a short time frame. The more iterations per time frame, the more your ads can evolve and improve. AdWords is a playground where both evolution *and* intelligent design rule.

You also lose money, because your campaigns are improving more slowly than they might. Ad groups that could achieve profitability in a few days, based on traffic, will take weeks or even months to start making money.

In the second-to-worst-case scenario, you don't learn anything about your market because you don't even pay attention to the differences between the winning and losing ads. You don't learn which headlines work best, so you can't improve your Web site, your e-mails, your expensive offline advertisements, and so on.

If you allow Google to optimize your ads, the absolute worst-case scenario involves Google killing off the more effective ads by mistake. Google decides ad effectiveness on the basis of CTR, not on whether the visitors who click an ad end up *buying*. Often the highest CTR ads *lose* money because they attract too many non-buyers.

Networks

As we saw in Chapter 1, you can show your text ad in any of three places: Google pages, search partner pages, and the content network. The default setting for each campaign includes all three networks. The trouble with this setting is that the three sources of traffic generally behave very differently, respond to different language and different offers, and don't command the same bid prices. You can set different bids for the content network, but a cleaner way to separate the networks is to put each one in its own campaign. See the later section, "Separating your account into three types of campaigns" for details.

Locations

Google allows you as much geographical precision as you could possibly need. The default setting is by country: Google gives you a list of countries and you choose the ones whose inhabitants will see your ads. Straightforward and uncomplicated, this setting is common for online businesses who can serve customers pretty much anywhere. If you sell downloadable software, or telephone consulting, for example, you don't have any reason to exclude customers from Belgium or Israel or New Zealand, assuming language compatibility. In my experience, certain African and Asian countries tend to be hotbeds of credit-card fraud, however — and if you don't think a particular country will add a great deal to your bottom line, you may want to leave it off your list.

Countries and territories

In its list of available countries and territories, accessible by clicking the Edit button next to Countries and Territories, Google lists the most commonly selected 24 countries at the top, beginning with the United States and continuing alphabetically from Australia to United Kingdom. The following is a list of dozens of countries from Afghanistan to Zimbabwe. Choose countries by selecting them and clicking the Add button (as shown in Figure 7-5). You can select multiple countries by holding down the Ctrl (Windows) or ⌘ (Mac) keys as you click the country names. When your list is complete, click the Continue button to return to the Edit Settings page.

You must save your changes on the Edit Settings page for them to take effect.

Figure 7-5:
You can show your ads to multiple countries and territories.

Location Targeting Options

Your campaign's location targeting option: **Countries and Territories**   [Change option] | Learn more]

Available Countries and Territories
Switzerland
Taiwan
United Kingdom
——————
Afghanistan
Albania
Algeria
American Samoa

Add »
« Remove

Selected Countries and/or Territories
United States
Canada
Denmark
Hong Kong
Netherlands

Continue | Cancel | Click 'Continue' to return to Edit Settings, where you can save these changes.

©2007 Google - AdWords Home - Editorial Guidelines - Privacy Policy - Contact Us

Regions and cities

If you want to target prospects more precisely, select the Regions and Cities Option after clicking Edit on the main setting page and Change Option on the Location Targeting Page. When you continue, you'll be able to choose regions from within a single country, as shown in Figure 7-6.

If the country is the United States, you can select the States/Regions/Metropolitan Areas radio button, and then select the areas you want from a list box. Or you can select the Cities radio button and enter your own list of cities in the format of city name state abbreviation: Durham NC or Roanoke VA. You can toggle back and forth between these two radio buttons to complete your list.

Figure 7-6:
You can target regions, individual states, metropolitan areas, and cities within one country.

Customized

If you run a local business, the regional and city targeting may not be precise enough for you. After all, no matter how good a dry cleaner you may be, few customers will drive 45 minutes across town to drop off their dress shirts. Enter Customized targeting to the rescue. You get to that page by editing the location targeting options, clicking the Change Option link, and clicking the Customized radio button on the Location Targeting Options page. You're given two options: a circular area, or a wild and wacky polygon of your creation.

✔ **Circular:** After entering a physical address or centering the map at your desired location (zoom way in by clicking the + button at the top left of the map), you can enter a radius around that spot in miles or kilometers. Figure 7-7 shows a radius of 30 miles around Charlottesville, Virginia.

✔ **Multi-Point Option:** Occasionally, a circle will not be precise enough. What if, in Figure 7-7, I don't want to show my ads in the Gordonsville area and points northeast? Google sends a multi-point option to the rescue. Below the map, click the Multi-Point Option link. Your map reverts to global scale, and you can either enter coordinates like you're a World War I ace, or zoom in to your map location and draw a polygon that defines your target area, as shown in Figure 7-8.

Figure 7-7:
Centering
the map on
Charlottes-
ville, VA and
selecting a
30-mile
radius
produces a
circular
area that
will see
your ads.

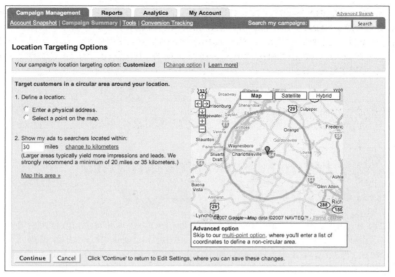

Figure 7-8:
Indulge your
inner artist
by creating
a polygon
within which
to show
your ads.

Working with campaign settings often produces an official-looking message
from Google, warning you that you're about to lose your current selection if
you do this or that. (See Figure 7-9.) As long as you keep saving the changes
you do want to make, just click OK and don't worry.

Separating your account into three types of campaigns

By default, Google wants to show each of your ads to as many people as possible. It's good business for them, and possibly for you as well. But until you separate out the traffic streams and evaluate each one individually, you'll never know. For most keywords, Google search converts best, search partners second best, and content network worst. So it makes sense to test your ads and keywords where they have the greatest chance of success before rolling them out globally. Google is a little bit like Frank Sinatra's "New York, New York": If you can make it there, you might be able to make it anywhere.

Separating your traffic by network is a little more complicated than it ought to be, but that turns out to be a good thing. If it were easy, everyone would be doing it and you would not be able to gain a competitive advantage.

Google Search

Your first campaign should probably be Google Search only. Creating a Google Only campaign is simple. On the Edit Campaign Settings page, uncheck the boxes next to Search Network and Content Network. Google has a little snit when you uncheck that last box — and tries to convince you to keep it checked and "pay less for content bids" (see Figure 7-10). Click OK to ignore the entreaty, and then save your changes.

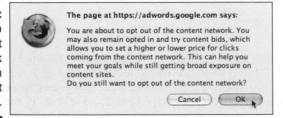

This campaign will now show your ads only on Google pages; not AOL search, not Earthlink, not Amazon.com. To confirm this setting, visit the Keywords tab of one of the ad groups in this campaign and make sure the status of the Content Network Total is Disabled.

Figure 7-11 shows an ad group with a messy campaign that mixed Search and Content results. While the content network received more than 5 times the impressions of the search network (78,396 vs. 17,565), it generated fewer than ⅕ of the clicks (36 compared to 203). My CTR on Search was a respectable 1.15%, but only 0.04% for Content. As a result, the noise from all those unclicked impressions overwhelms my valuable data. My two ad CTRs are 0.32% and 0.17%, respectively, far below the Search average of 1.15%. I can't tell at a glance which ad works best for Search.

Figure 7-11: Combining Content and Search traffic in the same campaign produces data that are hard to interpret.

Search Network

As you've seen, Google happily shares its search results with AOL, Earthlink, and other Search Partners. Google and AOL users are different from each other in meaningful ways, and those differences can affect how they respond to your ads. You probably can't predict how those differences will affect response, so the safest route is to separate the two streams and market to them separately.

On the Edit Campaign Settings page, uncheck the Google Search box but leave the Search Network box checked . . . just kidding! You can't do it; Google won't let you. You can't target AOL without also targeting Google. You can separate the streams by following this process:

1. **Create two identical campaigns (see Chapter 9 for some timesaving Campaign Modification tools).**

   The two campaigns should have the same settings, same ad groups, and same keywords. Add the letter **G** (for Google) to the end of one of the campaign names, and add **S** (for Search) to the other.

2. **Change their Networks settings as follows:**

   - **Campaign G:** Check Google Search, uncheck Search Network, uncheck Content Network.
   - **Campaign S:** Check Google Search, check Search Network, uncheck Content Network.

3. **For the Campaign S, reduce all your bids to about five cents below the Campaign G bids.**

You've created two campaigns that compete with one another for exposure. When they compete head to head on Google, the Campaign G will win because it has the higher bids. Only Campaign S will show for the Search Network, since Campaign G isn't configured to show for that network. *Voilà!*

Content Network

You can add the content network by creating a third identical campaign, this one with C after the name. For Campaign C, uncheck Google Search and check Content Network.

Figure 7-12 shows a neat AdWords account with three campaigns each receiving different streams of traffic. The Google Search only campaign has the highest CTR, 0.79%, the Search Network is second with 0.50%, and the Content campaign comes in lowest with 0.22%. Had those three traffic streams been intermingled, I would have seen only a cumulative CTR of 0.33%. Notice also the difference in average CPC: a Search Network click cost more than a Google click, while the Content click was cheapest. Because this is a young AdWords account, it's too early to tell whether different ads work better with different traffic streams, but experience tells me that's often the case.

 While people searching on Google expect organic listings and ads (after all, that's why they're searching), ads on the Content Network are interruptions. If you're reading an article in the *New York Times* or managing your Gmail, you haven't asked a bunch of advertisers to vie for your attention. Your Content ads must be extremely relevant, urgent, or curiosity provoking to compete against the editorial content of a Web page. Your search ads may only need to highlight a problem and offer a solution.

Figure 7-12:
Here the
Google (G),
Search
Partners (S),
and Content
(C) traffic
are sep-
arated by
campaign
so each
source
can be
evaluated
and
managed
intelligently.

Your bidding strategy for the Content Network must achieve the goal of getting your ad at or near the top position. Unlike a search-results page, AdSense
pages typically show from one to five text ads. Figure 7-13 shows the top of
the `tuaw.com` blog, with four AdSense ads between the header and the first
post. Three of them are iPod ads, but the fourth ("Find It All Right Here") is
simply an ad that seems to get clicks (and make Google money) pretty much
anywhere. So your Mac- or iPod-related ad needs to be in positions 1, 2, or 3
to get any play on this popular blog.

Figure 7-13:
Only the
top four
ads make
it to the
tuaw.com
home page.

Keyword and site targeting

If you show your ads on the Content network, how does Google decide which
AdSense publishers show your ads? You tell Google whether you want to bid

on pages that are optimized for your keywords, or whether you want to choose specific sites for your ads.

In the old days (before June 2007), if you select Keyword Targeting, you couldn't tell which sites were showing your ads. Imagine sending a check to a national TV network so your commercial would be shown on their affiliate stations, but they refuse to tell you where and when (and even whether) your ads will run. That's what Google's Content Network was like.

Just as this book was entering the "make another change and we'll break your fingers" stage, Google unveiled a new report that shows you which AdSense Web sites are showing your ads and how well the ads are converting on each AdSense page. To generate the Placement Performance report, you must first set up Conversion Tracking (which you find out how to do in Chapter 14). See www.askhowie.com/sitereports for instructions as well as examples of the power of this long-awaited feature.

Your first campaign uses Keyword Targeting by default, and you can't change it. Once your first campaign is configured, you can create a Site-Targeted Content Network campaign by clicking the Site-Targeted link next to + Create a New Campaign on the Campaign Summary page.

Name your new campaign and your first ad group, choose the language or languages your customers speak, and select your geographic target. Basically, you're selecting a group of people in some geographic area, from a small town to the entire world, who visit certain Web sites. You can choose Rap/Hip-Hop fans in the Midwest, Progressives in South Carolina, Evangelicals in Chicago, and so on. Interest groups merged with geography can provide very tight, responsive markets for your ads.

On the next page, you're prompted to create an ad. You can create a second ad to test, or just click Continue to choose the Web sites where you want your ad to appear. Google doesn't assume you know any specific sites. The wizard prompts you to select from categories such as games or health, enter topic words, name specific Web sites, or describe your audience and let Google suggest Web sites matching that demographic, as shown in Figure 7-14.

If you type the topic **Gout** (as shown in Figure 7-15), Google returns a list of 55 Web sites, along with information like impressions per day and supported ad formats (text, image, video). You can filter the results by clicking Choose Ad Format, so if you have a square 250 x 250 pixel image ad, you can choose only those Web sites that have elected to serve ads of that size and shape.

If your desired audience is in the United States and you choose to target the entire country, you can choose Web sites based on demographics. In the Figure 7-16, Google will show Web sites visited by 25–44-year-old women making more than $60,000 a year who have children in their household. Figure 7-17 shows the top Web sites returned for those criteria. You can select any or all of them to show your ad. The first one, vamoose.com, is a directory of vacation rentals. Ask yourself: Can I create an ad that will interrupt someone trying to rent a vacation home and make them act on my offer? If so, will that person be a good prospect? If both questions can be answered Yes, you may have a successful Content site.

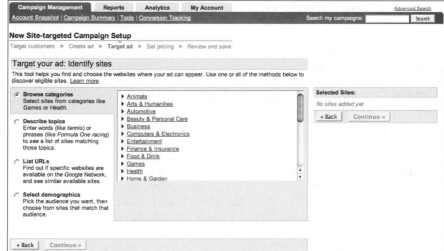

Figure 7-14:
Google can help you find the right sites for your ad in four ways.

Figure 7-15:
Choosing Content sites by describing topics.

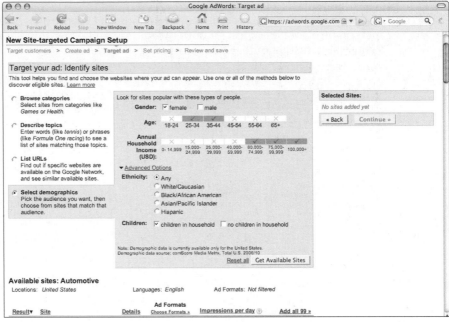

Figure 7-16: Demographic targeting allows you to show your ad to men or women of different ages, income brackets, and ethnicity, as well as if their household includes children.

Figure 7-17: Web sites whose visitors are deemed to meet the demographic criteria shown in Figure 7-16.

Bidding Smart

Earlier in this chapter, I urged you not to let Google automatically determine your bids. Eventually, when you have conversion tracking and analytics set up (see Chapters 14 and 15), you can adjust your bids intelligently in response to back-end conversion. When you first bid on a keyword, you want to balance three objectives: getting valid data quickly, generating high CTRs for your best keywords, and not losing the shirt off your back by paying too much for too many unprofitable clicks.

Initial bidding strategies

AdWords and SEO (Search Engine Optimization) expert Don Crowther of `www.greatresults.com` divides his keywords into three tiers for bidding purposes:

✔ **Money Makers:** Specific keywords with large amounts of traffic, often 3–5 words long, that you expect will generate high CTRs.

Examples: `gout foods to avoid`, `left-handed titanium driver`, `iPod shuffle blue case`

Bid to get those keywords in positions 1–3, the higher the better. Don reports that position 1 can return a much higher CTR than any other position. Think about it — position 1 is the first link the happy clickers will see, so it's likely to get more unqualified traffic than any other position. Ordinarily you want to discourage unqualified clicks, but the first thousand impressions help Google determine your keyword's quality score. A high CTR at the beginning may lower your maximum CPC by telling Google your keyword is well matched to your ad.

After the first thousand impressions, lower your bid to achieve positions 4–8 and then continually adjust according to ROI (see Chapter 14 for details on conversion tracking).

✔ **Generic Terms:** Category terms that lots of people use at the beginning of their search process; these are usually one-to-two-word, short-tail keywords.

Examples: `gout`, `golf club`, `iPod`

Bid for positions 4–8 for generic terms. Rarely will you convert enough of these searches to sales to justify the extra expense of positions 1–3, and the traffic for these words can bankrupt you if you generate too many clicks before optimizing your sales process.

✔ **Long Shots:** Keywords that may be extremely expensive or competitive, or just tangentially related to your ad.

Examples: [gout cure] (top bid $2.77), [golf vacations] ($8.27), [video ipod] ($6.61)

Bid wherever you can get some reasonable showing without breaking your budget. Typically that will be around positions 7–10 (the second page of search results typically cuts impressions by a factor of 10). Don notes, "Sometimes I'll be in spot 63, and I recognize that, and don't worry about it." Some keywords are hyper-competitive, and your competitors may have been testing and improving their campaigns for years. Learn what you can from them, but don't expect to be able to match their results on your first try.

If your campaign is showing on the Content Network, you should bid to appear in positions 1–3 for text ads, and position 1 for image and video ads. Otherwise your ads won't appear enough to for you to learn (or profit) from.

When you have data . . .

The initial bidding strategies should give way to data-informed bids as soon as possible. After you set up conversion tracking and analytics (described in Chapters 14 and 15, respectively), run keyword reports and adjust each keyword to be profitable. One position will give you the highest ROI for each keyword, and you can usually find it through trial and error within a few hundred clicks.

If your business doesn't lend itself to conversion tracking because you can't track sales online, you'll make adjustments on a much less precise basis. Aim for positions 4–8 one month, 7–10 another month, and see what happens to your business — keeping in mind any possible feedback lags due to the length of your sales cycle. If your offline sales are a big part of your business, you can learn about a fairly expensive strategy for including that data in your Google reports at www.askhowie.com/offline. This strategy isn't worth it for small sales, but if your average sales exceed $150, it may pay for itself quickly.

Chapter 8

Improving Your Campaigns through Keyword Management

▶ Managing your keyword sales force

▶ Increasing relevance by tightening ad groups

▶ Saving and resuscitating keywords

▶ Avoiding overwhelm with the 80/20 rule

*W*hen you place an ad in the Yellow Pages, you can't change it until the next edition comes out. After the ad is in the Yellow Pages, your job is to answer the phone, take care of customers, and pay the electricity bill.

Your AdWords account, on the other hand, frequently needs changes and requires much more of your attention than a static advertisement. If you like metaphors, you can equate your AdWords account to auto maintenance. If you never change the oil, the engine will eventually die. However, with regular maintenance and tinkering, you can get it to a high-performance state over time — and keep it there. Your AdWords account demands more attention up front, and then less and less as time goes on.

In this chapter, you discover tactics for improving your AdWords campaign performance over time. I show you how to identify unprofitable keywords, and what you can try before you fire them. I help you improve CTR by grouping similar keywords and targeting your ads more tightly to those keywords. I divulge a strategy for resuscitating keywords that have been rendered inactive because Google doesn't like them. Finally, I show you a triage system that allows you to focus your campaign management where it will bring the highest return.

Nurturing, Relocating, and Firing Keywords

Keywords connect people with ads. If the connection is right, the right people find the right ads. As your AdWords campaigns mature, you'll discover the best relationships between keywords and ads. Think of your keyword list as a commission-only sales force, with each keyword a different sales rep driving up and down the Internet looking for business:

- **Stars:** Some of keywords are stars, bringing in customers and profits on a regular basis.

- **Solid performers:** These are good performers, making their numbers without complaint but not setting the world on fire.

- **Long tails:** Still other keywords are harmless stay-at-homes, making you nothing but costing you nothing either.

- **Underperformers:** A large number of your keywords underperform and may be converted into solid producers by relocation to better territories.

- **Negative ROI:** Inevitably, you'll find keywords that just aren't worth keeping — they may bring you some business, but their expense accounts far exceed the value of their leads.

The following sections look at what to do about each of these keywords.

Star keywords

I'm going to take a wild guess about your AdWords account: I predict that 95% of your Web site traffic is coming from fewer than 10 keywords. Maybe fewer than five. I know this not because I'm psychic (I knew you were thinking that), but because in the five years I've been helping people with AdWords, I've rarely seen an account that wasn't tilted in that direction. In fact, it's not uncommon for an online business to live or die based on a single keyword.

Your most important AdWords job is to identify these star keywords and give them everything they need to be happy and healthy. Limos, special diets, bathtubs filled with Perrier — these keywords must receive ongoing attention if they are to perform at a high level.

Of course, keywords aren't really pampered Hollywood stars, so my suggestions in the previous paragraph are meant to be understood metaphorically. What keywords really want are relevant ads in the right positions taking the searcher to an appropriate landing page. All your keywords want this; your job as an advertiser is to give it to them to the extent you can. But if you're building your campaigns correctly, with hundreds or thousands of long-tail keywords, it's easy to lump your star keywords in with the hoi polloi and lose a lot of potential sales.

Give each star keyword its own ad group and landing page. The ads in that ad group include the keyword at least once, possibly twice, and you check your split tests regularly for a winner (see Chapter 13). The landing page tells your visitors within 1.3 seconds that they've come to the right place; to the Web site that has the answer to their deepest and most pressing desires.

If you didn't connect with the Hollywood-stars metaphor, here's one inspired by my visit to the North Carolina State Fair last fall: Your hundreds or thousands of keywords are like apples in your orchard, while the star keywords are your prize milk-fed pumpkins. Each pumpkin gets as much attention as an orchard of apples. (If you need more metaphors, you're on your own.)

Finding star keywords

To identify your star keywords, follow these steps:

1. **Log in to your AdWords account at www.google.com/adwords and get to the Campaign Summary page (you may be taken there by default).**

2. **Sort your campaigns by clicking the Impr. (impressions) column, so the campaign that has received the most impressions is at the top.**

3. **Click the top campaign name and repeat the sorting process with the ad groups in that campaign.**

4. **In the most-trafficked ad group, click the Keywords tab.**

    You should see all your keywords already sorted by impressions, as shown in Figure 8-1. The top one or two keywords are probably receiving a lot more traffic than the rest.

Figure 8-1 tells a typical story: The top two keywords, [gout diet] and gout diet, together have received 82% of the total impressions for this ad group. A closer examination shows that [gout diet] is significantly under-performing in terms of traffic: Its average position is 8.9, putting it on the second page of search results much of the time. Were I to raise its bid, that keyword alone would probably account for 95% of the impressions for this group. (Whether that would be a profitable move depends on the cost per conversion for that keyword, which you can explore in Chapter 14).

Moving a star to its own trailer

I know, back to the movie-star metaphor. It just amuses me to imagine [gout diet] running around in dark sunglasses and a designer shirt. Giving a star keyword its own ad group is a four-phase process:

1. **Create a new ad group in the same campaign as its current ad group, write an ad that connects strongly to the keyword, and add that keyword only to the keyword list.**

   If it's an exact match, with brackets, don't worry about negative keywords. If it's a phrase or broad match, include negative keywords.

2. **Bid a couple of cents higher on the keyword in the new ad group than you were bidding in the old ad group, either by lowering the old bid or raising the new one.**

3. **Create a new landing page specifically for that keyword.**

4. **When the keyword in the old ad group stops getting traffic in favor of the new ad group, pause the keyword in the old ad group.**

   If you run into problems, you can always pause the new ad group and unpause the old keyword.

Solid performers

Your *solid performers* are keywords that consistently generate decent numbers of impressions, but nowhere near the stratospheric output of the stars. In Figure 8-2, the first four keywords generate two-thirds of the total impressions. The next eight keywords are the solid performers, each generating between 1400 and 6900 impressions.

Figure 8-1: The top two keywords in this ad group have received 82% of the impressions.

Figure 8-2:
The keywords from "cold calls" to making cold calls are all solid performers.

Keywords of a feather should flock together

Look at your keywords and see if you can group them into more tightly focused ad groups, based on word similarity and CTR. For example, the keywords in Figure 8-2 need to be divided into more tightly targeted ad groups, based on word similarity and CTR.

The CTRs for the eight solid performers are as follows:

Keyword	Click-Through Rate
"cold calls"	2.25%
cold calls	2.01%
cold call techniques	0.81%
[cold call techniques]	1.20%
cold call scripts	1.14%
"cold calling techniques"	0.53%
[cold calls]	4.56%
making cold calls	1.91%

The range of CTRs is huge, with the best performing keyword, [cold calls], generating Web site visitors at almost nine times the rate of the worst performer, `"cold calling techniques"`. And they're all showing for the same ad or ads. What this means is that the ads in this group have the potential to achieve a very nice 4.56% CTR, if they're showing for the right keywords. The keyword `"cold calling techniques"` is poorly matched to the ads in this ad group, and should be moved to a different ad group with an ad and landing page more specifically targeted to that desire.

The keywords in this ad group that don't generate enough traffic to warrant their own group should be divided as follows:

✔ **Cold Calling Techniques ad group**

- `cold calling techniques`

- `[cold calling techniques]`

- `"cold calling techniques"`

- Any other phrases that include the three words `cold calling techniques` in any order

- Phrases with the three words with `technique` misspelled or mistyped (for example, `cold calling tehcniques`)

- Phrases with the words `cold call techniques` (then split those out if the CTRs are different)

✔ **Cold Calls ad group**

- `[cold calls]`

- `"cold calls"`

- `cold calls`

- `making cold calls`

- `[making cold calls]`

✔ **Cold Call Scripts ad group**

- `cold call scripts`

- `"cold call scripts"`

- `[cold call scripts]`

- Phrases with the three words with `scripts` misspelled or mistyped (for example, `scirpts`)

- Any other phrases that include the three words `cold call scripts` in any order

Determining your ad's true potential

Sort the keywords in your ad group by the Clicks column. The keyword that's received at least 30 clicks with the highest CTR represents your ad's potential.

All keywords that receive significantly lower CTRs don't belong with that ad. Typically, you'll find that the highest CTR keywords are the ones echoed in the headline of the ad.

Long-tail keywords

The long-tail keywords are the ones receiving low numbers of impressions, and the occasional click. They just don't get enough traffic to justify their own ad or landing page, but collectively are worth bidding on because they are cheaper than other keywords and convert better because there's less competition. These two factors lower your global average cost of customer acquisition, and can mean the difference between a struggling and a dominant business.

Each one isn't anything to write home about, but collectively they may be doing more for your business than any of your top performers — just like the hardworking character actors and lighting directors and third associate key grips and assistant best boys who don't get all the credit but without whom the movies don't get made. The names in the credits at the end of the movie are the long-tail keywords.

 Your long-tail keywords can be in big, undifferentiated groups with a generic "problem/promise" ad: Headline describes the problem, Description Line #1 makes a big promise, Description Line #2 includes a feature and call to action. (See Chapter 6 for details of ad writings)

You will improve performance by grouping the long-tail keywords by concept. For the gout-campaign example, I used the following concepts to group long-tail keywords:

- ✔ **Diet:** Keywords related to diet indicate, as best as I can tell, potential customers who desire to take control and change aspects of their lifestyle. Ads that reassure that such changes are quick and easy do well with this group.

- ✔ **Food:** Food keywords, on the other hand, reflect a narrower mindset related to specific foods to ingest or avoid, rather than a wholesale diet change. Ads that ask ignorance-uncovering questions (What are the 3 worst gout foods? Is cherry juice for real?) will motivate this group.

- ✔ **Remedy:** People who type `remedy` are looking for home remedies and folk medicine, as opposed to drugs or prevention. They like "secrets" and "what doctors won't tell you."

- ✔ **Symptom relief:** People searching for `gout pain`, `arthritis gout`, `gout symptoms`, and `gout treatment` view gout as a disease not entirely under their control. An ad that immediately offers information about diet and lifestyle change will alienate this group. Instead, empathize and offer quick results.

Some of your long-tail keywords may receive no impressions at all for months at a time. That's okay. Since you pay commissions only on clicks, the salesperson who never makes sales calls doesn't cost you a bit.

Underperforming keywords

As we've seen, a keyword will underperform if it points to an ad that doesn't address the right desires, or if that ad is positioned too high or too low (based on that keyword's maximum CPC). If the problem is too few impressions, check your average position for that keyword. Your ad may be showing on page 4, where few searchers are willing to go. Or your ad may be lower than third position in a Content Network campaign.

Sometimes your keywords deliver lots of impressions but few clicks. In that case, the problem is the ad itself: what it says or where it's showing. Move your keyword to an ad group that addresses the desire represented by that keyword. Increase your bid to a more desirable position.

Negative-ROI keywords

Once you set up conversion tracking (described in Chapter 14), you'll discover that some keywords appear to be doing well within the AdWords account — lots of traffic, good CTR — but don't convert to sales well enough to justify the cost of their clicks. This type of underperformance is especially insidious because it's hard to identify. I'll show you how to spot these Expense-Account Gluttons that cost you more than they make for you in Chapter 14.

You deal with negative-ROI keywords by first trying the tactic just described for underperforming keywords: point them to better ads. If the increased CTR doesn't make them profitable, add negative qualifiers like price and other disincentives to click (see Chapter 6). If nothing works, you have to let them go. Don't worry about them — someone else will blissfully (and cluelessly) continue losing money on those keywords. Just don't let it be you.

Resuscitating Poor-Quality Keywords

In July 2006, Google rolled out a change to its bid-price algorithm that left many advertisers bruised and confused. Its nickel keywords were now disabled, and required bids of at least $10.00 to reactivate. The big change was the addition of a new metric — Keyword Quality Score. Google returned to its roots as the provider of quick and relevant results, and began penalizing advertisers whose ads and Web sites weren't appropriate for the keyword.

The quality-score algorithm continues to evolve, and no one outside the hallowed halls of Google knows exactly what it is, but the trend is clear: You've got to give the people who see your ad a good experience all the way through to your Web site. To Google, a good experience means customers can find what they want quickly and easily, with no hassle.

Figure 8-3 shows the difference between keywords with Great and OK quality scores. The average bid for a Great keyword is 4 cents, compared to 10 or 15 cents for an OK keyword. If you could scroll down the page, you'd feel my pain at seeing a bunch of Poor-quality keywords asking me to ante up at 50 cents a throw.

The product I sell from this ad group is not expensive and does not lead to a big back end. If I can't get the click in under 10 cents, I can't survive in this market. My important keywords (the star and solid performers) must receive Great quality scores. The majority of the long-tail keywords must be deemed either Great or OK.

Figure 8-3:
The keywords with a Great quality score are much less expensive to bid on than those with OK quality scores.

To resuscitate a keyword, follow these steps:

1. **Move it to a new ad group.**
2. **Write a new ad with a message targeted specifically for that keyword.**
3. **Link the ad to a new landing page written with that searcher in mind.**

   (See Chapter 10 for landing-page dos and don'ts.)

Managing the 80/20 Way

This chapter is deceptively short, because the work it asks you to do can be time-consuming. It's maintenance, not setup — and it's tempting to do maintenance once and not peek under the hood again until you smell oil. (Yup, back to the car metaphor.) Especially after you've divided your campaigns into many focused ad groups, you can find yourself drowning amid the priorities competing for your attention. This section gives you some guidance in answering the only question that ever matters at this point: "What do I do now?"

The 80/20 Principle states that 80% of your efforts lead to only 20% of your results, while the remaining 20% of your efforts is responsible for 80% of your results. The top 20% of your keywords will generate 80% of your clicks and sales. Don't get hung up on the exact numbers — you'll probably find that the ratio in AdWords is closer to 95/5 or 99/1.

In any case, the moral is the same: Consciously spend your time and focus your attention on the parts of your AdWords account that have the biggest impact on your profitability.

Each AdWords account is different, so I can't give you a formula for how to spend your time. The key skills here are threefold:

- ✔ Knowing the key priorities for your business.
- ✔ Sorting your campaigns, ad groups and keyword lists by those priorities.
- ✔ Always addressing the issue that can provide the biggest boost to your bottom line.

The factor limiting the growth of most online businesses is the size of the reachable market. In AdWords, the reachable market consists of people searching for your keywords or visiting Web sites that display your ads. The AdWords metric for this market is *impressions* — instances of exposure to your ad.

After you log in to your account, click into a campaign. Look at the statistics for each ad group. You're looking to answer the question, "Which ad group's improvement will have the biggest impact on my business?" In general, I focus on the ad group with the highest potential number of impressions. In Figure 8-4, for example, the Causes of Gout PS group's average position is 8.3, meaning it shows on the second page of search results and not at all in the content network. If I increased my bids, the traffic would increase, probably to 10 times its current amount.

If the average position of an ad group is 7 or better within a search campaign, or 3 or better in a content campaign, then you are theoretically getting as many impressions as possible. If an ad group averages position 8 or worse (4 for content), your ads aren't getting seen by as many people as possible.

First, sort by impressions, and note any ad groups whose average positions are too low. They are potential sleepers, if you can afford the bids needed to get your ads in front of people.

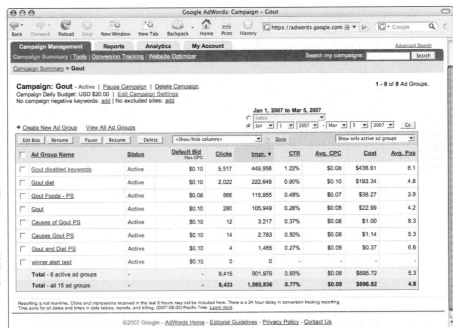

Figure 8-4:
Triage your ad groups by looking at areas of potentially big improvement.

Ad Group Name	Status	Default Bid Max CPC	Clicks	Impr. ▼	CTR	Avg. CPC	Cost	Avg. Pos
Gout disabled keywords	Active	$0.10	5,517	449,958	1.22%	$0.08	$438.61	6.1
Gout diet	Active	$0.10	2,022	222,648	0.90%	$0.10	$193.34	4.8
Gout Foods - PS	Active	$0.08	566	115,955	0.48%	$0.07	$38.27	3.9
Gout	Active	$0.10	280	105,949	0.26%	$0.08	$22.99	4.2
Causes of Gout PS	Active	$0.10	12	3,217	0.37%	$0.08	$1.00	8.3
Causes Gout PS	Active	$0.10	14	2,783	0.50%	$0.08	$1.14	5.3
Gout and Diet PS	Active	$0.10	4	1,465	0.27%	$0.09	$0.37	6.6
winner alert test	Active	$0.10	0	0	-	-	-	-
Total - 8 active ad groups	-	-	8,415	901,975	0.93%	$0.08	$695.72	5.3
Total - all 15 ad groups	-	-	8,433	1,085,836	0.77%	$0.08	$696.82	4.8

Let me plug a microphone into my head so you can hear my thinking about Figure 8-4:

> "Okay, let's see. I have four big ad groups, with over 100,000 impressions so far this year. The most expensive group is the top one. I've spent over $400 on it since January. Its CTR gets an OK rating, but I definitely can improve it. If I doubled the CTR, I would increase my Web traffic by 5500 people over the next couple of months. If I doubled the CTR on my next biggest group, Gout Diet, the same amount of effort would get me only 2000 more visitors. Oh, and look at the fourth group, Gout. The CTR is miserable, just 0.26%. I could probably improve it by a factor of 8, getting it to 2.00% with a little split-testing and rearranging of keywords. That would give me about 3000 additional visitors (280 × 8). And it's usually easier to improve a bad ad than an OK one, so maybe that's a good place to start."

I click the Gout ad group and view the keyword tab (see Figure 8-5).

> "Oh, look, the top eight keywords' CTRs are doing pretty well. While I'm here, I'll pause `"the gout"` because it got 332 impressions and not a single click. The big problem here is the content network — my ads are generating lots of impressions but few clicks."

Figure 8-5:
My keyword list tells that my CTR problem is caused by the content network.

Look at the total number of impressions in Figure 8-5: 19,122. Compare that to the total in Figure 8-4, which was over 100,000. That means about 80,000 impressions are from content.

> "Obviously my ads are aimed at people who are searching for a solution to their gout problem, rather than people who are reading about gout and need a powerful ad to interrupt them into taking action.

> "And goodness gracious me!" (Yes, sadly, that is how I talk to myself. You have no idea how annoying it can be.) "Except for the gout recipes keywords, my quality scores are just OK. I need to move the other high-potential keywords into their own ad groups and write better ads and send them to more tightly targeted landing pages. Then my dime bids can get my ads on the first page and skyrocket my traffic without harming my ROI."

When you install conversion tracking, you'll have another data point upon which to act. When you find an ad group that delivers negative ROI (see Chapter 14), do something at once. Either attempt a fix, or pause it, or delete it. But again, the order in which you act depends on the potential value of the improvement. A miniscule improvement in an ad group that gets lots of impressions is more valuable than a big improvement in an ad group consisting of seldom-seen long-tail keywords.

As you spend time in AdWords, you'll get the hang of where to focus, and you'll develop your own rhythm and intuition for what needs adjustment. The main thing to keep in mind is the 80/20 question: "What can I do now that will make the biggest difference in results?"

Split-testing ads and adjusting your bids are the sexy parts of AdWords management. Putting the right keywords together with the right ads and landing pages is more like nailing up the studs of a house than putting in the fancy trim. (Yes, campers, one final metaphor for today!) Nobody visits a show house and says, "My, those two-by-fours sure are straight." AdWords Consultant Greg Marsden e-mailed me these words of wisdom (so blame him for the metaphor):

> *Simply put, it's the solid scalable architecture of your campaigns that needs to come first before you pick the curtains out and decide what color to paint the door of your store. Virtually everyone I've worked with on AdWords completely misses that point and spends almost all of their time, effort and a ton of wasted money on frantically changing their ad texts just trying to find a "'super ad" that'll magically double CTR and save the day.*

Greg went on to relate that three items on his to-do list increased the amount of traffic to his Web site by 50% with no loss of quality:

- Separating content and search traffic (see Chapter 7).
- Building separate keyword lists for content and search.
- Expanding and tightly grouping keywords, particularly on the content side.

You can see the details of Greg's case study in Chapter 17.

Chapter 9

Getting It Done with AdWords Tools

In This Chapter

▶ Improving campaigns with the Account Optimizer tools

▶ Saving time with Google Campaign Management tools

▶ Checking your account's vital statistics with Diagnostic tools

*W*hen my father was 12 years old in 1930, his Uncle Freddie offered to take him to a Newark Bears minor-league baseball game. With the Depression raging, he couldn't afford the ticket on his own, so he accepted the offer from his notoriously stingy (and occasionally just notorious) uncle. Upon arriving at the ballpark, Uncle Freddie hustled them away from the turnstiles, around the stadium to the fence abutting the farthest outfield bleachers. Once there, Freddie knelt down and instructed my father to climb on his back and grab the top of the fence.

With a last-gasp boost by Freddie, my father vaulted the fence and toppled into the ballpark, right on top of a pair of cops hired to keep order at the raucous venue. One of the policemen roughly lifted my father up by the collar and inquired of the quivering youth, "Don't you know these games are free for kids?"

A whole industry of third-party tools has grown up around Google AdWords. Some of them, in my opinion, are indispensable (see my recommendations in Bonus Chapter 1, available as a PDF file at www.dummies.com/go/adwords). Others are convenient and may be worth it because of the time they save. But many are simply duplicates of free tools included (but buried) within your AdWords account. You may never need most of them. But in memory of my father's early brush with the law, I hereby introduce you to a bunch of tools that come free with AdWords. Don't let Uncle Freddie sucker you into missing out or paying extra.

The purpose of this chapter is to give you an overview of each of the free tools included with your AdWords accounts and its function, so you know to use it when you need it. This chapter is not intended to be an in-depth explanation of each tool's complete functionality. Visit www.askhowie.com/gtools for video tutorials that show you how to use them, one step at a time.

Improving Your Campaigns with the Optimizer Tools

Google offers free tools for your ad campaign on the Tools page. To go to the Tools page, log on to your AdWords account, go to the Campaign Management page, and then click the Tools link under the Campaign Management tab.

Google provides four tools under the heading Optimize Your Ads that, oddly enough, focus entirely on keywords rather than ads. I don't know if Google intended this title as a bit of cryptic wisdom, but wise it is: The quality of the ad is completely dependent on the match between it and the keyword that triggers it.

Keyword tool

You've met the Keyword tool in Chapters 4 and 5, so in this chapter I'll explore some additional features. It's great for generating ideas for additional keyword families that you might not have thought of, both from the pages of your competitors and from Google's vast database of search behavior (for example, people who search mortgage often end up on pages related to home loans and many people who type home loan return to Google a little later and search on mortgage as well). You can also use it to brainstorm negative keywords that your best prospects would not be typing.

You can generate new keywords either by entering one or more keywords in the text box under the Keyword Variations tab, or entering a Webpage URL under the Site-Related Keywords tab. Either way, Google will return a list of keywords related to your market. You can select the data that will display next to each keyword: search volume, bid price and ad position estimates, or search volume trends.

Search volume

If you request search volume data, Google returns two columns next to each keyword. The first shows the relative search volume for the keyword during the previous full month for which data is available. The numbers are updated quickly; I took the screenshot shown in Figure 9-1 on June 1 and it already included all of May. Google doesn't give you absolute numbers here, just comparisons. The Traffic Estimator tool (see the "Traffic Estimator tool" section) provides projected numbers of impressions.

Figure 9-1:
Keyword
variations
on the word
mortgage
include
more
specific
terms,
related
concepts,
and
synonyms.

The Advertiser Competition column shows, again in relative terms, how many competitors are bidding on that keyword. If the entire rectangle is shaded, the keyword is highly competitive, at least in terms of number of competitors. Don't let large numbers of competitors scare you away from a keyword or a market without researching further: The competitors may be easy to beat through split testing (see Chapter 13) and intelligent campaign architecture (see Chapters 7 and 8).

The right-hand column allows you to add any or all of the keywords to the ad group of your choosing. Notice that the column header prompts you for Match Type: Broad, Phrase, or Exact. The broad match keyword is the default. Try changing it to exact and see how the search volume and competition data change.

Don't confuse the broad, phrase, and exact terms at this stage of your keyword research — they are likely to perform very differently. If you do use this tool for adding keywords to your ad groups, do it carefully. I recommend scrolling to the bottom of the page and downloading the keywords to a text file or spreadsheet first, before dumping them into an ad group. You'll have much more control and will create better organized and better performing campaigns.

Cost and ad position estimates

You can also choose to display cost and ad position estimates for the keyword list, based on a Max CPC of your choosing. Select Cost and Ad Position Estimates from the Choose Data to Display drop-down list, and then enter a value for the maximum CPC in the US Dollars (USD $) text box. If a visitor to your Web site is worth $0.43, for example, you can use this tool to find keywords that will break even at worst. Enter **.43** and click the Recalculate button.

The Recalculate button didn't work about half the time I was playing with it. If this bug hasn't been fixed by the time you read this, simply click the Get More Keywords button again to display the estimated average CPC and ad positions for your keywords (shown in Figure 9-2). You can sort by Estimated Ad Position to find the profitable keywords that will position your ad advantageously. Figure 9-3 shows the phrase match keywords that you can afford to show on the Content network. If you're building a comprehensive list, remember to repeat the process for all three keyword types: broad, phrase, and exact.

To find out Google's estimate of the CPC for each keyword for position #1, enter **100** (for $100) in the US Dollars (USD $) text box.

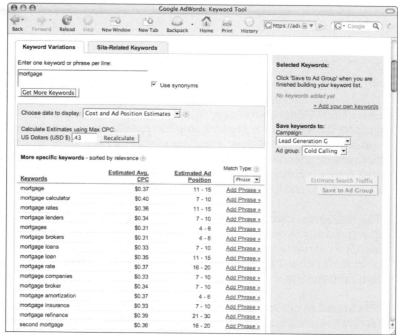

Figure 9-2:
These phrase match keywords are all available for $0.43 or less.

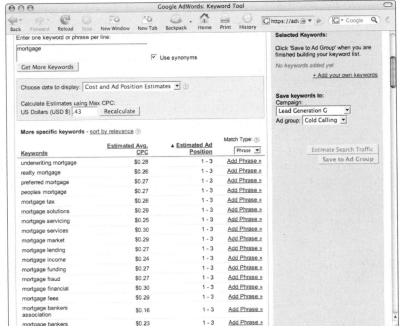

Figure 9-3:
Sorting by
Estimated
Ad Position
displays the
keywords
that can
attain top
positions on
your budget.

Search Volume Trends

The third option in the Choose Data to Display drop-down list is Search Volume Trends. This option gives you the average search volume along with two potentially interesting modifiers: the trend over the past 12 months for which data has been collected (the lag is usually a couple of months), and the month in which the search volume was highest.

The mortgage market is steady, with most keywords' trend lines staying pretty flat. A keyword like `gifts` shows huge seasonal fluctuation. The keywords `birthday gifts` and `wedding gifts` are steady, but `Christmas gifts`, `personalized gifts`, and `unique gifts` skyrocket in December and January and languish for the rest of the year, as shown in Figure 9-4.

I recommend a quick check on the seasonal trends in your marketplace as part of your online due diligence, so you don't start beating up on perfectly good campaigns in February because they've stopped sending you traffic.

Figure 9-4:
The Gifts
market
fluctuates
wildly by
season.

Possible negative keywords

The Possible Negative Keywords option from the Choose Data to Display drop-down list shows you related searches and gives you an easy way to hide your ads from searches containing irrelevant words. For example, if you sell soccer equipment and clothing in the United States, you would find many negative keywords upon entering Soccer in the text box, as shown in Figure 9-5. If you sell Diadora shoes but not Adidas, consider adding -Adidas to your keyword list.

Edit your campaign's negative keywords

This tool can save you time and hassle if each campaign represents a broad market. If one campaign includes ad groups for homeschooling math curricula, scuba gear, magic tricks, and seminars on how to take advantage of frequent-flier-miles programs, you have no need for campaign-wide negative keywords. If, on the other hand, your Whiteboards campaign consisted of ad groups for Magnetic Whiteboards, Porcelain Whiteboards, Commercial Whiteboards, Whiteboard Cleaners, Whiteboard Pens, and so on, you can use this tool to consolidate all the negative keywords in one master list. If you create a new ad group, you don't need enter the negative keywords into that group's keyword list. Some negative keywords might include these:

```
netmeeting
Microsoft
java
msn
```

These keywords refer to online *virtual* whiteboards, not the ones that hang on your office walls and get ruined by the schlemiel who uses a permanent marker by accident.

You can generate campaign-wide negative keywords in one of two ways. You can enter the negative keywords manually, or "sweep" them out of individual ad groups into the campaign.

- ✔ **Manual exclusion:** First, select a campaign from the Campaign drop-down list near the top of the page. If your campaign is new, place the negative keywords into the text box and click the Add Keywords button. You'll see them appear in the table at the bottom of the page.

- ✔ **Clean Sweep:** If your ad groups already contain negative keywords, you can consolidate them using Clean Sweep. You can choose to sweep nega-tive keywords found in every single group (choose All Ad Groups from the Campaign drop-down list), at least 75% of them, at least 50% of them, or keywords found in any ad group. Once Clean Sweep has run, you can decide which negative keywords to apply to the campaign as a whole and which to leave in their original groups only.

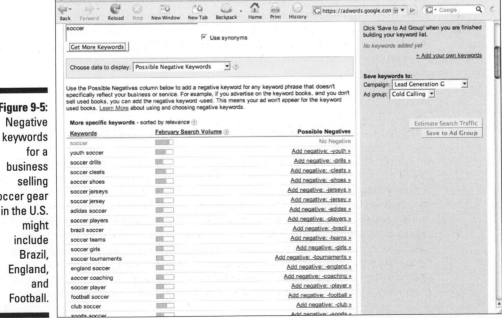

Figure 9-5:
Negative keywords for a business selling soccer gear in the U.S. might include Brazil, England, and Football.

Site Exclusion tool

The Site Exclusion tool allows you to choose particular Web sites (and parts thereof) where you *don't* want your ads to show. This tool is relevant only for campaigns that show in the Content network.

If you want to keep your ads off an entire Web site, enter the top-level domain with and without the www prefix: `www.fitfam.com` and `fitfam.com`. To keep your ads from showing in a specific cheesy subdomain or directory within a Web site, include that information: `cheesysection.fitfam.com` or `www.fitfam.com/cheesysection` and `fitfam.com/cheesysection`. You can also specify a particular page, such as `www.fitfam.com/embarrassingpage.html` for exclusion.

You must set site exclusion separately for each campaign.

Traffic Estimator tool

The Traffic Estimator can quickly help you avoid markets and market segments that simply don't generate enough search volume to justify a campaign, as well as help you estimate your sales volume and profitability. This tool calculates search traffic only, from Google and its partners. It does not include clicks you may receive from sites on the Content network.

Begin by entering a keyword or keywords into the text box at the top of the page. Next, enter a very high Maximum CPC. I always start with Google's maximum, $100, to find out what Google thinks I'll have to pay to get position #1. Ignore the daily budget for right now; since you're talking about $100 clicks, you can enjoy fantasyland a little longer.

Now, choose your customers' languages and locations, just as you would in setting up a new campaign (see Chapter 7). Click Continue to see how much Google thinks you'll pay for the top spot for each keyword, and how many clicks each one will generate. Google assumes your ads' CTRs will be the same as those of current advertisers bidding on these keywords. If your ads are more attractive, your average CPCs will be correspondingly lower.

In Figure 9-6, the top position for Whiteboard keywords can be had for $3–5 per click. Assuming your ads are as appealing (or unappealing) as everyone else's, Google thinks you'll be parting with $480–$660 per day for the privilege of showing your ads in position #1 to viewers in the U.S. and Canada. Based on its data for ads showing at that position for these keywords, Google estimates 108–117 visitors per day to your Web site (let's call it 112.5 on average). If your Web site can turn exactly 3% of your visitors into paying customers, and your average order amount is $500 at a 50% profit margin, then your gross daily profit from this campaign will be, on average, $843.75 ($500 × .50 margin × 3.375 sales). Subtracting the daily advertising spend (let's call it $520), your net at the end of each day is $323.75.

Download this table as a spreadsheet readable by Microsoft Excel by clicking the Download as .csv button at the bottom of the page. After you've saved the table, enter a saner amount in the Maximum CPC text box at the top left, and then click the Get New Estimates button. In Figure 9-7, you can see the results of capping your maximum bid at $2.00.

Now you get around 80 clicks per day for around $120. Assuming the same Web-site conversion process, you average 2.4 sales per day, for a daily profit of $600.00. Subtracting your AdWords costs leaves you with $480 net profit. Bidding lower and generating fewer clicks appears more profitable, based on this simulation.

The Web-site conversion for clicks *not* from position #1 is likely to be higher, because your ad attracts fewer happy clickers and more serious prospects. The lower bid is likely to be even more profitable than the preceding scenario projects.

Figure 9-6:
Google estimates your daily clicks and cost per day for your keywords, based on how much you are willing to bid and where you intend to show your ads.

Traffic Estimator
« Revise settings | Download as .csv
All estimates are provided as a guideline, and are based on system-wide averages; your actual costs and ad positions may vary. To view estimates based on your keywords' performance history, use the Traffic Estimator within the appropriate ad group. Learn more

Average CPC: **$5.49** (at a maximum CPC of $100.00)
Estimated clicks per day: **108 - 117** (at a daily budget of $660.00)

Estimates are based on your bid amount and geographical targeting selections. Because the Traffic Estimator does not consider your daily budget, your ad may receive fewer clicks than estimated.

Maximum CPC: 100   Daily budget: [   ]   Get New Estimates

Keywords ▼	Search Volume	Estimated Avg. CPC	Estimated Ad Positions	Estimated Clicks / Day	Estimated Cost / Day
Search Network Total		$4.39 - $5.49	1 - 3	108 - 117	$480 - $660
magnetic whiteboards		$3.39 - $4.24	1 - 3	0 - 1	$2 - $3
"magnetic whiteboards"		$3.68 - $4.60	1 - 3	0	$2 - $3
[magnetic whiteboards]		$4.13 - $5.16	1 - 3	0	$1 - $2
porcelain whiteboards		$0.00 - $3.55	1 - 3	0	$0 - $1
"porcelain whiteboards"		Not enough data to give estimates.			
[porcelain whiteboards]		Not enough data to give estimates.			
whiteboard		$4.02 - $5.02	1 - 3	40	$170 - $210
"whiteboard"		$3.97 - $4.97	1 - 3	35	$140 - $180
[whiteboard]		$5.24 - $6.55	1 - 3	4 - 5	$30 - $40
whiteboards		$5.59 - $6.98	1 - 3	14 - 17	$80 - $130
"whiteboards"		$5.42 - $6.78	1 - 3	12 - 15	$70 - $110
[whiteboards]		$5.01 - $6.26	1 - 3	2 - 3	$10 - $20
Search Network Total		$4.39 - $5.49	1 - 3	108 - 117	$480 - $660

« Revise settings   Download as .csv

Estimates for these keywords are based on clickthrough rates for current advertisers. Some of the keywords above are subject to review by Google and may not trigger your ads until they are approved. Please note that your traffic estimates assume your keywords are approved.

Figure 9-7:
Dropping
your bid to
$2.00
produces
almost as
many clicks
at a much
lower
estimated
daily cost.

Keep playing with the Maximum CPC until you find the scenario that produces the highest net profit. You can become even more granular by adding individual Max CPCs to the keywords, using the `keyword**1.50` format on the first page of the Traffic Estimator. Until you track the actual sales performance of keywords (so you know exactly the optimal bid for profitability), the Traffic Estimator is a good place to start.

Saving Time with the Campaign Modification Tools

In case you've forgotten, Google is pretty good at search. So it should come as no surprise that Google lets you search for keywords and snippets of ad text within your account, and lets you move or copy those keywords and ads from one location to another.

To access the Campaign Modification tools, log on to your AdWords account, go to the Campaign Management page, and click the Tools link under the

Campaign Management tab. Look under the Modify Your Campaign heading and click the appropriate tool's link.

Copy and moving keywords

To copy or move keywords, click the Copy or Move Keywords and Ad Text link on the Tools page. Select Search for Keywords, and then choose either to move or copy those keywords to a different ad group. Typically you'll move keywords within campaigns and copy them to different campaigns.

Narrowing the search terrain

When you click Continue, you'll see a dizzying range of search choices and delimiters (see Figure 9-8). You can search all campaigns, choose specific campaigns based on words in the name (a good reason *not* to name them Campaign #1, Campaign #2, and so on), and select campaigns based on status (active, paused, or deleted). You can also narrow the search to ad groups with specific words in their names.

Figure 9-8:
You can quickly search the entire account terrain for specific keywords and ad text.

Instead of narrowing your search landscape based on your input, you can click the Pick from a List link and choose particular campaigns and ad groups.

Selecting keywords

After you've told Google which campaigns and ad groups to search, the next step is to indicate the keywords you're looking for. You can enter one or many keywords in the text box, and search for them exactly as written — as whole words within larger keyword phrases, or as any part of the keyword. For example, selecting Matches Exactly from the Keyword drop-down list and entering **Cold** in the text box would find just the keyword Cold. Selecting the Contains option from the Keyword drop-down list would give you Cold Calling, Cold Calls, and Scold. Selecting the Contains Full Word option from the Keyword drop-down list eliminates Scold, but keeps all the keywords that contain the whole word Cold.

The more powerful search functions relate to the CPC and performance history of the keyword. You can find all keywords in your account with a current CPC of $2.00 or greater by leaving the $ text box blank and choosing Is Greater Than or Equal To from the Current Keyword CPC drop-down list and entering **2** in the $ text box. You can also select an option from the Performance History drop-down list to search for keywords by the following elements of their historical performance: cost, number of clicks, CTR, average CPC, average position, and number of impressions.

You can also select or eliminate keywords according to match type (by selecting the Broad Match, Phrase Match, or Exact Match check boxes) and status (by selecting the Active, Paused, or Inactive check boxes). Spend some time playing with the various settings and see what keyword lists Google gives you when you click Continue at the bottom of the page.

After you've generated a list of keywords (as shown in Figure 9-9), you can select and deselect individual ones, or do a batch move or copy. Click the Continue button to choose the destination ad group. If you want to move associated ad texts as well, select the Yes - Pick Ad Texts in the Next Step check box, and then click the Continue button.

If you elected to move or copy ad text, you'll be prompted to select the ads to move or copy in the next step. When you're done selecting ads, you go straight to a choice of one ad group — into which you dump all your choices, as shown in Figure 9-10. If you want to move keywords and ads into multiple groups, repeat the process for each group.

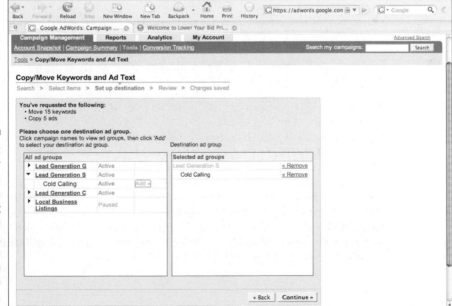

Figure 9-9:
You can accept all the keywords found by your search, or deselect specific ones.

Figure 9-10:
After selecting keywords and ad text to move or copy, choose one ad group as the destination.

Copying and moving ad text

The process for selecting ad text is almost identical to the keyword process. The main difference is a new set of criteria for ads. You can search the entire ad, or any of the five lines: Headline, Description Line 1, Description Line 2, Display URL, or Destination URL. You can also specify Active or Paused ads. Once you run the search, Google shows you the ads that fit your search parameters. Again, you can click the Continue button to move or copy those ads, or select the check box at the lower left that allows you to select keywords associated with those ads.

Getting Feedback from Google with the Ad Performance Tools

When you put an ad in your local paper or hire a kid to wear a chicken suit in July and hand out flyers for your Buffalo Wings Shack, it's pretty easy to tell whether the ad appears or the kid shows up and shakes his tail feathers. The world of online advertising is not so apparent, so Google provides some tools to help you monitor where and when your ads are showing.

To use the Ad Performance tools, log on to your AdWords account, go to the Campaign Management page, and click the Tools link under the Campaign Management tab. Click the link for the tool you want to try out under the Analyze Your Ad Performance heading.

The Conversion Tracking tool is important enough to merit its very own chapter, so I don't belabor it in this chapter. Flip to Chapter 14 to find out all about the Conversion Tracking tool.

Ads Diagnostic tool

Want to find out whether searchers are seeing your ads for your favorite keywords? Click the Ads Diagnostic Tool link on the Tools page. With the Ads Diagnostic tool, you can enter a keyword, choose parameters, and ask Google to indicate the ads that appear for a given search term. In Figure 9-11, Google will show the ads that appear in the Chicago, IL area for the phrase-match keyword IT consultant.

Figure 9-11:
Asking
Google
which ads
display
when
someone in
the Chicago
area
searches for
the phrase
match IT
consultant.

Note that you are not limited to the straight www.google.com search; you can also check other Google domains such as froogle.com, maps.google.com, google.co.za (the South African Google home page), and so on by entering the URL in the Google Domain text box. You can specify a geographic location, just as you do when targeting a campaign, choose the language(s) your customers speak, and even specify individual IP addresses for laser targeting. This is very useful for advertisers who can't see what their far-flung prospects in other regions or countries are viewing during searches.

Google offers a second option to diagnose a missing ad. Option 2: Search Results Page URL, at the bottom of the page, allows you to paste the entire URL of a search page into the Search Results Page URL text box. To use this option, open another Web browser window, perform a Google search, and then select and copy the entire text of the URL in the Address bar.

To be sure you've selected the entire address, perform the following steps:

1. **Right-click anywhere within the URL in the Address bar and choose Select All.**

2. **Right-click again and choose Copy.**

3. **Return to the Ad Diagnostic tool, right-click your cursor in the Option 2 text box and select Paste.**

4. **Click the Continue button.**

For either option, when you click the Continue button, Google shows you not only the ads that will show for that keyword, but also the ads that you would like to show, but aren't. Google also provides tips and strategies for fixing the problem, as shown in Figure 9-12.

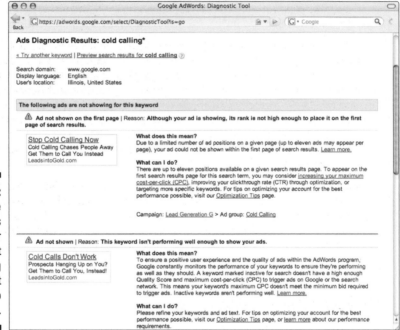

Figure 9-12:
Google
explains
why your
ads aren't
showing
and what
you can do
to fix them.

Your ad might be slacking off for a number of reasons:

✔ **Ad not showing on first page:** Your ad is showing, but not on the first page. Google suggests raising your minimum bid, increasing your CTR, or targeting more specific keywords.

✔ **Ad not shown because of low quality keyword:** Google gives each keyword a quality score (see Chapter 7). If your keyword quality is Poor or OK, Google penalizes you by making that keyword more expensive. Your options here include improving the keyword-to-ad-to-landing-page match (opening your mind) or bidding higher (opening your wallet).

✔ **Ad not shown because one of your other ads is showing for this keyword:** Google lets your campaigns and ad groups compete against each other, but will let only one win at a time. You won't see two of your ads showing for the same keyword, even if you bid on that keyword in multiple ad groups or campaigns. Google chooses the one with the highest ranking, which generally means the one that makes Google the most money (they aren't stupid). If you want the missing ad to show, either decrease the duplicate keyword(s) or raise your bid on this keyword.

✔ **Ad not shown because of paused campaign, ad group, or keyword:** If you've paused a part of your account, Google will stop showing it. Obvious, yes, but when accounts get large, it's easy to forget that you never turned that ad group back on after pausing it for maintenance.

✔ **Ad not shown because negative keyword or Non-Family Safe classification is preventing your ad from showing:** If you've dumped a lot of negative keywords into your campaigns or ad groups, you may have inadvertently caused a conflict between a positive and negative keyword. The Non-Family Safe classification means that your ad is deemed inappropriate for minors, and will be shown only to searchers who turn off the adult filters (few do). Unless you're selling adult entertainment (I love that euphemism!), make sure your ads would be at home on *Captain Kangaroo*.

✔ **Ad not shown because disapproved ads or keywords:** If your ad is disapproved due to a violation of Google's editorial guidelines (see `https://adwords.google.com/select/guidelines.html` for the actual document you "signed" when you gave Google your first five dollars), you can use the next tool to discover possible remedies.

Disapproved ads

I'm such a good boy, I can't show you screen shots for disapproved ads. The best I can do is let you see what happens when I try to write one, as shown in Figure 9-13.

Some ads can be fixed by requesting exceptions. If you sell MAS90 accounting software, originally created by Best Software, you may be able to use the Best brand name. If you use a medical term in an ad, you may trigger the "Uh-oh, it's a Canadian Pharmacy" policy. Click the Request an Exception link and explain to a live Google editor why this rule doesn't apply to your ad or keyword in 300 characters or fewer (now's not a good time to go into your childhood).

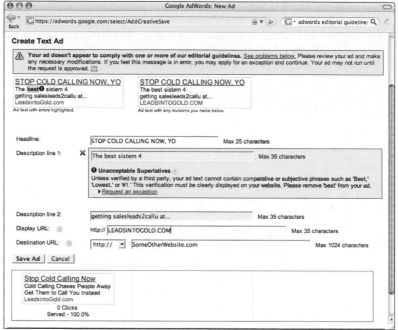

Figure 9-13:
The word
Best
triggers an
automatic
disapproval,
before
Google even
discovers
the mis-
spellings,
abbrevi-
ations, and
excessive
capitalization.

My Change History tool

The My Change History tool was created for those suffering from CRetTNS (Can't Remember to Take Notes Syndrome). You can find specific changes by filtering out the irrelevant ones. Google allows you to filter changes by date, campaign and ad group, users (in case you set up more than one user for your account), and type of change.

I find this tool useful when I want to examine my campaign or run a report to see the effects of a particular change. You can specify start and end dates in the Campaign Summary control panel and in reports. The My Change History tool helps you remember which dates to select to get a clean experiment.

For example, let's say you lowered a bunch of bids around the beginning of March, but you can't remember exactly when, and you want to see the effect this change has had on your business.

Figure 9-14 shows three Max CPC changes, two on February 13 and one on March 2 at 1:30 p.m. You can now look at the two weeks prior to March 2 and the two weeks following March 2 (for example) to compare your statistics for these two phases of the experiment. You can look at impressions, clicks, average position, total cost, conversions, sales, and such. If the only difference in the two periods is the change you identified, you have learned something by isolating that variable in time using the My Change History tool.

Figure 9-14: Filtering the change history by CPC shows all the bid changes in a given period.

Even though you can fall back on this tool, please spend a buck on a notebook and pretend you're in high-school chemistry class again. Taking notes on your questions and changes helps you monitor your account more seriously, and puts you in an observant and curious AdWords mindset.

Part IV
Converting Clicks to Clink

The 5th Wave   By Rich Tennant

©RICHTENNANT

"Oh, we're doing just great. Philip and I are selling decorative jelly jars on the Web. I run the Web site and Philip sort of controls the inventory."

In this part . . .

Up to this page, the book has been devoted to AdWords. In other words, you now know how to give money to Google. This is the part that shows you how to make money from paying customers — hopefully, more than you spend on AdWords.

In Chapter 10, I cover the vital importance of dedicated landing pages that quickly begin scratching the itch expressed in the keyword and inflamed in the ad. You'll uncover how to get your visitors to say, "This is for me" within one second of their arrival at your site.

I expound on my favorite topic, e-mail follow-up, in Chapter 11. No matter how wonderful your Web site, if you don't stay in touch with prospects and customers, they'll forget all about you. This chapter gives you the strategies to stay in touch with your Web site's visitors long after they've left your site, and shows you stunningly powerful and inexpensive tools that put follow-up on autopilot.

Chapter 12 covers a wide array of other Web-site strategies, all of them based on the time-tested principles of direct marketing: engagement, calls to action, and ascending levels of value exchange and intimacy.

Chapter 10

Giving Your Customer a Soft Landing on Your Web Site

*W*hen (potential) customers click your ad and your Web site appears, they will decide whether to stay and shop or return to Google within 7 seconds. Everything about your landing page will either persuade your visitor to stay and play, or hit the Back button and never darken your door again.

Don't just send customers to your site's home page. You have the ability to send your visitors to the page of their dreams, the one that quickly grants them their fondest wish, that scratches the itch they've never quite been able to reach before, that dreams the impossible dream — sorry, I was channeling Richard Kiley there for a minute. Deep breath. Orchestra fades. Where was I?

The text, the pictures, the design, the loading speed, the contact information, the logos, multimedia, and opportunities for interaction all combine to create a gestalt, an instant impression of Perfect Fit, Run Away Screaming, or something in between. Old-school direct marketers have favored text over graphics, based on years of experience with ugly magazine ads and Courier-font direct-mail sales letters. That works for some markets, but not most. The Web is a different medium from print, one in which design speaks as loudly as words.

Your AdWords landing page must impress two suitors: Google, and your Web site's visitor. This chapter shows you how to make landing pages that are highly relevant to the keywords and ads that point to them. You discover the most important purpose of a landing page, along with several strategies for achieving that purpose. You find out a few sneaky tricks for building multiple landing pages by doing the work just once. I show you the elements of a landing page than you can tweak to improve performance, and discuss briefly the things you need to know about search engine optimization to increase the quality scores of the keywords pointing to your landing pages.

Making Your Visitor Shout "That's for Me!"

Perry Marshall of www.perrysmarshall.com shares a wallet-walloping calculation that should convince you to spend a lot of quality time working on your landing pages:

> *Let's say you pay 50 cents for a click and Barbara in Oregon goes to your Web site and spends eight seconds seeing what you're selling . . . then leaves.*
>
> *50 cents divided by 8 seconds is $225.00 per hour.*
>
> *Barbara in Oregon's attention is pretty expensive, wouldn't you say?*

Now, maybe Barbara was never your customer. She clicked because your ad aroused her curiosity, or was cute, or implied or promised something for nothing. Oh, well, can't win them all. But most Web-site owners are told to be satisfied with conversion percentages that are pathetically low: half a percent, one percent. The Web is a numbers game, they're told. Get enough traffic and even a mediocre site can pay the rent.

The Web is a numbers game, true. But who says you have to be satisfied with the numbers? The entire premise of AdWords — in fact, the feature that rocketed it past what is now Yahoo Search Marketing within months of its birth — was the ease with which campaigns could be tested and improved. This improvement doesn't have to stop at the AdWords border with your Web site. You can deploy the market intelligence you gain by testing keywords and ad copy to create compelling landing pages that continue to attract and guide your best prospects.

The goal of each landing page is to build an instant emotional bond with your prospects, show them you understand their needs and can take away their pains. From that platform, you present your offer and guide them to take action. Your home page, the one that says, "Welcome to Acme Online Sock Emporium," is hardly ever the right place to take AdWords traffic. If someone walked into your retail Sock Emporium and told you, "I'm looking for red-and-white-striped, over-the-calf dress socks," you wouldn't take them back to the front door and say, "Welcome to Acme Sock Emporium, for the finest in men's and ladies' dress and casual socks, sporting socks, and never-washed vintage baseball stirrup socks worn by members of the 1958 Championship New York Yankees." Instead, you'll lead them directly to the wall displaying the red-and-white-striped, over-the-calf dress socks and ask them, "What size?" That level of specificity is the purpose of your landing page.

Your retail sock store is probably not located next to other sock stores. But your *online* store's landing page is precisely two clicks away from just about every other online sock store in existence. If your landing page doesn't look like the next point on the shortest distance between your prospect's A and B, whoosh! Barbara from Oregon is here one second, Oregon the next. (Hah! Chapter 10 and my first pun. My sister owes me a dollar.)

Achieving relevance based on keywords

As I discuss in Chapter 5, keywords are the keys to your search visitors' desires. You bundle similar desires into ad groups, and send the traffic from each ad group to a landing page focused on that desire. Everything true about ad copy is also true about Web-site copy; the message, the tone, the balance of features and benefits, the next call to action all must connect with the conversation already going on in your prospect's mind. The only difference is, on the Web site you are free from the space constraints and most of the editorial shackles imposed by Google. With great power comes great responsibility, as Peter Parker, another famous Webmaster, learned the hard way in the *Spider-Man* comics. Use the power of your Web site to focus not on your business, but on your customer's desires as suggested by their keywords and the ad that triggered their visit.

If your traffic is derived from AdSense, you don't have a specific keyword to build on. Instead, you know which ad interrupted them like a talking white rabbit and caused them to detour into the rabbit hole of your site. In that case, your landing page should continue the conversation begun by the ad.

For example, if you sell computer training videos on DVD, part of your AdWords account and landing pages might look like the example shown in Table 10-1.

Table 10-1	Linking Keywords and Landing Pages		
Ad Group	*Subject*	*Sample Keywords*	*Landing Page Headline*
Ad Group A1	Microsoft Access Tutorial Keywords	`Microsoft access tutorial, access tutorial, ms access tutorial, access database tutorial`	"Master Microsoft Access at Your Own Pace with this Award-Winning DVD-based Course"

(continued)

Table 10-1 *(continued)*

Ad Group	Subject	Sample Keywords	Landing Page Headline
Ad Group A2	Microsoft Access Training Keywords	`access training, access database training, Microsoft access computer training`	"Microsoft Access Training at Your Own Pace with this Award-Winning DVD-based Course"
Ad Group A3	Microsoft Access Best Performing Keyword	`[ms Access]`	"Become Certified in MS Access in Just 6 Weeks with this Award-Winning DVD-based Course"
Ad Group A4	Microsoft Excel General Keywords	`excel xp training, excel training, excel 2000 training, excel 2003 training`	"Receive Professional Excel Training from the Comfort of Your Home with this Award-Winning DVD-based Course"

Product-focused landing pages

If you sell physical products, like home office telephone systems or paper shredders or runners' watches with GPS, your landing page presents the most specific product you can offer, based on keyword and ad. The keyword `runners watch` takes visitors to your entire display of runners' watches. `Casio runners watch` produces a page dedicated to that brand (or, if you don't carry Casio, make it a turn-the-corner page that explains why your watches are superior to Casio's). And a search for `Casio GPR-100` should take them to a page devoted to that particular watch.

Concept-focused landing pages

Many online stores do not sell a wide variety of merchandise. Instead, they sell one or two items that solve a certain range of problems. For example, maybe you've invented a clever filing system that automatically purges old files, or reminds people when to pay the energy bill, or sends flowers and chocolate to key people on Valentine's Day. You probably will generate most of your traffic not from searches for the solution (since people don't yet know it exists), but from descriptions of the problem:

```
paper clutter
messy filing system
messy office
```

Or they search for the one aspect of a potential solution that resonates with them at that moment:

```
bill pay reminder system
self-purging files
holiday and birthday reminders
```

Each of the six keywords listed previously should go to a specific landing page that addresses that problem or need. The final destination will be the same for all buyers, but the paths they take from problem to solution will depend on where they're starting.

Turn-the-corner landing pages

Sometimes the thing you're selling is related only tangentially to what your prospect is looking for at first. The entire field of consultative sales is based on the premise that your prospects don't really know what they need, and your value as a salesperson is to help them discover "the need behind the need" and help them solve their problem at the most fundamental level. For example, many visitors to www.leadsintogold.com searched for ways to improve their cold-calling performance. The Web site doesn't offer any suggestions or tools for cold calling, except to stop doing it. The job of my landing page is to get my visitor to turn the corner from "I've got to learn how to make better cold calls" to "Cold-calling is a flawed strategy, and here's a strategy that will work much better."

Using PHP to increase relevance

Through the magic of a programming language called PHP, which either stands for Personal Home Page or PHP Hypertext Preprocessor (thrilling fans of recursiveness everywhere), you can increase the relevance of your landing page based on your visitor's keyword, geographic location, type of computer, and several other factors.

PHP marketing consultant Rob Goyette of www.vaelos.com has been quoted as saying, in a phrase borrowed from Napoleon Hill, "Anything the mind can conceive, PHP can achieve." Following are some of Rob's favorite uses of PHP on landing pages. You may be able to use dynamic keyword insertion (described in the next section) on your own, but the rest of the applications require considerable PHP expertise combined with marketing savvy. As they say in the car ads, "Professional driver on closed course. Do not try this at home." Meaning, of course, that the following sections describe what's possible with PHP, but you will need to be or work with an experienced Web site programmer to achieve those results. I can't go into detail about programming Web sites, because I don't know squat about it — I mean, it's beyond the scope of this book.

Dynamic keyword insertion

Chapter 6 shows how you can include the exact keyword in your ad through a technique called dynamic keyword insertion. You can configure your landing page to perform the same trick. For example, if your visitor surfed over to your site on the keyword `messy office`, you can insert that phrase anywhere you like in your headline, your page text, your call to action. You'll need to configure the destination URL for each keyword individually; then add PHP code where you want the keyword to appear on the landing page.

If your Web site consists of `.html` files (rather than `.php`), you will need to enable PHP in your `.htaccess` file. If you don't know what this means, ask your Webmaster or Web site host.

Magically changing the landing page based on keywords

The first *Harry Potter* book featured a cool gizmo called the Mirror of Erised. Each person who looked into the mirror saw an image of what their heart desired most. An advanced PHP application turns your landing pages into Mirrors of Erised based on keywords. This function allows you to create one single landing page that changes itself like a magic mirror. You save a lot of time by not having to create new pages for each keyword. A site selling college sports clothing and gear could create PHP code that would show Duke basketball shirts and sweatshirts to visitors who arrived with `Duke` and `basketball` in their keyword, and similarly create a UNC page for UNC fans.

Likewise, `baseball`, `lacrosse`, `basketball`, `Missouri`, `Gators`, and `Princeton` would all trigger the dynamic creation of other pages, specifically mirroring the desires suggested by the keywords. The program would also serve a default page for keywords not in its database.

Split-testing with cookies

Split-testing, which I cover in Chapter 13, is one of the most powerful tools at your disposal. You can use *cookies* (tiny snippets of code that identify an individual computer as having visited before — like having your hand stamped at a carnival, except each stamp has your name and address on it) along with PHP to discover which of two different landing pages is doing a better job of converting visitors into leads and sales. You can test headlines, bullets, offers, guarantees, frequently asked questions, placement of forms and buttons and links, as well as colors, fonts, inclusion or exclusion of video or audio, or just about anything else. Done correctly, you don't have to worry about your visitors seeing multiple versions of the same page. When a visitor returns to your page, the cookie your site placed on his or her computer will tell your Web server to show the first version the visitor saw (provided the visitor is using the same computer).

Survey to report/sales letter

Ask your customers what they're looking for before showing them content. Insert their answers into your page, or show them different content based on their answers. If you sell a diet plan, you can show different sales letters to vegetarians and meat eaters, people who travel a lot and people who don't, and people with diabetes or wheat allergies or berry phobias. If your site asks visitors to opt-in (see Chapter 11) in exchange for a free ebook or report, PHP can customize those as well.

Based on location

When you surf the Web, the sites you visit know a lot about you, including where your ISP is located. You could program your landing page to show Duke basketball tank tops to visitors from Hawaii and fleece hooded sweatshirts to visitors from Wisconsin. You can display local phone numbers and store locations, and even translate your site into different languages based on the physical location of your visitor.

Based on operating system

You can show different pages to Windows, Mac, and Linux users, a valuable feature if you sell software. Instead of prompting your visitor with too many choices, simply provide the download link appropriate to the visitor's operating system.

Scraping the Internet

You can triangulate your visitor's geographical location with other information you can find and scrape from the Internet, such as the local weather and traffic reports. I could program `www.fitfam.com` to greet you with, "Hey, it's noon your time, and it's sunny and warm today. Here's a great exercise you can do in your back yard that will only take five minutes."

Visit `www.vaelos.com/coolphp` for simulated examples of each of these PHP applications. You'll be amazed when you visit that page, when you discover what a Web site can tell about you without you telling them anything.

Scratching your customer's itch

Showing a "That's for Me" page will keep your visitor on your site for 30 seconds rather than 8. Your next task is to scratch their itch by fulfilling the promise of your ad.

Giving them what they want

If your prospects know exactly what they want, then give it to them. Are they ready to buy an Olympus DM-20? Put a photo, a price, a shipping policy, and a Buy Now button right on the landing page. Are they looking for more information to help them decide what to do next? Give them the information. Do they need to talk to a real human being? Put a phone number on your site and hire someone to answer it 24/7, or during business hours, or whenever your customers call.

Agitating the problem

I don't want to get too disgusting here (actually, I don't mind, but my editor does), but I have to point out something important about this itch metaphor. Scratching an itch feels good for a while, but actually makes the itch worse. Sometimes you can scratch so hard that it turns red and swollen and bleeds. Sometimes in the sales process you have to agitate the problem and make your prospect feel even worse before they will take action.

If you sell a product that prevents rather than cures, you must be willing to paint the awful picture of what happens when the preventable event — hard drive crash, flood, heart disease, death without a will, yellow teeth, whatever — occurs. Scratching the itch in a case like that means taking advantage of your visitors' momentary spasm of responsibility and making them quake with fear at the prospect of not addressing the issue this very minute, and trembling with relief at having found you.

Guiding them with a headline

Each page on your Web site is about something. The headline — a prominent phrase or sentence near the top of the page — helps your visitor decide whether to spend time on a page by summarizing the content, promising a benefit, or tickling curiosity. Imagine a newspaper without headlines, just articles. How would you decide what to read and what to skip? The headline is a relevance shortcut that also primes the reader for the message to follow.

Establishing credibility

In his popular book *Blink: The Power of Thinking without Thinking*, (published by Little, Brown and Company), Malcolm Gladwell shows how we make snap judgments about most things before we've even thought about them. The neural pathways that establish an emotional reaction are pre-thought. Before your prospect has read a word, identified the subject of a photograph, or listened to a word of audio, they've already decided whether they like you and trust you. They'll never be able to tell you why they feel the way they do, because those decisions are outside of consciousness. They'll come up with justifications for their gut reactions, but are usually clueless as to the real causes.

Overall look and feel

Visitors will react instinctively to the design of your landing page. They will assume things about you based on logos, colors, shapes, border styles, text fonts and sizes, and movement. Different markets respond to different gestalts. If you're selling a "secret" of some sort, don't put up a standard corporate Web site. If you want to appear like an established company, spend some money on elegant design elements rather than putting up an ugly sales letter. If you offer bereavement counseling, use a subdued color palette. If you sell violent video games, consider light text on a black background. And so on.

The Web site `www.probasketballreferee.com` tested two landing pages, identical in every respect except for the border and the header. (See Figure 10-1.) The second page, lacking the graphic elements, received twice as many opt-ins as the first.

Photographs can enhance credibility, especially in a medium comprised entirely of electrons. Show visitors your face, your store, your warehouse, your products. Asepco, a firm that manufactures valves for the pharmaceutical industry, put a photo slide show on its site that documented the odyssey of one of its valves from the mountain where the ore was mined to the finished product. It changes location frequently, so check `www.askhowie.com/valve` for the updated Web address.

Basically, you want to subliminally get across the message that "this trustworthy business will be around tomorrow." To achieve this, visit successful competitors' sites, talk to graphic designers, and test different designs just as the Pro Basketball Referee site did.

Specific visual cues

In addition to the overall look and feel, you can add specific graphical elements that lend credibility by association, as shown in Figure 10-2. These include credit card logos, PayPal, credit card processors like VeriSign; shippers' logos (such as those of UPS, FedEx, and the Postal Service); as well as Web-site certifications such as the Better Business Bureau's BBB Online Reliability Program, Hacker Safe, and Trust-e.

Another type of visual reassurance is the presence of subliminal "I Am Not a Crook" links, including privacy policy, Web site terms and conditions, shipping and refund policies, disclaimers, and so on. I'm not sure anyone actually *reads* these documents, but their very presence can be reassuring.

Finally, the more contact options you include, the less you look like a fly-by-night with something to hide. Post office boxes don't cut it; instead, get a real mailing address that gives the impression of an office. Give a phone number. Put your e-mail address where people can find it.

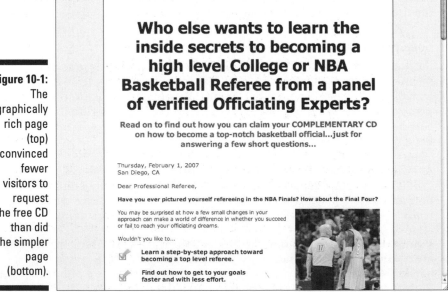

Figure 10-1: The graphically rich page (top) convinced fewer visitors to request the free CD than did the simpler page (bottom).

Figure 10-2:
The My Wedding Favors site devotes a large amount of space to "credibility-by-association" logos.

When you display your e-mail address on your Web site, put it in an image file rather than a live link. This will prevent spambots from harvesting it and sending you hundreds of unwanted e-mails every day.

Defining the Most Desirable Action for the Landing Page

Before creating your landing pages, as well as every page on your site, ask yourself the big question: What's the one thing I want my visitor to do as a result of visiting this page? The actions that are possible include reading, watching, and listening; clicking a link, completing a form, making or requesting a phone call, or engaging in live chat.

Most clients I've worked with can identify a "point of no return" for their customers; a place in the sales cycle that, once reached, typically leads to a sale. For example:

- "Once they request the free DVD, 90% of them become customers."

- "Once I get them to call, I sell 75% of them right there on the phone."

- "After they request a quote, almost all of them sign up for the service."

If you've got a step in your sales process that converts lookers to buyers, then everything about your landing page should be engineered to get as many visitors to that step as possible. And in most cases, the first step on the way to the point of no return is getting your visitor's e-mail address.

"Bribing" your visitor to opt in

Sometimes your landing page can go for the sale. In other cases, your prospect needs more information or more time before taking out a credit card. In either case, the big goal of your landing page is to make sure your visitors do not leave your site without giving you a way of contacting them in the future. If that way also includes a financial transaction, so much the better. But it's often more profitable to aim for a second date than to propose marriage on the first date.

Business on the Internet is a multi-step process — a series of small, safe, mutual commitments that allow your prospect to begin to trust you — and allow you to qualify the prospect. This process is the business equivalent of dating. Your job is to get on your prospects' wavelength so quickly and completely that they regard you as their "one and only." Remember, the page after your landing page is three clicks away from your competitor, using the Back button. The deeper they go, the more of a psychological commitment they're making to you.

An *opt-in*, in Internet marketing parlance, refers to a visitor who has given you an e-mail address, at the very least, before leaving your site. Essentially, an opt-in is permission to call them for a date. In the old days of the Internet (pre-2001), all you had to do was offer a free newsletter to get opt-ins. These days, with everyone protecting their e-mail inboxes from mountains of spam, visitors hesitate to sign up for anything. The last thing they need is more e-mail from someone else trying to sell them something, even if you're not peddling fake Rolexes and enlarged body parts.

In order to get their e-mail address and permission to follow up, you need to demonstrate value and promise future value. www.leadsintogold.com contains a long letter about cold calling and its alternatives, which many people have told me is eye-opening in its own right. In several places on the home page, I offer visitors a chance to download two free chapters of Leads into Gold, so they can sample the product before making a buying decision (as shown in Figure 10-3). The request for the opt-in makes sense, since I need their e-mail address to send them the free chapters. It is natural, not forced, so it works well. Note that I also ask for their names, which gives me the ability to address my follow-up e-mails to them personally ("Dear Ralph Lauren").

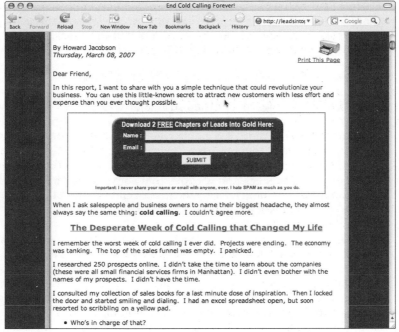

Figure 10-3:
Following up with prospects requires getting at least their e-mail address.

Perry Marshall's successful opt-in page at www.perrysmarshall.com offers an e-mail course, "5 Days to Success with Google AdWords." Perry includes two additional items in his opt-in form: phone number and toughest AdWords challenge. These optional fields can provide Perry with valuable information. If he or his staff take the time to call even 2% of his leads, he'll gain insights into their situations and their desires at the moment they arrive at his site. And the Biggest Challenge field tells him exactly what to offer on his site, in his prospects' own words. Perry calls this "reading them a page from their own diary."

The folks at www.novamind.com sell mind-mapping software. The top goal of their Web site is to entice visitors to download the free 30-day trial version of the product. Because they know that visitors who try the software typically buy the software, they don't even require an e-mail address.

If you can afford to spend real money on leads, you can collect snail mail addresses by offering a physical packet: a CD, DVD, book, report, 5-day supply of wrinkle cream, and such. E-mail is very cheap at the moment, but not very stable. A physical mailing address is not subject to spam filters or the whims of unreliable servers and switches. Also, the avalanche of spam e-mail that floods most people's inboxes daily makes it hard for your legitimate sales messages to get the attention they deserve. The motto for e-mail could be, "When you absolutely, positively don't really care if the message ever gets through."

Getting permission to continue the relationship is such a fundamental goal that I've devoted all of Chapter 11 to the opt-in and e-mail follow-up.

Engaging visitors in real time

The opt-in allows you to follow up with your visitors by e-mail, in what online geeks refer to as an *asynchronous* fashion. This fancy word (asynchronous, not fashion) means there is a gap between when the message is created and when it is received. This book is an extreme example of asynchronous communication, as I'm writing it long before you will read it (unless you believe, based on my prescience and wisdom, that I am actually a time traveler from the year 2036 who came back to the first decade of the 21st century and couldn't land a better gig than this book).

This form of communication fits well with the pie-in-the-sky dream of the Internet as a business medium where you never have to deal with customers: You just create a Web site, write a bunch of e-mails that get sent out automatically, and check your inbox for incoming orders. That strategy can work, to a degree, but everyone I've worked with has found that adding real-time live engagement to their Web site boosts sales significantly.

The telephone is a much-underused online marketing tool. Get a toll-free phone number, place it prominently on your Web site next to the calling hours ("24 hours a day, 7 days a week" is a good policy), and offer them a reason to call. Figure 10-4 graces the top of the `www.european-wall-tapestries.com` home page, while Figure 10-5 appears at the top right of the `www.myweddingfavors.com` site.

Figure 10-4:
Around the clock customer service.

Figure 10-5:
Set your phone hours to convenient times.

Ari Galper, proprietor of www.unlockthegame.com, wants to engage his visitors either on the phone or in a medium known as live chat. You can see from Figure 10-6 that the blue-bordered chat invitation, with a photo of Sharon announcing, "I'm Online," is the most prominent element on his Web site. When a visitor enters a question and clicks the Chat with Sharon button, a window opens in which Sharon and the visitor can type back and forth in real time, like AOL, Yahoo, or Skype chat services.

The visitor sees the chat box only, but the online merchant using live chat technology can see in real time all the visitors to the Web site, and what each visitor is doing and has done on the site. Live chat is the equivalent of a shopkeeper sitting in an invisible perch in the store, watching how all the customers are browsing, navigating, and buying.

Figure 10-6:
Live-chat technology can give you valuable insight into your visitors' desires and browsing behaviors.

Ari cautions against using live chat to go for the hard sell. Instead, chat with your visitors to find out their questions, their objections, and their goals. If a question comes up repeatedly, you know your Web site isn't doing a sufficient job in answering that question. You can improve your conversion rates by adding more useful and relevant information to your site. And even though you're not focused on making more sales in the chat, a consultative approach usually works better than a half nelson, especially in an online environment where your visitor has all the power. They can click you out of their lives in a second, and there's nothing you can do about it.

The www.unlockthegame.com chat box includes a second feature, known as Click to Call. When your visitors enter their phone numbers and click Call Now, the live-chat service uses the Internet to connect their phones to yours (one at a time, of course). Both phones ring, and you can be talking within seconds. Ari reports that many visitors who are reluctant to pick up the phone and dial his number will enter their own number and click. Somehow, he surmises, clicking is perceived as less risky than dialing.

If you are a one-person shop and wonder how you will ever get anything done if you have to field customer phone calls and chats all day, fear not. You can turn off the live-chat feature at any time and your visitors will simply see a box where they can ask a question and hear back from you later. And you can hire and train people for live-chat customer service just as you can for the telephone. But even if you can afford only a half hour a week to engage with customers, you should do it. The insights you'll gain into your market can't be gotten any other way.

The live-chat feature has been transformative for many of my clients, but the technology is not a cure-all. Just sticking a chat box on your Web site without understanding — and honoring — the principles of consultative sales will do more harm than good. Ari has posted a helpful article on the subject on my Web site; go to www.askhowie/chatwise to learn more about the strategy and philosophy, recommended live-chat vendors, and where to find out-sourced customer service staff trained in live chat.

Selling the Most Desirable Action

Once you've defined your sales process, your next big question is, "What stands between customers and the next step?" If you want them to download your free report, what do they need to be feeling and thinking in order to go ahead and do it? If you want them to call, what might cause them to hesitate and then bail? If you're asking for the sale, what action-freezing second thoughts might they be entertaining?

In the sales world, it's a cliché that you have to work as hard to sell a $10 item as a $10 million item. On the Internet, you have to work just about as hard to give something away for free. Your landing pages must answer your prospects' questions, reassure their doubts, assuage their fears, and guide them clearly to what they should do next.

I have an entire library filled with books and manuals dedicated to the creation of effective sales copy. The masters of persuasive copy know a lot of tricks and techniques, but the basis for their effectiveness is a deep knowledge of what their prospects want to have and want to avoid. As you can read in Chapter 4, marketing tricks without having your finger on the pulse of a substantial market is like doing a technically perfect triple gainer into an empty swimming pool. So the following copywriting tasks can be accomplished effectively only against the backdrop of market insight.

Using bullets

Sales bullets are the foundation for all effective sales copy, whether they appear in actual bullet form on the page or not. Ken McCarthy, my copywriting teacher, gave me a very useful phrase to focus on whenever I sit down to write sales copy: "Bullets Wound." (*Wound* here rhymes with *swooned*.) In other words, the purpose of the bullet is to highlight and stretch the gap in your visitor's mind between their current and ideal situations. The cure for the bullet is the next action you want them to take: read, click, download, call, chat, buy, whatever. Figure 10-7 shows some of Ken's bullets from a Web page describing the curriculum of the System Seminar.

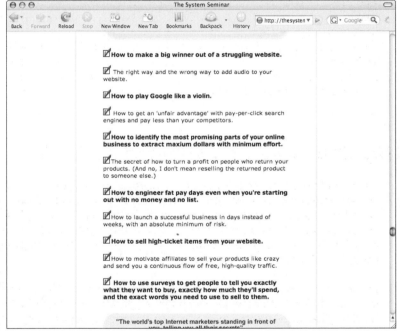

Figure 10-7: Bullets can arouse curiosity, make big promises, and bring facts to life.

Translating features into benefits

As sellers, we become intimately acquainted with the facts of our products and services. It glows in the dark; it comes in extra-large; it has a self-cleaning button; it's made from shea butter; and so on. After a while, we are in danger of operating under the illusion that our prospects understand why these features are important and beneficial. They don't have a clue, and if we fail to *translate* features into benefits, then we are asking our prospects to do interpretive work they have no interest in doing.

Here's a quick formula for figuring out whether a particular statement is a feature or a benefit. Write down the statement. Look at it. Ask yourself whether your most impolite and brash customer could conceivably read it and snarl, "So what?" If so, you've got yourself a *feature*, not a benefit.

To turn a feature into a benefit, write down the feature, add the words " . . . and what this means to you is . . ." and then complete the sentence. Ken McCarthy thinks of this as "bringing the facts to life." For example, one of my clients, poly-D, is a company that manufactures a metered dispensing system (MDS) for household, pharmaceutical, and industrial applications. Isn't that exciting?

Actually, the technology *is* exciting — and by the time you read this, I expect that you'll have at least one MDS-containing product in your home. But calling the feature a "metered dispensing system" asks the prospect — for example, brand managers in charge of cleaning products, toiletries, and food and beverage lines — to do way too much work.

The first pass at turning a feature into a benefit often creates not a true benefit, but a clearer feature set. For example, the MDS uses a button-operated vacuum pump to dispense the liquid, gel, or ointment it contains.

It's the job of the product marketer to bring each of these features to life. The fact that MDS dispenses product via a button-operated vacuum pump means the product

- ✔ Can be dispensed one-handed
- ✔ Gives a consistent dose
- ✔ Eliminates leaks and spills
- ✔ Gets 98% of the liquid, gel, or ointment out of the package

Each of those features is now ready to turn into a benefit:

- ✔ **One-handed dispensing:** Tired parents can hold a sick, thrashing toddler in one arm and pour the medicine into a cup with the other.

- ✔ **Consistent dose:** The tired parents don't have to worry about finding a measuring spoon or misreading the dosing directions.

- ✔ **No leaks or spills:** The tired parents don't end up with cough syrup running down their pajama tops or oozing between their toes into the shag carpet.

- ✔ **98% product evacuation:** The tired parents don't have to hold the cough syrup upside down for five minutes, waiting for the final drips to exit the bottle. No waste — they get to use what they've paid for.

The sales material we created for poly-D brings the features of the MDS to life for the brand managers, as well as for the end user. We didn't assume the brand managers would be able to translate the experience of a tired parent with a sick kid into a benefit relevant to them, so we did it for them. In the white paper available at www.poly-d.com we explained that the MDS instantly gave their existing products a new and dramatically different marketing story. We helped them see how effective their advertising campaigns would be, with a real consumer benefit to tout. Make sure your benefits relate directly to what you know or believe your prospects want. Your goal is to help your prospects visualize the movie of their future, a future made rosy by the action they're about to take.

Provoking curiosity

If the next action involves education of your prospects, you have to whet their appetites for the information you have and they don't. Bullets that provoke curiosity include teasers ("The most dangerous seat on an airplane — page 5"), hidden information ("Best-kept secret in the travel industry"), promise of valuable knowledge ("How to spot slot machines that pay off most often"), warnings ("Surprise! Choosing the wrong private school for your child can cost you a bundle in tax breaks"), and questions ("Would you know how to keep your ticket safe if you won the lottery?").

Useful But Incomplete: If I wanted you to go to www.askhowie.com/copy and view all the bullets in Ken McCarthy's sales letter, I would tease you with a partial list in Figure 10-7 and imply that the really good stuff is just behind the curtain.

Including third-party testimonials

For several reasons, third-party testimonials can sell more powerfully than you can. They can pull off this bit of magic because they are

- **Believable:** Your visitors have (unfortunately) been taught many times that salespeople will lie through their teeth to make a sale. Until you prove otherwise, you're presumed to be in that category. Your customers who say nice things about you don't have anything to gain by lying. On the contrary, they're risking their own "credibility capital" by going out on a limb and endorsing you.

- **Polite:** Grandma said that it's impolite to brag. If you can get your satisfied customers to do it for you, you can look bashfully pleased instead of boastful — while still getting your message across.

- **Benefit-based:** Testimonials are already formulated to highlight benefits, since they are created by customers rather than yourself.

You can deploy four testimonial media on your landing page: video, audio, written text, and contact for more information. Video can be extremely effective if done well, but tends to be expensive, time-consuming, and a pain for your customers to give you. Ken McCarthy uses video testimonials effectively at the `www.thesystemseminar.org` sales page. Because all his customers were in one place — his seminar — it was cost-effective to hire a video crew and collect the testimonials.

Audio testimonials can be almost as powerful, and are much less expensive and time-consuming to produce. You can collect audio testimonials just by asking your customers to pick up a telephone and talk. Try it now: Call (214) 615-6505, extension 6900 and say something nice about this book. I may post your comment at `www.askhowie.com/readercomments`. You'll have to pay long-distance charges (because I'm a cheapskate), but you can set up a toll-free audio line for just a few dollars a month. Visit `www.askhowie.com/audio` for recommended services and advanced testimonial-gathering strategies. You can listen to audio testimonial examples at `www.leadsintogold.com` near the bottom of the page.

Written testimonials by themselves are the least powerful, simply because you might have written them yourself. But adding the written text below an audio or video, you can have the best of both worlds: believability and multiple modes of message delivery.

Finally, you can let your visitors know you have "references available upon request." This can work for big purchases later in the sales cycle; on the landing page, focus on delivering needed information immediately.

Giving clear instructions in the call to action

Somebody once said, "A confused mind always says 'no.'" In fact, if you're reading this book out loud, you just said it. Make sure your instructions for the action you want visitors to take are so clear and free of ambiguity that a reasonably intelligent hamster could follow them.

Not only will you explain exactly how to fill out the form, where the form is located, and what to click, but you will also tell them what happens next. What page will be served after they click "Send me the two free chapters!"? What will appear in their inboxes; in what time frame? Do they need to add you to their spam filters' white lists? If they phone you, who will answer? What extension should they ask for?

Tony Robbins likes to say that humans have a simultaneous need for certainty and excitement — a balance between what is known and what is unknown. At the point where someone is considering entering into a relationship with your Web site, your job is to reduce the already-considerable uncertainty.

Chapter 11

Following Up with Your Prospects

*I*ndulge me for a moment and try this experiment. Think about the Web sites you browsed yesterday (or the most recent day you were online). Roughly how many were there? What were they? Take a minute and write down as many as you can remember. When you're done, open your Web browser and view your browsing history. How many sites did you forget? How many of those sites are you likely ever to visit again?

The point of this experiment: If you're anything like me, you visited a lot of sites, found some of them interesting, but got distracted and left without leaving yourself a convenient and reliable way back. Your Web site visitors are the same. You work like crazy to build a great AdWords campaign, pay real money for visitors, and most of them vanish like dust in the wind (to quote one of my favorite folk-rock songs of the 1970s).

You haven't bored your Web site's visitors, or offended them, or disqualified them. They just weren't ready to transact business with you at that moment. Or they got distracted by a phone call, incoming e-mail sound, fax, co-worker, daydream, flashback, or UFO sighting. What a shame, too. You spend so much time, money, and energy to get them into a sales funnel that turns out to operate more like a sieve.

In this chapter, I'll show you some strategies and tools for following up with prospects after they leave your Web site. You'll discover easy methods for deploying effective follow-up sequences that you create once and put on autopilot. You'll see how to use e-mail autoresponders and newsletters to become your prospect's one and only. And you'll be able to integrate telephone and mail strategies as well to keep your business on the radar screen.

Overcoming Your Prospects' Miniscule Online Attention Span

Your average Web-site visitor has the attention span of a guppy — deal with it. Online attention spans are notoriously short, but merchants have known for a long time that a sale delayed is generally a sale lost. The infomercial must get a couch potato to the phone, credit card in hand, before the thumb touches the TV remote. The direct mail subscription pitch must compel action before the reader puts the letter down to grab a cold drink from the kitchen, because soon that letter will be in a middle of a pile, instead of at the top. And the salesperson at the car dealership wants the prospect to commit today, before comparison shopping a better deal in the next county.

Pressure tactics don't work online

The traditional sales approach to any sort of buyer hesitation and reluctance has been to wrestle prospects to the ground, lock them into a half nelson (full nelsons prevent them from signing the credit-card slip), and shove a vacuum cleaner hose into their pocket or purse and suck out the money. In the offline world, this translates into pressure tactics, fake scarcity, fake urgency, aggressively overcoming objections, and various sleazy tricks. Salespeople are taught that "I'll think about it" means "No, and you can kiss your commission goodbye."

That attitude is crazy. Sure, prospects lie to avoid conflict and to keep from hurting our feelings. But sometimes prospects are telling the truth when they say they need to think it over. If they are forced into a decision before they're ready, the decision will almost certainly be *no*. If the high-pressure tactics work, the buyer's remorse refund rate will be astronomical. And those customers will not be likely sources of referral business, because they want to protect their friends from unpleasant experiences.

I could debate the relative effectiveness of these tactics in the face-to-face world, but it's clear that they don't work so well on the Internet. Don't like a Web site? It's gone at the click of a button, no hard feelings. Give yourself a reality check about online manners and inhibitions by visiting a Yahoo! chat group some time. Perfectly mild-mannered folks who wouldn't dream of so much as coughing if someone cut in front of them in the supermarket line turn into raving lunatics online, slinging mud and brimstone safe in the shelter of their anonymity. Trust me: The second your visitor is annoyed by your site, he or she disappears faster than Roadrunner in a cloud of smoke. (Insert your own sound effects.)

Build a relationship so you can make the sale when your prospect is ready to buy

Your mission, should you choose to run a successful online venture, is fourfold:

- **Get your prospects' contact information.** You want their e-mail at the very least, more if you can get it. The more you ask for, the fewer prospects will convert to leads (I define a *lead* as someone you can follow up with), and the more serious they will be.

- **Receive their explicit permission to stay in touch.** People don't always realize that you will be using their contact information to contact them, probably because it occurs so rarely in the offline world. Prospects are used to dropping their business cards into a fishbowl for a chance to win dinner for four, or giving the supermarket all their contact information in exchange for a loyalty card, and never hearing a peep after that. If you assume that an e-mail address represents an open invitation to visit their inbox, you'll be rudely awakened faster than they can hit the Report Spam button in their e-mail program. Enough spam complaints and your Web site is basically out of business.

- **Provide such helpful and credible advice, guidance, and support that your visitors never ever go searching on that topic again.** Perry Marshall refers to this as "taking your prospect off the market." When prospects are actively searching for information, they go wide, looking at a lot of sites and getting the lay of the land. They don't want to become the world expert; they're just looking for someone to trust, to hold their hand and lead them. Your follow-up will determine if you become that trusted resource or not.

- **Build a relationship that leads naturally to a win-win outcome.** Database marketing consultant Lori Feldman (www.thedatabasediva.com) reminds us, "The purpose of a business is to grow a customer." Not just to get the sale. A sale is a one-time transaction. A customer is a living, breathing asset. The relationship you build with leads may lead to sales, referrals of their friends, testimonials, and more. But the goal of the relationship is not to close the deal, but to determine if a sale is a win-win outcome or not. The most expensive customers in your database are the ones you shouldn't be selling to. They take up too much time, demand too much special help, and don't buy anything else from you.

Spinning a Web with an Opt-In

In Chapter 10, I identify the opt-in as one of the top goals of any landing page. An opt-in refers to a prospect who has opted into your database with the expectation of receiving follow-up communications from you. Depending on the market, the quality of traffic to your landing page, your offer, and how you describe that offer, you can aim for an opt-in from 20–50%, sometimes higher. If your opt-in rate is lower than 20%, you're doing something wrong. This chapter will help you fix your opt-in process.

Unlike a spider who spins a web to ensnare — and subsequently eat — its prey, you spin a customer-catching Web site to ensure a second date with your prospects. The opt-in takes all the pressure off the first visit. They can buy if they like, but, hey, no big deal if they don't. If your Web site has to make the sale on the first visit, your prose is likely to come across as desperate. And desperate is not attractive; not at junior high school dances, and not in sales. The more desperate you seem, the more it looks like there's something wrong with you.

The most common method of acquiring an opt-in is through a form on your Web site. Figure 11-1 shows an understated form, one that I use on www. fitfam.com/home to get visitors to download my Action Guide, "How to Raise Fit and Healthy Kids in a Crazy-Busy World." Opt-in forms can also be bold and attention-getting, as in www.loweryourbidprice.com, which shows an offer for a free eight-part mini-course called, "How to Lower Your AdWords Bid Prices." The graphics suggest a coupon, and the hand-scrawled ellipse highlights the action button.

Figure 11-1:
A short opt-in form offering an Action Guide.

When you download the FitFam Action Guide, you'll discover:

- **A 6-minute cardio workout that will burn calories for days**
- A 5-word StressBuster you can teach your kids for when things get crazy and overwhelming
- **A 4-minute brown bag lunch for school or office**
- An awesome cookie recipe that's healthier than 99% of breakfast cereals
- **Five Principles to Help You Create a Fit Family Culture**
- How to spell "Baba Ghanouj"

Get started now:

Email:
Name:

Send me the Action Guide!

Whatever e-mail service you use to send e-mails and manage your list will help you generate the HTML code or Javascript that puts the form on your Web site. Later in this chapter, I show you the vendor I use and recommend a few others for comparison.

If you thought you could do e-mail marketing using Outlook Express or Yahoo Mail, you were mistaken. If you have more than 20 leads in your database, you will need a specialized application to get the e-mails out, manage your list in accordance with anti-spam rules, and keep your sanity.

Generating an opt-in form using AWeber

For the purposes of this chapter, I'm going to use my preferred vendor, AWeber Communications, to show you how to set up and manage e-mail follow-up. If you already have a shopping cart with e-mail capabilities, you will have to adapt the instructions accordingly. If you don't yet have an e-mail-marketing provider, sign up for an account at www.aweber.com. (For a video tutorial and overview of the e-mail marketing process, visit www.askhowie.com/email first.) Currently, AWeber costs $19.95 per month, or $14.95 a month if you buy a year in advance. Just to put this cost in perspective, you can now send unlimited e-mails to up to 10,000 people at a time, as many times as you want. If you give $15 to the U.S. Postal Service, you can buy 36 first-class stamps and still have 24 cents left over for envelopes and paper.

Before you build the opt-in form, you need a place to send your visitor once they've completed the form. This page should confirm the success of their opt-in ("Thank you for signing up for the Nose Hair Removal Secrets 42-Day E-mail Course"), describe what they'll be receiving next and where and when to look for it ("Check your e-mail inbox in about 5 minutes for Installment 1: Don't Use a Butane Lighter While Waiting at a Gas Station"), and suggest a next action ("While you're waiting, let me tell you about an amazing new way to remove nasal hair without tweezers, dry ice, or gas flames . . . "). Don't worry about getting it perfect — for our purposes right now, all you need is a working URL to send your lead. Name the page something like www.*yoursite.*com/signupthanks.html and remember the name.

When the thank-you page is done, you're ready to sign up for an AWeber account as follows:

1. **Go to www.aweber.com and click the Order button at the top.**

   Choose any plan you like, from one month to a full year — you get 30 days during which you can get a full refund. If you like it, the annual plan is the best value; e-mail marketing is a long-term tool.

2. **After placing your order, you'll be taken to a page with a link to log in to the Control Panel. Click that link.**

   AWeber immediately sends you an e-mail with your login and password.

3. **Enter your new login and password, and then click Account at the top right and change your password to something you'll remember.**

4. **Return to the Home page and click the Getting Started — Setup Guide link.**

5. **Choose Web Form Wizard to create your first opt-in form.**

6. **On the next page, click the green Create Web Form button in the center of the page and fill out the form details (see Figure 11-2).**

7. **In the Form Name text box, enter a name for your form that you'll remember later.**

   Only you see the form name, so don't worry about being clever. Just describe it so you can find it later among the many forms you will create.

8. **Select the type of form you're using.**

   The form type can be in-line (that is, within the Web page itself), or a pop-up, pop-under, or pop-over/hover. Google won't let you use pop-ups, exit pops or pop-unders on a landing page, and they really annoy people, so forget about those options. The pop-over/hover isn't actually a pop-up; instead, it's a graphic that's technically part of your Web page even though it appears to float above it. Google has mixed feelings about this; sometimes it disables your ads if they point to pages with pop-overs, and sometimes it doesn't. Stick with an in-line form for now.

9. **Enter a URL that you created for your "Thank you for opting in" page in the Thank You Page text box.**

   The page must exist already, or else AWeber gets persnickety. If you don't have a thank you page ready, either enter your home page for now, or leave the AWeber default page. Just don't forget to come back and change it later. I talk about strategies for this page later in this chapter.

10. **As the instructions say, leave the Forward Variables check box blank if you don't know what it means.**

    Later on you can use this feature to customize the thank you page, just as you can do with PHP on the landing page (see Chapter 10).

11. **(Optional) Enable ad tracking by entering some unique description for this form in the Ad Tracking text box.**

    You can use ad tracking to segment your list based on the particular form your lead used to opt in. This ability to segment comes in handy, say, if each ad group leads to a different landing page. You can name the traffic source or the page in the Ad Tracking field so you can find all the leads who were interested in red wagons as opposed to green tricycles. If you place a form more than once on the same page (at the top of the right sidebar and below the landing page text, for example), you can even track which form collected the opt-in.

12. **Leave the Start on Message drop-down list at the default for now: (Default) 1 Autoresponse.**

    An *autoresponse* is an automatic e-mail that your leads get from you. The default setting means they will receive all the autoresponse e-mails in the sequence, starting with the first one.

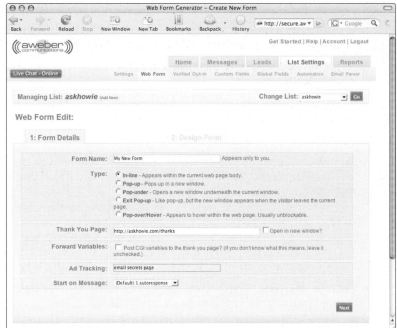

Figure 11-2:
Creating
an opt-in
form using
AWeber.

13. **Click Next to design the form:**

    The instructions for this part are pretty straightforward on the AWeber site:

    a. If you hover your mouse pointer over the Name field on the left, you see a plus sign. Click it to add that field to your form.

    b. Just below the Name field, you can click the Add New Field link to add more fields if you want to collect a visitor's address, phone number, pet's name, favorite flavor of Vice Cream, annual income, innie or outie belly button, and so on.

    c. When you add a new field, you see a check box labeled Subscriber Update. Check this box if you want your lead to be able to change this information later.

    d. You can change the order of the fields by clicking and dragging them up or down. Edit a field by holding your mouse over it and clicking the pencil icon. Four options appear to the left:

    Required: Does your prospect have to fill out this field to opt in, or is it optional?

    Type of Field: In addition to plain text, you can include drop-down lists and radio buttons for multiple choice questions, check boxes for yes/no, and a larger text area to give the prospect the visual cue that they can write a short novel here.

Label and Default Value: The Label text box is used in conjunction with the Default Value field (see the following) to segment your list later. For example, if you put this form on your Juggling Scarves for Kids page, you can include a hidden field called Product and make the default value Jr. Juggling Scarves. Later, you can search for this value and send a scarf coupon to people on your list who opted in from this page and haven't yet bought the scarves (see Figure 11-3).

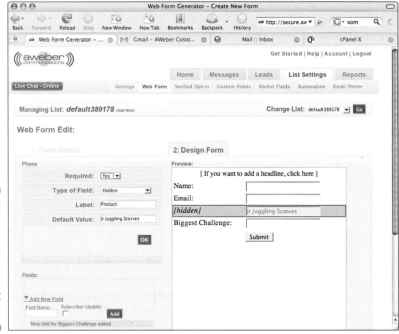

Figure 11-3:
Use hidden fields to include data that will help you segment your list.

14. **(Optional) Click the Submit button at the bottom of the form to rename it.**

    I generally give the button a title that sounds like my prospect making a request: "Send Me the Action Guide!"

15. **When you're done editing the form, click the Save button (bottom right), and you're ready to get the code for your opt-in page.**

Placing the form on your Web site

After you create your Web form on the AWeber site, you need to get the code that you'll place in your opt-in Web page. In the AWeber List Settings tab, select Web Form from the submenu. If you've created your first form, you will see it in the list. Click Preview to see what the form looks like all by itself. If everything is in the right order and you're ready to stick it on a page in your site, close the pop-up window and select Get HTML.

AWeber gives you a new window with two code options. The top one, shown in Figure 11-4, is in Javascript, and consists of a single line of code that you place on your page's HTML where you want the form to appear. The script goes to AWeber's Web site and pulls the form onto your page. As long as you don't need to change the look and feel of the form, this is a good option. It allows you to collect statistics on how many times the form was displayed, which you need to determine your opt-in rate.

Figure 11-4:
To use the form without making design changes, add this snippet of code to your Web page.

> Recommended: Copy and paste the following HTML code into your web page to use the web form titled "myform".

```
<script type="text/javascript"
src="http://forms.aweber.com/form/44/184178044.js"></script>
```

If you want more control over the design of the form, select and copy the raw HTML code from the lower box. Your Web designer can use this code to make the opt-in form blend in with the rest of your page. You can see an example of a designed AWeber opt-in form, visit www.poly-d.com and click through to the White Paper offer.

Visit www.askhowie.com/forms to see examples of both codes.

Generating opt-ins via e-mail

You can also generate opt-ins via e-mail. For example, if you send a blank e-mail to askhowie@aweber.com, within about a minute you'll get an e-mail with the subject line, "RESPONSE REQUIRED: Confirm your request for information from askhowie" or something like that. When you click the first link within that e-mail, you'll be added to my list and will start receiving my e-mail messages. (See the following section for a discussion of this double opt-in process.)

Importing and adding leads yourself

AWeber and most other e-mail marketing services allow you to import existing lists and add new leads manually as well. The better services — the ones you want to use — will send all these prospects a RESPONSE REQUIRED type of e-mail to make sure they want to receive your messages. It's a pain, but if your service doesn't require this, I predict that a lot of your e-mail messages will not make it through the spam filters. It's counterintuitive, but I won't use a service that *doesn't* make me verify my imported lists.

You and I are honest and ethical, of course, and would never send out thousands of spam messages to people who don't want them. But if the e-mail service I use allows *other* people to do just that, the spam filters will catch my e-mails as well as those of the spammers, because they are all being sent from the same server. Using a lax e-mail service is like putting the return address *Seedytown* on your envelopes. Don't risk it.

How to "Bribe" Your Prospects to Opt In

The mechanics of the opt-in are straightforward: Place a form on your site, tell people to fill it out, send them to a thank-you page, and start e-mailing. The only thing missing is the answer to your prospect's question, "Why on earth should I give you my name and contact information?" People protect their inboxes like geese protecting their nests. The last thing they want is a bunch of annoying e-mails trying to sell them something. The keys to achieving a high opt-in rate are to

- ✔ Give away something of value.
- ✔ Make the opt-in in a logical next step in the relationship rather than a form of online extortion.
- ✔ Offer your visitors something they really want.
- ✔ Reassure them.

Give away something of value

When I was little, my dad used to take me to Sonny Amster's bakery on Vauxhall Road in Millburn on Sunday mornings to get rolls and bagels for brunch. My most vivid memories of those trips were the hundreds of free cookies I consumed. Mr. Amster understood the power of giving away a free sample before asking for the sale. He knew that if he could give away something of value before asking for the sale, he was likely to ring up a bigger order than if he insisted on payment before the munching began.

Not only did my dad sometimes add a dozen cookies to our order, he felt compelled to buy as an act of reciprocity. As Robert Cialdini explains in his book, *Influence: The Psychology of Persuasion* (published by Collins), when someone does something nice for us, we feel a powerful urge to balance the scales by doing something nice in return. This principle is often used to manipulate us, but works even better when it's genuine.

You can give away something of value as a prequel to the opt-in. If you sell unicycles and generate traffic with a Unicycle Beginners ad group, give away a free guide on the seven steps to learning to ride. Put Steps 1 and 2 right on the landing page, and offer the remaining five steps in an e-mail. Make the first half of an article about choosing your first unicycle available on your site, and ask for an e-mail address to send them the second half. Put a video on your site showing the first step, and offer a series of how-to-ride videos in exchange for the opt-in.

Make the opt-in a logical next step

To grasp the concept of a logical next step, return with me to the metaphor of the museum where people go to find the love of their life. You're standing next to an attractive person whom you'd like to know better, looking at the post-modern painting of a 12-foot-high piece of lined notebook paper. The person glances in your direction, smiles, and says something like, "I wonder what music the artist was listening to while she was painting this." You say, "I'll tell you what I think if you give me your e-mail address." End of conversation, no?

The request for their e-mail address had nothing to do with the prior conversation. On your Web site, your opt-in will not work if it's just a thinly veiled attempt to build your list.

If you need inspiration, consider the tech-support hotline model. Have you ever waited on hold for 20 minutes for tech support, listening to cheesy music or endless repetitions of "Your call is important to us, and we will answer your call in the order it was received"? And then you get a live person, start explaining the problem, and 30 seconds later you hear a click and a busy signal? After years of this treatment, I finally got a technician who began the call by asking for my phone number and e-mail address "in case we get disconnected." Boy, I was never so happy to give away my information before. I had been given a logical reason to share that information, so I did.

Why do you need your visitors' e-mail addresses? What are you going to send them via e-mail? Why do they want it? If you ask for a phone number, how will they benefit from your call? Spell it out: "Leave your phone number if you'd like to talk about which perennials will thrive in your garden."

I asked Seth Godin (www.sethgodin.com), author of the very important book, *Permission Marketing: Turning Strangers into Friends and Friends into Customers* (Simon & Schuster), his thoughts about trying to compel your visitors to opt in because you're trying to build your list. Seth didn't beat around the bush:

> *What you want is irrelevant. Of course, it matters what you want if you have power, if you can force people to do what you want. The reality is that the new paradigm demands humility. You will either engage people on their terms or you will fail to engage them. Your choice.*

Offer your visitors something they really want

Every marketing campaign consists of three factors:

- ✔ **The market:** In the case of your AdWords landing page, the market is initially determined by the keyword and then funneled through your ad.
- ✔ **The creative:** This is everything you show your market to get them to accept your offer — text, graphics, audio, video, and so on.
- ✔ **The offer:** This is the bait, the thing they really want.

Marketers like to spend a lot of time massaging the creative part, because it's fun and because it's the part over which they have the most control. But the success of your campaigns will depend (95% of it, anyway) on one thing: how well the offer matches the market. In other words, is this bait something they want or not?

In dating, someone gives you their phone number for one reason only: they're hoping you give them a call some time. Your job is to become so appealing that your prospects actually want to hear from you again. They look forward to your e-mails. They get value (and perhaps entertainment) from every point of contact.

You already know what your AdWords traffic wants, because they told you by clicking your ad. You can use the ad to split-test features of your offer (free report, e-mail course, PDF delivered by e-mail, fax, small lead-lined box flown to your door by 72 carrier pigeons, whatever). See Chapter 13 for the details of split testing, and read the later section, "Creating a lead-generating magnet," for a discussion of types of things you can offer in exchange for your visitors' contact information.

Reassure them

Basically, human beings are motivated by three things: seeking pleasure, avoiding pain, and conserving energy. Of the three, pain avoidance is usually the strongest. Most of the time we're just acting out of damage control, asking ourselves, "What's the worst that can happen here and how can I prevent it?" At the threshold of opting in, our prospects want to be reassured that we won't spam them; that they can stop the flow of e-mails easily at any time; and that we'll respect their privacy and not sell, rent, barter, or give away their contact information to anyone else.

Legendary copywriter Gary Bencivenga puts the following sentence below his www.bencivengabullets.com opt-in form: "No obligation . . . Nothing to buy . . . Your e-mail address will never be shared or rented." Ken McCarthy offers this reassurance at www.thesystemseminar.org form: "I respect your privacy and will not share your e-mail address with anyone. You can easily unsubscribe at any time — Ken McCarthy."

To sell or get the opt-in?

When I present the opt-in strategy to clients, they sometimes object on the grounds that the opt-in strategy will get in the way of the main objective of the site: the sale. They understand the sales funnel, and worry that a sideways step will upset the process and destroy sales.

A sale is a fragile thing, and you can certainly sabotage your sales by creating a clumsy opt-in process. And you'll get fewer initial sales if you go for the opt-in first, rather than the sale. But if your sales conversion of a new visitor is 0.5% (meaning 1 out of every 200 visitors buys from you) and your opt-in percentage is 20% (meaning 1 out of five visitors opts-in to your list), you will almost certainly make more sales from ongoing follow-up than from the one-shot approach.

If your prospect wants to buy right now, don't put an opt-in in their way. Online sales include all the information you could ask for, including the lovely credit card number and expiration date. Consider the sale a super opt-in.

Make sure your thank-you page offers a path back to the sales funnel, rather than a dead end.

The thank-you page

Perry Marshall uses two clever techniques on his thank-you pages to keep the sales process going while the prospect is still hot. You can see his thank-you page by opting in to his five-day AdWords e-mail course at www.

`perrysmarshall.com`. Even though the first autoresponse e-mail actually hits your inbox within 30 seconds of clicking Start Your Mini-Course Now, Perry tells you to check your inbox "in about 10 minutes."

The second technique in use on this page is the dynamic redirect. The page tells the visitor, "In a few seconds I'm going to tell you about the latest tools for making the most of Google . . . ." And the page is coded to send you straight to a sales letter about 15 seconds after it first appears.

Here's the code, which you place between the `<HEAD>` and `</HEAD>` tags in the page's HTML code:

```
<meta HTTP-EQUIV="REFRESH" content="0; url=http://
www.yourdomain.com/nextpage.html">
```

Replace the two elements in bold. Instead of 0, put in the number of seconds you want this page to show before redirecting. Replace the example URL with the next page.

The thank-you page is also a great place to explain to your leads what to expect from you now, and what they have to do to get it. When you download the two free chapters from Leads into Gold at `www.leadsintogold.com`, you'll be taken to a download page that includes the download link and instructions on downloading the chapters in PDF format.

It also includes a mini-sales pitch for the autoresponder sequence you just signed up for (and may not have known about):

> *Important Note: I'll be sending you a series of e-mail tips to help you get the most out of the two free chapters. They have incredibly valuable insights, and a lot of subscribers think I'm crazy for giving it away for nothing.*
>
> *I've always been a show-off — just ask my sister.*
>
> *Here's the thing: Your ISP's spam filter may consider these e-mails to be spam, and will prevent you from reading them.*
>
> *To ensure you receive the e-mails (you can unsubscribe at any time), please add me to your trusted list of senders. Here's how . . .*

Notice that I put the download link right on the thank-you page. That strategy raises an interesting question: Do I care if someone can get to that page by giving me a fake e-mail address? If I put the link in an e-mail, I know that the e-mail must be real for them to get the two free chapters. In this case, I want to get the two free chapters into as many hands as possible, because those chapters do such a good job of selling the rest of the product. If you follow up with leads manually, or don't want your lead-generating magnet available except to your subscriber list, then don't put the link on the thank-you page.

To see an example of this without having to opt in to a list, visit www.askhowie.com/redirect and wait 12 seconds.

Creating a lead-generating magnet

You have many choices about what sort of lead-generating magnet (LGM) to create. You can offer information, a free sample, a demo version, a limited time free trial, or a coupon. If your Web site is a catalog store with many items available for purchase, the LGM can be as simple as an invitation to receive a 5% discount off the first purchase. Software vendors can offer demo versions, either time-limited or with features disabled.

If you sell high-margin consumables — such as skin care products, health supplements, and perfumes — you may find a free trial to be a cost-effective way to build your customer list. Jevene Cosmetics (www.jevene.com), for example, offers a free sample for $7.95 shipping and handling — presumably enough to break even on that shipment. It includes an interesting twist, waiving the shipping and handling fee entirely if the visitor also agrees to receive a promotional CD-ROM from Video Professor. Now you can remove wrinkles and manage your QuickBooks at the same time! Weird combo, but I bet it works.

Informational LGMs

The economics of the Internet favors giving away information. After you've created the LGM, digital copies are all free, so you incur no marginal expense by giving away a million as opposed to a hundred. When your business includes a healthy back end, you can afford to pay more up front to mail letters and packages.

Formats

Informational LGMs can take many formats:

- Free Report/White Paper (PDF)
- Newsletter (PDF, Web page, e-mail)
- Book (self-published)
- Magazine/Journal
- Resource Guide
- Analysis/Planning Template
- Electronic Book
- Recorded Message
- CD/Audiocassette
- DVD/VHS cassette

> ✔ Restricted Access Website
>
> ✔ Audio/Video download
>
> ✔ E-mail Course
>
> ✔ Live Seminar/Workshop
>
> ✔ "Cheat Sheet"

Content types

There are three basic types of information LGMs that lend themselves very well to the triple purposes of attracting, building trust, and selling. These are special reports, consumer guides, and how-to guides.

> ✔ **Special Report (often called *White Paper* in the corporate world):** The free report is the tool of choice when your prospect is not yet educated or motivated enough to take action of any kind. By contrast, the consumer-awareness guide works better when the prospects know they have a problem, know they need to solve it, and are looking at you and your competitors side by side.
>
> The free report essentially names a problem faced by your prospects, gets them emotionally involved in the horrible current and future consequences of the problem, unveils a generic solution, and then introduces and sells your version of the solution.
>
> Visit www.askhowie.com/reports for examples of a special report for consumers (by an indoor air specialist writing to parents of children with asthma) and a business to business white paper (about maximizing profits from your customer list).
>
> ✔ **Consumer Guide:** The consumer guide is most effective when your prospect is actively shopping for a solution and trying to figure out which solution to buy. A variation is the Consumer Alert, which warns prospects about all the ways they can get scammed or make the wrong decision. A popular format for this is the "Seven questions to ask before choosing a . . . ." You name your profession, and teach your prospect how to find a qualified and honest practitioner.
>
> ✔ **How-to Guide:** The third kind of informational LGM is the how-to guide. It doesn't have to refer to your product at all. What it does is teach your prospects how to solve a problem somewhat related to the problem that your product solves.

For example, if you sell bookkeeping services for small businesses, your prospects typically have grown to the point where they are overwhelmed by the amount of start-up stuff they haven't outsourced or hired for. Think about what other problems owners of growing small businesses have: inefficient purchasing systems, not enough time to market and sell, nagging questions about incorporation options, and so on. If you can offer information that solves those problems, you can be pretty sure that the people who raise their hands in interest are good prospects for you as well.

If you need to bid on turn-the-corner keywords, create a How-to Guide that qualifies your prospects and gets them into your funnel, even if it doesn't directly sell your products or services. You now have the ability to build the relationship through the most revolutionary communications medium of the last 50 years: e-mail.

Staying on Your Prospects' Minds with E-mail

Imagine for a moment that Google changes its policies and bans all your ads. Imagine further that it changes its search algorithm, thereby excluding your Web pages from its listings. What would happen to your online business?

Aside from pointing out the foolishness of putting all your business eggs into one Google basket, the scenario I just described points out the importance of having a customer list. As Fred Astaire sang to Ginger Rogers on a ferry deck in *Shall We Dance,* "They can't take that away from me."

As Ken McCarthy says, one goal of your list is to support your business if all your traffic disappears. The glue that binds your list to you is e-mail. In spite of all the spam, a person's e-mail inbox is an intimate space. Think of how much more upset people get about spam than junk mail to appreciate just how intimate we want it to be. Writing e-mails that grow the relationship is one of the most important skills you need to succeed online.

You can send two kinds of e-mail: autoresponses and broadcasts. They serve different purposes, and can complement each other to create a powerful e-mail customer-building strategy. Before I cover these methods, I want to discuss a much-debated topic in e-mail marketing: verified opt-in.

Verifying your lead

Suppose you come to my Web site and sign up for my newsletter. You enter the name U. Big Dope along with the e-mail address of some person you don't much like. What happens next is that your "friend" gets an e-mail from me addressed to U. Big Dope. You're anonymous, your acquaintance is mad at me, and I'm innocently confused by the whole thing. I may end up getting blacklisted by spam filters for enough of these lapses. (This actually happened to me a couple of years ago, but the actual name was much more offensive than U. Big Dope. The perpetrator targeted a couple of guys in his office as recipients of this prank, for which I got blamed. Needless to say, I've tended toward verified opt-in ever since.)

AWeber and other e-mail-marketing services have "solved" this problem, sort of, by creating a higher category of opt-in: *verified* or *double opt-in*. In this system, people who opt in receive one e-mail with a link they can click to really join the list. Essentially, this step says, "I'm going to make sure you are who you say you are by sending you this e-mail. If you didn't request this information, you don't have to do anything. Sorry about that."

Verified opt-in protects you from accusations of spamming. No matter how often you send out e-mails, some of your leads will wake up one morning with no recollection of your existence, find your e-mail in their inbox, and report it as spam with a single click. If they opted in using verified opt-in, you can prove to the spam police that you weren't e-mailing without permission.

Also, verified opt-in gives you a higher quality list. The more hoops people have to jump through to receive your e-mails, the hungrier they are for your information.

The one big problem with verified opt-in is that it depresses sign-ups. Especially if your market acts impulsively, your prospects may have cooled down in the 10 minutes it took your e-mail to meet their eyes. Instructions on your landing page and customization of the confirmation e-mail can improve your conversion rate, but you won't build as big a list with verified opt-in.

In AWeber, the default for a Web-form signup is unverified. You can change that setting any time for each list, but once verified, you can never change it back again. So think about your market, about how likely they are to mess with you or forget you, and how important it is for your business to have an easy time delivering e-mails through spam filters. As I said, I got burned once, and haven't looked back. All my lists are verified now.

Following up automatically with an e-mail autoresponder

The e-mail autoresponder is one of the coolest tools ever invented, right up there with Pez dispensers and bicycle brakes. You can preload a series of e-mail messages, and when someone opts in to your list, they receive the series in order, according to the schedule you set. You can merge fields to make the e-mail look exactly like a personal correspondence. Done right, your autoresponder sequence will mimic what you would write to each prospect if you had all the time in the world. You can schedule e-mails days, weeks, months and even years in advance. Figure 11-5 shows a very short autoresponder sequence of four e-mails, scheduled as follows:

Message 1: immediately

Message 2: 3 days later

Message 3: 3 days after message 2

Message 4: 3 days after message 3

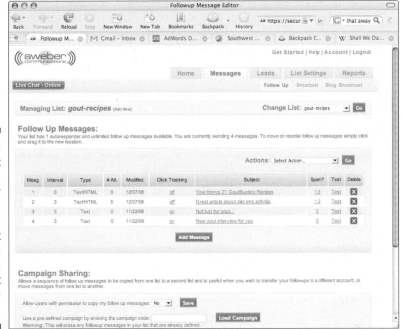

Figure 11-5:
A short auto-responder sequence consisting of an instant response and three subsequent follow-up messages.

But wait, there's more! You can create multiple lists, and set rules about subscribing and unsubscribing based on certain conditions. For Leads into Gold, my sequence consists of 18 messages sent over about two months. But what if someone buys on Day 17? Do I want to keep asking them to buy? Obviously not. I created a rule that says, "When someone on the list buys Leads into Gold, remove them from the prospect list and add them to the customer list." My customer sequence consists of 12 messages, also spread over about two months, that give advice, offer support, and tell them about other things they may want to buy.

I'll show you how to perform this magic again using AWeber, the service I use and recommend. You discover how to use the AWeber Control Panel to build an opt-in form earlier in this chapter. If you haven't yet signed up for an AWeber account, go to www.aweber.com and order now. You have 30 days in which to change your mind and get a full refund.

Changing your list name

From the AWeber home page, click List Settings to change the name of your list to something relevant to your business. If you use verified opt-in, the list name will be the main clue your prospects will see as they decide whether to opt-in.

Would you agree to receive e-mails from someone named default389178? If your ideal name is taken, think of variations — you have 15 characters to play with. My list names for my Gout e-book include gout-recipes, gout, and goutbook. For my marketing business, I use list names like adwords, adwordscoaching, askhowie, coachmarketing, email-club, emailstrategy, guide, and question. I improved my verified opt-in percentage when I changed the name of my Leads into Gold prospect list from 2freechapters to leadsgold-2free.

Changing to verified opt-in

To change to verified opt-in, follow these steps:

1. **From the List Settings tab, click the Verified Opt-in tab in the submenu.**

2. **Next to Web Form Submissions, click the OFF link to turn on Verified Opt-in for your Web forms, as shown in Figure 11-6.**

3. **Say yes to the pop-up warning and you're in complete compliance with e-mail-marketing best practices.**

   Give yourself a pat on the back.

Figure 11-6: Change to verified opt-in to prevent spam complaints and worse.

Next, you need to customize the verification message your prospects will receive. Your job is to get them to open the e-mail by choosing or creating the right subject line, and then getting them to click the link that puts them on your list. Click the Subject box to bring up the Pre-Approved Subject drop-down list and scan the subjects first. Which one most closely connects with what you promise? Is it a subscription? A request for information? Do you want to include a capitalized pre-head like RESPONSE REQUIRED? Do you want to include or omit the @aWeber e-mail suffix? (Hint: Omit it.)

The advantage of using a pre-approved subject line is, well, they're pre-approved. I prefer to write my own custom subject lines, enter the text in the Custom Subject text box, and wait for the AWeber folks to approve them. One of my favorites is, "Making sure you signed up on purpose for {!*listname*}." That helps them connect to me while saying exactly why I'm sending this e-mail.

In the Custom First Paragraph text box, simply repeat the offer and tell them what to do. For example:

```
Hi {!firstname_fix},

Congratulations on your purchase of Leads into Gold!
To receive the promised bonuses, simply click the
link below.
```

Save your changes by clicking the Save button at the bottom right, then review the verification message you've edited. When you're satisfied, click the Messages tab to start creating your autoresponder sequence.

Planning your e-mail sequence

When Abraham Lincoln was asked how long a man's legs should be, he famously retorted, "Long enough to reach the ground." When I am asked how long an e-mail sequence should be, I give the same answer and watch my clients' heads spin in confusion. Actually, I paraphrase Honest Abe and say, "Long enough to turn your best prospects into buyers." It really depends on the circumstances: the market, the keyword, the offer, the first sale.

Ask yourself: What is your prospects' interest cycle? How long will they focus on this itch before losing interest? Some itches go away by themselves after a few minutes or hours. In those cases, your best strategy is to go for the sale right away. Other itches can linger for years — soundproofing a noisy restaurant, losing 15 pounds, learning to play the ukulele. Your e-mail scheduling strategy depends on their interest cycle and the urgency of their need.

Your choices for e-mail content are so vast, I could write a book just on e-mail-autoresponder marketing. (Hey, maybe that will be my next *For Dummies* book!) Here are several strategies to choose from as you create your sequence:

✔ **Consumption of your LGM:** Just because people downloaded your special report or software demo doesn't mean they're going to read it or start using it. In fact, thanks to ferret-on-caffeine attention spans, they probably don't remember where they saved the file, or that they have the software. Your first e-mails should help them consume your LGM in manageable chunks. Reassure them: "If you haven't gotten to the white paper yet, I understand. You'll get to it when you get to it. When you do, I'd love to hear your thoughts."

Remind them why they wanted your LGM in the first place. Tell them about the great strategy on page 9. Show them a cool way to create a color-coded mind map using your software.

✔ **Soliciting engagement:** My most successful autoresponder message of all time goes out one day after my prospect has opted in. I've used this for my products and for various clients, and it always gets a great response:

```
Hi Betsy,

    Yesterday you visited FitFam.com and downloaded the Action Guide.

    (If you haven't gotten your copy yet, it's at www.FitFam.com/home/
Actionguide .)

    I just wanted to ask you, was it helpful? What were you looking for
when you came to the site? (If you haven't read it yet, I
totally understand. You'll get to it when you get to it.)

    If you'll hit reply, I'd love to hear from you. I want to make sure
the information on the site is as helpful as possible.

All the best,

Howie Jacobson, Ph.D.
www.FitFam.com
```

This chatty e-mail starts a dialog with prospects. They reply out of courtesy, because it looks to them like I sat down and wrote this just to them, and it would be rude not to reply. I always reply to their reply, thanking them for their feedback, and asking more questions about their situation. Before you know it, I'm doing consultative selling with zero sales resistance. I'll offer to help them over the phone, and very often can take the prospect to the next step in the sales funnel just by virtue of this e-mail.

✔ **Teaching and guiding:** My Leads into Gold e-mail sequence contains some very long e-mails. Each one is a short chapter on direct marketing. For people hungry for information on how to grow their business, these e-mails make me a valuable resource. Some of them reason, "If this is his free stuff, imagine how good his paid stuff must be."

✔ **Offering more good stuff:** If you have a second white paper, or an audio interview, or a free teleseminar, you can build goodwill and establish yourself as the expert by offering them to your prospects. Remember, most people start their search wide, looking in lots of places for information, but quickly narrow their informational intake filter to let in one primary source. Your goal is to be that one source.

✔ **Selling:** Yes, you can make offers and convince your prospects to take you up on those offers in e-mail. You'll be more successful in converting on those offers if they are the minority of your e-mails, and if the e-mails that do sell also educate or entertain (preferably both).

The best way to learn about what works is to get on a bunch of lists and experience various autoresponder sequences. Create folders in your e-mail program for each sequence, print out the e-mails and study them. What's the ratio of valuable content to sales pitch? Is the tone professional, folksy, in-your-face, or humorous? Are their motives transparent or veiled? Are the messages short, medium, or long? What's the purpose of each e-mail? Was it effective for you? Would it work in your market? And so on.

Go to www.askhowie.com/autoresponders for a list of autoresponders to study and model.

Pay special attention to the two most important elements on an e-mail: the Subject line and the From line:

✔ **The From line:** Before we read an e-mail, we look to see who sent it. If your leads know you only as Pat the Welder, they probably won't open an e-mail from Patricia McLaughlin. You can change the From address at the bottom of the Aweber List Settings page. The name next to the checked From/Reply box is the one your prospects will see in the From line.

✔ **The Subject line:** The subject line serves one function: to get the user to open the e-mail and read it. You can use curiosity triggers, benefit triggers, and any of the strategies discussed in Chapter 6. Your subject line is the headline of your e-mail, the thing your prospect spends a millisecond scanning before deciding whether to read the message or delete it.

Creating an autoresponder sequence using AWeber

Once you've renamed your list and set your verified opt-in preferences (described earlier in this chapter), you're ready to create e-mail messages. Click the Messages tab to see a list of your current messages (none, if you haven't created any yet). Click the Add Message button to create your first autoresponse.

If you are already collecting leads, they will receive your autoresponse e-mails. If you're just playing around, create a second list that nobody will see but you, as shown in Figure 11-7. You can create new lists by clicking the small Add New link next to the list name at the top left.

Creating a message

For now, my advice is to stick with plain text e-mails, not HTML. Plain text e-mails get delivered at higher rates, they're simpler to create, and they mirror the normal e-mails your prospects send and receive every day. They won't necessarily stand out and scream, "You can ignore me because I'm not from a real person."

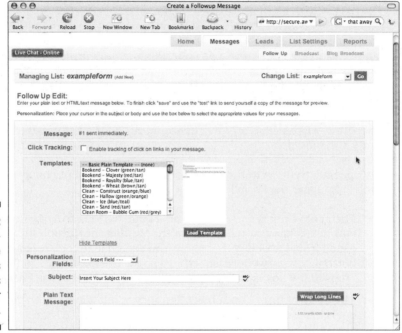

Figure 11-7:
Create auto-response messages on this AWeber page.

If you select the Click Tracking check box, you'll be able to see how many leads click links within your e-mails, which can be very useful information. The downside, if you're using plain text messages, is that your pretty links (www.fitfam.com/actionguide, for example) will turn into hideous AWeber links with lots of funny characters, and may scare people into not clicking.

Type your subject (the default, "Insert Your Subject Here" is not recommended) in the Subject text box, and then type your plain text message or import it from a text file or Word document into the Plain Text Message box. AWeber shows you its recommended width of 68 characters per line. If you click Wrap Long Lines after inputting your message, AWeber will automatically reformat it to that width.

I often make my e-mail messages half that width, or about 35 characters per line, to make them very easy on the eye and encourage my readers to scroll all the way to the end. After creating the message, save it (by clicking the Save button at the bottom right) to return to the message list.

Using personalization fields

You can personalize the e-mail message to each lead, using dozens of different fields, some of which are shown in Figure 11-8. I generally include the first name in the salutation, as follows:

```
Hi {!firstname_fix}
```

The `_fix` at the end capitalizes the first letter of the name and makes the rest lowercase, in case someone typed in his name as `HOwie` and you don't want to show him those two capital letters in every e-mail.

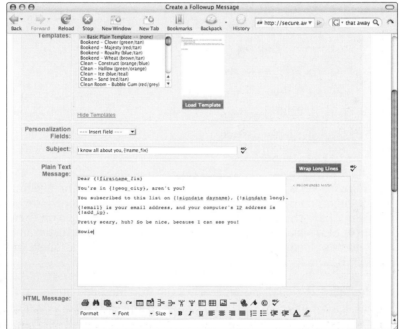

Figure 11-8: Using personalization fields, you can customize e-mails to each lead.

To view the actual e-mail generated by the message in Figure 11-8, visit www.askhowie.com/personal and complete the form. It's verified opt-in, so you'll have to confirm the first e-mail to receive the second. How close to your actual city did AWeber get? In my case, within about 270 miles — not very impressive. Oh well.

TIP

Click Test to send yourself a copy of the message. Do this with every e-mail you ever put into AWeber. Click every link within those e-mails. You'll save yourself a lot of "oops" e-mails, the ones where you say, "Gee, I'm sorry that the links didn't work in the last e-mail I sent out." Take the time to get it right, so you don't raise unnecessary doubts about your competence.

Scheduling your next message

For all autoresponder messages after the first one, you have to decide when you want the e-mail to be sent. AWeber allows you to choose any number of days, from 0 through 999, following the previous message. If you have a sequence that sends an e-mail a day for 5 days, then once a week for 4 weeks, and then once every 28 days forever, you configure it as follows:

Message 1: Instantaneous

Message 2: 1 Day Delay

Message 3: 1 Day Delay

Message 4: 1 Day Delay

Message 5: 1 Day Delay

Message 6: 7 Day Delay

Message 7: 7 Day Delay

Message 8: 7 Day Delay

Message 9: 28 Day Delay

Message 10: 28 Day Delay

And so on . . .

Generally, you want to send more frequent e-mails at the beginning of the sequence, and drop down to a stay-in-touch-once-a-month frequency after a month or so. The last thing your prospect wants is to go on vacation for a couple of weeks and return to an inbox full of you. (Actually, an inbox full of "Send this e-mail to 20 people within 10 minutes or your nose will fall off" might be worse, but you get the point.)

Scheduling an e-mail is simple: Click the Add Message button at the bottom of your list of e-mails to create a new one. At the top of the next page, the first field you can edit has the default number 4 in it. If you leave it as is, this message will be sent four days after the previous message. To send this message the very next day, change it to 1 (see Figure 11-9). If you're using a different autoresponder service, make sure you understand their format. Some of them ask you to schedule based on the signup date, rather than the previous e-mail.

Your autoresponse e-mails fall into one of two categories: obvious parts of a sequence, or simulated real time e-mails. If you offer an e-mail course, the messages that deliver the course don't have to "pretend" to be a note you just dashed off. Something as simple as

```
Hi Howie,
Here's Part 1 of the 17-Part E-mail Course, "How to Clean Your Fingernails"
+ + + + + + + + + + + + +
Part 1: Finding Your Fingernails

Many of my clients have such dirty fingernails, they can't even find them
anymore. Here's where to look: at the ends of your fingers, just opposite the
part with the fingerprint . . .

And so on . . .
```

will get the job done. After the course is over, you can start communicating in
a more chatty and natural way:

```
Hi Howie,
I was recently talking to a client who complained, "Fran, my fingernails are now
spotless, but my toenails are a mess. What do you suggest?"

Goodness, but I guffawed when I heard that one. Did he think I had another
17-part course about toenails?

The answer, obviously, is "Wear shoes and nobody will notice."

But then we started talking about the spring wedding season approaching, and it
occurred to me that you might find occasion to don footwear with open toes in
the coming months.

And so on . . .
```

Try to keep these messages "evergreen" by avoiding references that will date
them. Don't say, "I was watching the Oscars last night," because someone on
your list will receive your message in September and dismiss you as a liar or
TiVo addict. Do read over your messages once or twice a year to nip stale-
ness in the bud. If you talk about a celebrity who has died since you wrote
the e-mail, it may come across as offensive, if not just outdated.

The goal of the autoresponder is to automate what you would do anyway if
you had a million hours a day and nothing better to do. As you plan each
message and each sequence, ask yourself, "Knowing what I know about this
lead, what would I write to them today?"

The purpose of your first autoresponder sequence is to turn your lead into a
buyer (or at least to help your lead to decide if they should become a buyer).
Your e-mails continue to hammer at pain points, educate, offer solutions,
build credibility, invite feedback — everything you would do if you were the
account manager and this lead was a hot prospect.

Figure 11-9:
Change the scheduling of an e-mail by entering the number of days after the previous message.

Using autoresponders to move leads and customers through your sales funnel

Say you sell three products, and you want your customers to buy them in this order: Product 1, Product 2, Product 3. You can set up three autoresponders as follows:

- ✔ **Prospect List:** a sequence of e-mails to get your opt-ins to buy Product 1.

- ✔ **New Customer List:** a sequence of e-mails to get your customers to buy Product 2.

Here's the coolest feature of all: when someone buys Product 1, AWeber automatically adds them to the New Customer list and unsubscribes them from the Prospect List. You don't have to subject your customers to a sales pitch for a product they already bought. You can also avoid the worse-case scenario of offering a better deal for something they already bought.

- ✔ **Returning Customer List:** a sequence of e-mails to get your customers who already own Products 1 and 2 to buy Product 3.

Setting up automatic unsubscribe

To set up automatic unsubscribe, follow these steps:

1. **Create a second AWeber list by clicking Add New next to the list name at the top left.**

2. **On the next page, click the green Create List button and complete and save the forms on the Success page.**

   This new list will be for new customers who just bought your first product.

3. **Change the list to your first list by selecting it from the drop-down list next to Change List, as shown in Figure 11-10.**

Figure 11-10:
Select a list
to manage
using the
drop-down
list near the
top right of
the page.

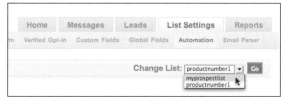

4. **Once you're managing the list that leads will unsubscribe from when they subscribe to the new list, go to the List Settings tab and click Automation from the submenu.**

5. **From the drop-down list in the center of the page, select Unsubscribe from List {*name of first list*} When Lead Subscribes To {*name of second list*} (see Figure 11-11).**

6. **Next, select the new list name from the drop-down list under the List column.**

7. **Click the Save button to save the changes and read the Action you've saved, to make sure it's what you want AWeber to do.**

If you have an online shopping cart, you can set it up to forward the customer information to AWeber after a sale is made. AWeber will then perform the automated rule, removing the customer from the prospect list and adding the name to the customer list. If you don't yet have an online shopping cart, go to www.askhowie.com/cart for some recommendations.

Don't be an accidental spammer

No discussion of e-mail would be complete without a foray into the wacky world of *spam* (junk e-mail). I know you get hundreds of them a week, if not each day, and you're saying to yourself, "But I would never send out an e-mail offering a fake Rolex. I don't even know where to find fake Rolexes." Or you're saying, "I've had enough of this chapter. I'm going to put this book down and try that new Indian restaurant, the one next to the beauty shop and the pizza place." (Sorry, I can't reveal how I do that trick.)

Figure 11-11:
You can set
up AWeber
to remove
people
automati-
cally from
one list
when they
are added to
a different
list.

Spam has become such a huge annoyance to e-mail users that many Internet Service Providers (ISPs) have become hyper-aggressive in their spam filtering. Your e-mails may be going to leads who opted in, they may be completely appropriate, and your leads may be hungering for them, but the big dumb filters are programmed to stop everything that doesn't come from Aunt Sadie and Uncle Lou.

If AOL or Earthlink incorrectly tags your e-mails as spam, you may find yourself sending 2000 e-mails and having only 400 get delivered. Spam is a big topic, but the following tips will help you steer clear of the worst mistakes made by innocent marketers.

Use plain text instead of HTML

Spammers use HTML to do all sorts of nefarious things in e-mails. A brand of spamming known as *phishing* creates e-mails that look exactly like they were sent by big companies such as financial institutions, or eBay and PayPal. Their goal is to get unsuspecting customers to click to fake sites that look like the real ones and enter sensitive data. If your e-mails are in plain text, it shows you're not hiding anything. Spam filters like that transparency, and bother plain text e-mails less.

Random e-mail tip

Leave a space after a URL before adding punctuation. Web browsers often include periods and commas that appear at the end of the URL, so someone might click your working link and end up with that nasty "Page Not Found" error.

Wrong: `www.askhowie.com.`

Right: `www.askhowie.com .`

Keep links to a minimum

Avoid putting lots of links in your e-mails. Remember, each e-mail should compel a single action. Too much choice is bad marketing, regardless of spam considerations. You can repeat a link at the top and bottom of a long e-mail, but don't give your reader half a dozen choices.

Avoid common spam trigger words

Words like `free`, `mortgage`, `pornography`, `spam`, `make money`, `enlargement`, and others alert filters that a message may be spam. In the past, you could fool a filter with punctuation tricks, such as `fr.ee` and `m@ke m0ney`, but the filters now look at tricks like these as spam markers.

So what do you do if you're in the mortgage business, or a similar legitimate enterprise that uses spammy words? One solution is to put your e-mails on your Web site, and write short e-mails with links:

```
Hi Bartleby,
Today's installment of "Affording a New Home" is available at
www.yoursite.com/newhome23

It talks about the three mistakes that can cost you big time, as well as a time-
saving resource you'll wish you had discovered years ago.

Enjoy,
Maury Gage Lender
```

Putting your e-mails online will reduce readership, so you'll have to work hard to entice your reader to click the clink and view your message.

Don't send attachments

If you have a legitimate attachment, like a PDF document or software demo download, put a link in your e-mail to a Web page where that file can be downloaded. Files attached to your e-mails can contain viruses. Also, large attachments can crash your readers' e-mail servers or just get your messages hung up in cyber-limbo.

For more tips on beating an undeserved spam rap, visit `http://www.askhowie.com/spam`. (See that extra space before the period? Just a subtle reminder, courtesy of the "Random e-mail tip" sidebar, elsewhere in this chapter.)

Broadcast e-mails

The other e-mail workhorse for your online business is the Broadcast. This works just like a combination of regular e-mail (you pick a recipient, type something, and send it) and the AWeber system (you can merge fields just like the autoresponses; you can schedule it to go out at a particular date and time; you can send it to hundreds or thousands of people at once).

To send a broadcast, go to the AWeber site, click the Messages tab, and choose Broadcast from the submenu. Click the green Create Broadcast Message button in the center of the page to get started. The first thing you notice is that this form is exactly the same as the form for creating an autoresponder, with only tiny yet crucially important differences:

- Instead of choosing a sending interval, you are prompted to enter a date and time. The default is right now.

- You can segment this list by creating a view and sending only to those leads who meet certain criteria (see the "Managing your e-mail list" section, later in this chapter for instructions on creating and using views.)

  The default views in the drop-down list use time and deliverability as the two criteria. You can send a broadcast e-mail to all leads who subscribed within a certain time frame. You can also resend a broadcast to leads who for some reason haven't been able to receive your regular e-mails due to spam filters or other problems.

- Instead of sending the message to just one list, you now can send it to multiple lists. You can also exclude lists. Just click the Send To Multiple Lists Or Exclude Lists link to open a table where you can choose the lists to include or exclude.

I use broadcasts to let my customers know about special events, time-sensitive information, and to send out newsletters. I also use broadcasts to fill up my autoresponders while making sure that my newest leads don't miss anything good.

Special events

Just today I sent an e-mail to several of my marketing-related lists, letting them know that the System Seminar tuition will be increasing in two weeks, and they should act now to save $700. Obviously, I can't put a message like that in an autoresponder.

Writing great newsletters

E-newsletter wizard Michael Katz, of `www.bluepenguindevelopment.com`, is one of the few people whose newsletters I read it as soon as they arrive. Michael teaches professional service providers like coaches, consultants, trainers, accountants and other people who sell their expertise to build relationships with prospects through regular e-mail newsletters. Here's Michael on the four commandments of e-newsletters:

What I'm about to tell you is so valuable, that I frankly wouldn't blame you if after reading it, you felt compelled to take $5.00 out of your wallet, stuff it in an envelope and send it directly to me. Here's why: What I'm going to share with you now are the four guidelines which we use to make sure that all the newsletters we're involved in stay on track. Here they are:

✔ *Make It Useful:*

With a business to business newsletter in particular, it's difficult to get any traction with readers if you don't give them some kind of actionable "aha" with every issue you send. They are barraged with e-mails, and eager to click the delete button as often as possible.

Your goal therefore, is to give them pause. To make them live in fear that if they delete your newsletter, they will miss some insight that would have made a significant impact on their success. Useful information rises to the top of the pile, and when your newsletter is on top, you need not worry about how big the pile is.

✔ *Make It Interesting:*

I don't know who started the rumor that significant and profitable businesses must also be serious and boring, but it seems to have caught on nonetheless. That's good news for you and me. Because with all the dry as dust E-Newsletters out there, all trying to sound like the front page of the Wall Street Journal, *we can make our newsletters shine with little effort.*

Personal anecdotes, conversational language and the occasional joke here and there will keep your readers involved long enough for them to hear the "real" information you're trying to give them. They probably won't read it just because it's interesting, but they certainly won't read it if it's not.

✔ *Make It Simple:*

An effective newsletter isn't a doctoral thesis; it's not even a case study. It's what I like to call, "a nugget." One insight or tip or concept that your readers can take in, understand, and hopefully remember long enough to put into practice. If you give me too much information (even if it's good), I'm likely to stockpile your newsletters until I delete them in one, "I'll never get around to reading these old ones anyway" frenzy. Give your readers something small enough to understand and remember.

✔ *Make It Authentic:*

Done right, your E-Newsletter is the voice of your company. It reflects your unique personality and culture, whatever that happens to be.

I've walked into enough companies to know that each of them — even the ones in seemingly straight laced, hard to differentiate industries — has its own language, pace, sense of humor and approach. Don't hide all that in an effort to sound "professional." Marketing is the opposite of fitting in — do yourself a favor and fit out!

For more of Michael's wit and wisdom, go to `www.bluepenguindevelopment.com` to read his latest newsletter and join his list. He might even reveal how to pronounce *ezine*.

You can use broadcasts for sales, announcements, coupons, news, opportunities; anything that is time-sensitive and of interest to a significant segment of your list.

E-newsletters

E-newsletters, also called ezines (which nobody knows how to pronounce), are regular communications from you to your customer base. You can create a publishing schedule or just send one out when the mood strikes. The most successful e-newsletter publishers I know stick to a schedule and never deviate. Because you can schedule a broadcast for a future date, you can create six newsletters and have AWeber send them out weekly while you drink yak milk and climb K2.

Repurposing broadcast e-mails to build your autoresponder sequence

Say you've created an autoresponder sequence that lasts five months, then stops. One day you're driving on the highway and this idea hits you for a great next e-mail for that sequence. You rush home and type the e-mail into your autoresponder sequence, 30 days after the last message. Let's call it the 180th day of the whole series.

Now everyone on that list who hasn't been on your list for more than 179 days will receive that message. But it's sad that the people who have been on your list for more than six months will never see your message. You could put it in your autoresponder and send it as a broadcast, but then all the new people will get the same e-mail twice.

The solution, as revealed to me by Perry Marshall during the intermission of a Blue Man Group performance in Las Vegas, is simple and elegant: Calculate how many days after subscribing someone will receive the autoresponse e-mail. Send the e-mail today as a broadcast, and make a note on your calendar to enter it into your autoresponder sequence that many days in the future.

Continuing with our example, let's say today is March 16. You will add the message to your autoresponder sequence on day 180. Send the broadcast to your list today, and on September 16, add the message to day 180 of your sequence. That way, everyone on your list will receive the message once, and no one will receive it twice.

Managing your e-mail lists

You can manage your e-mail lists by clicking the Leads tab on the AWeber site. You can search and sort by any of the data you collect. Click Select Field in any of the drop-down lists to view your choices. You can select filters and a sort order and save that view, in case you need to come back to it again. Once you generate the view (or just click Display View with All Leads showing to see your entire list), you can manage individual leads.

You can stop the autoresponder sequence for a lead by checking that person's box in the Stop column. You can reset the last message they've received to put them backward or forward in the sequence. You can erase them entirely — when someone complains to me about spam but don't unsubscribe via the link that appears at the bottom of every single e-mail I send them (what, me frustrated and bitter?), I erase them from the list to prevent future problems.

If you click the e-mail address, you can edit more information about your lead in the pop-over window: name, e-mail, ad tracking, last message delivered, and a miscellaneous notes field.

 As your list grows, you will benefit from tutorials on advanced list management techniques. You can find these and other AWeber tutorials at www. askhowie.com/aweber along with other articles about e-mail marketing.

Going Offline to Build the Relationship

When you start conducting business online, it's easy to be seduced by the automation and anonymity of e-mail and Web site. Imagine, a business that never requires you to talk with customers, lick a stamp, buy an envelope, or write a check. You could die and keep making money for years!

What many online-only businesspeople don't realize is they're sacrificing growth for convenience, or perhaps laziness. If you collect phone numbers, you can follow up via the telephone. Ditto for the fax machine, which is making a comeback as a permission-based follow-up medium that's considerably less cluttered than the e-mail inbox. (And faxes are less likely to be blocked than mass e-mail messages.) The mail, including the postal service as well as private carriers like FedEx and UPS, is a great way to stay in touch with prospects.

I can't begin to cover offline follow-up strategies in this book about AdWords. (Remember AdWords? This is a book about AdWords.) But they are so near and dear to my heart, I want to share one quick and clever way to use e-mail, your Web site and the telephone together to grow your business:

1. Choose a time and date for a teleconference call.

2. Go to www.freeconferencecall.com and sign up for a free 96-person conference call line.

3. E-mail your list to let them know about a teleconference you will be holding to answer their biggest questions. Include a link to a page on your Web site where they can take a short survey to register for the call.

4. Look over the survey results and pick the questions you will answer on the call.

5. Ask a friend or colleague with a nice voice to interview you by asking you the questions you've chosen. If you're brave, they can also moderate and help you field live questions from teleconference participants.

6. Record the call, using the www.freeconferencecall.com recording feature (free, but not such great quality), or an audio-recording service such as www.audioacrobat.com.

7. Download the recording, and either edit it with the free Audacity program (available at http://audacity.sourceforge.net) or the audio editing software of your choice, or post it as an .mp3 file to your Web site.

8. E-mail your list, letting them know that the teleconference is available for them to listen to online or download to their PC or iPod.

9. If you've said some good stuff, pay a transcription service to turn the recording into a Word document. (You can find freelance transcriptionists by posting a project at www.guru.com or any similar freelance brokerage site.) Edit it, make it graphically pretty, turn it into a PDF document, and put it on your Web site.

10. If you've shared some great material that your prospects and customers want, you can do any or all of the following:

    a. Give it away free on your site.

    b. Give it away free as an LGM in exchange for an opt-in.

    c. Turn it into a CD and/or printed manual and sell it as a product.

    d. Use it as a bonus to compel some other desired action.

    e. Let other people reproduce the CD and manual and include them as bonuses with their products.

    f. Come up with a brand new use that no one has ever thought of before.

Go to www.askhowie.com/phone for the detailed instructions and vendor list for the teleconference process.

Chapter 12

Building a "Climb the Ladder" Web Site

In This Chapter

▶ Understanding the goals of your Web site

▶ Discovering Web-site tools that turn visitors into buyers

▶ Using multimedia to get closer to your customers

▶ Turning your business into a testimonial farm

▶ Using PHP to personalize your site for returning customers

. . . .

*Y*our business is just a system for turning complete strangers into great customers. AdWords finds you the strangers, your ad invites them in, and your landing page opt-in and e-mail give you the ability to keep the conversation going. Your Web site contains the content that will turn leads into buyers, buyers into repeat customers, and customers into referral sources and advocates.

One way to look at your Web site is purely numerically: traffic in, money out. In a nutshell, the game of online marketing can be reduced to that equation. Your Web site, in this view, is a tool for extracting cash from visitors. You set up conversion tracking and analytics and reports to find out how good your Web site is at extracting a purchase from which visitors (see Chapters 14 and 15). You run split tests to increase the amount of money you get per visitor (see Chapter 13). But when you actually design and build your Web site, sales and money should be the farthest thing from your mind. Instead, you focus on growing customers.

The big goal of your Web site is to develop the relationship between you and your customers. Sales are part of that relationship, and an important part — after all, you can't take *satisfaction* or *good will* to the bank or the grocery store or the music store on Broad Street with the gorgeous Weber mandolins — er, excuse me, where was I?

Oh, yes: the relationship. The typical online business can identify several stages of customer: first-time buyer, second-time buyer, third-time buyer (now the customer is a habit, not a fluke), referral source, and advocate. You may be protesting that your business is different, because you only have one thing to sell to a customer. That may be true, for now, but the real competitive advantage online is not the best AdWords campaign, or the best Web graphics, but the best relationship with customers. If your customers are worth more to you than your AdWords competitors' customers are worth to them, you eventually win — and win big.

Your Web site can be a potent partner in farming the seeds of leads into fruit-bearing customers. (Hey, that last sentence was poetically metaphorical. Excuse me while I high-five myself.) This chapter shows you how to use various tools on your Web site to grow customers, clients, and an enthusiastic volunteer sales force.

Identifying the Rungs of Your Business Ladder

Take a few moments now to sketch the perfect trajectory of a new visitor to your Web site. What's the first measurable outcome you desire? An opt-in? A sale? To engage you in a chat? To ask a question via a form? To call your business phone?

Once they've taken that step, what's the next one? If they've opted in, it may be a sale, or a second opt-in to a new list, or attending a teleseminar, or scheduling a phone call. If they've already bought, maybe you have an upsell they should get. Maybe you want them to send you a testimonial, or to refer five friends, or to use the product they've bought, instead of putting it on a shelf unopened.

What's the top rung of your customer ladder? Think of the top 20% of your current customers — what puts them in that category? If you have customers who've maxed out your business, can you build a new rung at the top so they can ascend even higher? A private coaching club? A membership site? A chocolate-themed cruise?

Every business is different; take a few minutes now to identify the rungs of your business before continuing. Once you know where you want to go, it's much easier to help them get there. Let's look at a few rungs that are common to most businesses:

✔ **The Lead:** The bread and butter of the online business is the *lead* — the visitor with whom you can communicate even after he or she leaves your site. In Chapter 11, I cover strategies and tactics for getting visitors to opt in to your list. I also share how you can use e-mail to bring them back to your Web site. E-mail is great, but limited. The e-mail inbox is too competitive and distracting a space to hold an intimate conversation. It's like trying to have a date in a restaurant booth surrounded by comedians, competitors, fake-Rolex peddlers, and all their friends and family. Also, spam filters make it hard to say much of anything related to selling. The wise online marketer uses e-mail to bring leads back to the Web site.

The lead has uttered a soft, tentative "Maybe" in response to your overtures. Your job is to make the leads glad for the chance they've taken, and provide value far beyond their expectations. You are aiming for the three magic verbs: *know*, *like,* and *trust*. When your leads think they know you, feel warmly toward you, and believe you to be trustworthy, they will take a chance with a first purchase.

✔ **The First-Time Buyer:** The one-time customer has taken a leap of faith. The "Yes" is followed by "Okay, show me what you've got." Don't think of the first sale as *closing* anything. You customer just opened the door and invited you into the front hall. The customer hasn't taken your coat, or invited you to sit down. Now is the time to prove yourself.

✔ **The Second-Time Buyer:** The second sale shows that you've passed the first customer test. Your product or service did what you said it would, or more, and you haven't alienated the person with poor customer service. Your job now is to take your prospects off the market entirely, so they will never consider patronizing a competitor's business. They must feel that you are their protector, watching out for their best interests and more concerned for their needs than your own.

✔ **The Third-Time Buyer:** The third-time buyer has established a trend and a habit. These buyers have committed part of their own self-esteem to proving themselves right, and will continue to buy from you as long as you don't ignore or mistreat them. Your goal is to get them to the point where they feel comfortable telling their friends about you.

✔ **The Referrer:** Visitors to your Web site who have been referred by someone they trust is completely different from search engine or pay-per-click traffic. They come with positive expectations and an optimistic filter, and will doubt and argue less than a complete stranger. When your customers take the time and effort to send others to you, you have a business than can survive just about any change in Google's algorithm. There's just one more rung to take them to. . . .

✔ **The Loyal Advocate:** Is there a business in your town that you feel so good about, you would be angry if a competitor opened up? Those feelings are what you want to inspire in your customers. You want them act as your advocates, your advisors, your eyes and ears around the marketplace. You want them to post comments and questions to your blog, to agree to be recorded and filmed for testimonials, and to shout to the world that you run a great business.

Using Web Tools to Help Your Visitors up the Ladder

Let's simplify human behavior for a moment. Peter Bregman (www.bregman partners.com), author of *A Short Guide to Leading a Big Change*, points out that people take action when three things are true:

1. They know what to do (knowledge)

2. They can do it (capability)

3. They want to do it (motivation)

This chapter focuses mostly on the third element, motivation. How to get people to know, like, and trust you; to show them that the action you want them to take will help them avoid pain and gain pleasure; and that it's the easiest and quickest and cheapest way for them to get there. But the first two points are just as important. If your Web site is poorly designed, it doesn't matter how magnetic or persuasive you are. You can't convince someone to click a Buy button they can't find.

Design

The design of your Web site will either guide your visitors toward rungs of your ladder or make those rungs invisible or inaccessible. I've seen too many Web pages that look like they were designed to *prevent* sales: tiny fonts, distracting graphics, gratuitous Flash animation (as Lemony Snickett would say, "'Gratuitous' here means 'your Web designer spent a lot of time and money learning how to use that animation software and by golly, they're going to use it every chance they get'"), navigation systems determined by a template rather than what will get the visitor's attention, and shopping carts that require more clicks than a Wheel of Fortune booth in Point Pleasant Beach.

Is your navigation self-evident? If visitors wanted to buy *kettlebells* (big hunks of iron with handles used by hardcore fitness fiends), could they figure out how to find them from your home page? Do you use graphics and borders to shine a light on the most-looked-for links on your pages? Or do they have to drill through pages like Shop and Weights and Free Weights and Miscellaneous to find your Kettlebell selection?

I often coach online entrepreneurs who show me Web sites where the most important links are buried in long navigation bars or hidden below the scroll bar. When I tell them that I can't find how to get to the page for restaurant owners, they say things like, "It's in the submenu on the left. Just click Most Popular Pages and you'll see it."

As Mike Psenka of Universal Data (`www.universaldata.net`) points out, if you have to train your visitors to use your site, the navigation isn't, to use a software-design buzzword, *self-evident*. For Mike, *self-evident* isn't nearly strong enough a term. He strives to create software and reporting that is, in his words, "User Ridiculously Obvious." Take a look at your Web site with new eyes: Is it User Ridiculously Obvious?

The next time you're surfing and searching, pay attention to sites that seem easy and obvious to use. Notice where they place their buttons and links, and what they call them. Avoid the mystery buttons with icons and no names. Keep your design clean and functional — use everything you need, but no more. Look at the difference between the home pages of American Airlines (Figure 12-1) and JetBlue (Figure 12-2). The Continental page is busy, with lots of links, multiple offers, and several competing graphics. The big graphic at the top is animated, and keeps changing as you try to figure out where to go to conduct your business.

JetBlue's home page is simple and sparse, with few colors and a big obvious form for the number-one action on this page: booking a flight. The headline, "Free TV with purchase," next to a graphic of the video monitor in the back of an airplane seat, emphasizes the JetBlue difference: 36 TV channels on every flight.

Figure 12-1:
American Airlines' home page is cluttered and confusing.

Figure 12-2:
JetBlue's
home page
is simple
and clear,
focusing the
visitor on
the flight
booking
form.

When you start clicking into the site, the differences become even more apparent. Clicking American's Reservations navigation button brings down a long sub-menu with a huge array of options. (Figure 12-3). By contrast, when you click Where From to start booking your flight on the JetBlue site, a beautifully designed list of departure cities appears above the page, as shown in Figure 12-4. User-friendly? User Ridiculously Obvious.

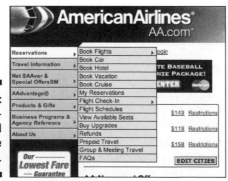

Figure 12-3:
Avoid hard-
to-read
menus like
this one.

Figure 12-4:
JetBlue's
menus are
slick and
easy to
read.

And if you're not convinced of the power of simplicity, perhaps you haven't seen this page: www.google.com. Google got to be the 900-pound gorilla of search partly by making it so easy to conduct a search. No competing graphics or links — just a plain box in the center of a nearly empty page. Other search engines competing with Google in the late 1990s were trying to cram every pixel on their home page with juicy content. Google won by not intimidating or confusing its users, as well as by delivering quick and relevant content.

Sales copy

Sales copy refers to the words you use to convince your visitor to take some action. You sell opt-ins, you sell free downloads, you sell phone calls, and of course you sell products and services.

Even in the dawning multimedia era of the Web, words matter. Your sales copy is what ultimately persuades visitors to take actions. We're creatures of inertia and hesitation when it comes to doing business. We don't want to get burned (again). We don't want to make big mistakes that will be cumbersome and costly to undo (again). As you write, focus on two elements: proof of performance and risk reduction. I will buy from you, assuming I want the big benefit you're promising, if I believe it will work for me and if I'm not taking a risk.

Proof can come in many forms. If you can demonstrate effectiveness, that's the best. Think of the vacuum-cleaner salesperson who shows that the vacuum can suck up a bowling ball — hard to argue with that! Online, many products defy demonstration, although video is expanding the horizon. The next best thing is to get testimonials and endorsements from real customers, describing in their own words what your product or service has done for them.

How long your sales copy should be has been the subject of a long (and utterly pointless) debate in marketing circles for decades. It should be exactly long enough to get the job done, and not one word longer. The comprehensiveness of your sales pitch depends on the price of the product (more expensive items generally require more substantiation), the severity of the need (the ER doctor doesn't need to give a long speech about why it would be good to staunch the flow of blood from the patient's aorta), and your visitor's familiarity with the product or the producer (I could probably sell J.K. Rowling's next book in five words — "Buy J.K. Rowling's New Book" — but it would take me considerably longer to convince you to buy my new Yiddish-style magic/fantasy novel, *Chaim Mendel and the Enchanted Phylacteries of Thomashevsky*).

Think about the length of your sales copy this way: How long would you talk on a live sales call if your prospect was interested? Would you say 25 words and then shut up? Don't underestimate your prospect's capacity for interest in solving a problem or attaining a goal.

Articles

Not every word on your Web site needs to convince. You build credibility, trust, and reciprocity by sharing your expertise. Remember, your sales copy is only as good as your reputation. Well-written and helpful articles establish your reputation as someone who knows what's good, and who seeks to be helpful.

Articles support the sales process not only by building your credibility. You can write articles that build the need for what you're selling. For example, if I sell meditation CDs for parents and kids, I could include articles about meditation: health effects, methods, instructions, stories about transformation brought about by meditation, and so on. If I sell special dichromatic green light bulbs for use during meditation, I can include articles about the healing properties of green light.

Articles can also dispel confusion and help your visitors take action. If you sell four brands of flat-screen TV, your visitor may become overwhelmed at all those choices — and do nothing. You can write reviews that compare the brands and models, and help visitors decide which one is right for them.

Blog

A Weblog, or *blog*, is a way of publishing Web content without requiring any design or coding skills. If you can write an e-mail, you can publish a blog. The way blogs have evolved, with bloggers linking to each other and carrying on hyperlinked discussions and arguments back and forth, lend themselves to platforms for expertise.

From its origins as a communications outpost for the hopelessly techie and its phase as a self-absorbed tell-all medium for high school kids, blogging has evolved into a powerful business tool. To be a credible blogger, you not only have to know your stuff, but have your pulse on the rest of your market. You'll discuss industry trends, amplify or argue points made by other blogs and Web sites in your industry, and act like a key opinion leader in your space.

Another feature of blogs is reader interactivity. Your visitors can add comments and questions, engaging in a conversation with you and each other. It's *your* blog; you benefit from being the host of the party.

Dave Taylor of www.intuitive.com teaches clients to blog for business purposes. Go to www.askhowie.com/blogrules to find his article on the 7 Don'ts of Business Blogging.

Your keywords' quality scores can benefit from an active blog on your site. Google spent much of 2006 and 2007 raising the relevance requirements of AdWords listings. You can improve the relevance of your landing page if it links to dozens or hundreds of other relevant pages. Google schedules its inspections of your site according to how often it thinks you update the site. An active blog, including comments by visitors, induces Google to visit more frequently. The more your site changes, the more up-to-date and relevant Google assumes it to be.

Live chat

I introduce live chat in Chapter 10, as part of a landing-page strategy. Live chat can live on every page of your Web site, so your visitors can ask questions whenever they feel confused or overwhelmed, or are close to a buying decision. E-mail responses take too long. Phone calls are too scary. Chat combines the instantaneous nature of the phone with the safety (and relative anonymity) of e-mail.

Chat as an engagement tool

You can include chat boxes wherever they will be the most beneficial on your site. Some good places to include a chat box are

✔ **On sales letter pages:** If it's a long letter, place chat buttons alongside or within the page in several places, so the reader doesn't have to scroll back up to the top to engage you.

✔ **On your order pages:** Chat boxes can prevent cart abandonment by allowing your visitors to voice final objections and get reassurance before placing the order.

✔ **On articles pages:** You or your staff can answer questions and demonstrate your knowledge and concern.

With some chat software, you don't have to wait for visitors to initiate the chat. You can invite visitors to chat; the invitation appears on-screen as a pop-up they can accept or decline.

Effective chats aren't aimless conversations, as the word *chat* may mistakenly imply. Ari Galper of www.unlockthegame.com recommends making them closed-loop conversations. Here's his flow, in a nutshell:

1. Introduction

2. Find out their situation

3. Reassure them that their problem can be solved

4. Wrap-up — recommend your solution

Ari teaches specific phrases that interrupt gently, generate trust, and create a space for discovery and problem-solving rather than heavy-duty selling. I've posted an in-depth interview with Ari on using live chat to improve Web site conversion on my Web site. Go to www.askhowie.com/chatwise to listen online, or to download the interview to your computer or MP3 player.

Chat as a tool for improving your Web site

When a visitor asks a question about your Web site, they are telling you where your site is missing the boat. Ari told me that one of his recurrent questions for a particular product was, "Does it comes with a guarantee?" After telling a number of visitors where they could read about the guarantee, he realized that the fact of the repeated question meant it wasn't obvious enough. He made the guarantee stand out more by changing its background color and border, the questions went away, and his conversation rate went up.

You can also use the chat interface to "spy" on your visitors as they browse your site. Figure 12-5 shows the interface for Ari's www.unlockthegame.com Web site provided by live-chat provider Live Person (www.liveperson.com). The top window shows a dozen current visitors, sorted by length of time on the site. The highlighted visitor's browsing history appears in the lower window. Additional tabs below the bottom window show you each visitor's chat history, as well as information about geographical location, operating system, and Web browser. A recent release of Live Person includes information about which AdWords campaign, ad group, and keyword brought the visitor to your site. You can even see what's on the visitor's computer screen by selecting the Page Viewer.

Figure 12-5: Chat software allows you to see all the current visitors on your site, how long they've been there, and what pages they view in what order.

The capability to watch your visitors' browsing behavior can be enlightening. Imagine a shopkeeper who couldn't see the aisles in the store, and never realized that an applesauce spill in Aisle 7 was preventing the sale of canned fruits and fruit juices. The path each visitor takes on your Web site tells you something about how you're guiding them, intentionally or not.

You can find gaps in your Web site by first asking the question, "What's the perfect path?" If a visitor came to your landing page, opted in, and then followed your Web site in a logical way to the next sale, what would that look like?

When you start observing the actual behavior of your visitors — how they jump around from page to page, refresh pages, go back to your home page, leave completely, and so on — you can identify the obstacles and poor signage that's confusing or alienating your visitors. When you identify a page that's breaking the flow, you can fix it.

Audio

The biggest drawback to the Internet as a business medium is its impersonal nature. Since people can't look each other in the eye and shake hands, trust will always be a big hurdle in developing business relationships online. Psychologists tell us that most human communication is nonverbal — body language and tone of voice. The sound of your voice on your Web site can go a long way toward making you more real and trustworthy.

You can easily spend thousands of dollars on Web-audio equipment, and in some cases the investment can be well worth it. But if you just want to see if the additional of a human voice can improve your conversion, start with a tool you already own and know how to use: the telephone.

Audio Acrobat offers a service for $20 a month that allows you to create audio files for your Web site by talking into a telephone or recording them on your computer. You can easily embed the files in your Web site or send them via e-mail. Visit www.askhowie.com/audio for a demonstration of the service, as well as a video tutorial that shows how to get audio onto your Web site within minutes.

Four ways to spice up your Web site with audio include these:

- ✔ **Welcome messages and guidance:** Robert Middleton puts his message and personality right in the center of his home page with an audio introduction. He qualifies the prospect, introduces himself and his Web site, acknowledges common objections, and ends with a clear call to action. The message lasts about a minute, and gives the visitor time to browse the home page and see Robert's smiling face to the left of the audio button. By the time the message is over, Robert's visitors have been welcomed, agitated, reassured, guided, and gently pushed toward the next step. Experience it for yourself at www.actionplan.com — and make sure your computer speakers are turned on.

- ✔ **Mini audio sales letters:** Mike Stewart takes the introductory audio message approach one step further with a mini sales letter. He includes two snippets of audio testimonial, and explains why information publishers need to add audio to their product mix. You can listen at www.internet audioguy.com by clicking the Play button at the right.

- ✔ **Testimonials:** Audio is a perfect medium for testimonials, which I cover near the end of Chapter 10. The more testimonials you can collect, the more credible your sales message. Ken McCarthy of www.thesystem seminar.org once remarked at a seminar that business owners should think of their business as a machine to create testimonials. I've collected many testimonials for Leads into Gold by requesting them at the end of a surprise bonus consultation that I offer. I e-mail some of my customers and offer them a 15-minute action consultation, and I set aside half an hour. After the consultation, I ask if they would do me a favor and phone in what they would say to someone who was on the fence about buying Leads into Gold. You can hear some of the best ones at `www.leadsintogold.com` near the bottom of the page.

Audio Acrobat (`www.audioacrobat.com`) allows you to create multiple testimonial lines, each with its own phone number, so you can provide recorded instructions specific to the product or service your caller is praising.

✔ **High perceived value in your content:** You can answer questions, interview experts or have other people interview you, read articles you've written, comment on current issues, solve common problems, and do it all over the phone without having to suffer writer's block. I discuss a teleseminar strategy at the end of Chapter 11; you can extend this method to collecting and deploying many kinds of valuable audio content.

One way to increase the perceived value of your online audio is to offer the same audio for sale as a CD. Your visitors have the choice to buy the CD for $24.95, or they can simply download the audio in MP3 format for free.

If you find you need to edit your audios, you'll find that a well-constructed sound-editing program is easier to use than a word processor. For PCs, I love Sony's Sound Forge Audio Studio program because it's cheap, powerful, and simple. The URL for Sound Forge is ridiculously long, so I'll post it at `www.askhowie.com/sonyaudio` as a live link. A more complicated but free program is the open-source sound editor Audacity, available at `http://audacity.sourceforge.net`. Audacity is also available in a Mac version.

Stick with two forms of online audio:

✔ **Streaming audio:** One format, used by Robert Middleton at `www.actionplan.com`, is streaming audio that can be heard online but not saved or downloaded. It's great for short clips, but a pain for long messages.

You can use the inconvenience factor to your advantage, by offering a downloadable version of the streaming audio in exchange for contact information. You can also sell the same audio on your Web site as a shippable CD, but allow people to download it for free. Knowing something has a price automatically increases the perceived value of a free item.

✔ **MP3 files:** The second format is the MP3 file, a format that can be played online through a player or downloaded and saved on a computer, where it can be synced with an iPod or other MP3 player. Think of your customers listening to your wisdom while driving in their cars or working out at the gym — what a rush!

Stay away from Real Media and Microsoft's Windows Media as formats — their players annoy users with constant pop-ups and reminders to buy or upgrade. MP3 is a universal format that sounds great and plays on virtually all players.

How to use Web video to increase sales

by Joe Chapuis (www.webvideozone.com)

Adding video to your Web site can help attract visitors, add value, and increase site visibility. But you've got to do it right. If you're not careful, putting video on your Web site can actually backfire, chasing people away and causing a lot of headaches for you in the process.

It's never been easier to create and add video to your Web site. But just like with anything else, there is a learning curve, and there are pitfalls. Just because it can be done, doesn't mean it should be done. You need to know when and where to use Web video — and when not to.

In addition, not everyone has the same programs and players on their computers. For example, if you produce all of your videos in QuickTime .mov format, people who don't have (or want to use) QuickTime will never see your video.

Your goal should then be to create videos that are accessible to the greatest common denominator. You'll want to make sure any video you offer is viewable to as many visitors as possible, while minimizing hassles and tech problems for your viewers.

And while it's true that placing video on the Web is now quite easy, that doesn't necessarily mean it's always a good idea. Sometimes, your message can be better told using text with a few images. In other instances, an audio message will suffice. Video isn't the end-all solution for everything you have to say.

So before you rush into posting video on your Web site, consider these important points:

1. Web video done poorly is worse than no video at all.

   This is especially true if your video clips don't play properly, or if the quality of the video reflects poorly on you or your site. In these cases, it would be better not to use Internet video on your site.

2. Internet video may not work for all visitors.

   Some Web surfers are still using Windows 98 or older operating systems. Many of these older systems do not support the playing of video very well. One solution is to offer your video clips in as many different video formats as possible. Unfortunately, this can be a frustrating and time-consuming process for you.

3. Know your target market.

   Not everyone experiences the Internet the same way. People access the Web at very different connection speeds. While more than half of the U.S. Web-connected population now enjoys a high-speed broadband experience (and for these people, video is no problem), there are still many people connecting via painfully slow telephone modems.

   By knowing who you are targeting, you can better determine if video makes sense for your site, as well as the best way to deploy it.

4. Video requires a lot of storage space.

   On average, a one-minute video clip of average quality and resolution often requires at least 2MB of Web hosting space. If you offer that same clip in the six most popular formats, it is possible that you would need 20MB of space — just for that one minute of video! And if you offer a total of 20 minutes of video, and provide it in all different formats, you could easily consume 400MB of Web space.

5. Video is a bandwidth hog.

   If 100 people click to view your 5-minute video at the same time, they could jointly require and consume 2GB of bandwidth, all at the same time! Depending upon your hosting package, that alone could exceed your allocated monthly bandwidth.

Imagine what would happen if 1,000 people clicked to view your 5-minute video . . . your Web host would likely crash, due to the inability to fulfill the huge bandwidth request. And your Web host won't be very happy. And neither will you, when they send you their bill.

6. Clicking away from your site and your Internet video is effortless.

Even with the fastest Web connection, viewing high quality video on a computer monitor can be tedious — especially compared to watching that same video on TV. For best results, Web video clips should be short (under 3 minutes) and to the point.

Once the novelty wears off (and it will, once video becomes commonplace — very soon), people are going to be less willing to sit there and watch some idiot skateboarding off his roof.

In order to grab and hold attention, and get some kind of result, Internet video needs to be: compelling, useful, and/or entertaining.

7. Be careful when choosing an Internet video format.

Whether the video you plan to offer is a computer screen tutorial, or live video footage shot with a camcorder, you may want to offer your video in multiple formats, making it viewable by as many people as possible.

But at the same time, too many choices may confuse and overwhelm your audience. In addition, there are time and cost considerations for creating and deploying your videos. If you offer five different choices, you need to create and upload five different videos (and what happens if you need to make a change to the video?).

Joe Chapius is the founder of www. webvideozone.com, *which offers tools, tips and tutorials to help businesses profit from Web video. Go to* www.askhowie.com/video *for Joe's reviews of various video formats and methods of hosting video files, as well as his take on the right and wrong way to use YouTube/Google Video.*

Video

As more and more Web users upgrade from dialup to broadband connections, the Internet is ready to serve as an interactive multimedia channel. YouTube has already trained us to watch video online. If you sell products, you can combine the visual and auditory richness of a QVC or infomercial with the click-to-buy immediacy of a Web page with AdWords' ability to show the right message to the right person.

You can use video to demonstrate products, to show even more of your personality to your visitors, to display powerful testimonials, to chat with your market, and much more. With a decent video camera and good lighting, certain types of video content are almost as easy to create as text and audio.

Saying "make yourself at home" with video

Online video can serve as a warm welcome to your Web site; a way to say hello, orient your visitor, and create an immediate emotional bond. If you think of your Web site as your home, and your visitors as, well, your visitors, you can open the door, smile, invite them in, take their coat, and offer them a chair, a cup of tea, and directions to the bathroom. Joy Milkowski accomplishes this with a short video welcome at www.nefiber.com.

Giving a shop tour with video

Josephine Canovas is a professional horse breeder and trainer in Spain. She sells Andalusian horses internationally. Obviously, most of her customers will not travel to her horse farm to view the horses and their living conditions. She uses video to show, rather than tell, about her horses and the care they receive. At www.andalusians-for-you.com/break-page-1.html you can view raw video of the stable and its daily happenings.

Running a Home Shopping Channel on your site

The Web boasts several significant advantages over TV shopping shows:

- ✔ The production costs are much lower.

- ✔ You are showing products to people who are searching for those products, rather than just channel surfing during commercials.

- ✔ Your visitors can program your channel to show the exact product they're interested in right now, rather than wading through hours of knives and dehydrators to get to the levitating steamer basket.

- ✔ You can make money with small market items because you're attracting high-quality traffic and you don't have to keep paying to air your show.

- ✔ You can complete the transaction in the same medium as you're selling. When you watch TV, you can't buy the product using the TV — you need to pick up the phone.

At www.myweddingfavors.tv (shown in Figure 12-6), you can watch a home shopping style show and choose among Beach Favors, Seasonal Favorites, Bridal Shower Favorites and others. When the hosts show and describe an item, the Web page changes to display that item to the right of the video, along with buttons for More Info, E-mail a Friend, and Buy This Item.

Displaying customer testimonials

Ken McCarthy of www.thesystemseminar.org has been collecting video testimonials during his seminars since 2002. He makes them available on a brilliant site, www.askagrad.com. The home page of the site invites visitors to self-identify based on their current situation, and then serves the video testimonials most relevant to that group. If you visit the site and describe yourself as a Smart Beginner, you'll be taken to a page that includes a testimonial that I gave in 2002 (shown in Figure 12-7), when I had short hair and no dragon tattoo across the bridge of my nose. Oh, wait, I still don't have a dragon tattoo on the bridge of my nose. I must have been thinking of someone else.

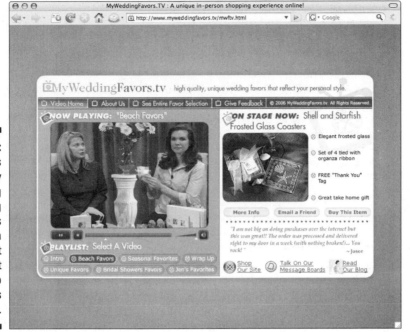

Figure 12-6:
The videos on My Wedding Favors bring products alive in ways that static text and photo Web pages cannot.

Figure 12-7:
The author gives a testimonial for the System Seminar at www.askagrad.com.

Teaching with video

Whatever your business, you have expertise that other people lack. When you make that expertise available online, you gain credibility as an expert helper, not just a self-interested peddler. Video offers the highest emotional bandwidth for your visitors to assess your knowledge and your character. Oliver Sachs wrote in *The Man Who Mistook His Wife for a Hat* about a group of patients in the aphasia ward who were laughing hysterically at a speech given by then-president Reagan. Although the patients had lost the ability to understand language, they ascertained he was lying by observing his facial expressions, gestures, and vocal tones and cadences. Just as video can destroy trust, it can also build trust when your goal is to be helpful and straight with your market.

The Kabbalah education site `www.arionline.info` features instructional videos that introduce the subject of Kabbalah and the instructors. Through music, spoken word, and moving images, the videos not only instruct but elicit emotional reactions. Just as many of us have developed crushes on total strangers because we see them in Hollywood movies (I still have a thing for Amy Irving in *Crossing Delancey*, heaven help me), skillful video can create relationships with customers you haven't met yet, and may never meet in person.

The *For Dummies* people wouldn't let me include actual videos on these pages, even though I know it can be done from watching *Harry Potter* movies. Even thought I can't show you any video examples in these pages, you can go to `www.askhowie.com/video` for links and discussion of good and bad uses of Internet video.

Recognizing and welcoming returning visitors with PHP

In Chapter 10 I show you how the PHP programming language can serve your visitors customized Web pages straight from the AdWords click. You can also use PHP to recognize returning visitors, so you can present them with relevant information and offers.

You've seen this in action if you're an Amazon.com customer. You're greeted by name, which is nice, but the really powerful application is the personalized recommendations based on your previous shopping history. In Figure 12-8, Amazon.com asks me if I'm aware that it sells organic food. Actually, I wasn't aware of it, because I've never bought groceries from Amazon.com before. So how did it know/figure out/guess that I'm into healthy eating? Hmmm, do you think my prior purchases of *Disease-Proof Your Child: Feeding Kids Right* by Joel Fuhrman (St. Martin's Griffin) and *The China Study: The Most Comprehensive*

Study of Nutrition Ever Conducted and the Startling Implications for Diet, Weight Loss, and Long-Term Health by T. Colin Campbell and Thomas M. Campbell II (Benbella Books), had anything to do with it?

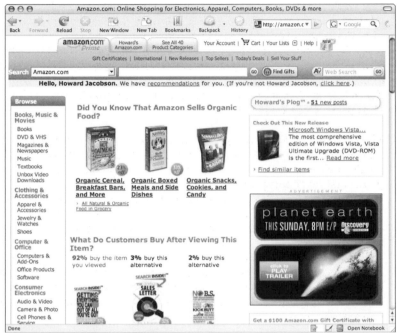

Figure 12-8: Amazon.com offers me organic food, probably based on my history of buying and browsing healthy cookbooks and other books on natural health.

Amazon.com uses its enormous database of customer behavior to make targeted offers. You can accomplish the same thing, on a much simpler scale, by engaging a PHP programmer to create a script that recognizes people who've visited your site before, and make the next offer. Rob Goyette of www.vaelos.com gives the following example of a simple returning customer page headline for an online sporting goods store: "Welcome back, Howie, I hope you're enjoying your new ping-pong table. Do you want to see our line of tournament-quality paddles and balls?"

Part V
Testing Your Strategies and Tracking Your Results

The 5th Wave   By Rich Tennant

"We're using just-in-time inventory and just-in-time material flows which have saved us from implementing our just-in-time bankruptcy plan."

In this part . . .

One of my favorite things about the Internet is how cheaply and quickly I can fail — and how much I can learn from each failure. This part reveals simple strategies that virtually guarantee success if you implement them diligently, no matter how many failures you encounter.

Chapter 13 explains how to continually improve your ads by running multiple ads simultaneously and showing the different versions randomly to Google searchers. (Hint: Write two ads — Google does this automatically if you know how to change the default campaign settings.) Here's where you also get a handle on split-testing pages on your Web site.

The immensely powerful AdWords conversion-tracking feature is covered in Chapter 14. I show you how to add code to your Web site so Google can tell you how much money you're making or losing from every single ad and keyword. Armed with this intelligence, you can dramatically improve profitability and reduce your AdWords spend.

In Chapter 15, I introduce Google Analytics, a comprehensive Web site statistics program that ties in with AdWords to give you even more information about how to design an effective Web site.

Chapter 13

How You Can't Help Becoming an Advertising Genius

Most people find that writing an effective AdWords creative is challenging. In the old days (2004, actually), advertisers found their ads swatted down constantly by the 0.5% CTR (Click-Through Rate) threshold. That is, not even 5 in 1000 searchers would click their ad, and Google felt that an ad so unattractive did not deserve to remain active.

The difficulty of successful ad creation is understandable — you've got 130 characters to convince someone to choose your offer over 19 other close-to-identical ads on the same page. Plus, writing good ads is tough in the best of circumstances.

Many elite Internet marketers attend the annual System Seminar (`www.thesystemseminar.org`). At one of these events, Perry Marshall of `www.perrysmarshall.com` demonstrated the need for split testing by challenging audience members — professional marketers all — to choose the more effective ad or headline from a series of 10 split tests. The best of us got no more than 4 or 5 out of 10 correct. As we held our hands up high and proud for having achieved 50 percent on the test, Perry shot us down: "If I had flipped a coin, I would have done as well as you. Congratulations. You guys are as smart as a penny."

If you want to be smarter than a penny, you must apply the most powerful tool in the marketer's arsenal: split testing.

In this chapter, I show you how to set up split testing with AdWords and ana-lyze the results. I tell you about split-testing landing pages, as well as your entire sales process. Also, you discover only what you need to know about *statistical significance* (which, in this case, relates to your confidence level that the split-testing results are repeatable) to make the best choices about your ads.

Capturing the Magic of Split Testing

Nothing leads to improvement faster than timely and clear feedback. While a million monkeys typing would eventually produce the entire works of Shakespeare, they would get there much faster if they got a banana every time they typed an actual word, and an entire banana split when they man-aged a rhymed couplet in iambic pentameter. (Can you tell I've been reading *Shakespeare For Dummies*, by John Doyle and Ray Lischner?) And for every nonword, someone would chuck a copy of *Typing Shakespeare For Monkeys* at them.

Now suppose the monkeys could keep and understand a written record of the characters that produced bananas, banana splits, and no reward. After a while, you would see more and more real words and Shakespearean phrasing, and fewer xlkjdfsdfsr. Ouch!

AdWords contains the world's simplest mechanism for getting timely and clear feedback on your ads. You can create multiple ads, which AdWords shows to your prospects in equal rotation, and you can receive automatic and ongoing feedback.

Split testing is not an AdWords innovation — direct marketers have been test-ing customers' response rates since Moses got two tablets of command-ments. *Readers' Digest* used to choose headlines for its articles by sending postcards to readers, asking which articles they would be interested in read-ing in an upcoming issue. The list of articles was actually a list of headlines for the same article.

Here's how split testing works in AdWords:

1. **Run two ads simultaneously within a single ad group.**

2. **Monitor the effectiveness of both ads at eliciting the customer response you want.**

   Continue monitoring until one of those ads has proven itself better at its calling.

3. **Declare the proven ad the winner (or, in marketing geek-speak, the *control*).**

4. **Retire the less successful ad, replace it with a new challenger, and repeat the contest.**

   If the challenger does better, it becomes the new control. If the control maintains supremacy, you send a different challenger up against it.

The beauty of this split-testing system is that you can't help but improve your results over time. If a new ad proves worse than your control, simply delete it. And the added beauty is that you don't even have to know what you're doing to improve your ad's effectiveness. While market intelligence, creativity, and writing skill help, mere trial and error — when funneled through split testing — can boost your results significantly.

One of my early AdWords projects was an ad for a direct-marketing home-study course for small businesses (see the series of ads in Figure 13-1). An early ad, headlined "Cold calling — now illegal," achieved a 0.7% CTR. The final ad I used — "Cold calling not working?" — nearly quadrupled that with a 2.7% CTR. The big lesson from this long series of ads is this: I had no idea what I was doing at the time, yet I still succeeded. Take a few minutes and examine each of the ads carefully. Be honest — could you predict which of these ads would do better than the rest? I couldn't. I still can't. But the numbers don't lie, and I was able to turn a marginal product into a success thanks to split testing.

Cold calling not working? Discover a powerful alternative. Free report and 2 chapter download. www.LeadsIntoGold.com	2.60%	**End cold calling forever** Small business marketing system. Download 2 chapters for free. www.leadsintogold.com	1.35%	
Cold calling not working? Discover an effective alternative. Free report and 2 chapter download. www.LeadsIntoGold.com	2.35%	**Stop cold prospecting.** Small business marketing system. Free report and 2 chapter download. www.leadsintogold.com	1.04%	
End cold calling forever Lead generation system explained. Free report and 2 chapter download. www.LeadsIntoGold.com	2.28%	**End cold calling forever** and make more money. Free report and 2 chapter download. www.leadsintogold.com	1.00%	
End cold calling forever Lead generation system explained. Free report and 2 chapter download. www.leadsintogold.com	2.26%	**End cold calling forever** Small business marketing system. Free report and 2 chapter download. www.leadsintogold.com	0.83%	
Cold calling ineffective? Discover a powerful alternative. Free report and 2 chapter download. www.LeadsIntoGold.com	2.22%	**Stop cold calling forever** Small business marketing system. Free report and 2 chapter download. www.leadsintogold.com	0.82%	
End cold calling forever Attract customers automatically. Free report and 2 chapter download. www.LeadsIntoGold.com	2.18%	**Cold calling -now illegal** Effective alternative explained. Free report and 2 chapter download. www.LeadsIntoGold.com	0.76%	
End cold calling forever Attract customers automatically. Free report and 2 chapter download. www.LeadsIntoGold.com	2.04%	**End cold calling forever** Free report and 2 chapter download. Attract customers automatically. www.leadsintogold.com	0.00%	
End cold calling forever Free report and 2 chapter download. Lead generation system explained. www.leadsintogold.com	1.95%	**Stop wasteful advertising** Small business marketing system. Free report and 2 chapter download. www.leadsintogold.com	0.00%	
End cold calling forever Small business marketing system. Free report and 2 chapter download. www.leadsintogold.com	1.76%			

Figure 13-1:
The author ignorantly split tests his way to profitability.

Conducting Split Testing with AdWords

Split testing with AdWords follows the four-step process outlined by in the preceding section. You can prepare yourself to launch a series of split-testing ads by getting curious about what messages will be most compelling to your prospects. Turn each message into an ad and get ready to have fun.

Creating a challenger ad

Creating your second ad is even easier than creating your first (see Chapter 3 for step-by-step instructions):

1. **From the Campaign Management tab, click the campaign that contains the ad group you're working on.**

2. **Click the Ad Group to which you are adding an ad.**

3. **Click the Ad Variations tab.**

4. **Next to + Create New Ad, click the Text Ad button, as shown in Figure 13-2.**

   An ad template with sample copy appears on-screen.

Figure 13-2: Creating a new ad on the Ad Variations tab.

5. **Type over the existing copy and URL with your challenger ad's copy and URL.**

6. **Click the Save Ad button.**

7. **Below the ad at the top of the Ad Group summary page, click the small View All link to confirm the existence of a second ad.**

After your challenger ad is in place, you want to make sure that your two ads will compete fairly. Google assumes you're too busy (or lazy) to monitor your split tests, so the default setting is for AdWords to show the ad with the higher CTR more, and gradually let the poorer-performing ad slip into oblivion.

You want to override this setting for two reasons:

- ✔ An ad with a lower CTR may still be the more profitable ad (see Chapter 14 for details of this apparent paradox).

- ✔ When you let AdWords evaluate the ads without your supervision, you don't learn anything that makes you a smarter advertiser. The faster you declare winning and losing ads, the faster your marketing improves.

Here's how you override the AdWords default setting that may kill an ad without your approval. (*Note:* You establish this setting on the campaign level, so you may need to do this with each campaign.)

1. **From the Campaign Management tab, click the campaign that contains the ad group you're working on.**

2. **Click Edit Campaign Settings.**

   A page with various campaign-level settings appears.

3. **Under Advanced Options, the fourth setting is called Ad Serving. Select the Rotate: Show Ads More Evenly radio button.**

4. **Click the Save Changes button at the bottom of the Campaign Settings page.**

Now you're split testing properly. Once you install conversion tracking (see Chapter 14), you have the ability to compare the profitability of your ads. Until then, the only thing you can compare is the CTR.

Monitoring the split test

Just as you wouldn't put a cake in a 350° F oven and not pay attention to when it was done, you wouldn't set up a split test and then ignore the results. There are three ways to check up on your cake to make sure it doesn't burn and the fork comes out clean:

✔ **Haphazardly:** Check up on your cake when you think of it. As long as you catch it before the smoke alarm does, the cake might turn out okay.

✔ **Annoyingly:** Set your watch to beep every few minutes to remind you to check the cake.

✔ **Geekily:** Install a sensor in the oven that alerts you when the cake is done.

These three methods are available for monitoring your AdWords split tests as well:

✔ **With the haphazard method,** you can look at each ad group once a day, once every three days, once a week, whenever Dartmouth wins a football game, and so on. The interval you choose should relate to the amount of traffic your ads are getting. For example, if you get 50 click-throughs per day, you might want to check your ads every day. A huge stream of traffic will give you a winner much quicker than a trickle, all other things being equal. But even if your traffic is massive, wait at least a couple of days before declaring a winner. Visitors checking out your ad at three o'clock in the morning on Sunday are likely to be very different from Monday afternoon visitors. You want to collect a representative sample to be sure your results are accurate.

✔ **With the annoying, repetitive method,** you can create reports within AdWords and schedule those reports (see Chapter 14).

✔ **With the geeky, pass-the-buck method,** you can subscribe to a third-party service that monitors all your split tests and e-mails you when you have a winner (see the section, "Automating your testing with Winner Alert" later in this chapter).

Declaring a winner

Okay, so you're watching your split tests with eagle eyes and keen concentration. How do you know when one ad has outperformed another? After all, as the investment ads say, "Past performance doesn't guarantee future results." Fortunately, the testing process is simple and straightforward when you're running a single test of two different ads. You just want to answer the question, "Is this result real, or just a random coincidence?" That's where your friend and mine — statistical significance — makes a welcome appearance.

Understanding statistical significance

If I flip a coin twice and it lands heads both times, should I assume that coin will always come up heads? Of course not — two flips don't give me enough data to reach that conclusion. What about four flips, all heads? Less likely, but still plausible? What about ten flips, all heads? Are we getting a tad suspicious now? It could still be due to random chance — after all, every single flip of a fair coin has an equal chance of landing heads or tails — or, possibly, this is no fair coin. If I get to 20, 30, 100 flips with no tails in sight, I can be pretty sure something's up.

In your AdWords split testing, you're looking for information that will tell you that something's up. You want to know that one ad is truly better than another, and that the difference in CTR is not due to randomness. If you run two ads with identical text but different URLs (`www.ComfortSoap.com` versus `www.YouProbablyNeedaShower.com`), and the first URL gets clicked three times and the second not once, is that enough data to retire the second ad and bring in a new challenger? Just as with the coin, you can never know for absolute certain. Statistical significance tells you the probability that you're making the right choice.

Testing for significance

If you're doing it yourself, here are the steps to assessing the significance of your results and deciding whether to declare a winner:

1. **From your AdWords account, click through to the Ad Group you want to test.**

2. **Click the Ad Variations tab, and write down the following numbers:**

   - Number of clicks for Ad #1

   - Impressions for Ad #1

   - Number of clicks for Ad #2

   - Impressions for Ad #2

3. **Go to `www.askhowie.com/split` and enter the four numbers in the appropriate fields.**

4. **Look at your confidence interval and see whether you have a winner.**

I'm willing to accept a 95% threshold for my split testing. I can live with the knowledge that 1 out of every 20 split tests is giving me a bogus sense of confidence. Below that, and I want to keep running the test until I achieve significance, or until I'm satisfied that there really is no difference between the two ads.

What if you have no winner?

Let's say you're testing two ads, and they're running neck and neck for days. Weeks. Months. In this case, you're losing money by continuing the test. Sure, at some point the data might tip one way or the other, but the simple fact is, the difference isn't going to be important in real life. Drop the challenger (keeping the control makes sense because it's got more history behind it) and get a new challenger. Pull the plug on a test when each ad has at least 100 clicks.

Strategies for Effective Split Testing

Many AdWords beginners understand the concept of split testing, but do it haphazardly and without strategy. They learn that split testing is too confusing and complicated, and give up on the most powerful weapon in their marketing arsenal. The following sections discuss three strategies to assure a streamlined and effective split-testing process.

1. Start wide, get narrow

When you begin split-testing in an ad group, choose two very different ads. You may want to focus on different markets (stay-at-home dads versus divorced/widowed dads with full custody), different emotional responses (greed versus fear), or different benefits (lose weight versus prevent heart disease). Get the big picture right before drilling down to the details. It does you no good to test *easy* versus *simple* in a headline if your prospects don't care about ease or simplicity, but just whether it can run on batteries.

Once you discover the right market, key benefits, and the emotional hot buttons of that market, you can start testing more specific elements (see the upcoming section, "Generating Ideas for Ad Testing").

2. Keep track of your tests

Remember high-school chemistry class? You had to buy a marble notebook and keep track of all your experiments, including date, hypothesis, experiment design, and results.

Chances are that your bright ideas about ad testing are not new. If you don't keep track somehow, you'll find yourself repeating experiments to which you already know the answer. Keeping track of your results in a marble notebook, or its digital equivalent (a Word document, private blog, or Excel spreadsheet), is crucial to moving forward efficiently.

3. Split testing is just asking questions

Split testing can become so mechanical, it's easy to forget the purpose is to make you smarter by learning what makes your customers tick — er, *click*.

Perry Marshall distinguishes between true market research and what he calls "opinion research." Opinion research is what people *say* they'll do. Market research is what they *actually* do. Split testing is a powerful form of market research that will provide answers to whatever questions you ask. As the computer programmers are fond of saying, "Garbage In, Garbage Out." If you ask intelligent questions, you'll get useful answers.

So before you run a split test, take a moment to write down (in your lab notebook, of course) the question you want your prospects to answer for you. Then design a split test that asks that question.

The following figures show some examples of good questions and the split tests that were set up to answer them:

How much traffic do I give up if I put the price of the product in the ad? (See Figure 13-3.)

Figure 13-3:
Including the price in an ad cuts my traffic in half.

Variations	Clicks	Impr.	CTR ▼
Beat Gout with Food. End the pain - take control. Downloadable book - quick read. VitalHealthInstitute.com	66	31,931	0.20%
Beat Gout with Food. End the pain - take control. Downloadable book - $17.77 VitalHealthInstitute.com	34	32,024	0.10%

Will positioning my product as a "professional shares his secrets" increase clicks, compared to flagging the benefit of family fun? (See Figure 13-4.)

Figure 13-4:
The "pro-tells-all" approach is a clear winner.

Variations	Clicks	Impr.	CTR ▼
Get started Beekeeping. Set up hives, harvest honey - stay safe and have fun! A pro tells all. www.Beekeeping-Secrets.com	287	6,071	4.72%
Get started Beekeeping. Set up hives, harvest honey - be safe and have fun! Family activity. www.Beekeeping-Secrets.com	203	4,781	4.24%

Generating Ideas for Ad Testing

You want to test broadly different ideas before getting into details. Don't worry about whether description line 2 should have a comma in it before you've figured out the answers to your big questions. Imagine that you're searching for the most delicious plum in the world. First you test the orchard to make sure it has plum trees and not orange trees. Once you've found the plum orchard, start testing trees to find the tree with the best plums. Once you've found the best tree, see whether you prefer the plums near the top or closer to the ground. On the north or the south side. Then taste the fruit on different limbs, and once you've found the most promising limb, see which branch yields the best fruit.

David Bullock's (www.davidbullock.com) list of big questions from Chapter 6 comes in handy here:

- ✔ Who is looking?
- ✔ What are they looking for?
- ✔ Why are they looking for it?
- ✔ What will be the end result of their search?
- ✔ What does the searcher want the ultimate outcome to be?
- ✔ What is the emotional good feeling they seek?
- ✔ What emotional outcome are they trying to avoid?
- ✔ Who does the searcher care about?
- ✔ What does the searcher care about?

In other words, split test the ads to discover the demographics and psychographics of your market. Who are they — working mothers or single career women taking care of aging parents? What big benefit are they looking for in your product — saving time or assuaging guilt? Are they angry at their company or do they feel grateful? Who do they want to help them with this problem — Walter Cronkite or Jon Stewart?

Use your split tests to answer these questions as best you can. Write down a hypothesis and brainstorm two ads that will prove or disprove it. Once you've tested the big ideas, turn your attention to the little things that can make a big difference:

- ✔ **Order of lines:** If you're highlighting the benefit on line 1 and explaining a feature on line 2, try switching the order of the two lines.

- ✔ **Display URLs:** If you buy a bunch of domain names related to your main domain, you can point them all to the same Web site and test which domain name attracts the right customers. If you have the .com and .org for the same domain, will one outperform the other?

- ✔ **Capitalization:** Finding the right capitalization of your URL to make its meaning stand out is an art form. For example, I found that LeadsintoGold.com did better than leadsintogold.com in almost every test.

- ✔ **Synonyms:** Try variations of your benefits: simple/easy/quick/no sweat.

✔ **Punctuation:** Perry Marshall talks about the cadence of an ad — the way the searchers hear it in the mind's ear can subtly influence whether they resonate with it. Use punctuation to make the phrase more melodic and persuasive. Figure 13-5 shows what happened when I used a comma to put the emphasis on *You* instead of on *Instead*:

Figure 13-5: In this split test, a comma quadruples the CTR.

Variations	CTR ▼
Cold Calls Don't Work Prospects Hanging Up on You? Get Them to Call You, Instead! LeadsintoGold.com	2.02%
Cold Calls Don't Work Prospects Hanging Up on You? Get Them to Call You Instead! LeadsintoGold.com	0.49%

The ad with the comma is four times as effective as the other one. Without testing, there's no way I would have predicted the effect would be so profound.

Tools for Split Testing

With the proper tools, split testing can be the most powerful tactic in your entire marketing strategy. The following tools allow you to split test faster to improve faster.

Automating your testing with Winner Alert

My AdWords account is quite large at this point. I have 27 separate campaigns. Many of the campaigns include dozens of ad groups. Each of these groups is running a split test pretty much all the time. I probably have to monitor well over 100 split tests simultaneously. If I were to go into each ad group and pull out the data, and enter it into a statistical significance calculator, it would take me the better part of a day just to assess the tests. And that doesn't even include the time it takes me to think up new ad variations to challenge the winners.

If you're just starting out and you're running fewer than 10 ad groups at a time, you won't feel my pain. But once your campaigns grow, you'll either stop tracking the results of your tests, or you'll wait too long to find winners. Waiting too long means you're ignoring profit-growing market data, and you're showing prospects suboptimal ads.

To help alleviate this problem, I created a tool called Winner Alert that automates the process of tracking the statistical significance, and e-mails you whenever one of your split tests produces a winner. It's a great tool, and when you're ready for it, you can try it free for a month. Go to www.askhowie.com/winner for video demos and your coupon code.

Turbocharging your testing with Taguchi

The Taguchi Method lets you test hundreds of variations in a fraction of the time it would take if you used a standard A-B split. It's not for beginners; the methodology is so complicated, it's easy to fall into the Garbage-In-Garbage-Out trap and believe you have the answer to Life, the Universe, and Everything because the printout looks so impressive.

You should consider Taguchi testing if and only if your keywords get at least several thousand daily impressions each, and if the person setting up your test has experience using Taguchi for marketing. Taguchi testing was originally developed to reduce manufacturing errors, and many practitioners misapply a manufacturing mindset to the marketing process. David Bullock is the premiere Taguchi marketer who applies the method to AdWords. You can find an article he wrote to protect you from incorrect and unnecessary use of Taguchi at www.askhowie.com/taguchi.

Split Testing Web Pages

You can split test other elements of your Web site (and your sales funnel) using AdWords' split-testing capabilities. For example, you can run two visually identical ads with different destination URLs. If you have conversion tracking set up (see Chapter 14), you'll be able to see which Web page produced more leads and sales just by comparing your two ads' cost-per-conversion.

Once you've mastered the techniques in Part V, you can benefit from some third-party tools that make it almost as easy to test and track Web pages as it is to split test Google ads. Bonus Chapter 1 (available as a PDF file at www.dummies.com/go/adwords) describes a couple of the best of these tools — and tells you where to get them.

Chapter 14

Slashing Your Costs with Conversion Tracking

Say you're split-testing two ads, and one gets a conversion rate of 1.00%, while the other converts only 0.77%. The first ad is definitely a keeper, right? Without conversion tracking, you might think so. But what if the first ad attracts lots of non-buyers, while the second ad gets clicks from buyers? Remember that a click on your ad means one thing for certain: You've just paid Google. When you think about it this way, your AdWords strategy shifts from trying to get the highest CTR to enticing only the most qualified prospects to your site. In order to tell which ad leads to sales and not just clicks, you need to install conversion tracking.

By *conversion*, Google simply means an action that you want a visitor to take on your Web site. When you can track a visitor's actions on your site, you know what clicks lead to sales. Conversion tracking also allows you to bid more intelligently on keywords. You may find that a high-traffic keyword that's costing you a lot of money isn't actually generating leads and sales. You can then lower your bid, change your offer, or fire the keyword. Without conversion tracking, all your campaign-management efforts are shots in the dark, tinkering with inputs without really knowing what's happening at the other end. It's like learning to shoot free throws in basketball with no feedback about whether your shot went in or missed left, right, too far, or too short.

Conversion tracking is simply a snippet of code added to your Web site that places a cookie on your visitors' computers. This cookie tells Google where the visitors came from, down to the keyword and the ad, and what they did on your site. You can see which ads and keywords are making you money, and which aren't. In this chapter, I show you how to set up conversion tracking correctly (do it wrong and you'll suffer from the GIGO — Garbage In, Garbage Out — Syndrome and make lots of bad decisions). You'll see how to read and interpret the data generated by conversion tracking, and how to improve your account based on this new intelligence. You'll also discover how to design quick-scan reports that can be generated automatically and e-mailed to you on a regular basis.

Setting Up Conversion Tracking

From the Campaign Management tab, click Conversion Tracking from the sub-menu (see Figure 14-1). Before getting started on the next page, watch the step-by-step Flash demo (either from the link in the body of the page, or from the link Understanding Conversion Tracking under Helpful Documentation on the right. When you're ready, click the Start Tracking Conversions button to continue.

Figure 14-1:
Initiating
conversion
tracking.

| **Campaign Management** | Reports | Analytics | My Account |

Account Snapshot | Campaign Summary | Tools | Conversion Tracking

Choosing a conversion type

Google identifies five different types of conversion that you may want to track: sales, leads, signups, views of a page, and other, as shown in Figure 14-2. You can track as many different conversions as you want. The following list gives you a look at the five types of conversions so you determine when it makes sense to use each one:

- ✔ **Purchase/Sale:** If you sell products online, you can determine exactly how much money you make from each ad and keyword.

- ✔ **Lead:** If you collect contact information so you can follow up with Web site visitors, you can track leads. If you don't sell products online, and use the Web mostly for lead generation, you can get very powerful information on cost-per-lead for your ads and keywords.

- ✔ **Signup:** Google distinguishes between signups and leads; I don't. If someone subscribes to my online newsletter, then by golly, I think of them as a lead. If you maintain two lists, you can distinguish them by treating one as a list of leads and the other as a list of signups.

✔ **Views of a Key Page:** Let's say you have a certain page that you want visitors to see because you've noticed a connection between traffic to that page and the success of your business. Maybe it's the About Us page; maybe a powerful testimonial; maybe your daily menu. You can determine which ads and keywords reliably generate visitors who get to that page.

✔ **Other:** I can't think of any others. If you can, this is the one to use.

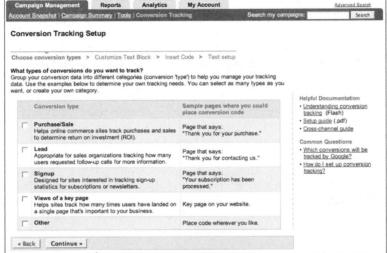

Figure 14-2: You can track several types of conversion simultaneously.

Choose one of these types for your first conversion to track, and click Continue at the bottom of the page. On the next page, you'll be able to design the block of text that lets your Web site visitors know that Google is monitoring their online activity. The default is one line of white text on a gray background. Google will automatically adjust the text color — either white or black — to be visible against the background you choose. Customize this text block to keep it from standing out on your Web page. Generally, I leave the default alone and just click Continue at the bottom.

Selecting language and security level

Before generating the tracking code, you need to tell Google two more things: the language of your Web page (English, Spanish, Russian, and so on), and the security level of the page on which you will place the code.

✔ **Language:** From the drop-down menu, select the language of your text block. Google will translate the `"Google Site Stats — send feedback"` text block into that language.

✔ **Security Level:** The tracking code goes on the page following the conversion. You are concerned only with the security level of that confirmation page, the one where you put the code. You have two choices, based on the URL prefix:

```
http:// - normal security
https:// - heightened security
```

In other words, if the URL of the page your visitor goes to *following* the conversion starts with `https://`, then choose the https:// option from the Select a Security Level drop-down list. Not doing so will cause your visitor to see a nasty little security-alert pop-up.

Generating and copying the code

You now can generate the code that goes on your Web page (for example, if you're tracking sales, you'd insert the code into your "Thanks for your purchase" page). Scroll to the bottom of the page and click anywhere in the text box to select the entire code snippet, as shown in Figure 14-3.

I recommend copying the conversion code and pasting it into a plain text document (a `.txt` file, not a `.doc` or `.rtf`) for safekeeping, rather than immediately dropping the code into your Web page. That way you'll have a saved version of the code if you ever need it again. Make sure you give the text document an obvious-but-descriptive name, such as `Google Conv Tracking.txt`.

Figure 14-3:
Clicking
inside the
text box
containing
the code
selects the
entire
snippet.

That's it! You've generated the tracking code. You don't need to click the Continue button; simply go back to the Campaign Summary tab in the Campaign Management submenu. You should see two new columns — Conv. Rate and Cost/Conv. — filled completely with zeroes. Once you place the code on your Web site, Google will replace the zeroes with your conversion numbers.

Assigning a value to a conversion

Before I show you where and how to put the conversion code onto your Web site, let's talk about the Advanced Option: Conversion Value link just to the right of the text box.

Click that link if you want to assign a monetary value to the conversion. The easiest example is a sale: If you sell a product for $37, that conversion is worth $37 to your top line. Enter the value of the conversion, click Refresh, and click in the text box to the left to copy the code that includes the conversion value.

You can enter the sale price or your net profit as the conversion value, whatever makes more sense. I prefer to use net profit, so I can see that a keyword with a CPC of $0.35 is worth $0.75 in my bank account, after expenses.

You can create conversions of many different values. If you sell three versions of the same product, you can put different-valued conversion code on the thank-you pages for each version, as shown in Table 14-1.

Table 14-1		Sample Conversion Values by Product	
Product	*Price*	*"Thank You for Buying" Page*	*Conversion Code Value*
Product A: Basic	$17	/productAthanks.html	17
Product B: Value	$97	/productBthanks.html	97
Product C: Deluxe	$497	/productCthanks.html	497

Putting code on your Web site

The code snippet goes on the Web page that your visitor reaches *after* successfully taking the action you're measuring. In other words, if you want them to opt in, the code goes on the "Thank you for opting in" page. For conversion tracking to be accurate, three things must be true about this page:

1. *Every* visitor who performs the desired action goes to the confirmation page (into which you insert the conversion code) following that action.

2. A visitor who *doesn't* perform the desired action will not get to the confirmation page.

3. Visitors can't refresh the confirmation page to create false multiple conversions. (See www.askhowie.com/norefresh for details.)

If the conversion is a page view, then the code goes on the viewed page itself. In other cases, the confirmation page is the next page. If you are using an e-mail-management service such as AWeber (see Chapter 10), put your code on the page you designate as the Thank You page in the autoresponder setup.

Where to place the snippet

The conversion-tracking code should go just above the `</body>` tag on your confirmation page, as in Figure 14-4.

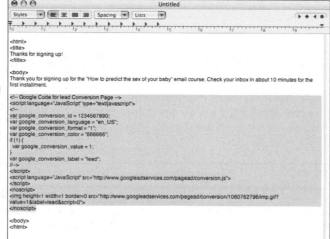

Figure 14-4:
Place the conversion tracking code in your HTML editor, just above `</body>`.

Visit www.askhowie.com/conversioncode for a video tutorial on putting code on your Web site.

Common tracking-code mistakes

The following list gives you a rundown of the common mistakes people make when inserting the conversion code (by reading this list and taking it to heart, you can avoid these mishaps!):

✔ **Putting the code in the header or footer.** If you place the tracking code in the header or footer of a page, it may show up on every single page in your Web site. Every page view will then be counted as a conversion.

✔ **Putting code on the wrong page.** Don't put the tracking code on the conversion page itself, but on the page that is served following successful conversion. (An exception is a page view conversion, where the confirmation page and the page itself are one and the same.)

✔ **Putting the code on the same page multiple times.** With complicated Web pages, it's easy to forget that you've already placed the tracking code on the page.

If you're not sure whether your tracking code is currently on your Web page, view the source code of the page. Here's the drill:

1. Choose View➪Source in your browser.

   The source code appears in a text editor window.

2. Choose Edit➪Find, and enter **Google Code** in the Find What text box.

3. Click the Find Next button to search the code.

Tracking sales from a shopping cart

You can configure conversion tracking to record the total amount your visitors spend by using dynamic fields generated by your e-commerce system. For example, if you use Yahoo! Stores or eBay/PayPal shops, you can modify the code snippet to tell Google how much a visitor spent on your site. You can also get this information from a shopping cart written in ASP (Active Server Pages), JSP (Sun Java Server Pages), or PHP.

If you aren't a proficient coder and don't know what CGI means, please don't try this yourself. Send your Webmaster to `https://adwords.google.com/select/setup.pdf` for full documentation on configuring dynamic shopping carts for conversion tracking.

Testing conversion tracking

To see whether Google is tracking the conversion you set up, you have two choices: the quick and (possibly) expensive way, or the natural way. The quickest way to confirm correct setup is to search Google for your keyword, click your ad, and perform the desired action. You should see that conversion in your campaign summary screen as a non-zero number somewhere in the two new columns (see the following section). If you don't want to waste a click, your other choice is to wait for a real visitor to convert. Unless your clicks cost several dollars each, I recommend spending the money yourself and making sure you're getting useful data.

Introducing Two New Columns

Once you've triggered conversion tracking by generating the code snippet, Google shows you two new columns in the campaign management pages: Conv. Rate (conversion rate) and Cost/Conv. (cost per conversion), as shown in Figure 14-5. Until you place the conversion code on your site and visitors start converting, you will see zeroes in those columns. Also, expect a 24-hour delay in reporting a conversion.

Figure 14-5:
The columns
Conv. Rate
and Cost/
Conv.
appear after
you initiate
conversion
tracking.

All Campaigns

Feb 1, 2007 to Feb 28, 2007

+ Create a new campaign : keyword-targeted | site-targeted ⓘ

Campaign Name	Current Status	Current Budget [?]	Clicks	Impr.	CTR	Avg. CPC	Cost	Conv. Rate	Cost/Conv.	Play Rate [?]
Lead Generation G	Active	$10.00 / day	12	1,477	0.81%	$0.35	$4.20	0.00%	$0.00	0.00%
Lead Generation S	Active	$10.00 / day	1	198	0.50%	$0.43	$0.43	0.00%	$0.00	0.00%
Lead Generation C	Active	$10.00 / day	14	5,989	0.23%	$0.28	$3.99	0.00%	$0.00	0.00%
Local Business Listings	Paused	[$1.00 / day]	0	2	0.00%	-	$0.00	0.00%	$0.00	0.00%
Total - all 4 campaigns	-	$30.00 / day active campaigns	27	7,666	0.35%	$0.32	$8.62	0.00%	$0.00	0.00%

Conversion rate

The conversion rate is the percent of visitors from that campaign, ad group, ad, or keyword who complete a conversion. Let's drill down to the ad group level to make this clear. In Figure 14-6, you can see six ad groups in the Gout campaign. Two of the groups have led to sales, which is the only conversion I'm tracking in this case. A sale equals one conversion. The first group, Gout Disabled Keywords, received 2211 clicks and converted 0.81% of them to sales. When I do the math (2211 × 0.0081), I find that this ad group is responsible for 17.9 sales. (I'm going to round up to 18 sales because I don't see how I can make nine-tenths of a sale.) You can also hover your cursor over the conversion rate percentage to see the actual number of sales.

The next ad group, Gout Diet, turned 958 clicks into 7 sales (958 × 0.0071). None of the other groups led to sales during this time period.

Cost/Conv.

The second new column, Cost/Conv., refers to how much you spent on AdWords, on average, for each conversion. In the Gout Disabled Keywords group, for example, I spent $9.71 to make a sale. Whether that's good or bad depends on how much I earned from each sale. In this case, the Gout e-book sells for either $17.77 or $37.77, depending on whether the visitor purchases the basic or deluxe version. Assuming the worst case — that all the sales were the basic version — I'm still making a gross profit of $8.06 per sale. I'll take that.

Figure 14-6: Conversion rates and costs per conversion help me calculate the ROI of my ad groups.

Actually, I'm making less than $8.06 per sale, since I have to pay for credit-card processing. When your margins are tight, make sure you're accounting for *all* costs as you determine your ROI.

The second ad group is bringing in customers for $11.29 each, or a profit of $6.48 per sale. Still okay, but not as good as the first group. In general, the lower this number, the better you're doing. The exception is if the cost-per-conversion is zero.

Look at the next four groups to see this clearly: no sales, so a $0.00 cost per conversion. Zero is the worst number to see in this column, because it means you've achieved nothing. Luckily, my AdWords expenditures for these groups are low (see the numbers in the Cost column). Also, they haven't generated enough clicks during this time period to yield statistically significant results (see Chapter 13 for a discussion of split testing and statistical significance).

Tracking ROI of Ads and Keywords

The information at the level of campaigns and ad groups is nice, but not particularly useful. Where conversion tracking becomes a powerful driver of action is at the levels of specific ads and keywords.

Identifying the profitable ads

After you have conversion tracking in place, you can compare two ads competing in the same ad group, not just to see which one attracts more clicks, but which one attracts more qualified clicks. The method I outline works both with text ads purchased on a CPC basis and image ads bought on a cost-per-thousand-impressions basis, because you will reduce all the data to a single number: *profit per thousand impressions*.

I began this chapter with a hypothetical example of two ads with CTRs of 1.00% and 0.77%, respectively. Without conversion tracking, you would declare the 1.00% ad the winner and start testing a new ad. As you can see in Figure 14-7, you could be making a big mistake.

Figure 14-7:
The lower-CTR ad is almost four times more profitable than the higher-CTR ad.

Variations ▼	CTR	Conv. Rate	Cost/Conv.
Never cold call again. Get prospects to call you instead. The System Revealed - download now www.LeadsintoGold.com	1.00%	9.1%	$9.19
Never Cold Call Again. Get prospects to call you instead. Free Report and 2 chapter download www.LeadsintoGold.com	0.77%	33.3%	$2.37

The conversion in this case was an opt-in, to receive two free chapters of the Leads into Gold home-study course. The first ad, the one with the "better" CTR, converted fewer than 1 in 10 visitors to leads. The second ad, while attracting fewer clicks, converted 1 out of 3 visitors to leads. You can see the difference in dollars and cents when you compare the two ads' cost per conversion metrics. Each lead cost me $9.19 when the first ad was shown, compared to only $2.38 when the lead saw the second ad.

Why is the second ad so much more effective at delivering qualified prospects? Look at the call to action in the second description line: "Free report and 2 chapter download." Visitors are enticed by the promise of a two-chapter download; the real question isn't why so many of them converted, but why so many more *didn't* opt in to download the two chapters.

Higher CTR often means lower site conversions

Lest you think the previous example was a fluke, I'm going to draw back the curtain a little more on my AdWords campaign. Figure 14-8 shows a second set of ads, almost identical in language, in which the same inverse relationship exists between CTR and site conversion.

Figure 14-8: One word makes a world of difference in this split test.

Variations ▼	CTR	Conv. Rate	Cost/Conv.
Cold calling not working? Discover a powerful alternative. Free report and 2 chapter download. www.LeadsIntoGold.com	2.53%	10.5%	$7.45
Cold calling not working? Discover an effective alternative. Free report and 2 chapter download. www.LeadsIntoGold.com	2.28%	14.0%	$5.58

Why should the word *effective* improve my site conversion from 10.5 to 14% compared to the word *powerful*? I can't know for sure, but my guess is that *powerful* is a more attractive word and therefore casts a wider net than *effective*, while *effective* attracts more of the serious business owners who are predisposed to take the time to study my Web site and accept my offer.

Please take the moral of this story to heart: CTR is usually far less important than the cost per conversion. But until you set up conversion tracking, you're like the guy in the joke (for some reason, it's always a *guy* in the joke) who's looking for his keys under the street lamp, even though he lost them in the dark on the other side of the street. When asked why he's looking in the wrong place, he answers, "Because the light's better here." As business strategist Peter Senge reminds us, "We can't expect what we don't inspect." If you want higher CTRs, you can get them without paying attention to conversion. But if you want higher profits, you must inspect your site conversion data.

Balancing CTR and cost per conversion

CTR still matters. It's related to profitability, because of Google's bid price formula: The higher the CTR, the lower the CPC. Also, you might run an ad with a miserable CTR that nevertheless converts at a high level. But because it sends so little traffic to your site, the high conversion rate contributes little to your bottom line.

You can balance an ad's CTR and cost per conversion by calculating a metric based on initial input and ultimate output: How much are 1000 impressions worth to you? Table 14-2 presents an example.

Table 14-2				Balancing CTR and Cost per Conversion		
Ad	Impressions	Clicks	CTR	Total Cost	Conv. Rate	Cost/Conv.
Ad #1	5000	300	6.0%	$150	12%	$4.17
Ad #2	5000	150	3.0%	$100	18%	$3.70
Ad #3	5000	25	0.5%	$25	60%	$1.67

Which ad do you keep? If you look solely at CTR, it's easy: Ad #1 is the clear winner. But now that you've added conversion tracking, you can compare the ads' respective cost per conversion. By that measure, Ad #3 is the winner, generating a conversion for $1.67, compared to the Ad #2's cost per conversion of $3.70 and Ad #1's bloated $4.17.

The trouble with Ad #3 is the tiny amount of traffic it generates. What you really want to know is which ad makes the most money? To calculate profit per ad, you need two more numbers: total number of conversions and value of a conversion.

Calculating the total number of conversions is easy: just multiply number of clicks by the conversion rate and divide by 100. Ad #1's total conversion is $300 \times 12 \div 100 = 36$.

The value of a conversion answers the question, how much is one of that action worth to your business? If you're tracking hard sales data, Google can give you this information in the Reports section (see the "Creating Easy-to-Understand Reports" section, later in this chapter). If you're tracking throughput data such as leads or page views, you may need to estimate the value of a conversion to your business. In this example, let's assume that a conversion is a $45 sale, of which you get to keep $40 after cost of goods and processing fees. Now you can redo Table 14-2 as shown in Table 14-3.

Table 14-3				Conversion Values		
Ad	Impr.	Tot. Cost	# Conv	Conv. Value	Total $ (Profits — Cost)	Cost/1000 Impr.
Ad #1	5000	$150	36	$40	$1290	$258.00
Ad #2	5000	$100	27	$40	$980	$196.00
Ad #3	5000	$25	15	$40	$575	$115.00

When you deposit your check in the bank, it doesn't give you extra money for having a high CTR or a low cost per conversion. When split-testing ads within a single ad group, the most important number is the amount of money you make per thousand impressions, after paying for your clicks.

The preceding example reflects a situation where your first sale is your only sale. If you make the lion's share of your profits from back end sales (meaning sales after the first one), if those sales occur online, you can still use the average cost per impression metric to choose a winner. If you can't track the lucrative back end sales through Google, you may just want to treat your AdWords campaigns as pure lead generation: whichever ad produces the most leads (in the case just cited, Ad #1) is the winner.

Keywords

You can also track ROI for each keyword in your Google search, and search partners' campaigns. Armed with this information, you can tighten your ad groups, lower or raise your bids on individual keywords to improve ROI or increase traffic for profitable keywords, and pause or delete keywords that cost more than they make.

Figure 14-9 shows an ad group for Leads into Gold. The overall cost per conversion for this ad group is $23.80, far too high to be profitable. Let's say that my break-even is $18.00 per conversion. All the keywords whose cost per conversion is greater than $18.00, or at $0.00, are current money losers. They include `cold calls` at a whopping $75.70 per conversion, all the way down to `cold calling techniques` at an almost-acceptable $19.94. The keywords with cost per conversion between $17.15 and $4.73 are all fine, but the one below those are generating no conversions at all, just costing me Google clicks.

The keyword-conversion data can be fed back into campaign management (see Chapters 7 and 8) to continually lower your costs and increase your profits.

Dealing with multiple conversions

The trouble with the Leads into Gold example we examined in Figure 14-9 is that I'm actually tracking more than one conversion at a time. I have the tracking code on the page following an opt-in, as well as on the pages following the sales of the three editions of the product: $247, $337, and $489. The campaign-management console adds all the conversions together, and doesn't distinguish between an opt-in and a $489 sale. Obviously, sales are more interesting to me than opt-ins, as I can go to a grocery store and buy food when a sale happens.

Figure 14-9:
Only six
keywords
out of 33
in this ad
group are
generating a
positive ROI.

When you run multiple conversions (and you should, if you have more than one desired outcome on your Web site), you can't rely solely on the conversion data presented in two columns in the campaign-management tab. No, grasshopper, you now need to enter the Wonderful World of Conversion Reports.

Creating Easy-to-Understand Reports

Google allows you to create reports that distinguish between leads, signups, page views, and sales. You can see which ads and keywords are making you money, and exactly how much. You can identify the keywords that are doing their job — that is, generating more money than they cost. And you can automate the reporting to receive exactly the numbers you need in your inbox on a daily, weekly, or monthly basis.

To create a report, follow these steps:

1. **From within your AdWords account, click the Reports tab.**

2. **Click the Create a Report Now link in the center of the page to create your first report, as shown in Figure 14-10.**

   If you've already run reports, you'll see a list of the last five reports that have run, as well as any saved report templates at the bottom of the page.

Figure 14-10:
Click the link
shown by
the hand
to start
generating
reports.

Types of reports

Google enables you to choose from several different types of reports, including:

- **Keyword Performance:** This report tells you how each keyword is doing. As we saw earlier in this chapter, the two conversion columns in the campaign-management console mushed all the conversions together into one undifferentiated pile. In a report, you can separate out multiple conversions and assign a monetary value to each one.

- **Ad Performance:** This type of report lets you know which ad in a split test is the most profitable, based on ROI and total profit. Depending on your Web site's sales process, you may place more value on generating leads or on sales numbers; you can configure reports that give you exactly the numbers you need in order to make profitable decisions.

- **URL Performance:** This report evaluates your destination URLs. You can split-test landing pages this way, but it's messy. You're better off using a third-party tool (see Chapter 13 for the details of split-testing) to test landing pages; you can swap pages in and out in one place, rather than in the destination URLs of perhaps dozens of different ads.

- **Ad Group, Campaign, and Account Performance:** These three report types (Ad Group, Campaign, and Account Performance) are useful mostly for their ability to show you hourly results. You can find out what time of day you receive the most impressions, the highest CTR, the most clicks, and the highest and lowest CPC. This information can help you schedule ads so they don't show at certain unfavorable times of day.

Settings

Your settings choices change depending on the report type. Basically, you have to make three choices:

- **View (unit of time):** How do you want the data chunked by time? You can view a summary of all the data; or look at individual years, quarters, months, weeks, or days. Some of the reports allow you to look at the data on an hourly basis. Hourly (by date) shows each individual hour. Hourly (regardless of date) combines the data to show the average hourly activity — that is, over the entire date range you're looking at, how does your traffic at 3:00 a.m. differ from traffic at 10:00 a.m. or 3:00 p.m.?

- **Date range:** Over what time period do you want to examine the data? You can choose a default time frame from the drop-down menu, or specify an exact range. Depending on your traffic, you want to choose a time period that can give you statistically significant results. In other words, if you receive only 100 impressions a day, it doesn't make sense to view one day at a time. Instead, choose a period that allows trends to emerge — say, a week or a month.

- **Campaigns and ad groups:** You can choose to show every ad group in every campaign, or look at select ad groups. I like to choose a single ad group per report, so I can focus on just the relevant data that can help me make decisions. As you'll see, the amount of data you can generate with reports is staggering. The art of running reports is not to generate as much data as possible, but as *little* as allows you to take intelligent action. When you choose to manually select campaigns and ad groups from a list, a drop-down list of campaigns will appear. You can add the campaign directly, or click a campaign name to view its ad groups, which you then can add individually.

Advanced settings

Configure the advanced settings to create truly useful reports:

- **Add or Remove Columns:** You can select the data to appear in your report. Depending on report type, you may have half a dozen options, or as many as 50. See the upcoming section, "Customizing Your Reports to Show the Most Important Numbers," for suggestions on which columns to display and which to ignore.

- **Filter Your Results:** You can limit the scope of the report by showing keywords, or ads, or ad groups, or campaigns that match any of a number of search criteria, as shown in Figure 14-11. Here are just two examples:

- You can choose to display only active ads in active ad groups in active campaigns.

- You can look at content targeted campaigns only, or keywords whose average CPC is (say) greater than $3.25.

If you find yourself overwhelmed by gigantic report spreadsheets, spend some time looking at filters to see whether any of them will reduce complexity while retaining the key information.

Figure 14-11:
Use filters
to create
smaller
reports that
are easier to
understand.

> **3. Advanced Settings (Optional)**
>
> ▸ Add or Remove Columns
>
> ▾ Filter Your Results
>
> Show only keywords that match all of the following criteria:
>
> | Ad Group Status ▾ | is one of | Active
Deleted
Paused | Remove |
>
> | CTR ▾ | Is less than ▾ | 0.5 | Remove |
>
> | Avg Position ▾ | Is greater than ▾ | 10 | Remove |
>
> Add another restriction
>
> ☐ Include keywords with zero impressions

Templates, scheduling, and e-mail

You don't have to go through the whole report-creation process every time. You can save reports as templates and schedule them to run automatically on a daily, weekly, or monthly basis. I like to schedule reports to run weekly that show me activity for the previous 30 days. I can print them out, study them, and archive them in a binder to understand trends and compare results from one month to the next.

I create new reports to answer questions, test hypotheses, and explore my campaigns from different angles. When I find a new report to be valuable, I schedule it to run on a weekly or monthly basis. My accounts don't justify daily reports, but if you get a lot of traffic on a daily basis, you may want to devote 10 minutes a day to glancing at the day's reports. In general, you want to spend more time monitoring new campaigns than mature ones.

Create a report as a template to save yourself the time and effort of making the same choices over and over again for different reports. You can create a template with specific columns and filters, and just change the ad group, instead of creating each new ad group report from scratch.

You can view reports in HTML format from the Report Center, and/or download them in several formats. I like the HTML view for sorting by different columns, just like the campaign-management interface; I like the .csv Excel format for printing and performing additional calculations.

Customizing Your Reports to Show the Most Important Numbers

Some numbers matter more to your business than others. Let's explore customizing the columns for the Keyword Performance and Ad Performance reports.

Customizing Keyword Performance reports

Your column choices for keyword reports are shown in Figure 14-12. Basically, your goal is to remove as many columns as you possibly can and still get the information you need. So before you choose columns, get clear on what are the important questions you want a report to answer:

✔ If you have an e-commerce Web site, your most important keyword question will likely be, "Which keywords are making money and which are losing money?"

✔ If the primary purpose of your site is lead generation, you want to know how much each lead costs you.

✔ If you are generating traffic for clients, you are probably most interested in page views.

Figure 14-12: You can choose from dozens of columns to create keyword performance reports.

Sometimes you want to see a bunch of statistics next to each other. I often am interested in leads versus sales for particular keywords, so I'll select leads count, sales count, and sales value. I may discover that a certain keyword attracts a disproportionate number of buyers, even though it doesn't compel more opt-in conversions.

For example, in Figure 14-9 earlier in this chapter, we saw that most of the keywords in the ad group weren't generating positive ROI, based on the average value of a conversion. The keyword `cold calls` was the top offender at over $75 per conversion. The problem with this data is that I can't distinguish between an opt-in and a sale. When I run a keyword-performance report — choosing the conversion metrics of cost per conversion, value per click, sales count, and sales value (shown in Figure 14-13) — I discover a much more nuanced and useful picture.

The keyword `cold calls` turns out to be my best, not worst, keyword. I pay an average of $0.86 per click and make an average of $2.18 from each click. None of the other keywords led to sales at all.

The bottom-line number for keywords is value per click, also known as *visitor value*. This number answers the question, "How much money is a visitor to my Web site worth to me, on average?" You should know this number for each of your sales channels. When you know your visitor value, you know exactly how much you can spend on advertising. The higher your visitor value, the more you can afford to pay for traffic. And when you discover that a promotion produces less or more revenue than you would expect given your averages, you can decide whether it's worth repeating.

Figure 14-13:
The key-word cold calls cost $134.24 to show and earned $337, for an average value per click of $2.18.

Google AdWords: LIG cc techniques all time: Mar 28, 2007 11:12:11 AM PDT

Keyword	Keyword Matching	Keyword Status	Impressions	Clicks	CTR	Avg CPC	Cost	Avg Position	Cost / Conversion	Value / Click ▲	Sales Count	Sales Value
cold calls	Phrase	Active	6,904	156	2.26%	$0.86	$134.24	2.1	$67.12	2.18	1	337.00
cold calling	Phrase	Active	31,701	615	1.94%	$0.85	$525.07	3.4	$16.94	1.61	2	958.00
making cold calls	Phrase	Active	237	6	2.53%	$0.79	$4.73	1.5	$4.73	0.17	0	0.00
no more cold calling	Exact	Active	116	7	6.03%	$0.86	$5.99	5.3	$5.99	0.14	0	0.00
cold calling	Exact	Active	13,422	378	2.82%	$0.89	$335.59	4.2	$13.98	0.11	0	0.00
cold calling techniques	Phrase	Active	3,180	17	0.53%	$0.91	$15.40	2.7	$15.40	0.06	0	0.00
cold calling techniques	Broad	Active	15,992	219	1.37%	$0.86	$189.43	2.3	$19.94	0.05	0	0.00
cold calls	Exact	Active	2,716	124	4.57%	$0.69	$85.73	1.5	$17.15	0.04	0	0.00
cold call techniques	Broad	Active	6,101	50	0.82%	$0.66	$33.03	2.2	$30.44	0.02	0	0.00
cold calling	Broad	Active	25,134	721	2.87%	$0.82	$592.31	3.1	$51.57	0.02	0	0.00
cold calling techniques	Exact	Active	5,297	64	1.21%	$0.91	$58.45	2.6	$58.45	0.02	0	0.00
cold calls	Broad	Active	6,115	123	2.01%	$0.76	$93.54	2.4	$75.70	0.01	0	0.00
[no cold calling]	Phrase	Active	54	2	3.70%	$0.74	$1.47	7.8	$0.00	0.00	0	0.00
cold call	Broad	Deleted	83	0	0.00%	$0.00	$0.00	1.5	$0.00	0.00	0	0.00
cold call script	Broad	Deleted	437	5	1.14%	$0.68	$3.41	2.0	$0.00	0.00	0	0.00
cold call scripts	Broad	Active	3,577	41	1.15%	$0.68	$28.06	2.5	$0.00	0.00	0	0.00
cold call scripts	Exact	Active	871	11	1.26%	$0.62	$6.80	3.2	$0.00	0.00	0	0.00
cold call scripts	Phrase	Active	627	15	2.39%	$0.74	$11.14	1.8	$0.00	0.00	0	0.00
cold call selling	Broad	Deleted	1,473	8	0.54%	$0.76	$6.07	1.9	$0.00	0.00	0	0.00
cold call techniques	Exact	Active	362	9	2.49%	$0.92	$8.28	2.5	$0.00	0.00	0	0.00

Perry Marshall often talks about the Unlimited Traffic Technique: Start with AdWords, but don't end there. Use AdWords to improve your sales process — meaning, to increase your visitor value. Once your visitor value is high enough, you can buy all the traffic you want. You can hire search engine optimization consultants to boost your organic rankings. You can advertise your site on other Web sites, on the radio, in magazines, wherever — because you know exactly how much a visitor is worth to you.

Customizing Ad Performance reports

Your Ad Performance reports should answer the primary question, "Within each ad group, which is the best ad?" In an e-commerce situation, this means the ad that puts the most money into your bank account per impression. As of this writing, Google does not include a Value/Impression column in its reports, so you need to figure this out manually or add a column in a spreadsheet. Figure 14-14 shows my recommended selections for an e-commerce ad performance report. I eliminate as many details as possible so I can see all the numbers on one page.

Figure 14-14: Customize reports by choosing what you want to see and deselecting what isn't necessary.

In Figure 14-15, you can see the results of the choices I made in Figure 14-14. Some columns are mandatory in the report, such as Ad ID and Destination URL, but I can easily remove them in Excel because they don't help me. I can also move columns around in Excel, putting related numbers next to each other. Most important, I can create additional columns that give me the numbers I really need.

Figure 14-15: The shaded rows show that some ads are much more profitable than their competitors.

In this case, I created a new column (in bold) called **Value/Impression*100**, which is how much every impression is worth to me, multiplied by 100 so I can make better sense of the data. The absolute number is less important than the comparison of the ads that I'm testing. In rows 13 and 14, the two ads in question are identical, except for the end of the Display URL: the one with `VitalHealthInstitute.com/BeatGout` is almost twice as profitable as the one with the URL `VitalHealthInstitute.com` on its own: $0.63 versus $0.32.

Rows 15 and 16 feature two ads, identical except for quotes around "Gout Cure" in one. The ad without quotes is almost three times more profitable than its competitor, $0.35 versus $0.12. Rows 17 and 18 show again that adding a subdomain to the main Display URL has increased profits, $0.24 versus $0.14.

You can create a Value/Impression*1000 Column in Excel by dividing the sales value by the number of impressions, and multiplying by 1000. Go to `www.askhowie.com/valueimp` for a video tutorial on creating the Value/Impression*1000 column in Excel.

Discovering What to Do with the Data

Before taking action based on the data, make sure the data is accurate. Google is usually not the culprit when data is faulty; instead, you most likely made an error in placing the code on your Web pages. If you're measuring opt-ins and sales, it won't take long to verify the data. Count the number of leads Google says you've acquired over a given period of time, and compare it to the number of opt-ins to your autoresponder or newsletter list for the same date range. If the two numbers are fairly close, you can be confident that you're reading useful data. (Expect the numbers to be slightly off to account for time delays between initial click and conversion.) Similarly, compare the sales count and sales value for an e-commerce site with the actual sales data from your shopping cart or merchant account. Again, they should be close, not necessarily identical.

Use the report data to split-test your ads — not on CTR, but on profitability (refer to Figure 14-15). As a rule of thumb, wait until each ad has generated at least 30 clicks before declaring a winner to make sure your results are statistically significant and not just a fluke occurrence.

You're looking for keywords that aren't paying for themselves, or aren't as profitable as they could be. When you find these keywords, you can adjust your bid price (and average position) to reflect their value, you can move them into a different ad group and match them to a different landing page (see Chapter 8), or you can pause or delete them to stop the bleeding.

If you find a keyword that costs $0.35 per click and has a value per click of $0.27, you're losing 8 cents every time someone clicks your ad. Before deleting the keyword, lower your Maximum CPC to $0.26. You may find your visitor value increasing because lower positions tend to generate higher-quality clicks. Worst case, you're slightly better than break-even for the keyword.

If your break-even bid doesn't generate enough traffic because it puts you on page 9 of search results, or is below Google's minimum bid, then you can try moving the keyword to a different ad group and matching it more closely to the ad and the landing page. Sometimes getting the keyword quality score to Great is all you need to do.

The goal of keyword bid management is to maximize profits per keyword. Test your high traffic keywords in different positions. Pay for position 1 for a week, and then drop it to position 7 for another week. Tally your sales and costs: Which position is more profitable? Over time, you'll find the sweet spot for each keyword. Obviously, if your campaigns contain thousands of keywords, you'll want to focus on the top traffic keywords.

Chapter 15

Making More Sales with Google Analytics

In This Chapter

▶ Activating Google Analytics

▶ Observing and measuring your visitors' behaviors

▶ Identifying Web site roadblocks and detours

▶ Making your Web site friendlier and more effective

$\mathbf{I}$n *Why We Buy: The Science of Shopping* (Texere Publishing), Paco Underhill share the insights gleaned from 20 years of his study of the science of shopping. Some of these include

✔ Putting shopping baskets all over bookstores.

✔ Making the women's clothing aisles wide to avoid the irritation of "butt-brush."

✔ Putting fitting rooms next to the men's clothing section since men buy mostly on the basis of fit, while women consider many other factors.

These findings may seem like common sense to you, but I wouldn't have come up with them in a hundred years. And neither did the giants of retail until they hired Underhill to study shopper behavior and redesign their stores. Underhill's company Web site, www.envirosell.com, describes the methodology for a typical engagement:

> *Twelve Staples stores were studied in different markets across the country for two days each.*
>
> > • *Shoppers were observed throughout their visit by in-store observers.*
> >
> > • *Video, focused in different areas of the store, recorded shopping patterns for eight hours each research day.*

> • *Shoppers were intercepted and interviewed after they completed their shopping visit.*
>
> • *A manager and an associate from each store were interviewed by researchers to gather their insights on the store.*

I bring this up to explain how incredibly lucky you are as a Web site proprietor to *not* to have to go through this to improve the effectiveness of your site. You can observe your customers without hiring armies of consultants, without intercepting them for interviews, and without watching hours of video. All you have to do, in fact, is install Google Analytics tracking code on your site and you'll be able to evaluate and redesign your online store with greater accuracy, less risk, and greater speed than you could ever manage offline.

You can view — in minute detail — the parts of your site that frustrate or detour your visitors. You can compare this month to last month. You can define goals and funnels and watch your visitors convert or bail at every point on the navigation path. You can identify pages that don't work, and replace them in minutes. And you can automatically connect all this data to your AdWords cost-and-conversion data to segment your traffic by keyword (and other characteristics).

In this chapter, I draw heavily on the expertise generously provided by Timothy Seward of ROI Revolution, online at www.roirevolution.com. (Especially since Google completely overhauled Analytics three weeks before my book deadline — thanks, Sergey and Larry!) Including even one-tenth of what Timothy has taught me would have turned this book into a medicine ball, so I'm limiting the information on Analytics in two ways:

- ✔ **I just show you how to track AdWords traffic.** You can configure Analytics to tell you cool stuff about all your visitors; in fact, it will tell you all about organic search-engine traffic by default. I'm going to ignore all that and let you explore it on your own. (Once you understand how Analytics deals with AdWords traffic, the rest isn't hard.)

- ✔ **I don't get into complicated installations**, including integration with e-commerce shopping carts or the tracking of downloads or outbound links. If you are (or know) someone who's a code jockey or has years of IT experience, feel free to play with these settings. Otherwise, start simply — and hire an Analytics expert when you're ready for advanced tracking.

Instead, I show you how to install and configure Analytics to get clean and actionable data. I introduce you to some very powerful data screens, and show you how to set up experiments and answer interesting questions with these data. Once you have the data, you discover what to do with it to get more leads and sales.

Installing Analytics on Your Web site

The Google Analytics installation process consists of three steps:

1. Creating and configuring an Analytics account

2. Adding tracking code to your Web pages

3. Creating filters to keep your data clean and useful

Creating an Analytics account

Within your AdWords account, click the Analytics tab. Click the Continue button to enter Web site information for your first profile (each Web site requires its own profile), as shown in Figure 15-1. You can create multiple profiles, but for right now let's keep it simple.

Figure 15-1:
Make sure
the two
check
boxes are
checked
so your
AdWords
data is
included.

Analytics: New Account Signup

General Information > Accept User Agreement > Add Tracking

Please enter the URL of the site you wish to track, and assign a name as it should appear in your Google Analytics reports. If you'd like to track more than one website, you can add more sites once your account has been set up. Learn more.

Website's URL: http:// ◦ www.cheesemongr.com
(e.g. www.mywebsite.com)

Account Name: www.cheesemongr.com

Destination URL Auto-tagging: ☑ Automatically tag my ad destination URLs with additional information useful in analytics reports. Learn more.

Apply Cost Data: ☑ Automatically apply your AdWords cost data to all profiles in this Analytics account for reporting calculations.

(Cancel) (Continue »)

Enter the Web site URL, and give this account a name. Very important: Make sure the check boxes are checked next to Destination URL Auto-tagging and Apply Cost Data. Auto-tagging adds information about which keywords your visitors typed and which ads they clicked to arrive at your site.

Google warns that a small percentage of Web sites can't handle Auto-tagging. If you start getting errors when you click your ads, turn off Auto-tagging and tell the following to your Webmaster: "Please configure my site to allow arbitrary URL parameters." When your Webmaster has done this, turn Auto-tagging back on.

Checking the Apply Cost Data check box connects AdWords bid costs to your Analytics data, so you can calculate the costs and values of various Web site conversions.

On the next page, read the epic novel titled *Google Analytics Terms of Service* — and if you agree with each and every provision, check the agreement box at the bottom and click the Create New Account button to get started.

Adding tracking code to your Web pages

On the next page, you'll see a text block containing the Analytics tracking code. Click inside that box to select the whole thing, then copy it and paste it into every page on your Web site that you are planning to track. The code goes just above the </body> tag, near or at the bottom of the source code for each page. Your source code may end something like this:

```
<script src="http://www.google-analytics.com/urchin.js"
    type="text/javascript">
</script>
<script type="text/javascript">
_uacct = "UA-1234567-1";
urchinTracker();
</script>

</body>
</html>
```

Don't copy my code! No ethical objections, just practicality: Each account comes with a unique number, which follows the UA- prefix in the code.

If your Web site is built on a template, you can add this code just once and it will automatically be added to every page. If you don't know what I'm talking about, just e-mail the code to your Webmaster and tell him or her, "Place this code just above the </body> (close-body) tag on every page of my site."

When you click Continue, Google prompts you to check the status of your tracking code. Unless you've added it already, when you check you'll get a message telling you that the tracking code has not been detected on your home page (as shown in Figure 15-2). The pink warning box will remain at the top of your Analytics control panel until it's satisfied that you've added the code correctly.

Be cautious about installing the Analytics tracking code yourself if any of the following conditions exist:

✔ You want to track visitors across more than one domain (for example, http://unicyclesforkids.com and http://whoneedstwo wheels.com).

✔ Your site includes subdomains (such as `http://stunt.unicycles forkids.com` and `http://distance.unicyclesforkids.com`).

✔ You want to track visitors on a secure server (such as `https://unicyclesforkids.com`).

✔ You want to track file downloads (PDFs or MP3s, for example).

✔ You have a third-party shopping cart or an e-commerce site.

✔ Your visitors can pay you with PayPal or Google Checkout.

✔ Your site uses frames (if you're not sure, ask your Webmaster).

✔ Your site generates pages dynamically but the URL remains static (if you're not sure, gently let go of your mouse and move away from the computer).

Figure 15-2:
Check the status of your tracking once you've had the code added to your Web site.

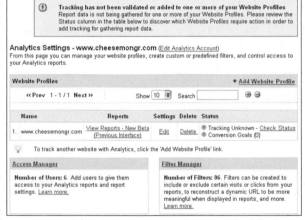

Check out Michael Harrison's cautionary blog post at `www.roirevolution. com/config` for a case study of a mismanaged Analytics installation that generated junk data long after the error was corrected.

If you want to add more Web sites to your Analytics account, click the + Add Web Site Profile link and repeat the process.

Configuring Analytics

While you're waiting for tracking validation, you can configure your Analytics account to allow other users full or restricted access, and to eliminate junk data. From the Analytics home page, choose the profile you want to configure and click Edit. From this page, you can edit your profile information, create conversion goals and funnels, apply filters, and manage additional users.

Adding users

You may want to give other people full or restricted access to your Analytics account and data. You can add more users and specify their rights to change and view the account. For example, you can give your Webmaster access to Webmaster reports only, and you can allow an assistant to view data but not change the account configuration.

Add users by clicking the Access Manager link near the bottom of the Analytics control panel (refer to Figure 15-2). Click Add User at the top right, enter their e-mail and name, and choose an access type: View Reports Only, or Account Administrator. See Figure 15-3. If you've selected View Reports Only, select the profile(s) you want the user to see, and then click Finish.

Figure 15-3: Give additional Analytics users limited access to reports by creating profiles just for them.

You can configure limited access to reports by creating a new profile that's a copy of your main one. Click + Add Web site Profile in the Analytics Control Panel and select Add a Profile for an Existing Domain. Enter a name the new profile (for example, enter **My Web site - Raphael** if Raphael is the user who will have limited access to reports), and click Finish. You should see an additional profile in your list.

Click Edit to select the reports that the user can see. Scroll down to Available Reports, and uncheck the reports to exclude. Later in this chapter, I introduce you to some of the reports, charts, and graphs, so you can make informed decisions about user access.

Choosing a default page

Every Web site has a default page, defined as the page your Web server shows to visitors who enter your Web site name only. For example, someone typing `www.askhowie.com` is automatically redirected to the page `http://askhowie.com/index.php`. In this case, `index.php` is the default page. If you aren't sure of the name of your default page, ask your Webmaster.

If you don't tell Analytics your default page, then views of your root domain (`www.askhowie.com`) will be counted separately from default page views (`www.askhowie.com/index.php`), even though these two pages are actually the same.

From the Profile Settings page, click Edit to configure the Main Web Site Profile Information. Enter your Web site's default page, not including the root domain. You will enter something like this:

```
index.html
index.htm
index.php
```

Click the Save Changes button at the bottom of the page when you're done.

Filtering out internal traffic

A Jewish folk tale from the mythical town of Chelm tells of when Schlemiel and his wife opened a lemonade stand on the outskirts of the town market. Early in the day, one customer bought a glass for 25 cents. After that, nobody bought. Finally, Schlemiel picked up the 25-cent coin and gave it to his wife, requested a glass of lemonade. Shortly thereafter, Mrs. Schlemiel returned the coin to her husband in exchange for a glass. So they went back and forth the rest of the day, until the entire supply of lemonade was gone. They celebrated their good fortune at having sold out their stock, but couldn't figure out where all the money had gone, and why they had only 25 cents to show for their efforts.

You may laugh, but if you don't create a filter to exclude internal traffic to your site, you're making the same mistake. Internal traffic refers to visits to the site by insiders — you, your Webmaster, your colleagues. You don't want these visits to contaminate the important data: the visits by prospects and customers.

A filter to exclude internal traffic is pretty simple to set up:

1. **From the Analytic's Profile Settings page, scroll down to the Filters section and click + Add Filter.**

2. **Select Add New Filter for Profile.**

3. **In the Filter Name text box, enter** Internal traffic.

4. **From the Filter Type drop-down menu, select Exclude All Traffic from an IP Address.**

   Google fills in the next field with `63\.212\.171\.12` (shown in Figure 15-4).

5. **Replace the numbers with your own IP address and the addresses of anyone else you consider internal traffic.**

   Each computer has its own IP address, so if you work at multiple computers, you'll want to filter them all. You can find your IP address at www.whatismyip.com. It consists of four blocks of numbers, separated by periods.

   If your IP address is 12.34.56.78, for example, you enter the following into Analytics:

   ```
   12\.34\.56\.78
   ```

   The \ character is called a backslash, located just above the Return or Enter key on most keyboards.

   When you've created filters for all internal users, you can apply those filters to all Analytics profiles (see the next step).

6. **Select Apply Existing Filter to Profile and you can choose from a list of filters to apply to that profile.**

Analytics allows you to create many different kinds of filters. You can find a list if you select Custom Filter from the Filter Type drown-down menu. For now, don't worry about adding more filters. When you start receiving data, you'll quickly see pages that are unnecessarily segmented by Analytics, and you can create filters to correct the problems.

Figure 15-4:
Ignore internal traffic by filtering out the IP addresses of internal users.

For more information about how to configure filters and how to determine that you need them, check out www.roirevolution.com/filters on the ROI Revolution blog.

Configuring goals and funnels

A *goal* refers to something you want your Web site visitors to do — such as fill out a form, buy something, visit a particular page, download a file, and so on. Except for file downloads and clicks on links to other Web sites, you configure a goal by identifying the page your visitor goes to after completing the conversion.

If the goal is an opt-in to your newsletter, the Goal page is the thank-you page visitors arrive at after completing the opt-in form. For a goal page to work, two things must be true: The only way someone ends up on that page is by doing what you want them to do, and everyone who takes that action ends up on that page.

Creating a goal

Next to the first goal, labeled G1, click the Edit link. On the next page (shown in Figure 15-5), enter the Goal URL, name, and make sure the goal is active. Scroll to the bottom of the page and click the Save Changes button. If you'd like to define a navigation funnel for that goal (an optional step), see the following section for details.

Defining a funnel

Google defines a *funnel* as "a series of pages leading up to the Goal URL." Sometimes you won't be able to define a funnel. Your visitors may choose their own path to a particular goal, or there may be many equally plausible paths to the same goal.

If the goal is a purchase, you can usually identify several required steps that must occur in order. Shawn Purtell of www.roirevolution.com offers the hypothetical example for an online cheese shop in Figure 15-5.

If you're not sure of the path, set up your best guess as a funnel. Even if you're completely wrong, you'll see graphically how visitor behavior on your site deviates from the ideal.

Determining a goal value

If your goal is an ecommerce goal, a configuration beyond the scope of this book, leave the value blank or at $0.00. If the goal is a lead, a page view, or a download, you can estimate the value of that goal and input it in the Additional Settings section. For example, say you generated $24,000 in income last month from 750 leads. Each lead is worth, on average, $32 ($24,000 ÷ 750 = $32). You can set the value of that goal at 32.00 (making sure to omit any currency sign), and then save your changes by clicking the Save Changes button.

Goal Settings: G1

Enter Goal Information

Goal URL: http://www.cheesemongr.com/catalog_request_succ (e.g. http://www.mysite.com/thankyou.html)
When the user navigates to this page, they have reached the conversion goal (Checkout Complete, Registration Confirmation, etc.).

Goal name: Catalog Success!
Goal name will appear in Conversion reports.

Active Goal: ● On ○ Off

Define Funnel (optional)

A funnel is a series of pages leading up to the Goal URL. For example, you might define the checkout steps that lead up to a completed purchase as a funnel. In this example, the funnel generally would not include individual product pages -- rather, it would consist only of those final pages that are common to all transactions.

The Defined Funnel Navigation report will show you how effectively you retain visitors throughout the conversion process.

	URL	Name	
Step 1	http://www.cheesemongr.com/index.	Home	☐ Required step
Step 2	http://www.cheesemongr.com/catalo	Catalog Request	
Step 3			
Step 4			
Step 5			
Step 6			
Step 7			
Step 8			
Step 9			
Step 10			
Goal (see above)	http://www.cheesemongr.com/catalo	Catalog Success!	

Additional settings

Case sensitive ☐
URLs entered above must exactly match the capitalization of visited URLs.

Match Type [Head Match ▾]

Goal value [10]
How do I use actual e-commerce values as my goal value?

[**Save Changes**] [Cancel]

Figure 15-5: Configuring the funnel for a catalog request.

E-commerce setup

If your Web site includes an e-commerce shopping cart, you definitely want to get it hooked up to Analytics. You'll discover which keywords are making you money and which are not. You'll find the optimal path for your AdWords visitors, from keyword through ad through landing page all the way through your site.

Unfortunately, there are simply too many variables for me to explain how to do it: brand of shopping cart, Web server, and so on. If you think you can configure it yourself, you can learn a lot from Google's tutorials at `www.google.com/support/analytics`. If you're looking for a consulting company to set up your Analytics correctly, you can choose with confidence from Google's own list of accredited Analytics partners, located at `www.google.com/analytics/support_partner_provided.html`. Google vouches for all 10 (the current number of North American partners); I can't speak highly enough about the talents of my Analytics advisor, Timothy Seward of ROI Revolution. Visit `www.roirevolution.com` to sign up for their free Webinar, get their newsletter, or pick up tips on their blog.

Actually, the fact that e-commerce Analytics is so complicated is a good thing — the harder something is, the bigger your competitive advantage when you implement. Analytics can provide you with black-belt skills in a white-belt world.

Making Sense of the Data

Analytics allows you to track much more than AdWords traffic, but if I got into the entire range of Analytics' capabilities, this book could double as *Weightlifting For Dummies*. I'm going to limit this section to AdWords only, and ignore organic search traffic, banner ads, newsletters, offline promotions, and direct entries. But once you've mastered the AdWords part of Analytics, you will definitely want to explore the whole range of possibilities.

Checking for data integrity

Before studying your Analytics data, compare the number of clicks between AdWords and Analytics to see if your Analytics profile is working properly. I once placed Analytics code on a redirect page and the actual landing page by mistake — and got reports of twice as many visitors as I actually received. Comparing the clicks in your AdWords control panel and your Analytics tables can tell you if there's a problem, but not what that problem is.

Shawn Purtell of ROI Revolution cautions that the numbers should be close, but probably won't be identical. Analytics and conversion tracking handle repeat visitors differently, and if a visitor clicks today and converts in a week or a month, the data in the two systems will log those events in different time frames. As long as the data are basically telling the same story, you're okay.

Viewing your data in the Dashboard

Once your tracking is correctly set up and verified, it's time to start amassing insights on your visitors' behavior. From the Analytics tab in your AdWords account, click the View Reports link for the profile you want to examine. You'll begin with the Dashboard, which you can customize by adding views that you'll want to see a lot.

The Dashboard consists of, as you might expect, the just-the-facts graphs and charts that give you a quick picture of how your Web site is doing, as shown in Figure 15-6. It includes a graph of visits by day, as well as more in-depth information about those visits.

Figure 15-6:
The Dashboard screen includes overview information about your visitors.

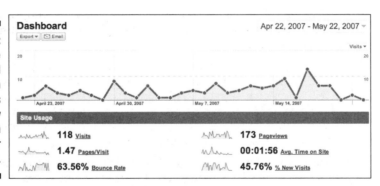

Visits-by-day graph

You can play with the visits-by-day graph, which by default shows you the last 30 days of data, by clicking the arrow to the right of the second date. You can change the date range by length and start date, either by clicking a date or several in the Calendar view, or (much easier and more elegantly), selecting the Timeline tab above the calendar. Click your cursor inside the box and hold your mouse down to drag it backward or forward, or click and select either edge to expand or contract the date range.

Below the Date Range boxes is a check box labeled Compare to Past. Check that box to superimpose a previous date range over the current one. For example, you can quickly compare your Web traffic in May and March.

Analytics will automatically generate a range of the same number of days as the current one.

Many other screens also feature a top graph similar to the visits-by-day graph, and you can manipulate them all the same way — by changing starting and ending points, and by comparing two time periods.

Playing with Analytics is really simple, once you've seen it done. Head over to `http://askhowie.com/dates` for a series of short video tutorials that will have you playing with your data in no time.

Site Usage statistics

The Dashboard shows you important data about how often your site is visited in the Site Usage section. The Site Usage section provides the following data:

- ✔ **Visits, Pageviews, and Pages/Visit:** For a given period, how many visitors came to your Web site, and how many pages did they all look at? In Figure 15-6, 118 visitors were served a total of 173 pages over the week, for an average of 1.47 pages per visitor.

- ✔ **Avg. Time on Site:** How long did the average visitor hang around before leaving your Web site? Figure 15-6 shows a rather pathetic time of one minute, 56 seconds.

- ✔ **Bounce Rate:** Google defines a *bounce* as a single-page visit. If people leave your landing page without going deeper into your site or opting in to a list, your landing page isn't doing its job. Figure 15-6 shows a bounce rate of 63.56%, which means that the majority of visitors to this site are indifferent to the landing page, and I'll probably never get the chance to do business with them.

- ✔ **% New Visits:** What percentage of your visitors have never been to your site before? (Remember, Analytics tracks computers, not people.) Figure 15-6 shows 45.76% of the visitors are new to your site.

Visitors Overview graph

The Visitors Overview graph shows you the number of unique visitors, rather than the number of visitors. If Sean from Toronto comes to your site on Sunday, Tuesday, and the following Saturday, that counts as three visits, but only one visitor (assuming, of course, that he used the same computer all three times).

The Visitors Overview and following sections can all be removed from the dashboard by clicking the small X in the right-hand corner of the header.

Map Overlay

A world map shows you at a glance where in the world your visitors live. The darker the shading, the more visits from that location. Click on a land mass to zoom in to a continent. Keep clicking to go deeper, into countries, states/provinces/regions, and cities.

Traffic Sources Overview

This graph shows you the comparative traffic production of direct visitors (those who type your URL directly into their browser), search engine traffic by engine, and other referring Web sites. Click the small View Report link for a detailed breakdown of which search engines and referring sites. Note that Analytics distinguishes between paid search (cpc) and organic for Google, Yahoo, and MSN.

Content Overview

You can see the five most viewed pages on your site, based on the number of *pageviews* (how many times visitors saw that page). The % Pageviews column shows what percent of all the pageviews on your site were generated by that particular page.

Goals Overview

The Goals Overview gives you a quick look at the number of visitors completing your defined goals.

The AdWords Campaign screen

In the Dashboard, you can see the number and percentage of visits generated by each AdWords campaign. Click the View Report link to go deeper into the AdWords reporting, the part of Analytics I describe in the rest of this chapter.

In addition to a link off the Dashboard, you can access this screen directly from the left navigation by clicking Traffic Sources, then AdWords, and finally AdWords Campaigns.

The top chart, as usual, shows visits over time. Below, a table segments your traffic by campaign and shows the number of visits, pages/visit, average time on your site, percentage of new visits, and bounce rate for each campaign. Click a campaign name to get the same information on the ad group level, and click an ad group to see the same data for each individual keyword. Figure 15-7 shows how Analytics drills down into the French campaign (which cost a total of $74,544.64) to the Brie ad group (accounting for $40,164.41, or 53.88% of the total) and even deeper to the individual keyword brie (which cost $1718.42, or 2.31% of the advertising spending for the entire campaign).

If the traffic comes from the content network, it's labeled (content targeting), and appears at the top of the keyword list. You can search for specific keywords using the search box below the keyword list.

Clicking on an individual keyword brings up actionable data in three tabs:

✔ **Site Usage tab:** How visitors from that keyword behaved on your site: average time on site, bounce rate, pages/visit, and percentage of new visits. Interesting, to be sure, but the next two tabs will really blow your mind (if you're into that sort of thing).

✔ **Goal Conversion tab:** How visitors from that keyword converted to each of your defined goals, and the goal value per visit (that is, how much the average customer who types that keyword is worth to you). Armed with this information, you can set your AdWords bids so that no keyword is costing you more than you're making back on your site.

✔ **Clicks tab:** The monetary value of a click generated by that keyword: including total number of clicks, value of each click (RPC — Revenue-Per-Click, the average revenue you received for each click based on ecommerce sales and the value you assigned to your goals), your profit (or loss) margin, and the overall ROI of that keyword.

Figure 15-7:
You can discover how each AdWords campaign, ad group, and keyword produces different business results.

Ad content segmenting

Choose Ad Content from the Segment drop-down list to see the same data, this time by individual ad. (You can find the Segment drop-down list above the Site Usage, Goal Conversion, and Clicks tabs.) Only the headlines are shown, so if you're running different ads with identical headlines, you're not going to find this particular view very useful.

Views

To the right of the Site Usage, Goal Conversion, and Clicks tabs, you'll find five views to choose from. From left to right, they are Table, Pie Chart, Horizontal Bar Graph, Comparison Against Site Average, and Mini-histogram (that's a line chart, not a medical test).

Showing you all the views here would fill up another book. Check out www. roirevolution.com/graphs for a more in-depth discussion of the Analytics graphs. Play around with different segmenting options and views, and feel free to explore. You can't break anything in the Analytics report section — it's all read-only.

The Keyword Positions view

From the left navigation, choose AdWords and then Keyword Positions. Below the obligatory line graph of visits over time, you'll see a list of your keywords, and the number of visits generated by each one. Click any keyword, and a magical view appears to the right of the keyword list. This view shows you how many clicks were generated by that keyword in each position on the search-results page. The view itself is a mockup of the search-results page, on which ads can appear on top of the organic results to the left (labeled Top 1, Top 2, and Top 3) or down the right side (labeled Side 1 through Side 10), as shown in Figure 15-8. You can use this information to find and bid on your keyword's "sweet spot" on the search-results page.

Figure 15-8: The Keyword Positions view shows which ad positions generate clicks for a given keyword.

You can also determine position for ads showing on the content network. If an advertiser runs an AdSense tower of five ads, your ad could be in positions one through five in that ad block.

Automating Analytics reporting

At the top of almost every screen, Analytics gives you the option to export or e-mail the results in one of four formats: PDF (for Adobe Acrobat Reader), XML (a Web language), CSV (for Microsoft Excel) and TSV (Tab Separated Values, for other spreadsheet applications). You can also add the view to the main Dashboard.

When you create an e-mail report, you can customize it and schedule it to be sent to whomever you want at regular intervals. You can even include a date comparison, so you can see changes in the key numbers each week or month. Under the Schedule tab, just check the box labeled Include Date Comparison.

Acting on Your Data to Make More Money

Throughout this chapter, I show you examples of data that you can act on to improve Web site conversion. In this section, I recap some of the low-hanging fruit that you can pluck with even a simple, non-e-commerce Analytics setup.

Optimizing your site for your visitors

The more you know about your visitors, the more successfully you can create a Web site that serves their needs and invites their business. Begin with the Web Design Parameters screen in the Webmaster view. View and print your visitors' browser versions, screen resolutions, and connection speeds for the past week, month, and three months. Note the most popular types of each characteristic.

The next step will take a little work, but it's well worth the effort. Go and navigate your Web site using the browsers, resolutions, and connection speeds used by your visitors. How long does you site take to load via dialup? What part of your landing page is visible on an 800 x 600 screen? What does your order form look like in Safari or Firefox?

If you interact with your site using only your own computer, you have no idea what your visitors are experiencing. Take the time to put yourself in their shoes, or on their mouse, and you may discover simple design tweaks that will double conversion literally overnight.

Improving site "stickiness"

If visitors leave your site after viewing only one or two pages, you may have a "stickiness" problem. A *sticky site* is one that keeps visitors engaged for a long period of time, so they have a chance to get to know you, answer their questions, and feel more comfortable with the idea of doing business with you.

The Average Pageviews per Visit metric, available on many screens, is a good indicator of how sticky your site is. If you spend all your energy on your AdWords campaigns yet lose visitors within a page or two on your site, you know where you need to improve.

From Timothy Seward of ROI Revolution: "To calculate your target for pageviews per visit, count how many pages it would take to complete the core goal of your site. For example, if your site is an ecommerce site, then count how many pages it takes from the homepage to make it all the way to the receipt page. That resulting number is a good target to shoot for."

Loyalty and recency

Loyalty refers to the number of times visitors return to your site. *Recency,* like it sounds, refers to how recently they've been back. Most successful businesses display high loyalty and recency metrics: Their customers come back again and again, and a large percentage of their customers have purchased recently.

Click Visitors on the left, then Visitor Loyalty, then Loyalty. You'll see a bar chart showing the number and percentage of visitors who have visited your site once, twice, three times, all the way up to 25–50 visits (as shown in Figure 15-9). If your online business depends on repeat customers to be profitable, you should improve the effectiveness of your e-mail follow up sequences and other means of generating repeat traffic.

Figure 15-9:
The vast
majority of
visitors to
this site are
first-time
visitors, a
problem if
the site
depends on
repeat
business
to be
successful.

The report just below Loyalty is Recency. A healthy site attracts its visitors back at regular intervals, whether it be daily, weekly, or monthly. Figure 15-10 shows a site that encourages visitors to return on roughly a bi-weekly or monthly basis. The site, www.peaceweavers.com, does so by means of a regular newsletter and an updated photo blog.

Figure 15-10:
Over 10% of
the site
visitors over
the past
month had
been on
the site
between
one week
and two
months
previously.

As AdWords matures and competition heats up, the value of the first transaction will trend toward break-even. If you want to be successful, you must cultivate recency and frequency in your customers. E-mail autoresponders and broadcasts (see Chapter 11), special events, teleseminars, referral contests, quizzes, new articles, and sales can all make your Web site a recurring destination rather than a one-shot deal.

Evaluating Web site changes

You can apply the date range comparison function to goal tracking and goal conversion. For example, say that you made a change to your opt-in landing page on July 1, and you want to determine the effect of that change. You can compare the goal conversion for your opt-in for July 1–30, compared to June 1–30 of the same year.

In your AdWords Campaign report (or most other reports), first click the date range at the top right of the screen. Set the date range by clicking and selecting the start and end date, and then check the Compare to Past check box. By default, you'll see the previous week or month, depending on your current date range. To change the comparison range (for example, to the same month last year), choose the Timeline tab and drag the slider to the left until you reach the beginning of the comparison date range.

The graph now contains bars of two different colors, representing the different time periods. In Figure 15-11, the total number of visits and unique visitors were up from March to April, but the time on site, average pageviews, and bounce rate all got slightly worse. The owner of this site needs to spend more time improving the site, rather than generating new traffic.

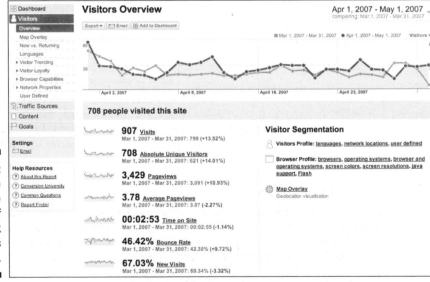

Figure 15-11:
Compare two date ranges of data to track changes over time.

Page and funnel navigation

The visually coolest part of Analytics is the navigation. You can see how visitors abandon the funnel you've defined, and where they go. You can also analyze any page on your site in terms of where visitors come from before landing on that page — and where they go afterward (shown in Figure 15-12).

Figure 15-12:
For any page, discover where your visitors come from before viewing and where they go after viewing.

66.98% Entrances		53.16% Exits	
33.02% Previous Pages		**46.84% Next Pages**	
Content	% Clicks	Content	% Clicks
/index.htm	8.39%	/products/brie/index.htm	8.48%
/learn/about.htm	4.54%	/index.htm	8.39%
/catalog_request.htm	3.32%	/products/index.htm	8.32%
/products/gouda/index.htm	3.22%	/learn/about.htm	5.36%
/products/brie/index.htm	3.05%	/catalog_request.htm	3.75%
/products/cheddar/index.htm	2.69%	/products/cheddar/index.htm	3.53%
/products/index.htm	2.31%	/products/gouda/index.htm	2.36%
/products/bleu/index.htm	0.91%	/sitemap.htm	1.54%
/sitemap.htm	0.77%	/products/bleu/index.htm	1.30%
/products/brie/details/briezybrie.htm	0.58%	/contact.htm	0.99%

Page navigation

Click Content from the left navigation. Identify your most viewed pages on the left, under the Top Content header, and click each URL to see how that page fits in your visitors' navigation. You can learn how visitors found that page by clicking the Navigation Summary link. You'll discover that some of your pages are sending visitors in the wrong direction, and you can take steps to correct the problem. You can make links bigger and more noticeable. You can move buttons and forms left or right, above the fold, or repeat them several times on a page. You can highlight text, use arrows or animation to draw eyeballs, or deploy audio or video.

Funnel Visualization

From the Goals section in the left navigation, choose Funnel Visualization. You can select any of your (up to four) goals. You will see how well your funnel moves visitors from entry to goal achievement, and where and why they are abandoning your funnel, as shown in Figure 15-13.

Timothy Seward offers the example of a detour from the shopping cart checkout page to the guarantee page instead of the completed sale. Upon discovering that, a clever merchant would add the guarantee to the checkout page and keep their visitors on track to a sale.

Figure 15-13:
3116 visitors
entered the
funnel, and
104 exited
success-
fully by
requesting a
catalog.
Funnel
Visualization
shows
where the
other
visitors
went.

Reverse Goal Path

Also under Goals, check out Reverse Goal Path. This view shows you how vis-itors actually get to your goals; not what you think your funnel is, but what your visitors think it is. You may uncover your visitors' unanswered ques-tions and objections by studying the reverse path to each goal. If a lot of visi-tors are coming through your privacy policy page, a page usually ignored by viewers, perhaps your site doesn't seem trustworthy enough. You may want to add credibility elements such as logos, anti-spam assurances, and more professional design.

Part VI
The Part of Tens

The 5th Wave   By Rich Tennant

THE FUTURE OF AD PLACEMENT IN VIDEO GAMES

"Watch out for the Necromancer behind the Toyota with the Snapple in his hand."

In this part . . .

This part covers important stuff that didn't quite fit in the rest of the book. I gathered these tidbits and assembled them into top-ten lists.

I gathered together the worst beginner's mistakes I've encountered in my years as an AdWords consultant and coach for Chapter 16. Avoid these and you've shaved two years off your learning curve.

Chapter 17 contains case studies that highlight the principles revealed in this book. You'll find a broad range of businesses, challenges, and solutions that are meant to bring the concepts to life and inspire you to make your own AdWords success stories.

Because I had so much fun writing Chapters 16 and 17, I wrote two more top-ten lists and made them into Bonus Chapters 1 and 2. You can view and download these chapters as PDF files at www.dummies.com/go/adwords.

In Bonus Chapter 1, I share a bunch of the online tools I use personally and recommend highly. Some are free and some are paid; start with the free ones and start paying for tools out of your AdWords profits.

Bonus Chapter 2 was my excuse to contact some of the best copywriters in the world and get them to return my e-mails. You'll get a first-class education from these tips on writing great Google ads.

Chapter 16

The Ten Most Serious AdWords Beginner's Mistakes

AdWords can have a steep learning curve, as well as an expensive one. In this chapter, I quickly run through the most common and expensive mistakes I've seen as an AdWords consultant and fixer.

Neglecting to Split Test Your Ads

Even the world's best marketers are wrong more often than they're right. If you run a single ad, the chances of that ad being the best of all the possible ads in the universe are laughably small. When you compare two very different ads head to head, one of them will almost always be better than the other — more compelling, more attractive, or more in tune with the innermost desires of your market.

When you've run the test long enough to have statistically significant data, you gracefully retire (or unceremoniously fire, whichever you prefer) the losing ad and put up another challenger. You continue the process, directing the survival of the fittest ad until you find the one unbeatable control that maximizes your business goals.

In the old pre-Internet days, split testing was complicated and expensive, a high-level business process reserved for huge companies with giant mainframe computers and millions of dollars on the line. Now, Google AdWords makes split testing as easy as sending e-mail; when I see advertisers neglecting this fundamental improvement strategy, I feel like the mom telling her kid to eat his peas because there are children starving somewhere else in the world. I want to shake them and shout, "Don't you realize how lucky you are to be able to split test so easily and cheaply and achieve such quick and conclusive results?"

If you aren't split testing at this point, contact my office. I'll pack my WrestleMania Split Test Avenger outfit, fly (business class only, please) to your place of business, and shake some sense into you.

Practical advice:

- ✔ When you set up a new ad group, always have two different ads ready.
- ✔ Think of split tests as experiments you're conducting to satisfy your curiosity. Keep a journal of questions, prioritize them, and always have another split test waiting in the wings.
- ✔ Split test wide variations first, and then narrow down to smaller details.
- ✔ Check for statistical significance before declaring a winner. Don't mistake randomness for rock-solid trends.
- ✔ Split test landing pages and e-mail sequences as well as AdWords ads. With the right tools, these split tests are almost as easy as the AdWords split-testing interface.

See Chapter 13 for best practices in split testing.

Letting Google Retire Your Ads without Testing

Another campaign setting that you need to override is the Ad Serving option in the Advanced Options section. From your campaign management console, click into a campaign and then click the Edit Campaign Settings link near the top. On the next page, Campaign Settings, find Ad Serving under Advanced Options (on the left). Do not optimize ad serving. Do not let Google show better performing ads more often. Instead, select the radio button next to Rotate: Show Ads More Evenly.

If you're split testing, you have two goals: You want to identify the winner as quickly as possible, and you want to learn something from the test that will help you connect better with your market in the future.

When you let Google take control behind the scenes and quietly retire your low-CTR ads, you allow tests to drag on unnecessarily. It's like holding a race, not specifying its length, and running it until the winner is miles away and the losers are gasping for breath at the side of the road. A much more efficient method is to establish a finish line and identify the winner as soon as the tape is broken. When Google retires your ads behind your back, you lose the market intelligence that your split tests often provide.

Finally, as I show in Chapter 14, the ad with the best CTR is often the least profitable. Yet Google chooses winners based on CTR, not conversion.

Split Testing for Improved CTR Only

Ads that generate high CTR can be wonderful. They attract more visitors to your site at lower cost, and rank higher than other ads bidding the same amount. They also teach you about your market's desires and fears.

But when you split test two ads and choose the winner based solely on CTR, you are in danger of worshipping a false god. Understand that the AdWords game is based on one rule: Get more outputs for your inputs than anyone else. Okay, CTR is a key throughput — but leads, customers, and dollars are what you're after.

A mention of Paris Hilton in your ad text may generate a high CTR, but just like the old magazine ads with the four-inch red headline of the word sex, she may be attracting eyeballs belonging to nonbuyers. Remember that lots of clicks translates into lots of money for Google, not for you. Getting the right clicks is more important than getting lots of clicks.

When you split test your ads, make sure you run conversion reports, and don't rely on CTR alone.

Ignoring the Display URL Line in Your Ad

After the headline, the Display URL line is the most important one in your ad. It constitutes as much as 25% of the entire ad. Yet the typical beginner simply puts the name of his or her Web site, and doesn't even try capitalizing — let alone adding subdomains or subdirectories, or experimenting with other URLs that redirect to the main Web site.

The Display URL is the name of your store, in the eyes of the searcher. Search is an activity based on speed — people want quick results, and they want the right information and the right product served to them right away. If someone is looking for a three-hole punch, and their choices are `thunder mountainofficesupplies.com` or `threeholepunchesforall.com`, they will assume that the latter site is likelier to satisfy their desire — and do it more quickly.

To test different domain names, you can use a redirect service such as `www.zoneedit.com` or just buy a bunch of domains at `www.getgoing online.com` and redirect them manually.

Even easier and cheaper is the use of subdomains (such as `holepunches. ecoofficesupply.com`) and subdirectories (say, `ecoofficesupply. com/3holepunches`). Again, `www.zoneedit.com` makes quick work of creating and managing multiple subdomains, and your first five domains with them are free.

Creating Ad Groups with Unrelated Keywords

The easiest way to set up an ad group is to write an ad, dump every keyword you can think of into that group, and send it to your home page. Heck, that should take you about 10 minutes of work if you're using some of the powerful keyword tools I talk about in Chapter 5. It's much more complicated and time-consuming to create tight ad groups, based on a narrow set of related keywords matched closely to the ads and the landing page. But your results will be well worth the extra time and effort.

Keywords unrelated to ads and landing pages produce poor CTR and conversion results — and cost a lot of money because of the poor `quality score` penalty. Remember that each keyword represents a mindset; take the time to group your keywords by similar mindsets, and write your ads and landing pages to address the desires and fears attached to those mindsets.

You can tell when your ad groups are too broad if the CTRs of different keywords in the same group vary wildly. You may discover that the successful keywords are found in the ad headline and repeated in the description or URL. Peel the underperforming keywords out of that ad group and stick them into their own group, with an ad written just for them.

Muddying Search and Content Results

Many beginners rely on Google's default settings when creating campaigns. Remember that Google's defaults usually serve to simplify your account and to increase Google's revenue. Sometimes those two goals are compatible with your goals, and sometimes they aren't. One of the campaign settings you need to change right away, because you prefer profitability to simplicity, is Networks. (See Figure 16-1.)

Figure 16-1:
Separate
content
from search
network
from Google
traffic
on the
Campaign
Settings
page.

If you run all three steams of traffic (Google, search partners, and content network) through the same ad group, you lose the ability to distinguish among the very different kinds of traffic. *Content network traffic* consists of people who were interrupted while they were reading or surfing or watching something else. *Search network traffic* consists of people who are actively looking for your keywords. Not only do they arrive at your site driven by different motivations and desires, they respond differently to your ads and offers.

In many cases, content traffic overwhelms search traffic. When that's true, you lose the ability to split test ads properly; your accurate CTR and conversion data from the search traffic is drowned out by the flood of content traffic. Figuring out what your market is telling you is like trying to hear a cricket at a heavy-metal concert.

When you choose winning ads and identify profitable keywords based on poorly converting search traffic — and try to apply those lessons to your search marketing — in essence you're surveying penguins to try to sell to chimpanzees. The two market channels are very different, and should be studied and treated differently.

See Chapter 7 for detailed instructions on how to split Google, search partner, and content network traffic into three different campaigns.

Ignoring the 80/20 Principle

The 80/20 principle, applied to AdWords, states that the vast majority of outputs (impressions, clicks, leads, sales, and such) are caused by a very small minority of inputs (ad groups, ads, and keywords). Instead of diffusing your efforts, focus on the vital few rather than the insignificant many.

When you follow my advice and create Best Practice AdWords campaigns, you inevitably create a fair amount of complexity. With so many variables to monitor and juggle and adjust, it's common to become overwhelmed and wonder, "What do I do now?"

I often see consulting clients who have spend days massaging an ad group that has no potential to make a significant contribution to their bottom line, while ignoring the big keywords in the important ad groups.

Keep reminding yourself that the AdWords game is about maximizing outputs from fixed inputs. In this case, inputs are impressions and advertising cost. Spend your time fixing the things that will make the biggest difference:

1. Sort your campaigns by impressions.

2. Sort that campaign's ad groups by impressions.

   Assess the ads in that group — do you have a clear winner?

3. Sort keywords by impressions, and look at the top five keywords.

   Are they making you money? Do you need to adjust their bids? Peel and stick them into a new ad group? Pause or delete them?

Here the number of impressions is your limiting factor. If you have two ad groups, one with 50 impressions a day and the other with 20,000, a 50% improvement in conversion might translate into one additional sale a month for the smaller group and one to two more sales a day for the larger group. Where do you want to spend your time?

One exception: you may be artificially limiting impressions in two ways:

- ✔ By ignoring potential high-traffic keywords
- ✔ By bidding for a position on page two or worse

Make sure you check your average position for each keyword, ad, ad group and campaign before assuming you've maxed out its traffic.

Declaring Split-Test Winners Too Slowly

Once you set up split testing, you want to identify winners as quickly as possible, so you can learn and improve faster than your competition. If you can double your CTR and maintain the same quality of traffic, you get twice as many visitors for the same amount of money. When you double your Web site's traffic, you can run your landing-page and sales-page split tests twice as fast as well. The faster you split test, the faster you improve.

I commonly look at new clients' accounts and point out that they have been running a split test for weeks longer than they need to. Not only are they showing an inferior ad half the time, they're also wasting the most precious resource of all: *meaningful insights about their market.*

Set up reports to run on a regular basis that just look at ad performance. Make it a habit to run the numbers through the statistical significance tester at www.askhowie.com/split and identify split tests that have yielded conclusive, action-producing results.

You can automate this process and receive e-mail notification of split-test winners by subscribing to www.winneralert.com.

Declaring Split-Test Winners Too Quickly

If your ad group receives a lot of traffic, your split tests may achieve statistical significance after only an hour or two. The problem with this speedy outcome is that the people searching during that particular window of time may be different from people searching at other times. If you choose a winner based on the traffic from 2:00 to 4:00 in the morning on Sunday, you may be picking an ad that has less appeal to people searching at noon on Wednesday.

To be safe, run each split test for at least a week, so you don't put too much weight into a cyclical blip. You can run reports by date and time to identify differences in impressions, CTR, and conversion by day of the week and time of day.

If your week-long split test threatens to become too expensive because of the volume of traffic, you can limit your traffic geographically by creating a campaign that targets a few low-population metropolitan areas but shows your ad 24/7.

Forgetting Keywords in Quotes (Phrase Matching) or Brackets (Exact Matching)

When you put a keyword in quotation marks, you tell Google that the quoted words or phrase must appear exactly as written somewhere in the keyword. Brackets are even more specific: They signify that the searcher must enter the keyword exactly as it appears within the brackets, with nothing added or removed.

When you use broad match keywords only (putting no quotes or brackets on the keyword), you don't really know what your visitors actually entered as search terms. You lump many different searches into a big vague basket and miss out on some valuable market intelligence.

Phrase and exact match keywords often achieve higher CTRs than broad matches, because you can create ads that speak directly to the exact words and phrases your visitors type.

 Because of the hierarchy among broad, phrase, and exact match keywords, be aware that phrase match keywords cannibalize their broad match counterparts, and exact match keywords steal impressions from both. If the CTRs differ among the three match types for high-traffic keywords, peel the underperformers and stick them into their own ad groups. (See more about keyword matching in Chapter 5.)

Ignoring Negative Keywords

Negative keywords keep certain searchers from seeing your ads. If you get significant traffic from broad or phrase match keywords, you may find that Google is matching your ad to some irrelevant searches. If you want to deter tire-kickers from costing you clicks, you may want to add negative keywords like `free` and `complimentary`.

If you target upscale buyers, you can improve your ROI by eliminating `dis-count` and `cheap`, as well as certain brand names that have low-end connotations. If some of your search terms are ambiguous (for example `anthrax` refers to both a disease and a heavy-metal band) or could refer to two different niches of the same market (`auto glass` and `plate glass` windows), save your click money by adding negative keywords to your keyword list.

Monitor your keyword-conversion performance over time to find new negative keywords. If you sell golf clubs and none of your `golf instruction` keywords convert, you can add `instruction` as a negative keyword.

Keeping the Keyword Quality Score Hidden

Google introduced the keyword quality score in 2006, without much fanfare or documentation. It's not even shown in the default ad group Keyword tab screen. You must add the Quality Score column to the ad group Keyword tab to be able to manage this crucial metric.

Quality score tells you how much you must bid in order to show your ad for a given keyword. Poor quality scores put you at a huge competitive disadvantage in your market; for this reason, I advise my clients to fix their quality scores before dealing with anything else on their sites or AdWords campaigns.

AdWords was the first advertising medium in the world to penalize advertisers for showing irrelevant content to their users. Their algorithms are based on years of comprehensive data collection — the keyword quality scores contain information based on far more than your measly account. Ignoring it means you are missing the opportunity to make your whole sales process more customer-friendly and effective.

Activate the quality-score column by going to the ad group, clicking the Keyword tab, and clicking the Customize Columns link. Select Quality Score from the Customize Columns drop-down list.

Spending Too Much or Too Little in the Beginning

Marketing Consultant Joy Milkowski of www.adwordstoolbox.com reminded me of another big beginner's mistake: Over- or under-spending during the first weeks and months of your AdWords campaigns.

If you open your wallet too much by specifying too high a monthly budget or daily spend, you'll lose all your money before you have time to learn the ropes. When you've figured out that something isn't working, turn it off right away while you make changes. Chances are — even with this book under your belt — you will take some time to get the feel of AdWords and develop proficiency. If you rush, you'll blow through your budget several times and walk away going, "This stuff doesn't work."

If you ever took a driving lesson, you may remember that your instructor made you drive slowly for a long time, showing you how to steer and brake and stop fiddling with the radio dial, before ever letting you open up on a highway. Your AdWords budget is your MPH — take it easy until you learn how to drive safely.

Other clients are so hesitant that they set daily and monthly budgets far too low to generate enough traffic. They don't get enough impressions to split test and improve their ads and keywords, and they give up in frustration. Without enough statistically significant data, they don't know how to improve their campaigns and quit in frustration. That's like learning to drive by never going faster than five miles per hour. The experience of going 55 MPH (or 85, which I wouldn't know about, especially not on I-95 in Maryland just south of DC, I swear) is qualitatively and not just quantitatively different from inching along in an empty parking lot. The super-slow experience just doesn't transfer to the real thing.

The happy medium involves setting a learning budget and sticking with it. Do your homework (see Chapter 4) to estimate the amount of traffic you can expect. Your advertising spend (as well as the daily or weekly attention you'll need to give your account) depends on the velocity of that traffic. At first, don't expect to make money, or even come close to breaking even. You're not advertising to earn it back; instead, you're running market tests so you can come out swinging when you open up your wallet and your traffic. Your goal is to get your ROI into the black within a few months.

Chapter 17

Ten AdWords Case Studies

*T*he best way to see the strategies and concepts from this book in action is by viewing actual examples. I can't show you all the details, because successful advertisers guard their keywords, strategies, and metrics like the recipe for Coca-Cola. I've compiled case studies from consultants who hope you'll think they're clever enough to hire them, from clients who hope you'll go to their Web sites and buy their products, and from friends egotistical enough to want to see their names in a book. Among these three groups, you'll see enough gems to keep you busy for a while.

Adding a Welcome Video to the Landing Page

Ken Evoy, president of www.sitesell.com (a turn-key Web hosting and e-commerce business-building system), thought that he had fully optimized his Web-site conversion process through years of comprehensive testing. Nothing he tried could beat his control site. But he found that adding a short, friendly Welcome to My Website video to his home page dramatically increased sales for his Site Build It! service. The video helped increase sales by 30% by explaining the product and building an emotional connection with visitors.

With the help of Web video consultant Joe Chapuis of www.webvideozone.com, Ken created a 3-minute video shortcut for the SiteSell homepage that walks prospects through a quick tour of his site and service. Ken explained, "Site Built It! is a big product that takes a lot of words to explain. Video enables us to get so much more information across so much more efficiently."

Ken added the video to the top of his home page, using the Flash video player available at www.webvideozone.com. Joe Chapuis explained the importance of video placement: "If you want someone to watch your video, you need to have it at the top of the page where it will get noticed, as well as on a Web page that prospects are likely to visit."

Ken reported that sales increased by 30% since he added video to the home page: "Video is incredibly powerful, especially for a product like SBI. . . . We have never been able to communicate so precisely, effectively, nor with such emotion."

As Seen on TV Ads and Web Copy

Dremu.com sells skin-care, wrinkle-removing, and anti-aging products formulated with emu oil. They have used an ad strategy that I call *media credentializing* to generate high CTRs and robust sales conversions. Their ads include phrases like these:

> as seen on NBC
> as seen in *Vogue* and *Allure*
> as seen on [*name*'s] show

Mass-media convey much more credibility than online media. Anyone can have a Web site — heck, your nephew who flunked high-school math probably has a Web site — but not anyone can get interviewed on television or get quoted in a magazine or newspaper. The money Dremu spent on PR to get a few local media mentions or TV spots has paid off many times over, not in immediate sales following the media appearance, but in the consistent use of the original exposure to build credibility.

On the Dremu.com Web page is a list of media that have included mention of Dremu's Deception cream. On the same page, www.dremu.com/deception, you can watch a video clip from a local ABC-TV affiliate demonstrating the product. The media appearances have snowballed — national news and entertainment outlets scour local media for interesting stories, and consider the fact that a story has run somewhere else proof that it's newsworthy.

Within four months of including media appearances in their ads and Web pages, Dremu.com's sales volume had doubled.

Dremu.com also bid on the names of celebrities who have been quoted as using or recommending their products. When Cindy Crawford introduced her new line of anti-aging products, Heavenly Beauty, via late-night infomercials, Dremu.com bid on Cindy Crawford Heavenly Beauty and saw a huge spike in sales whenever the infomercial ran. Apparently, Heavenly Beauty had not included AdWords in its marketing mix, so many of the people who looked her up online were directed to a different anti-wrinkle cream with an equally impressive client list.

Plugging in the Blender with Risk Reversal

Sometimes you do 99% of the things right and still can't achieve success, a situation that seems to fly in the face of the 80/20 Rule, the Golden Rule, and the Rule of Thumb. I think of that situation as the *blender bafflement:*

I'm preparing to make a delicious and nutritious fruit smoothie. I've got water, rice milk, pitted organic medjool dates, frozen berries, a banana, walnut pieces, a little bit of frozen spinach (you can't taste it), ground flax seeds, and my awesome Vitamix blender. I put the lid on the blender (I hate it when globs of smoothie hit the ceiling and drip down my neck for the next half hour), and press the switch. Nothing happens.

The blender isn't plugged in, of course. The plug is just two inches away from the outlet — and gee, in the grand scheme of things, that's good enough, isn't it? Especially since everything else is configured perfectly. But no — blender bafflement is unforgiving.

John Lercari of `www.thememoriesplace.com` was suffering from a bit of the blender bafflement. The Memories Place sells customized rugs and throws with photographs on them, and despite all his best efforts, John could not figure out how to achieve his goal of doubled sales. Then he hit upon the concept of risk reversal from a classic marketing book, Jay Abraham's *Getting Everything You Can Out of All You've Got: 21 Ways You Can Out-Think, Out-Perform, and Out-Earn the Competition* (St. Martin's Griffin). John realized that no one in his industry offered a satisfaction guarantee on their products. After all, if you don't like the shower-curtain-sized photo of you and your brother drinking beer and playing beach volleyball, it's not like John can turn around and sell it to anyone else.

When John went back through his records, he confirmed something he already knew — almost all his customers were delighted with their rugs and throws and pillows and other items, and he could count the number of refund requests and complaints over the last couple of years on the fingers of one hand. He prominently added a guarantee to his site: "If you are not completely satisfied with your throw from The Memories Place, we will remake it for you." He pointed out that this guarantee was unlike anyone else's in the industry — featuring it on pop-overs, navigation buttons, and text throughout his site. Without changing anything else, his daily sales tripled overnight. The two inches between the blender plug and the wall outlet was, in John's case, the concern in his prospects' minds that they wouldn't like the finished product and would be stuck with it. When he erased that concern, sales increased significantly.

Getting the Basics Right

Kelly Conway of www.ctrexpert.com kindly saved me several hours of work by providing the following case study. Notice the simple steps that cumulatively produced stellar results.

I met David O'Hara, a product-development expert, when he was looking for help in selling one of his products, the Breatheasy blood-pressure reduction system, via PPC advertising. David's goal for this ad campaign is to drive visitors to a landing page where he makes a one-time sale of either a CD or downloadable product. Two landing-page examples include
www.highbloodpressurehq.com and
www.highbloodpressurehq.com/about_me.html

The campaign includes 30–40 ads, which we continuously split-test. Examples include:

```
15 Minutes to Lower Blood
Pressure - 6 Weeks to a Better Life
Free from High Blood Pressure
HighBloodPressureHQ.com
2,070 Clicks | 3.49% CTR | $0.12 CPC


These Breathing Exercises
Lower High Blood Pressure
Naturally - Just 15 Minutes a Day
HighBloodPressureHQ.com
220 Clicks | 4.90% CTR | $0.24 CPC


How To Lower Blood
Pressure - 15 Minutes/Day - 6 Weeks
to Freedom from High Blood Pressure
HighBloodPressureHQ.com
137 Clicks | 6.82% CTR | $0.23 CPC


Lower Blood Pressure
Start Immediately - 15 Minutes/Day
Simple, Practical & Affordable!
HighBloodPressureHQ.com
101 Clicks | 3.63% CTR | $0.16 CPC
```

The state of the ad campaign, at the time that David contacted me, was similar to many other campaigns I've seen. He was bidding on 600–800 keywords, all of which were in a single ad group. None of the keyword phrases were making use of anything other than Google's broad-match option. David's initial request was to get the minimum cost-per-click of many of his keywords below the $1 and $5 Google was requesting.

Improve Web Site to Increase Keyword Quality Score and Lower Bid Prices

The campaign's overall CTR had been around 0.50%. My immediate goal was to raise that number dramatically. I knew by doing that, I would be able to decrease the minimum bid and our average CPC. The initial cost per click was $0.23. However, David still had hundreds of keywords he wasn't bidding on due to the $1 and $5 minimum-bid requirements. In addition, I recommended that David add content to his Web site so that Google would find his keywords more relevant. He went to work on that while I worked on increasing the CTR.

Add Quotes and Brackets to Every Keyword

First, I created phrase- and exact-match versions for every keyword in the campaign. Those keyword variations often have less competition, which means their bid prices can be lower. Additionally, they often attract better-targeted visitors than the broad-match versions of the same phrases.

Delete Poorly-Performing Keywords

Next, in order to quickly raise the campaign's CTR, I needed to delete the keywords that were performing poorly. I deleted phrases that, after 200 or more impressions, had resulted in no sales and had not achieved at least a 0.80% CTR.

Interim Results after Two Weeks

Implementing these strategies helped us increase the campaign's cumulative CTR to 1.02% by the end of the second week. Additionally, we managed to lower our average CPC by nearly 10%, to $0.21, during that period. By the end of the first month, our overall CTR was 1.67%. Google reported our average ad position for the first month as 5.6; indicating that our ads appeared, on average, in fifth or sixth position within Google's sponsored listings.

Segment Keywords into Ad Groups

The next step was to segment the keywords into groups of related phrases. This work was time consuming, but not difficult. I reviewed all of our keywords and identified 18 targeted groups. For example, a person searching for "hypertension cure" may have a very different mindset from someone who searches for "lower blood pressure quickly", though both are good prospects for David's product. Segmenting the overall market allowed us to write specific ads targeted to the apparent internal dialog of each person searching for a solution. A valuable side benefit of this exercise was that the resultant shift in perspective from the market as a whole to market segments allowed us to unearth additional search phrases that doubled the size of our keyword list.

Continued Split-Testing

We had, of course, been split-testing ads all along. One particular ad (the first one displayed above) had consistently out-pulled all contenders. In the new groups, we split-tested that control ad against ones specific to each group's market segment. In about half of the cases, the control ad still won; proving that you never know what will work best until you test. We continue to write market-specific ads and split test them against the control, however, and new winners emerge each week.

Discouraging Unqualified Traffic

In the interest of increasing sales conversions, we took a few actions that reduced our CTR. For example, as soon as we got the overall CTR above 1%, we introduced several negative keywords (such as `"-free"`). This combination of forward and backward steps resulted in an overall CTR of 3.88% over the first five months of the campaign. At that point, several of our ad groups had achieved a CTR over 4%; the highest was 4.98%. Dozens of specific keyword phrases garnered double-digit CTR.

Current Results

In summary, over the first five months of this campaign, we increased the CTR by 597% (0.65% to 3.88%), while reducing the average CPC 22% (from $0.23 to $0.18) and maintaining an average ad position just over 5; as low as 3.5 in one ad group. Additionally, at the five-month mark, no keyword phrase had a minimum bid amount over $0.40. As a result of all this work, David's blood pressure is even lower today than when we started.

You can find an expanded version of this case study at Kelly's Web site, `www.ctrexpert.com`.

Letting Visitors Choose Their Own Sales Funnels

Glenn Livingston of `www.ultimateadwordsresearch.com` never begins a Web project without conducting a "Will I Make Money, and If So, How?" survey. One of his projects provides information on body language — how to interpret it and how to use it. After performing keyword due diligence to determine whether the size and hunger of the market would make the project financially worthwhile, Glenn launched the site by driving AdWords clicks to a survey that promised a free copy of the finished product in exchange for answering questions that would help the author provide useful information. The survey found several different market segments, and correlated those segments to specific keywords. Once the survey was complete and Glenn finished the product, he wrote different sales copy for each segment, focusing on their hot-button issues and highlighting bullets of specific interest to them.

When someone enters the site, www.howtousebodylanguage.com, from the home page, Glenn offers them a free subscription to his Body Language Newsletter, and asks them via drop-down menus about their interest. Where they go then is based on their choices; they are taken to the appropriate sales letter.

This site makes several thousand dollars a month in almost entirely passive income, and has generated a large list of people interested in body language and persuasion, upon which Glenn can build a large back-end business.

15-Cent Click to $1700 Customer in Minutes

Mike Stewart of www.internetvideoguy.com doesn't spend hours creating new ads or designing amazing Web sites. He doesn't research hungry markets or spend hours creating long e-mail follow-up sequences. He buys cheap clicks on AdWords on keywords related to recording teleseminars and phone calls. He split-tests his ads but doesn't generate enough impressions to make significant changes very often.

Mike's landing page (at www.teleseminartools.com) features a prominent two-minute video commercial for a home talk show recording studio priced at $1695. The video cost almost nothing to make, compared to tens or hundreds of thousands of dollars for television commercial production. But the decreased quality doesn't matter on this site, because the AdWords traffic is so highly qualified. A commercial airing during a break in *The Office* is shown to everyone watching the program; only a tiny percentage of the viewers will be interested in a given product at a given time. That's why commercials on mass media need to be repeated so often. But a commercial on an AdWords landing page can specifically respond to the itch represented by the keyword.

For the low-traffic keyword teleseminars and its variations, Mike generated 134 clicks at $0.15 CPC over a three-month period, for a total advertising spend of around $20.00. These clicks generated 13 sales totaling over $22,000 over the same period. Mike cautions that these numbers are possible for two important reasons:

1. The keyword teleseminars generates a customer who is likely to be qualified for the offer.
2. The product for sale lends itself to a video demonstration.

Mike teaches others how to create inexpensive Internet commercials at www.internetvideoguy.com.

Local Search with Video Web Site

One of Mike Stewart's clients is www.carpetdepotdecatur.com, a local carpet store in Decatur, Georgia. The owner, Brad Flack, bids on about 30 keywords in the Atlanta market only, and drives traffic to a Web site that uses video to introduce the store and answer frequently asked questions. The ads are simple, and include the call to action, *watch online video*.

The video on the home page features Brad introducing himself and explaining the benefits and dramatic difference of his store. He references the map below the video screen and the phone number above it, and invites viewers to call or visit the store. Below the video is the first blue hyperlink, offering a "Measure Your Home" how-to video.

Customers now come to the store feeling like they already know Brad from viewing several minutes of video. He has stopped running ads in the Yellow Pages, since most customers use Google first, and some rely on online search exclusively. Since none of his competitors are advertising with Google at this point (and he hopes they don't read this book!), his ad is the only one that prospects see. With no competition, clicks are cheap and his number-one position is guaranteed.

Generating B2B Leads Without Cold Calling

Joe DiSorbo of www.webgistix.com uses the Web to generate targeted business to business leads for e-commerce companies who want to automate or outsource the packing and shipping of orders. Because his service is a complex business to business sale, he uses the Web strictly to generate leads. Joe explains how he went from AdWords zero to hero in 12 months by employing very basic strategies. He explains:

> *Prior to using AdWords, we engaged in the painfully slow process of surfing the Internet, locating a potential target (an existing e-commerce company), finding their contact information on their Web site, and then cold-calling them to pitch our services. We opened an AdWords account in May 2005, made a list of all possible keywords, and got started.*

> *Our first twelve months using the system can be broken into three distinct 4-month periods with significant jumps in CTR.*

Phase 1 — The Beginning (May 2005 through Aug 2005)

Impressions: 146,028
Clicks: 467
CTR: 0.32%
CPC: $0.71

During the first four months we established two things:

1. *People were actually searching online for fulfillment services and clicking our ad.*

2. *We didn't yet know how to attract and convert enough prospects to make AdWords cost-effective.*

We started with a single campaign that contained a single ad group. That ad group consisted of every related keyword we could think of (broad match only and a single ad). When we ran a new ad, we shut off the original one. We didn't know how much the campaign was going to cost so we limited our daily budget and kept our bid prices low, which gave us a low position. Over that period our highest CTR was 0.77%.

The good news was that prospects were in fact clicking on our advertisements and coming to our Web site. Some even filled out a form and requested more information. Once we had their information, we could call them back. These calls were much easier to convert to sales than the cold calls we had been making previously.

Phase 2 — The Big Leap (Sept 2005 to Dec 2005)

Impressions: 169,616
Clicks: 2,583
CTR: 1.52% (376% increase over Phase 1)
CPC: $1.62

During the second four months our AdWords efforts started to pay off. Beginning in September 2005 our CTR increased to 1.52%. We had significantly more people visiting our Web site and were converting more of them to sales. Over that period we tried various ways to increase our response rates. Three tactics in particular improved our campaigns the most:

1. *We got rid of the poorly performing and non-related keywords. This lowered our overall impressions but improved the connection between keywords and the ad.*

2. *We broke out like words into their own ad group so we could customize each headline for each set of keywords.*

3. *We began split-testing ads.*

Because these changes were working well, we added new keyword groups in November 2005. Impressions rose along with CTR as we applied our newfound skills to the new ad groups.

Phase 3 — Continuous Refinement (Jan 2006 to Apr 2006)

Impressions: 393,021
Clicks: 10,990
CTR: 2.80% (83% Increase over Phase 2, 774% increase over Phase 1)
CPC: $1.23

In January 2006 our CTR took another big leap upward. We had been split-testing vigorously for the past 4 months and refining our ad groups and keywords. The big leap came when we tested a display URL that matched, or was closely related, to the search term the person typed in. Now, both the headline and the display URL were related directly to what the person was searching for.

Up to this point we had been using our corporate domain, Webgistix.com, only. Once we started using targeted URLs we again saw a big increase in CTR. We went out and bought all the URLs we could get related to our industry and started using them in the display URL for our top search terms. These included:

Keyword	*Display URL*
Fulfillment Center	www.FulfillmentCenter.biz
fulfillment costs	www.fulfillmentcosts.biz
kitting	kitting.biz
pack and ship	packandship.info
literature fulfillment	literaturefulfillment.biz
ecommerce fulfillment	ecommercefulfillment.biz

In addition to customized display URLs, we set up Web sites with those URLs to act as landing-page gateways to the main www.webgistix.com *site. We optimized those Web sites for different keywords, creating, in effect, landing sites instead of just landing pages. We kept the corporate logo at the top, but the important text and URL reflected the keyword. The Web site* http://fulfillmentcenter.biz *is optimized for the keyword* "fulfillment center".

This change increased our Web-site conversion from 1% to 3% instantly, without any split testing.

The overall business result has been 80% sales growth three years in a row.

Understanding and Answering Customer Objections

Jaco Bolle of `www.savefuel.ca` sells a small generator that can be installed in cars and trucks to add hydrogen gas to the engine for better gas mileage and lower emissions. When he came to me for help in improving his Web site conversion, he faced several marketing challenges:

1. Very few people have heard of supplemental hydrogen.

2. Most people are skeptical when they hear that they can improve their gas mileage by adding hydrogen to their gas tank.

3. People associate hydrogen gas with the *Hindenburg* disaster and are scared to generate it near their vehicle engine.

Through informal market research (talking about the product with everyone we could find and reading posts in online forums dedicated to hydrogen technology and fuel savings), we identified these and other objections that were preventing sales. Then we put together a nine-day e-mail course, titled "Supplemental Hydrogen Secrets Revealed." Each day addresses a different objection head-on — educating and entertaining the reader, building a bond of trust, and moving them closer to buying.

The first e-mail has the subject line, "Hydro-Gen, Iran and Poison Ivy." It lists the big benefits of hydrogen supplementation, includes several testimonials, and is chatty and engaging. The references to Iran and Poison Ivy in the subject line, which were included to pique curiosity and get the e-mail read, are echoed in this text from the e-mail:

> *For most of us, saving money and time (fewer fill-ups) is a pretty good motivation all by itself. But in this case, there [are] a couple of very strong "non-selfish" reasons to want to consume less fuel.*

> *Everyone has a different take on world politics, but I've never met anyone who thought that the U.S. should become more dependent on Middle Eastern oil. It's a little crazy to think that we're worried about Iran's nuclear program and that we've been funding that program at the pumps for years.*

> *And I don't know about you, but I'm starting to believe the signs of global warming. There [have] been reports on the news about poison ivy plants growing faster and being itchier as the carbon dioxide levels in the atmosphere rise.*

On the third day we tackled the big objection: safety. An excerpt from the e-mail, titled "The Hindenburg, *Die Hard,* and Sad Toddlers: Is Hydrogen Safe?", follows:

> *Of course, we get a lot of questions at SaveFuel.ca about the* Hindenburg. *People want to know, "Is my car going to burst into flames over central New Jersey if I install a Hydro-Gen unit?"*
>
> *It's a good question. It's the first thing I'd ask before installing anything in my car: Is it safe?*
>
> *First of all, nothing is without its hazards. Forks, staplers, bicycles, cars, toasters — they all can be misused in dangerous ways. So the real question is, Is the Hydro-Gen safe if used properly?*
>
> *Here's why the Hydro-Gen is safer than the gasoline or diesel you currently use:*
>
> *+ + + Hydrogen is less of a fire hazard than gasoline + + +*
>
> *The Hydro-Gen uses a small amount of electricity to turn water into its two component elements, hydrogen and oxygen. Hydrogen is much less flammable than gasoline. Gasoline bursts into flames at anywhere from 228–501 degrees Celsius (442–933 degrees Fahrenheit), while hydrogen doesn't ignite until 550 degrees Celsius (1,022 degrees Fahrenheit).*
>
> *All those scenes in the* Die Hard *movies where the car flips over and bursts into flames — that's ordinary gasoline, not hydrogen. Now, cars don't actually burst into flames very often in real life, but still — gasoline is far more likely to ignite than hydrogen gas.*
>
> *Here's another thing: If you were ever forced to memorize the first row of the periodic table, you'll recall that hydrogen is the first — and therefore lightest — element. How light? Fifteen times lighter than air. Twice as light as helium.*
>
> *Did you ever give a helium balloon to a small child at the amusement park? And they let go? That balloon really took off, didn't it? Next time you comfort a sad toddler about the loss of their helium balloon, imagine a balloon twice as buoyant in air, filled with hydrogen.*
>
> *Because it's so light, hydrogen disperses upwards. Quickly. It doesn't stick around and burn, like gasoline does. If you watch a video of the* Hindenburg *fire, you'll notice something amazing: That giant ship burns hydrogen only for 30 seconds. Rescuers run to the scene almost immediately.*
>
> *(Check it out yourself in this video:* `http://tinyurl.com/lue73`*)*
>
> *Here's a startling fact: 62 out of 97 passengers on the* Hindenburg *survived the disaster on May 6, 1937, many of them relatively unharmed. The ones who died either fell, or were burned by dripping diesel fuel.*

Note the chatty yet authoritative tone, the use of story to make the point, and the non-salesy nature of the e-mail. This e-mail ends with a by-the-way call to action: " . . . if this e-mail has just put your mind at ease regarding safety, here's the lift to order a Hydro-Gen and get started saving gas and money right away: `www.savefuel.ca/oxy-hydrogen`."

Another e-mail addresses concerns about the unit voiding a vehicle's warranty or harming the engine. Day 5's installment answers the objection, "This sounds too good to be true. If hydrogen supplementation works, then the big car companies would be using it."

Slowly, the autoresponder sequence answers objections, provides more and more testimonials, explains the technology, and culminates with an ironclad risk-reversal guarantee. Borrowing language from a Robert Collier sales letter of the 1930s, we write, "By ordering, you obligate me, not yourself. If it doesn't work the way I say it will, I insist that you return the Hydro-Gen for a full and prompt refund."

The result of this e-mail sequence, coupled with several other improvements to site, including tested headlines, the addition of live chat and live phone operators available 20 hours per day, was a doubling of the site conversion, from roughly 1.75% to 3.5%. Jaco relates that a competitor approached him in despair, asking whether he would consider selling the competitor's product on the `www.savefuel.ca` Web site.

Making Money in an Impossible Market

David Bullock of `www.davidbullock.com` believes so strongly in rigorous testing of the sales process that he decided to put his methodology to the test in a nearly impossible situation: buying AdWords clicks for $0.25 and sending the traffic to a Web page promoting an affiliate product that produces $4.25 per unit sale for David. In order to break even in this scenario, David's site needed to produce 1 sale for every 17 clicks. In other words, if the affiliate site — over which he had no control — could convert a very healthy 5% of its visitors to paying customers, David could not have made money on the front end, even if he had been able to send every single visitor to that site!

His goal for the campaign was a net profit of $30/day, stable and predictable. He gave himself one advantage: He chose an inexpensive product with built-in continuity — an impulse purchase that would lead customers to buy more over time.

During the intense testing phase, David limited his Web site traffic to 100 clicks per day. His conversion at the start of the experiment was 2%: one sale for every 50 visitors to his site.

Task #1: Lowering the bid price

The first task was to lower the bid price. At a quarter a click, there was no way to turn this campaign into a financial success. David employed two strategies: improving the ad CTR and firing underperforming keywords.

He employed Taguchi multivariate testing to find the ads with the highest CTR. Taguchi testing uses matrices to create several ad variations at a time, simulating the actual testing of thousands of ads. This method works only with a very significant traffic stream. If you only get a few hundred impressions a week, Taguchi testing will actually slow you down. From an initial figure of 0.25% in January 2006, David's CTR rose to 0.95% in February, 1.25% in March, and 1.73% in April. It now holds steady at approximately 2.00%, an eightfold improvement.

Second, he tracked his initial list of 335 keywords, and fired words that weren't leading to sales. Ultimately, the campaign contained only 85 keywords. David's CPC is now $0.12, less than half its original cost.

Task #2: Improving Web-site conversion

David focused his tests on three elements of his landing page: the headline, the presence or absence of a photograph of the product, and the text on the page. The original headline was "How to Buy X." The eventual winner became, "How to Get X Without Any Hidden Harmful Y" (sorry, he's not going to reveal the product or the Web site).

He found that an image of the product improved conversion, and that a long-copy Web page did better than a short-copy Web page. Once the page format was established, David performed Taguchi testing on the first few paragraphs of the copy to establish the right words in the right order.

Now the site sends 50% of its AdWords visitors straight to the affiliate site where they can purchase the product. One visitor out of every 24 makes a purchase. His overall conversion rate from click to sale is 4.37%, significantly higher than the breakeven requirement of 3.32%. And because of the continuity, the back-end profits make the site even more lucrative. In April 2007 David spent $109 on AdWords and earned $1122 in affiliate income. In addition (he'll be embarrassed for me to reveal), it took over an hour for him to look up all these numbers because he locked down this campaign over a year ago and hasn't touched it since.

A single AdWords campaign to a single Web page selling a product he doesn't make, stock, or ship — and it pays the mortgage month after month. All because David focused on the fundamentals and tested and tracked his results rigorously.

Index